Lean Manufacturing Systems and Cell Design

Lean Manufacturing Systems and Cell Design

J T. Black
Steve L. Hunter

Society of
Manufacturing
Engineers
Dearborn, Michigan

Library of Congress Catalog Card Number: 087263-647-X

International Standard Book Number: 2003102335

Additional copies may be obtained by contacting:

Society of Manufacturing Engineers
Customer Service
One SME Drive, P.O. Box 930
Dearborn, Michigan 48121
1-800-733-4763
www.sme.org

SME staff who participated in producing this book:

Cheryl Zupan, Editor
Bob King, Editor
Chris McGorey, Graphic Designer/Cover Design
Rosemary Csizmadia, Production Supervisor
Kathye Quirk, Graphic Designer
Jon Newberg, Production Editor
Frances Kania, Production Assistant

Printed in the United States of America

About the Authors

J T. BLACK

J T. Black is professor emeritus of industrial and systems engineering at Auburn University, where he also served as the director of the Advanced Manufacturing Technology Center.

He was born in Rahway, N.J., and lived in New York, Ohio, Pennsylvania and Delaware while growing up. He graduated from high school in Edgewood, Penn., and attended Lehigh University (B.S.I.E.), West Virginia University (M.S.I.E.), and the University of Illinois at Urbana (Ph.D.).

Black has been teaching manufacturing engineering since 1960, when he became an instructor in the industrial engineering department at West Virginia University. He has taught manufacturing processes and systems at West Virginia University, University of Illinois, University of Vermont, University of Rhode Island, Ohio State University, University of Alabama-Huntsville, and Auburn University.

J T. Black is the author of over 70 technical papers and numerous books on manufacturing processes and systems, including the widely held *Material and Processes in Manufacturing*, now in its 9th edition. He resides in Auburn, Ala., with his wife Carol. His other interest is tennis (he has been ranked #2 in 50 and 55 doubles and #1 in 60 doubles in Alabama).

Many people have asked him about his name. Black said his mother named him J (just the letter with no period) after a Pennsylvania Railroad (PRR) control tower. The towers coming out of Johnstown eastbound on the PRR are identified by letters, according to Black, and the 10th tower is J tower. Black's middle initial is T and it stands for Temple, after his Uncle Temple who was buried under a coal car during a train wreck at Horseshoe Curve. Black was the first of his generation to turn away from the railroad, much to the distress of many of his relatives, particularly his grandfather and his father, an electrical engineer for the PRR.

STEVE L HUNTER

Dr. Steve L. Hunter is an associate professor at Mississippi State University's Forest Products Laboratory. There, he is working with Mississippi and Southeast U.S. furniture man-

ufacturers to improve their productivity and international stance. Hunter was born in Rome, Georgia. He earned a BS degree from Berry College in manufacturing engineering technology and a Master's Degree from Auburn University, with a major in manufacturing systems engineering and a minor in industrial engineering. He earned his Doctorate, again from Auburn University in industrial and systems engineering manufacturing with a minor in ergonomics.

Hunter has been interested in manufacturing systems design since 1980 and has designed and implemented many lean production systems. His recent research has included the ergonomic ramifications of manufacturing system design using computer simulation. This research attracted the attention of NASA where he was honored as a NASA Fellow. He carried out primary human engineering research on the ergonomics effects of micro-gravity on astronauts for NASA's Marshall Space Flight Center. Before NASA, Hunter taught manufacturing engineering courses at the University of Memphis. Earlier, he worked as a civilian at the Air Force and Naval Aviation depots serving as an engineering project manager. His work in lean production includes the design and implementation of many commercial manufacturing cells, as well as the design of an 18 cell system for manufacturing and assembly for the Navy. While working for the Department of Defense, Hunter won numerous outstanding service awards for his contributions to national defense. He is married and his wife is a nurse.

J T. Black dedicates this book to his wife Carol.

Table of Contents

Preface xv

Acknowledgments xvii

Chapter 1: Introduction to Lean Manufacturing Systems and Cell Design

Industrial Revolutions 1

Empowered Workers 8

Production and Manufacturing Systems 16

Understanding a Company's Business 21

Product Life Cycles 22

A New Manufacturing System 22

Chapter 2: Ten Steps to Lean Production

Successful Lean Manufacturing 25

Summary 43

Chapter 3: Manufacturing System Design

Introduction 45

System Design Trends 45

Optimization of the Manufacturing System 46

Evolution of Functional Structure 46

Systems Defined 47

Manufacturing Versus Production Systems 48

Classifications of Manufacturing Systems Designs 49

Standardized Work 59

Linked-cell Systems 59

Group Technology 59

Design For Flexibility 62

Comparing Lean Production to Other Systems 62

Summary 66

Chapter 4: Axiomatic Design Principles

Introduction 67

Key Concepts 67

Decompose the Problem 69

Sample Design 70

Creativity, Flexibility, Controllability, and Productivity 74

Honda's Uniqueness Requirement 75

Design Process Hierarchy 76

Functional Requirements 78

Constraints 78

Role of Information 79

Design Axioms and Corollaries 79

Summary 82

Chapter 5: Manned Interim Manufacturing and Assembly Cells

Introduction 83

Linked-cell Manufacturing System 84

Interim-cell Design Example 84

Decouplers in Manufacturing and Assembly Cells 93

Work-in-process Versus Stock-on-hand 94

How an Assembly Cell Works 94

How a Manufacturing Cell Works 98

Cycle Time for a Cell Based on Takt Time 100

Achieving Superior Quality 101

Flexibility in Cell Design 102

How and Why Cells are Linked 106

Standard Operations Routine Sheet 107

Design for Customers 108

Other System-design Tools 109

Group Technology 110

Production-flow Analysis 110

Coding/Classification Methods 111

Other Methods 112

Pilot Cells 112

Benefit of Conversion 113

Conversion Constraints 113

Summary 115

Chapter 6: Setup Reduction

Introduction 117

Single-minute Exchange of Dies 117

Economic Setup-reduction Techniques 118

Changing Processes to Meet Changing Volumes 121

Motivation for Single-minute Exchange of Dies 125

Basic Steps for Reducing Setup Time 128

Power Clamps 138

Apply Methods Analysis 140

Abolish Setup 143

Single-minute Exchange of Dies Phases 143

Summary 144

Chapter 7: Integrated Quality Control

Introduction 145

Statistical Quality Control 146

Integrated Quality Control 149

Process Analysis Tools and Techniques 153

Making Process Capability Studies 167

Motorola's Six Sigma 171

Teams and Quality Circles 175

Poka-yoke 176

Quality Control Department 178

Summary 179

Chapter 8: Integrated Reliability

Introduction 181

Role of Maintenance 181

Integrate Preventive Maintenance 181

Manufacturing Engineering 184

Total Productive Maintenance 185

Zero Downtime 186

Lean Production 186

Benchmarking 186

Pilot Areas 187

Predictive Maintenance 187

Computerized Maintenance Management System 187

Continuous Improvement 187

Kaizen Activities 191

Reliability..192

The Second Shift...195

Total Productive Maintenance Implementation..197

Summary..197

Chapter 9: Refining Lean Production

Leveling...199

Mixed Model Final Assembly...203

Long-range Forecasting...205

Balancing...206

Manufacturing Cell Types...210

Synchronization..211

Summary..213

Chapter 10: Production and Inventory Control

Kanban..215

Constant Work-in-process...226

Integrated Inventory Control..230

Inventory: An Independent Control Variable...230

Supply-chain Management...236

The Paperless Factory of the Future...238

Summary..241

Chapter 11: Making the Vendors Lean

Introduction...243

Lead Time and Expediting...243

Lean Supply Chain...244

The Plant Trip...246

Rules for Lean Cell Design..258

Fourth Industrial Revolution..260

Chapter 12: Ergonomics in Cell Design

Lean Production and Ergonomics...261

Health Issues..263

Ergonomic Solutions...265

Physiology..268

Human and Machine Interfacing..270

Conclusion...272

Chapter 13 Automation and Autonomation

Automaticity 273

Automation in Lean Manufacturing 277

The Factory With a Future 286

Chapter 14: Simulation

History 290

Advantages and Limitations 291

3D Computer Simulation Tools 293

Industry Success 305

Summary 306

Chapter 15: The Toyota Production System Today

Introduction 307

Eliminating Waste 307

Roots in Ford's System 308

TPS History 309

Roots of Autonomation 310

Getting Ready for Lean 311

JIT Production 313

Level Production 314

Pull System 315

Lean Manufacturing 316

Integrated Quality 320

Internal Customer Satisfaction 322

Standardized Work and Cell Design 323

Toyota Supplier Support Center 325

References

References 327

Index 333

Preface

J T. Black began teaching an engineering course on manufacturing system design in 1983 at the University of Alabama in Huntsville. He decided to call the course integrated manufacturing production systems. The course title suggested that the manufacturing system be integrated with critical control functions that normally reside in the production system.

Integrated manufacturing production systems became a strategy for the redesign of an existing factory into a factory with a future. This strategy is based on a linked-cell manufacturing system that provides for a continuous flow (or smooth movement) of materials through a plant. While some may disagree, there is strong evidence that the linked-cell system was invented at the Toyota Motor Company by vice president of manufacturing, Taiichi Ohno, who referred to it as the Toyota Production System. This system was simple and flexible for even complex products like automobiles. Many U.S. companies have since implemented the strategy in various forms.

In *Lean Manufacturing Systems and Cell Design*, the authors examine the implementation of lean manufacturing by many companies. The lean production strategy stands in marked contrast to the well-advertised computer-integrated manufacturing approach.

Recently much has been written about agile manufacturing, which means a company is able to respond quickly to changes in the marketplace and bring new products to market quickly by using advanced versions of computer-integrated manufacturing. However, computerizing an existing system does not make it agile or integrated. Companies that successfully implement some version of Ohno's system are agile. This book presents that experience in a logical ten-step methodology.

The ten-step method embodies lean manufacturing, setup reduction, and pull production-control methodologies. Quality control, production control, inventory control, and machine-tool maintenance are also integrated into the linked-cell manufacturing system. This methodology produces superior quality at a low cost, with minimum throughput time. It provides the proper structure for automation to solve quality or capacity problems. The new word for this is autonomation.

The authors believe the linked-cell manufacturing system is the manufacturing system of the future. Common practice in the future will be to link manufacturing with assembly cells. In the 1990s, companies implemented manned cells that used multifunctional workers who walked from machine to machine. Cells are designed to be flexible so they can readily adapt to changes in product design and product demand. They can be readily integrated with the critical control functions. Cells that make families of parts using a set (or group) of manufacturing processes replace the functional job shop structure.

The last time an industrial revolution happened in manufacturing systems was in 1913 when the world came to Detroit to see the Ford Motor Company's moving assembly line. The linked-cell system Ohno invented was a logical extension of the Ford system. Ohno studied and understood how the system of mass production functioned. However, he recognized that the Ford system was designed to handle large volumes of the same parts with no variety. Over time, a new system invented by Ohno emerged. This new manufacturing system evolved into a hybrid of the flow shop and the job shop designs. The Ohno system was designed to handle large or small volumes of a variety of parts using the same economies of volume as the Ford system. Many people now say that Ford invented lean production. This is simply not so; the inventor of lean manufacturing was Ohno, and he should be so recognized.

Ohno got the idea for his kanban system after visiting an American supermarket, where he observed people pulling goods from the shelves to fill their shopping carts. The empty space on the shelf was the signal for the stock person to restock by reordering cases of the consumed item. In effect, the shopper provided a totally flexible final assembly for the custom order. In applying this idea to manufacturing, Ohno developed a system whereby downstream use of parts dictated upstream production rates. The materials were pulled through the factory by consumption of parts in final assembly. An empty cart returned to the manufacturing point was the signal to make more parts. Ohno quickly discovered that it was more productive to move machines closer together so that the workers could make one, check one, and pass it on to the next machine. Thus, manufacturing cells evolved through the factory-wide desire to eliminate waste. There is no record of Toyota using group technology, a well-known method for finding families of parts around which cells can be designed.

Many decision-makers have resisted converting to lean manufacturing because it is not high-tech or they perceive that it may be difficult to implement. However, lean production may severely impact the political and social structure of the entire company. It takes many reasons for a company to undertake such an effort and many excuses for not doing it. However, this much is clear: companies that have the courage to undertake this change will be survivors—the factories with a future. Those who resist will become history.

Acknowledgments

There are many people who made significant contributions to this book. Co-author, Dr. Steve Hunter is one of the world's experts in cellular manufacturing system design and implementation. He is now at Mississippi State University continuing his research into manufacturing system's design while assisting the Mississippi furniture industry with the design and implementation of lean manufacturing systems.

Author J T. Black thanks his wife, Carol, who did all of the typing and helped with editing prior to submission. She also made many suggestions that greatly improved the readability of the final manuscript. Thanks also to Dr. Dan Sipper, Rich Wilson, Angeline Honnell, and Dr. Brian Paul who provided many suggestions for improvement.

The authors give thanks to students from all courses at Auburn University and earlier at the University of Alabama in Huntsville. They contributed greatly to the book with their questions and discussions, both during and after class. Some of the students, Dave Hanning, Yen Shi "Hopper" Tsai, Doris Lizotte, Jill Williams, Alice Carter, Jack R. "Rick" Wade, Carlos Engle, Dr. Lewis Payton, and Kavit Antani, provided written contributions. Jason Wang and Allen Chen did the figures for the first version. Dr. Steve Hunter and Ranjit David developed many of the new figures for this book, along with extensive commentary and editorial.

The authors would like to thank the engineers and managers at Delmia Corporation for their continued support of manufacturing system design and ergonomics research. They would like to especially thank Delmia's president, Bob Brown, and David Papp, Southeastern sales manager, for their continued support through the use of Delmia's remarkable ENVISION ERGO® high-level 3D/virtual-reality software.

The axiomatic design material was extracted from the unpublished work of Nam Suh, a professor at MIT whose work on axiomatic design has long been admired. This text also reflects the work of David Cochran, a former student of Black, who is now on the faculty at MIT and leading the axiomatic systems design work there.

Two people inspired this book. Tom Gelb is an engineer at Harley-Davidson, who described with great passion the conversion of Harley-Davidson to lean manufacturing. The second great influence on the book was Dick Schonberger. Drs. Schonberger and Black presented many Just-in-time seminars in the early 1980s and they are considered pioneers in this field.

The authors would also like to thank the SME editorial staff Cheryl Zupan, Bob King, Chris McGorey, Kathye Quirk, Jon Newberg, Frances Kania, and Rosemary Csizmadia for their work on the book.

Chapter 1
Introduction: Lean Manufacturing Systems and Cell Design

INDUSTRIAL REVOLUTIONS

Black's theory of industrial revolutions proposes that new designs of manufacturing systems spawn industrial revolutions. A new manufacturing system design brings one or more manufacturing companies to the forefront in the industrial world. Each new design employs a unique enabling technology such as the assembly line or assemblage of machine-powered tools. In every case, a new system is adopted quickly by a few companies, before it slowly disseminates to other manufacturers around the world.

At the dawn of humanity's need for tools, weapons, and later, consumable goods, there were no manufacturing organizations comparable to those of today to fulfill those needs. With the arrival of commerce and trade, there were organizations for the manufacture of commercial items, but a few tools and one or two pieces of equipment did not comprise a real factory. Rather, these organizations were large-scale cottage industries. By the turn of the 17th Century, however, the forerunner of the modern factory was emerging. Earlier, manufacturing operations were largely performed in home-based workshops by skilled craftsmen. These artisans were master gunsmiths, blacksmiths, utensil makers, etc., who produced goods under a master/apprenticeship system. The machines they used to form and cut their materials were man-powered.

As outlined by Amber and Amber (Amber and Amber 1962) in the industrial yardstick for automation, the first step in automating facto-ries was to power manual machines to increase cutting and forming speed. The need to power machine tools efficiently created the need to gather machine tools to one location where a source of power existed. Around the late 1700s, steel and cast iron were becoming available to build machines. By the early 1800s, the U.S. population rapidly expanded and fueled the demand for more goods and services. By the middle 1800s, railroads transported more people to cities where consumable goods were being produced to supply an increasing demand.

Powered machine tools, an abundance of inexpensive labor, and reliable and relatively fast transportation were the enabling technologies that drove the first industrial revolution and influenced factory design (see Table 1-1). The craft/cottage production era in America was popular prior to 1700 to around 1850.

The first industrial revolution, also called the *American Armory System*, began with the creation of factories using powered machines, mechanization, and interchangeable parts. The first industrial revolution had job shops or functional layouts and spanned from 1840 to approximately 1910. Today, there are many examples of these job shops still in existence.

The second industrial revolution, sometimes called the *Ford System*, featured the moving assembly line or a flow-line type of product layout. Under this system, manufacturing companies learned about economy of scale. Many historians called this the *mass production era*. During this time, automation became common. The third industrial revolution, sparked by the

Table 1-1. Industrial revolutions are driven by new objectives				
	1st Industrial Revolution	**2nd Industrial Revolution**	**3rd Industrial Revolution**	**4th Industrial Revolution**
Time period (era)	1840–1910	1910–1970	1960–2010	2000–Future
Manufacturing system design	Job shop	Flow shop	Linked-cell TPS*	Integrated Manufacturing, Computerized
Layout	Functional layout	Product layout	One-piece flow via Linked-cells	Linked assembly of large modules or subassemblies
Enabling technology (physical implementation)	Power for machines Steel production Railroad for transportation	Moving final assembly line Division of labor Standardization leading to true interchangeability Automatic material handling	U-shaped cells; Kanban Rapid die exchange Zero defects Total preventive maintenance	Virtual reality/simulation 3D design using low-cost High-performance computers
Historical company names	Whitney, Colt, Remington	Singer Ford	Toyota Motor Co. General Electric, HP, Omark, Harley Davidson	Boeing, Lockheed, Dell, Mercedes Benz
Economics	Economy of collected technology	Economy of scale High volume— Low unit cost	Economy of scope Wide variety of low unit cost	Economy of modules Smaller factories
*System developed by Taiichi Ohno who called it the Toyota production system (TPS)				

Toyota production system, is now referred to as *lean production*. The Toyota production system uses a system design often called the *linked-cell manufacturing system*. This system is simpler, produces lower cost, higher quality parts, and is more flexible than the first two manufacturing industrial revolutions' manufacturing system designs. The third industrial revolution's critical control functions are integrated into the design of the basic building blocks of the Toyota production system. The basic building blocks of the Toyota production system are manufacturing cells.

First Industrial Revolution

In 1800, approximately 80% of Americans worked on farms. The first industrial revolution began with the advent of powered machine tools, the creation of factories, and a movement of people from farms to towns and cities. This mass movement to metropolitan areas was a megatrend of the first industrial revolution. Now 200 years later, only about 2–3% of Americans work directly on farms, but the productivity and yield of farms continues to increase. Large, often special-purpose farming equipment, decreases the number of direct laborers (the number of people working in the fields). A similar trend occurs in the number of direct laborers in factories. Modern factories are continually decreasing the amount of required labor due to improved factory designs and better equipment.

The design of most manufacturing systems operating today is often a combination of both the job and flow-shop designs. The job-shop design was developed during the early 1800s and is a functional layout where processes are arranged by department or process type. In the flow-shop design, processes are laid out in manufacturing sequence with one worker per process.

The first factory design was the job shop. It replaced craft or cottage manufacturing as the need to power machine tools was used to increase productivity by increasing cutting and forming speeds. Therefore, the method needed to drive or power the machines developed into a functional design.

The first factories were built on the banks of rivers and streams so that the machines and processes could be powered by water pressure turning waterwheels. Waterwheels drove shafts that ran into the factories (see Figure 1-1). Machines and processes were aligned underneath appropriate power shafts, since individual shafts turned at speeds required to drive particular sets of machines. For example, lathes were collected under their own power shaft, likewise, milling machines and presses. Belts transferred power off the shaft to deliver a single, set speed to a particular group of machines. Later, waterwheels were replaced by steam engines, which allowed factories to be located beyond riverbanks where spring floods were often a problem. Eventually, large electric motors replaced steam engines. Finally, individual electric motors replaced large electric motors. Nevertheless, the job-shop design continued and the functional design held on blindly to the original system design (see Figure 1–2). This era became known to historians as the *American Armory System* because most early factories manufactured weapons such as muskets. The industry leaders of the world came to view the revolutionary American Armory System and it was disseminated throughout the industrial world.

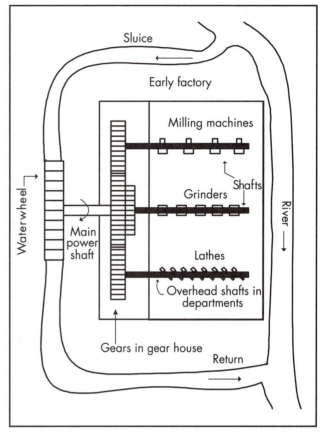

Figure 1-1.Early factories used water power and a system of shafts to drive machines.

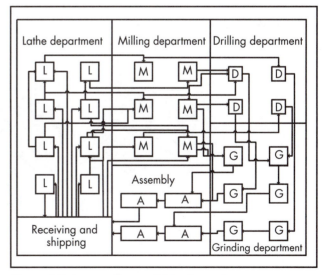

Figure 1-2. Layout of a small job shop where processes are functionally gathered into departments.

Second Industrial Revolution

The second industrial revolution began in the early 1900s with the advent of assembly lines and the Ford Motor Company concept of mass production. This led to the development of the flow shop where large assembly tasks were broken down into smaller tasks. Products were assembled station to station, where distinct tasks were carried out at each station (see Figure 1-3). By the 1940s, large, expensive, and complicated manufacturing processes, called transfer lines, were part of the trend (see Figure 1-4). Complex processes developed in the 1940s included large automatic material-handling mechanisms from which the term *automation* evolved. Inadvertently, designers of manufacturing systems developed "islands of automation." These systems, called transfer lines, were inflexible to change in volume or product. This same type of automation today is called *fixed automation*, a contrast with flexible automation, which features programmable machines. Over the years, flow-line manufacturing was adapted for the production of small items and culminated with the moving assembly line at Ford (Womack 1991). Around 1913, Ford's production engineering group developed flow-line manufacturing, lead by Charles

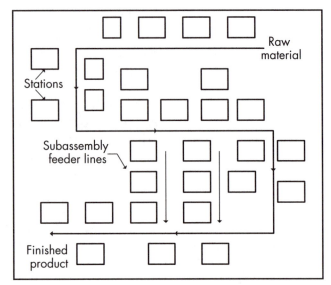

Figure 1-3. Schematic of a flow-manufacturing system.

Sorenson (Ford 1919). Just as they did in the early 1800s with the advent of the first industrial revolution, the industrial world came to America and then went home to implement a new manufacturing system design.

From the second industrial revolution, a hybrid system evolved, a mixture of job and flow shops. It permitted companies to manufacture large volumes of identical products at low

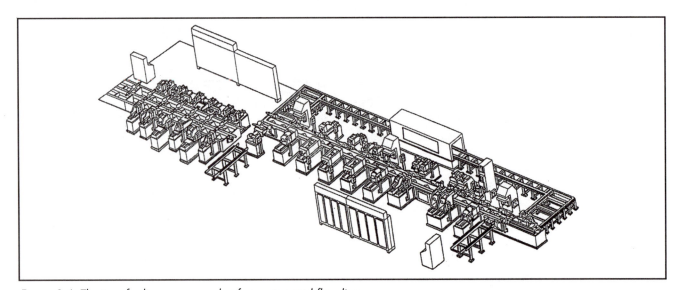

Figure 1-4. The transfer line, an example of an automated flow line.

unit costs and it allowed the concept of mass production to evolve. The job shop made product in large lot sizes according to the *mass production system*, or economic-order-quantity equation.

Figure 1-5 shows a schematic diagram of a mass production system with a job shop, flow shop, and final assembly line. The job shop is where large volumes of goods are produced in small batches. This manufacturing design groups the processes functionally. The material moves from process to process through the plant as dictated by the schedule developed by a production control department. This department schedules each machine and, thus, each operator. A route sheet document tells material handlers and forklift operators the next stop where parts are to go. Production control has the responsibility of determining when (timing), where (which machine), and how many (lot size), so work on parts is carried out in a supposedly orderly and timely manner.

Figure 1-5 details a schematic of a final assembly line—a type of flow-line manufacturing system design. A modern-day automobile assembly plant with a moving assembly line is a good example of a flow line. The moving assembly line for automobile production is broken into hundreds of stations sequenced to systematically build an automobile. This requires work at each station to be balanced, or equalized, so each task takes about the same amount of time. This system requires interchangeable parts with the repeatability of each manufacturing process based on precise measurement standards. The moving assembly line produces vehicles one at a time, in a method sometimes called one-piece flow.

The transfer line is an extensively automated flow line for machining products in large volumes. The enabling technology of the transfer line is the use of repeat-cycle automatic machines. This system also requires interchangeable parts based on precise measurement standards. The transfer line was designed to produce large volumes of identical goods, a process that was often required to economical-

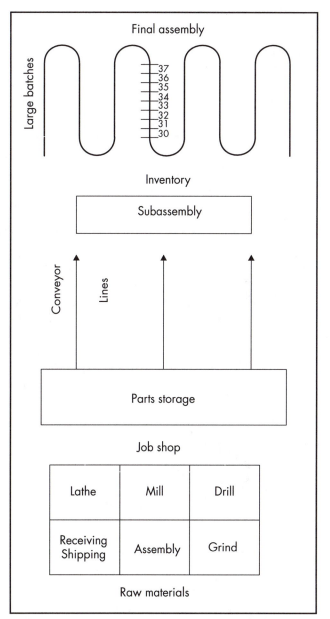

Figure 1-5. The mass-production system for automobiles is a moving assembly line (stations 30-37 shown).

ly justify expensive capital investments. Transfer-line systems were not only expensive, but they were inflexible. Automatic repeat-cycle machine tools on transfer lines were replaced with computer numerical control machines or flexible manufacturing systems. Today, flexible manufacturing systems are more expensive and complex than transfer-line systems. They have been adopted by less than 1% of manufacturing companies in the US.

Parts that feed automated flow lines, transfer lines, and flexible manufacturing systems are most often produced by job shops in large lots. Component parts are often held in inventory for long periods of time and eventually brought to the transfer line where a particular product is being assembled. The line produces one product during a long run and then switches to another product. The changeover setup can take days or even weeks.

Transfer lines were in place during World War II and were clearly responsible for America having the military equipment and weapons to win the war.

This massive production system thrived after World War II, permitting automobile producers to manufacture vehicles in large volumes using economy of scale. Just when it appeared that nothing could top this manufacturing system, a new player, Toyota, devised a system design that thrust the manufacturing world into the third industrial revolution.

Third Industrial Revolution

At this writing, the third industrial revolution is over 40 years old. The third industrial revolution is not based on hardware or any particular process, but on the design of the manufacturing system—the complex arrangement of physical elements characterized by measurable parameters. Figure 1-6 illustrates this manufacturing system. Toyota was the first to develop this design scheme. Among the Japanese manufacturers, Toyota Motor Company distinguished itself as the best. Many factors made this company the top automobile manufacturer in the world. There was a time when the world looked to Japan and observed a tiny nation. Now this small country has become a giant in the global manufacturing arena.

A new manufacturing system design vaulted Colt and Remington to the manufacturing forefront in the first industrial revolution; Ford, in the second industrial revolution. The develop-

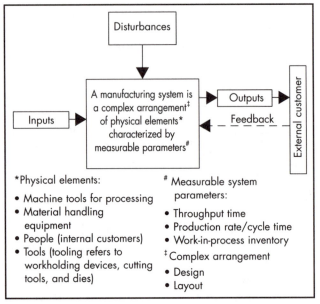

Figure 1-6. The manufacturing system with inputs and outputs, the portion that actually makes the products.(Black,1990)

ment of the unique cellular manufacturing system, however, is what made Toyota the top car maker in the world. The new system linked cell manufacturing, known as the Toyota production system, the Just-in-time (JIT) system, or world-class manufacturing system. See Table 1-2 for an extensive listing of linked-cell manufacturing system names. In 1990, the system was called lean production. Lean production was coined by John Krafcik, an engineer working in the international motor vehicle program at MIT (Womack, et al 1991).

What was different about this linked-cell manufacturing system was the development of manufacturing and assembly cells designed to be linked to final assembly. Figure 1-7 shows cell-to-cell and cell-to-other system-component relationships. The fundamental linking function of this manufacturing philosophy produces a functionally integrated system for inventory and production control. The results of this system are low unit costs, high productivity, superior quality, and on-time, every-time delivery of unique products from a flexible system.

Table 1-2. Names for the linked-cell manufacturing system	
Name	**Sources**
Lean production	MIT group of researchers, (Womack 1990)
Toyota production system	Toyota Motor Company (Ohno, Shingo, Monden)
Ohno system	Taiichi Ohno, inventor of TPS
Integrated pull manufacturing system	AT&T
Minimium inventory production system	Westinghouse
Materials as needed (MAN)	Harley Davidson
Just-in-time/total quality control (JIT/TQC)	JIT/TQC (Schonberger)
World-class manufacturing (WCM)	Schonberger
Zero inventory production systems (ZIPS)	Omark and Bob Hall
Quick-response or modular manufacturing	Apparel industry
Stockless production	Hewlett Packard
Kanban system	Many Japanese companies
The new production system	Suzuki
One-piece flow	Sekine (1990)
Continuous-flow manufacturing	Chrysler, IBM

The linked-cell manufacturing system is unique in that lean production methodologies requires the creation of manufacturing and assembly cells. When one compares a new design to a job-shop-system design, the simple and orderly array of processes in a lean production system contrasts sharply with the chaotic job-shop design. In a new manufacturing design, enabling technologies are the U-shaped manufacturing and assembly cells. Figures 1-8 and 1-9 show detailed examples.

Cells in a linked-cell system operate on a one-piece-flow (Sekine 1990) basis, just like the subassembly and final-assembly lines. In lean production, the final-assembly line is redesigned to handle product mixes of different models, or small quantities of one automobile model, and quickly switch to another model. In 1985, Honda was building its Civic® and Accord® models on the same final assembly line. Harley Davidson was building 14 different motorcycles on the same line every day. Nedcar in the Netherlands was building two different automobiles, each with two different models, on a single final-assembly line. The demand for components pulled from subassembly and manufacturing cells to be assembled into the final product was smoothed (Monden 1983).

Fourth Industrial Revolution

If it is true that the future is always here, but not everywhere, then it can be said that the fourth industrial revolution exists somewhere in the world today. The first industrial revolution was driven by the manufacture of weapons of war via the armories. The second industrial revolution made equipment and weapons for World War II. The third industrial revolution reduced the cost of remanufacture of weapon systems' components while providing state-of-the-art weaponry for national defense. The fourth industrial revolution has been assisted by technology developed to design a Boeing 747 aircraft that carries a super-laser capable of shooting enemy missiles hundreds of miles away. The same computer system Boeing used to design the 777 was also used by an airborne laser team to combine the work of 22 design teams in 11 states. Both the weapon system and its manufacturing system were completely designed and functionally simulated by computers. This enabling technology was also used to simultaneously design commercial manufacturing systems and products. Products resulting from this technology are large modular subassemblies of the airborne laser that can be

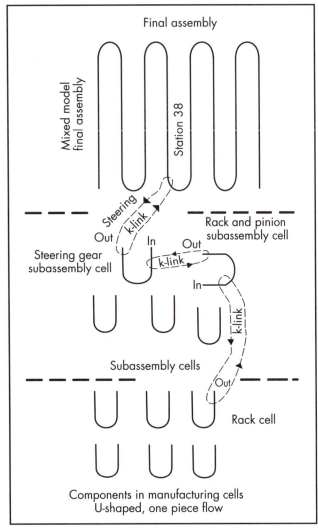

Figure 1-7. The lean manufacturing system is a linked-cell system.

delivery of subassemblies, but they will also supply labor to perform installations on customer's assembly lines. Today, there are some vehicle assembly plants in Brazil that are test beds for future lean manufacturing system designs that apply this new concept.

Powerful computers will permit graphical-3D, or virtual-reality, simulation of the entire product assembly that includes the simulation of each workstation on the assembly line. Ergonomic factors for factory workers are becoming more of a concern to engineers and managers. Computer simulation of workstations with any of the latest software packages for good workplace design can prevent or reduce ergonomic and physiological problems for workers. Similarly, manufacturing and assembly work cells with walking workers or robots can be simulated in detail.

In the fourth industrial revolution, the enabling technology will be 3D/virtual-reality simulations of the workplace, including ergonomic and human engineering analyses of workers. These virtual-reality simulations have already shown dramatic reductions of throughput, product development times, and manufacturing costs by improving communications across global, multidisciplinary design teams and facilities. In addition, the high-level software is helpful in the design and analysis of various components, ensuring that product design changes can be implemented faster than by using conventional methods.

EMPOWERED WORKERS

Although many people do not realize it, manufacturing is in the midst of the third industrial revolution, and it is just as dramatic as its forerunners. This revolution is heralded by the systematic formation of manufacturing and assembly cells. As the third revolution matures, control processes supply real-time information on entire systems. The same trends are happening in factories that happened on farms over the last 200 years. Over time (vastly shorter than the time that affected agriculture), fewer people will

assembled on a final assembly line anywhere in the world.

In the commercial automobile industry, final assembly lines are shorter, leaner, and with fewer stations. The stations have longer station and takt times because they must install larger subassemblies. *Takt time* is a German term that translates as "drumbeat of the production system," or simply, the production rate of the final assembly line.

Fourth industrial revolution vendors will not only be responsible for JIT manufacturing and

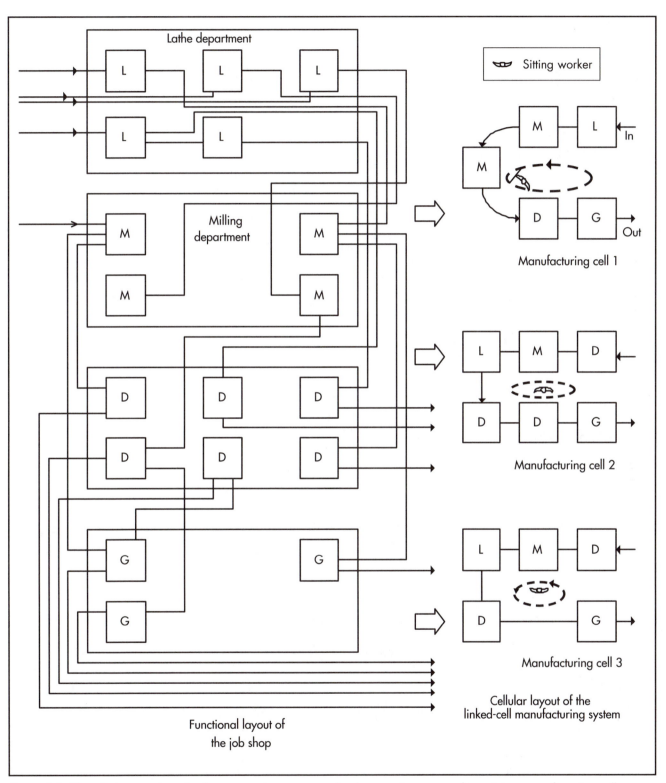

Figure 1-8. The job-shop portion of a factory requires a systems-level conversion to reconfigure it into manufacturing cells.

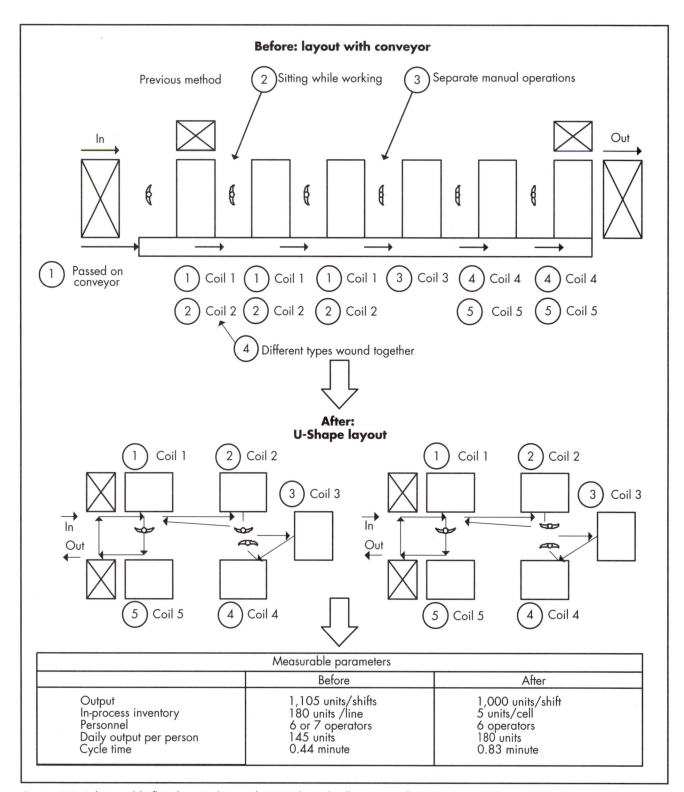

Figure 1-9. Subassembly flow lines redesigned into U-shaped cells using walking workers. (Sekine 1990)

work on the factory floor itself and more will be involved in the production of goods. Value will be added and wealth created only through the conversion of raw materials by manufacturing.

There is a general trend toward more labor saving automation in factories, but this should not be an undue concern. Factory automation creates more jobs every year than it eliminates. Tomorrow's factory will require greater levels of worker knowledge and more effective modes of transferring information on the quality and quantity of goods manufactured. The knowledge base of factory workers must be increased to improve productivity. Knowledge has a market value, particularly technical knowledge, thus, one can expect to pay factory floor workers more in the future.

The United States tends to give technical knowledge away or sell it to the lowest bidder. For example, Japan purchased much of the technical knowledge it needed to build vehicles, electronics, machine tools, and even electron microscopes. The early Japanese transmission electron microscopes were essentially duplicates of the precision-made Siemens instruments. A common thread of high, or sophisticated, technology binds Japanese product areas. Precision machining of magnetic lenses, along with the fabrication of high-voltage electronics, are key to the construction of quality electron microscopes.

The factory with a future needs superior information systems and people who can program, analyze, and otherwise deal with the information flowing to and from the factory floor. Unlike energy, knowledge and information do not follow the laws of conservation. Rather, they are synergistic, each promoting growth in the other. As the factory worker becomes better educated and knowledgeable about how the entire manufacturing production system works, the system subsequently begins to function better.

Manufacturing processes and systems must become simpler with automation. Often products are redesigned so that they can be automatically processed or assembled. In the 21st Century, significantly fewer workers on the

plant floor will be seen. The workers remaining will be better educated, more involved in solving daily production problems, work to improve the entire system, and make decisions about how to improve industrial jobs and manufacturing systems.

The Evolution of Lean Manufacturing

What spurred the third revolution was the competition of the Japanese in a wide variety of products and markets. Japanese prices were competitive and the quality superior. The country financed its remarkable transformation through low-interest government and private loans. More significantly, it developed lean production techniques to reduce inventory levels. Better cash flow resulted because of the vastly increased frequency of inventory turnovers.

Americans have theorized that Japanese manufacturing success can be attributed to their dumping of excess products in United States markets; governmental support given to targeted industries; or cultural differences. The Japanese are known to be hardworking and industrious citizens, like many of their colleagues worldwide. The theory that the success of the Japanese is simply the result of working long hours for substandard wages does not ring true because of the complex, quality products being built. The Japanese developed a new manufacturing system design, specifically Toyota, that is functionally and operationally different from any other manufacturing system—lean production. At the outset, it is important to understand this new system so that these principles can be implemented into factories.

Lean production is flexible, yet still delivers products on time, at the lowest possible cost, and on a continuing basis. They educated their work force and placed their best engineering talent on the production floor, rather than in the design room. Rather than invent a new mousetrap, the Japanese developed a better way to make mousetraps of superior quality at a lower cost.

The creative process technology of the Japanese spurred the manufacturing cell concept. Suppliers to final-assembly plants have captured much of this creative process technology. This is one reason why lean manufacturers today opt for single-source suppliers, where the proprietary-process technology is captured in one place. Toyota and many other Japanese manufacturers do not write about their technology or manufacturing systems (not even in their technical journals). The Japanese are sensitive to the fact that they have received much of their knowledge by picking up an American journal and reading about it. Japanese organizations sometimes make it very difficult for outsiders to get access to proprietary-process technology.

The Toyota Production System was designed to produce superior quality products. Toyota has taught the concept of total quality control to everyone, from company presidents to production workers. Japan has changed from a country that made junk to a nation that gives customers high-quality, robust, and reliable products. The Japanese accomplished this world-class manufacturing status through manufacturing system design.

W. Edwards Deming, the famous quality expert, said that the reduction of variation is the key to success (Deming 1982). If this is so, then reducing variation is the goal for continuous improvement, a cornerstone of the lean production philosophy. Types of variation important to a manufacturing organization are:

- quality (defects/million);
- output (parts/day);
- throughput time (hours/part); and
- cost (dollars/part).

All of these can be reduced through the implementation of lean manufacturing philosophies and methodologies. Additionally, continuous change and redesign of the manufacturing system design are key to the lean production philosophy. Here, the entire organization is like a single mind, strongly focused on making the system better everyday.

Cultural Change

Coupled with the redesign of manufacturing and production systems is a required cultural change in the operating philosophy within a company. Employee involvement and teamwork are rooted in the idea that no one employee is better than any other. All employees are addressed as associates. There is no executive lunchroom—the CEO eats lunch with supervisors and workers. There are no preferred parking places, except for the associate of the month.

The old system of management telling workers what to do and how to do it must change. However, this change usually requires that the CEO have the courage to shift a portion of the decision-making responsibilities from management to the factory floor. Restructuring manufacturing and production systems helps this most difficult transition.

The biggest and perhaps most difficult change is cultural. Employees' mentalities must change along with the factory floor design. Workers must be convinced that what they think and feel about the manufacturing system is important to the success of the organization. For this to work, achievement must be tracked closely and rewarded. People will "give it an extra mile" if there is a strong reward system. Rewards do not necessarily need to be monetary; there is strong evidence that verbal recognition and certificates work equally well.

Introduction to Lean Manufacuring

Lean manufacturing implementation requires a systems-level change for the factory—a change that will impact every segment of the company from accounting to shipping. Table 1-3 presents an outline for a 10-step methodology that converts a manufacturing system from mass to lean. This is a design task, so if machines are not being relocated, lean production is not being

Table 1-3. Lean production methodology for implementation (see Chapter 2)	
1. Develop and simplify the flow of materials	• Develop one-piece flow • Design/implement manufacturing cells • Use U-shape
2. Reduce and/or eliminate setup in the cells	• Use single-minute exchange of dies (SMED)
3. Integrate quality control	• Inspect to prevent defects • Use seven tools
4. Integrate preventative maintenance	• Improve capability and reliability • Use total preventive maintenance
5. Level and balance, sequence, synchronize	• Mixed model final assembly to level the demand for parts from the cell. • Balance the output from the cells to match demand from final assembly • Arrange subassemblies in sequence with order of assembly • Where possible, produce components in time with final assembly
6. Integrate production control	• Link the cells to final assembly with a pull system (kanban)
7. Integrate inventory control	• Gradually remove inventory from kanban links, exposing problems
8. Integrate the vendors (technology transfer)	• Teach vendors steps one through seven
9. Autonomation	• Develop processes and devices in the processes that automatically prevent processes from making defects or overproducing
10. Restructure the production system	• Use concurrent engineering
Once the manufacturing system has been designed for flexibility, controllability, uniqueness, and efficiency, products that can be made in this system can be designed along with processes to make those products (product development). The company is restructured into teams, often along product lines.	

implemented. The design and implementation of manufacturing cells is absolutely critical for a manufacturing organization to convert to lean production.

Before a factory embarks on the 10 steps, everyone must be educated on the concepts of lean production. Top management must be committed to the venture. If the top manager is not convinced and giving 100% support to a factory conversion, then the prospects of lean production success drop significantly. Every employee must be involved, motivated, and ultimately committed to the change process—this is a top-down initiative.

The conversion to linked cells is a system-level change affecting the factory environment and functional and cultural relationships within it. Lean production and implementation of its methodologies are long-term strategies. Changing the manufacturing system is equivalent to heart transplant surgery. It is major

and usually not elective. Changing the manufacturing system, especially the culture, is often difficult.

It is the manufacturing system that produces goods that the customers demand. There are two groups of people the manufacturing system must satisfy: those who use the products and those who use the system that makes the products. The manufacturing system's external customers buy or use products made by internal customers. The internal customers are workers who use the system to manufacture goods. Internal customers are usually a smaller group of people than the external customers. The manufacturing system must be restructured for the benefit of internal customers, the users of the manufacturing system. External customers of the manufacturing system also must be satisfied. External customers demand competitive prices and goods that are high in quality, robust, and delivered on time.

External customers, the buyers of internal customer-produced goods, determine prices. Everyone in a plant must understand that cost, not price, determines profit. Americans have always thought that cost plus profit equals price. The Japanese think that price minus cost equals profit. Thus, it is easier to understand the Japanese obsession with reducing waste by reducing costs. The external customer wants low cost, superior quality, and on-time delivery; the system must fulfill those needs. "Reduce cost by eliminating waste," is the operational motto of lean manufacturing. Waste is viewed as anything done to the product that does not add value and quality.

Here are some lean production implementation suggestions:

- Top-down commitment and involvement from management is critical. The entire company must must be committed to the change. Leaders must set examples, be active and enthusiastic, and be present on the factory floor regularly.
- The selection of measurable parameters is critical to track change. Everyone must understand that cost, not price, determines profits. Every employee must be committed to the elimination of all forms of waste.
- Internal customers must be encouraged to set high goals. They need to know who the best manufacturers in the class are by benchmarking. Rather than following industry leaders, companies should strive to leap ahead of them.
- Education and training helps workers understand why there is a need to change and how to implement that change. Workers must be empowered to implement quality control, machine maintenance, production control, inventory control, process improvements, setup-time reductions, and other tenets of lean production.
- The company must share the gains with those who contribute to company success by rewarding deserving teams. Many believe that bonus payments are the best way to share company success.

To summarize, it is important to educate and communicate an entire plan to the entire work force. The fundamental system-design concept is to develop manufacturing and assembly cells throughout the factory using cellular manufacturing for one-piece flow everywhere possible in the system. The restructured lean production system is simple enough for everyone who works in the system to understand.

Background on Manufacturing Systems

Civilization is linked to the ability to convert raw materials into usable goods. This began with the Stone Age and continued through the Bronze Age into the Industrial Age. The age of steel, with its sophisticated ferrous and nonferrous materials, has dominated the material world for the past 100 years. Civilization is now entering an era of custom-made materials such as plastics, composites, and ceramics. Nonetheless, metals still represent a significant portion of usable (and reusable) materials.

As material varieties expand, so do the variety of processes. Manufacturing processes are developed to efficiently add value to materials. Advances in manufacturing technology often account for productivity improvement. When a manufacturing technology is proprietary, competition can often gain quick access to it in the mass production world because technology is purchased over the counter from vendors. Lean manufacturing protects itself against this practice by capturing proprietary processes in manufacturing cells supplied by sole-source vendors. The mature lean manufacturing company designs and develops its own unique processes. For example, an engineer for Honda may visit the supplier making racks for the Accord steering gears. The engineer will visit the Honda cell for racks, but will not tour through other cells operated by this contract vendor. All the processing technology that the engineer needs to see is in one cell that makes racks for the Honda Accord.

Materials, people, and equipment are interrelated factors in manufacturing that must be combined properly to achieve low cost, superior quality, and on-time delivery of goods. Typically, as shown in Figure 1-10, 40% of the selling price of a product is its manufacturing cost. Since the market determines the selling price, maintaining a profit often depends on reducing manufacturing costs. Direct labor is usually the target of automation and accounts for about 5–12% of manufacturing costs, even though many view it as the main factor in increasing productivity.

The lean manufacturing strategy attacks material, general administration, and labor costs. Material costs include capital costs and the costs of storing and handling materials within the factory. The lean strategy eliminates material handling, except as needed to make products. Eliminating material handling is not the same as automating it.

Total expenses equal the selling price less the profit. Of those expenses, approximately 68% of the dollars are spent on people. This includes about 15% on engineers, 25% on marketing, sales, and general management people, 5% for direct labor, and 10% for indirect labor.

The average US labor cost in manufacturing was $14.85 per hour for hourly workers in 2001. Thus, reductions in direct labor had only a marginal effect on overall costs. A systems approach, or taking into account all factors, must be used when searching for waste-cutting measures. This requires a sound understanding by decision-makers of materials, processes, and equipment, followed by an understanding of the manufacturing systems.

Changing World Competition

In recent years, major changes in the world of goods manufacturing have occurred. Some of these changes are:

- worldwide competition by world-class companies (global companies);
- advanced manufacturing-process technology; and
- new manufacturing-system structures, strategies, and management.

Worldwide competition is now a fact of manufacturing life. In automobile manufacturing, foreign competition is relocating on American soil, demonstrating that the new lean production system works just as well in the United States as it does in Brazil or Japan. The future will bring

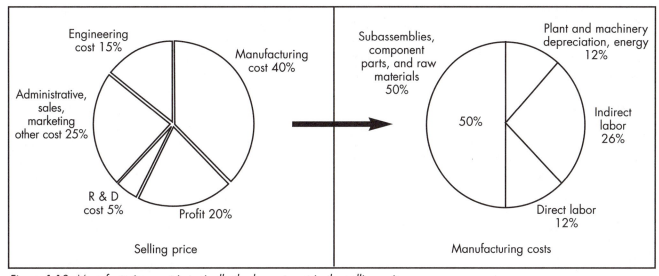

Figure 1-10. Manufacturing cost is typically the largest cost in the selling price.

more, not fewer, world-class competitors into the manufacturing world. Everyone with enough capital has access to new manufacturing-process technology because technology can always be purchased. Thus, technology alone does not ensure manufacturing competitiveness. The secret to success in manufacturing is to build a company that can deliver on time (short throughput time), superior-quality products to the customer at the lowest possible cost (with the least amount of waste), with the ability to be flexible and robust.

PRODUCTION AND MANUFACTURING SYSTEMS

Manufacturing is the economic term for making goods and services that will be available to satisfy human wants and needs. Manufacturing is creating value by applying useful mental and/or physical labor and, thus, converting raw materials into useful products demanded by consumers.

Manufacturing processes are combined to form *manufacturing systems*. Manufacturing systems take input and produce product for customers. *Production systems* include and service manufacturing systems. Thus, a production system refers to the total company and includes manufacturing systems as shown in Figure 1-11. The following football analogy helps to distinguish between manufacturing and production systems.

Imagine that college football is an example of a service industry. Football players would be the equivalent to the machine tools (see Figure 1-12). The actions that the players perform such as punting, passing, running, tackling, and blocking could be equated to manufacturing operations. Different players, or tools, have different functions, and some perform better than others.

The arrangement of machines (often called the factory layout) defines the basic design of the manufacturing system within the company. In football, this arrangement is called an offensive alignment or defensive formation. Modern teams use "pro-T" sets and "I-formations," but many US factories are still using the archaic single-wing version called the job shop.

The job shop is a functionally designed manufacturing system where like processes are typically put together into departments. The same organization occurs in football, with all the linemen segregated from the backs. Coaches are equivalent to foremen, and the head coach is the supervisor.

In the football analogy, the production system would be the athletic department that sells tickets, runs the training room (machine maintenance and repair), raises operating capital, arranges material handling (travel), and does whatever is needed to help keep the manufacturing system operating. The production system does not perform the actual manufacturing processes, just as no one in the athletic department actually plays in the football games. Production system personnel are more indirect, such as managerial and staff employees. In the plant, the production system personnel service the manufacturing system. This division is called staff, while people who work in direct manufacturing are called line workers. The production system includes the manufacturing system personnel, plus other people in functional areas of the plant who provide information, design, analysis, and control. When the manufacturing system is a job shop, the production system is functionally designed.

The subsystems are connected to one another to produce goods, services, or both. Goods refer to material items. Services are nonmaterial. Customers buy services to satisfy wants, needs, and desires. Service production systems include transportation, banking, finance, insurance, utilities, health care, education, communication, entertainment, sporting events, etc. These services involve labor that does not directly manufacture a product or create wealth.

Production ranking has a definite rank of importance. This is simple and easily understood, for example confusing *system* with *process* is similar to mistaking a CEO for the floor sweeper. Knowledge of rank is necessary

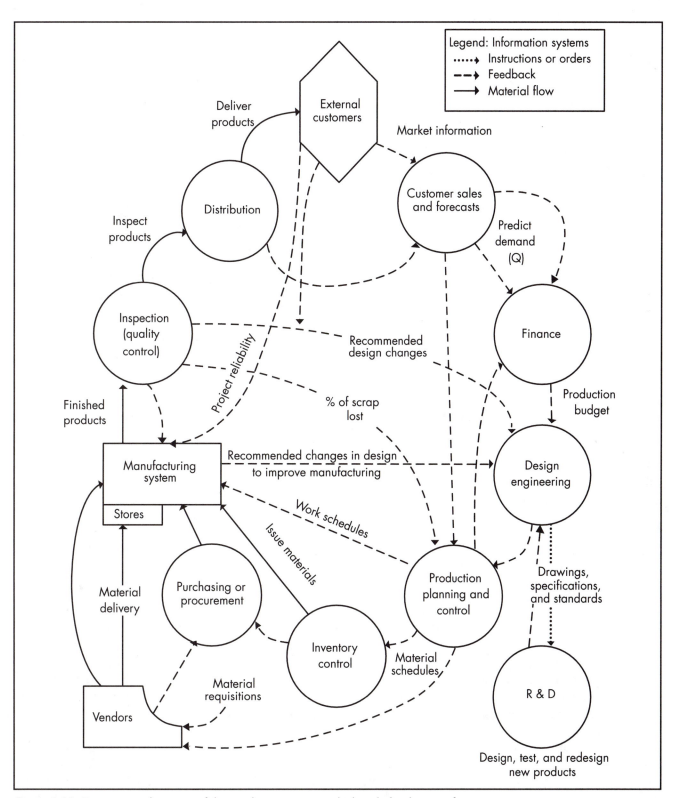

Figure 1-11. Functions and systems of the production system, which includes the manufacturing system.

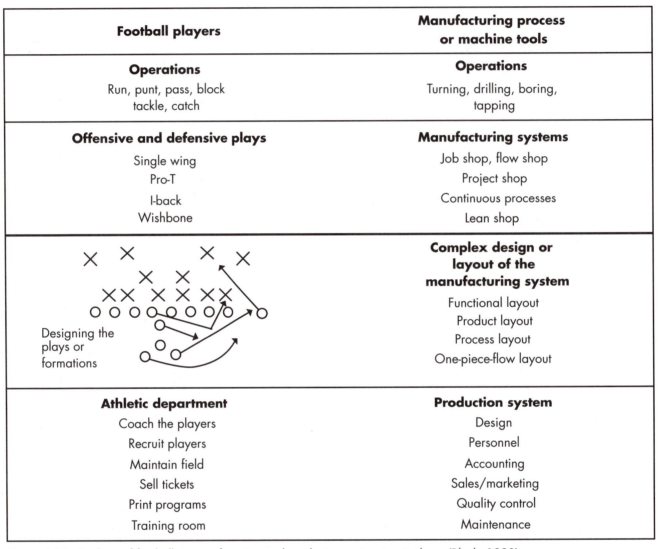

Football players	Manufacturing process or machine tools
Operations Run, punt, pass, block tackle, catch	**Operations** Turning, drilling, boring, tapping
Offensive and defensive plays Single wing Pro-T I-back Wishbone	**Manufacturing systems** Job shop, flow shop Project shop Continuous processes Lean shop
Designing the plays or formations	**Complex design or layout of the manufacturing system** Functional layout Product layout Process layout One-piece-flow layout
Athletic department Coach the players Recruit players Maintain field Sell tickets Print programs Training room	**Production system** Design Personnel Accounting Sales/marketing Quality control Maintenance

Figure 1-12. Analogy of football to manufacturing and production system terminology. (Black, 1990)

(see Table 1-4). The terms tend to overlap because of the inconsistencies of popular usage.

Production System

The highest-ranking area in the manufacturing hierarchy is the *production system*. A production system includes people, financing, funding, equipment, materials, supplies, markets, management, and the manufacturing system. In effect, all aspects of commerce (manufacturing, sales, advertising, profit, and distribution) are involved.

Much of the information given for the production system is relevant to the service production system, which, by design, is usually a job shop. The job shop, which contains elements of the flow shop when volume is large enough to justify special-purpose equipment, is a common system worldwide. The job shop with flow-shop elements is called the *production job shop*. Most manufacturing systems require a service production system for the most effective product sales. This is particularly true in industries such as the restaurant industry where cus-

Table 1-4. Production Terms for Manufacturing Production Systems		
Term	**Meaning**	**Examples**
Production system (the whole company)	The entire company or enterprise—all aspects of people, machines, materials, and information, are considered collectively.	Company that makes engines, assembly plant, glass-making factory, foundry.
Manufacturing system (collection of processes)	A series of manufacturing processes resulting in specific end products; the arrangement or layout of all the processes, material handling, equipment, people, and tooling (workholders).	Series of connected operations or processes; a job shop, flow shop, continuous process, project shop, or linked-cell system.
Manufacturing process (machine or machine tool)	A specific piece of equipment designed to accomplish specific processes, often called a machine tool; machine tools gathered together to make a manufacturing system.	Spot welder, milling machine, lathe, drill press, forge, drop hammer, die caster—manufacturing process technology.
Job (sometimes called a station, a "job" is a collection of tasks)	A collection of or sequence of operations done on machines or a collection of tasks performed by one worker at one location on an assembly line.	Operate machine, inspect part, assemble A into B. The machine tool operator has the job of running the machine.
Operation or task (sometimes called a process)	A specific action or treatment, the collection of which makes up the job of a worker.	Drill, ream, bend, solder, turn, face, mill, extrude.
Tools or tooling (cutting tools, workholders)	The implements used to cut, shape, or form the work materials, called cutting tools if referring to machining; also refers to jigs and fixtures used for workholding and punches and dies in metal forming.	Grinding wheel, drill bit, tap, end-milling cutter, die, mold, clamp, three-jaw vise, plate jib.

tomer service is as important as quality and on-time delivery.

Manufacturing System

A *manufacturing system* is a collection or arrangement of operations and processes producing desired products or components. It includes the actual equipment and machines composing the processes and the arrangement of those processes. Control of a system implies total control of all, not individual, processes or pieces of equipment. All users of the manufacturing system should understand how the system works, that is, behaves. The entire manufacturing system must be controlled to regulate inventory levels, movement of material through the factory, production output rates, and product quality.

There are many hybrid forms of manufacturing systems, but the functional design, also called the job shop, is the most common system. Charles Carter, from Cincinnati Milacron analyzed his company's manufacturing system for milling machines (Carter 1971). Carter tracked the frame of a machine through the factory and discovered that because of its design, the job shop proved to be the least productive and most difficult to control of all the manufacturing systems. Parts in a typical job shop spend only 5% of total manufacturing time on machines and the rest waiting or moving from one functional area to the next. Carter studied the machines themselves to determine what happens once a part is on a machine. He found that as a part is being processed, value is added only 30–40% of the time by changing its geometry (see Figures 1-13a and b). The remainder of the time the part is being loaded, unloaded, inspected, etc. The advent of numerical control machines has increased the percentage of productive machine time because tool movements are programmed and the machine can automatically change tools or load and unload parts.

However, because these machines still are in a job-shop environment, there remains a high percentage of waiting and delay time.

The percentage of time a machine spends making chips (40%) multiplied by the percentage of time on the machine (5%), yields a 2% productive time for an eight-hour shift. Suppose it is recommended that the process be upgraded, increasing the percentage of time making chips to 50% (using a faster machine), or even 60%? Such an improvement might cost $300,000. If no change in the manufacturing system takes place, the effect on the bottom line will be small, in the neighborhood of 1%. If the manufacturing system

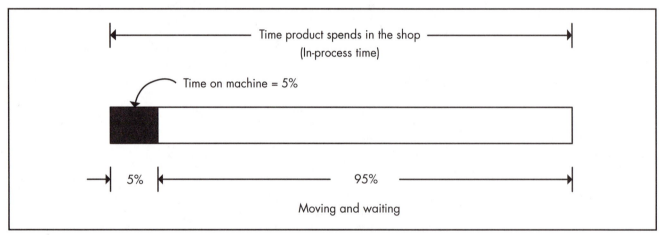

Figure 1-13a. Throughput time is mostly wait or delay time.

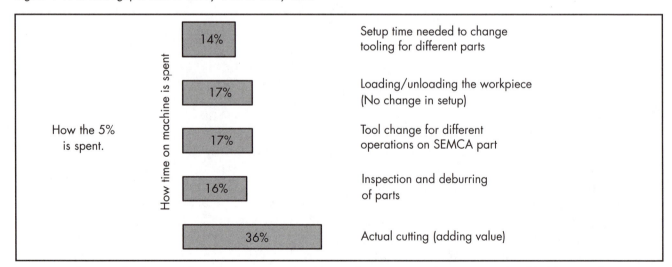

Figure 1-13b. Typical utilization of production time in metal-removal operations with conventional tool holding, workpiece loading, setups, and inspections.

is restructured to raise the time on the machine to 50%, the process will result in a significant 20% overall improvement in productivity.

UNDERSTANDING A COMPANY'S BUSINESS

Understanding process technology is important for everyone in the company. Manufacturing technology affects the design of the product and manufacturing systems, the way the manufacturing system can be controlled, the type of personnel employed, and the materials that can be processed. Table 1-5 outlines process technology characteristics. One valid criticism of American companies is that managers seem to have an aversion to understanding the industrial revolution's effect on their own companies' manufacturing technologies. This may be related to the argument presented in the previous section: why worry about process improvements when they have such a small impact on the bottom line?

Failure to understand the company's business, especially its fundamental process technology, can lead to failure. The way for a CEO to overcome an aversion to manufacturing technology and acquire a true understanding of it is to go to the factory floor and run the actual process. Suppose a job on an assembly line is to tighten bolts to a specific torque. How will a

Table 1-5. Process Technology Characteristics	
Mechanics (statics and dynamics of the process)	How does the process work? What are the process mechanics? What physically happens, and what makes it happen?
Economics/costs	What are the tooling and engineering costs? Which costs are short term and long term? What are the setup costs?
Time spans	How long does it take to set up? How can this time be shortened? How long does it take to run a part once it is set up? What process parameters affect the run time?
Constraints	What are the process limits? What cannot be done? What constrains this process (size, speeds, forces, volumes, power, cost)? What is very hard to do within an acceptable time/cost frame?
Process capability	What are the accuracy and precision rates of the process? What tolerances do the process meet? (What is the process capability?) How repeatable are those tolerances?
Uncertainties/process reliability	What can go wrong? How can this machine fail? What do people worry about with this process? Is this a reliable, stable process?
Skills	What operator skills are critical? What is not done automatically? How long does it take to learn to do this process?
Flexibility	Can this process easily work on parts of a new design or material? How does the process react to change in part design and demand? What changes are easy to do?

worker know if the right amount of torque has been applied? Only someone who has run a drill press can understand the sensitive relationships between feed rates, drill torque, and thrust. All processes require skill. The CEO who spends time learning the processes by working on the plant floor will be well on the way to being the head of a successful company. It is equally important for those who run the processes to have a part in the decision-making process on any issues concerning the factory processes and manufacturing systems.

PRODUCT LIFE CYCLES

Products have a life cycle (birth, growth, maturation, decline and death) and, therefore they are dynamic and change with time. A company's products may change, the volume of product they produce may change, or the actual process may change. There is relationship between a product's life cycle and the kind of manufacturing system that produces it. Figure 1-14 simplifies the life cycle into these steps:

1. The startup step involves a new product or company, low volume, and a small company.
2. The rapid-growth step occurs when products become standardized and volume increases rapidly. The company's ability to meet demand often stresses its capacity.
3. The maturation step evolves when standard designs emerge. Process development is important here.
4. The commodity step includes the long life, standard-of-the-industry product.
5. The decline-and-death step occurs when a product is slowly replaced by an improved product and then dies.

In Figure 1-14, the horizontal axis is time, usually in years. Preceding the startup step are the initial design and prototyping steps that may take more years. The maturation of a product in the marketplace generally leads to fewer competitors, with competition based more on price and on-time delivery than

unique product features. As the competitive focus shifts during the different stages of the product life cycle, the requirements placed on manufacturing cost, quality, flexibility, and delivery dependability also change. The stage of the product life cycle affects product design changes and the commonality of components— all of which have implications for the manufacturing processes and system. The first line of Figure 1-14 shows that the manufacturing system is changed during the product's life cycle.

The product life-cycle concept provides a framework for thinking about both the product evolution through time, and the types of market segments likely to develop. The different designs of manufacturing systems reflect a company's ability to manufacture at various volumes while decreasing the cost per unit over time. The general trend has been that product life cycles are becoming shorter, leading to two consequences. First, the time to develop new products must be shorter since the old products are being phased out quicker. Second, the manufacturing system must be designed to be flexible enough to deal with new products as they emerge from the development process.

The linked-cell approach has changed the classic life-cycle concept. Linked cells enable a company to decrease cost per unit significantly, while maintaining flexibility and, concurrently, making smooth transitions from low- to high-volume manufacturing. That is, the same flexible system can accommodate large changes in volume without needing to make major changes in the design of the company's manufacturing system.

Toyota and Honda are examples of companies with years of experience in the development of linked cells. They have been able to introduce new models (designs, styles) every three years, and both believe a two-year styling change is within reach.

A NEW MANUFACTURING SYSTEM

Many countries have achieved an equal level of process and machine tool development. Much of today's technology was devel-

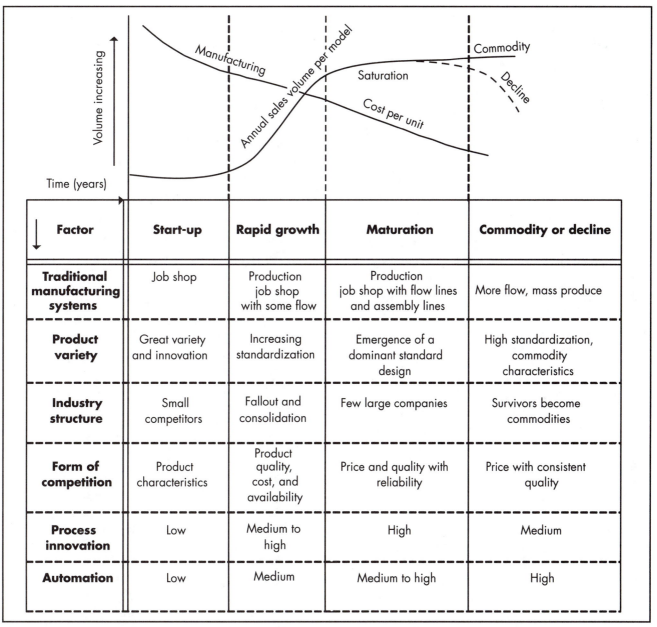

Factor	Start-up	Rapid growth	Maturation	Commodity or decline
Traditional manufacturing systems	Job shop	Production job shop with some flow	Production job shop with flow lines and assembly lines	More flow, mass produce
Product variety	Great variety and innovation	Increasing standardization	Emergence of a dominant standard design	High standardization, commodity characteristics
Industry structure	Small competitors	Fallout and consolidation	Few large companies	Survivors become commodities
Form of competition	Product characteristics	Product quality, cost, and availability	Price and quality with reliability	Price with consistent quality
Process innovation	Low	Medium to high	High	Medium
Automation	Low	Medium	Medium to high	High

Figure 1-14. Traditional relationship between product life cycle and manufacturing system development/evolution.

oped in England, Germany, the United States, and Japan. Now, Taiwan and Korea are also making great inroads into American markets, particularly in the automotive and electronics industries. What many American managers and engineers have failed to recognize is that methodology is as powerful as technology. The lean production system permits functional integration of critical subsystems into the manufacturing system. In future years, this new system based on linked cells will take its place with the Taylor system of scientific management and the Ford system of mass production. The original working model for the lean production system is the Toyota Motor Company. The system is also known as just-in-time, the Toyota Production System, or the Ohno system, after its chief architect, Taiichi Ohno.

Many American companies have successfully adopted some version of the Toyota system. The experience of dozens of these companies is condensed into 10 key steps that will be discussed in detail in Chapter 2, which, if followed, can create a future for any company. There is an order to implementing the 10 key steps. Many American companies have visited Japan to superficially look at the Toyota production system. The companies returned to the US and did one of three things. They either reduced inventory; cut vendors sharply, but still made them deliver daily; or they implemented a kanban system with parts delivered JIT. What the companies failed to do was implement the second, third, and fourth steps.

Quality is the overall critical step. For the lean production system to work, 100% good quality units flow rhythmically without interruption to subsequent processes. To accomplish this, an integrated quality control program must be developed. The responsibility for quality must be given to workers on the factory floor, with a required company commitment to constant quality improvement. The goal? To produce perfect product the first time, by making it easy to see quality, by stopping the line when something goes wrong, and by inspecting items 100% if necessary to prevent defects from occurring. The results of this integrated quality control subsystem are astonishing. Six of the 10 problem-free automobile models for 1985 were from Toyota. This quality record has continued for more than 17 years. Building manufacturing cells and reducing setup does not need to be the first effort, but it is the best way to proceed. The effort implements the lean production quality motto of make-one, check-one, and move-one-on to the component manufacturing level. Improving cell quality to produce zero defects and avoid machine tool failures is a necessary prerequisite to implementing kanban and reducing inventory. Step three, the utilization of kanban, can reduce variance, which will yield high-quality parts and assemblies every time.

The most important factors in successful, economical manufacturing are people, followed by materials, then capital. All three must be organized and managed to provide effective coordination, responsibility, and control. Part of the success of the linked-cell system can be attributed to a holistic approach that includes:

- consensus decision making by management teams, coupled with decision making at the lowest possible level;
- mutual trust, integrity, and loyalty between workers and management;
- working in teams or groups with pay based upon team performance, a natural outgrowth of linked cells (elimination of hourly wages and piecework);
- incentive pay in the form of team bonuses for company performance; and
- stable, even lifetime, employment for all full-time employees, coupled with a large pool of part-time temporary workers.

Many companies in the United States employ some or all of these elements, and a company can be organized and managed in many different ways and still be successful. Nonetheless, the real secret of lean manufacturing lies in designing a simplified system that everyone understands, where the decision making is placed at the correct organizational level. In manufacturing, low-cost, superior-quality products are the result of teamwork within an integrated manufacturing production system. This is key to producing superior quality at less cost with on-time delivery, all goals of lean production.

Chapter 2
Ten Steps to Lean Production

SUCCESSFUL LEAN MANUFACTURING

The 10 steps to lean production (Figure 2-1) are a result of many years of research into successful lean manufacturing processes both in the United States and abroad. These 10 steps were taken from hundreds of successful functional manufacturing systems conversions to lean manufacturing. The steps are numbered and the order of implementation should exactly follow the step order. Otherwise, a successful factory conversion will be highly unlikely. The 10 steps are similar to building a house. Step 1 in house construction is building a strong and sustainable foundation. Likewise, in manufacturing, Step 1 must design and build a strong and sustainable linked-cell manufacturing system—lean production's foundation. The manufacturing system practitioner will be on the road to a successful factory conversion to lean production with this proven methodology.

Step 1: The Manufacturing System— Form U-shaped Cells

In a lean production, linked-cell manufacturing system scheme, manufacturing and assembly cells replace the functional job shop. The first task is to restructure and reorganize the basic manufacturing system into cells that produce families of parts. This prepares for systematically creating a linked-cell system where there is one-piece parts movement within cells and small-lot movement between cells. Creating cells is the way to integrate production, inventory, and quality control with machine-tool maintenance.

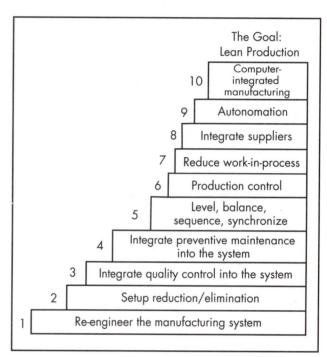

Figure 2-1. Ten steps to lean production.

Conversion of the functional system into a flexible, linked-cell system is a huge design task. Most companies design their first cell by trial-and-error. The first cells are often designed around a product family that defines a set or sequence of processes needed to create that family of parts. The rack bar for an automobile is an example. A given model of an automobile may have 10 variations of racks (right-hand drive versus left-hand drive, power steering versus mechanical steering, etc.). Variations of auto racks are made in one cell. The cell makes racks for every auto of that particular model.

Operations in the cell include metal cutting, heat treating, inspection, and assembly. Grinding and superfinishing are also completed in the same cell. By grouping similar components into part families, a group or set of processes can be collected to manufacture parts families. Arrangement of machines in a cell is defined by the sequence of manufacturing processes performed on the parts.

Many companies begin with a pilot cell so that everyone can see how cells function. It requires time and effort to train operators. In addition, they may need time to adjust to cellular operations. Selecting a product or group of products for a cell is a simple, but risky, design method.

Cell operators should be involved in the early stage of designing the cell if possible. Otherwise, they may not take ownership of the operation. The pilot operation shows everyone how cells operate and reduces the setup time on each machine or process. Some cell processes or machines may not be used 100% of the time. The machine-utilization rate may or may not improve in an archaic job shop. Process utilization is likely to be higher in a functional system where overproduction is allowed.

Overproduction is considered a high form of waste in the lean production philosophy. The objective in a manned linked-cell manufacturing system is to utilize people and non-depreciable assets fully, enlarging and enriching jobs, and allowing workers to become multifunctional.

Workers learn to operate many different kinds of machines and perform many functions including quality control, machine tool maintenance, setup reduction, and continuous improvement. In unmanned cells and systems, the application of equipment is important. This is because the most flexible and intelligent resource in the cell, the worker, is removed and replaced by a robot.

Manned cells are designed in a U shape so workers can move from machine to machine to load and unload parts with the shortest walking distance.

Figure 2-2 shows an example of a simple-manned cell. The cell has one worker who can make a walking loop around the cell in 110 seconds. (See the breakdown of time in Figure 2-2). The cycle time for the cell is 110 seconds.

This can be found by:

$$CT = \frac{1}{PR} \qquad (2\text{-}1)$$

where:

CT = cycle time, seconds
PR = production rate

Machines in a cell are usually single-cycle automatics; they can complete the desired processing untended and turn off automatically after the processing cycle. If an operator comes to a machine that has just finished its production cycle, he or she will unload, check, and load the next part into the machine. The operator then starts the machining cycle by hitting a *walkaway switch* before stepping to the next machine. The cell usually includes all of the processing equipment and machines required for a completed part or subassembly.

Figure 2-2 shows the average manual time and walking time. Times for the machining cycle are given as machine time. The cell is designed so the machining time for any part in the family on any machine in the cell is less than the necessary cycle time. That is, machining time is less than cycle time. Thus, machining times are uncoupled from cycle time. However, note that the machining time for the third operation is greater than the necessary cycle time. That is, 180 seconds is greater than 110 seconds. Therefore, this operation must be duplicated and the worker must alternate between the two lathes, visiting each lathe every other trip around the cell.

This makes the average machining time:

$$\frac{180}{2} = 90 \text{ seconds}$$

Therefore, the turning process stays below the required 110 seconds; that is, 90 seconds is less than 110 seconds.

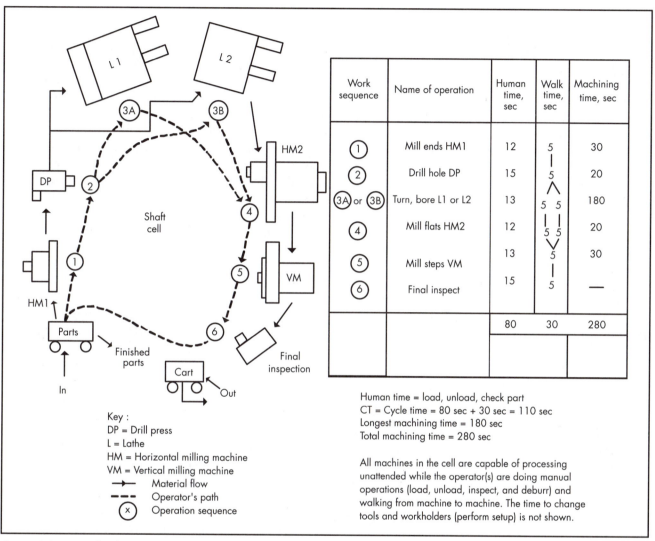

Work sequence	Name of operation	Human time, sec	Walk time, sec	Machining time, sec
①	Mill ends HM1	12	5	30
②	Drill hole DP	15	5	20
③A or ③B	Turn, bore L1 or L2	13	5 5	180
④	Mill flats HM2	12	5 5	20
⑤	Mill steps VM	13	5	30
⑥	Final inspect	15	5	—
		80	30	280

Human time = load, unload, check part
CT = Cycle time = 80 sec + 30 sec = 110 sec
Longest machining time = 180 sec
Total machining time = 280 sec

All machines in the cell are capable of processing unattended while the operator(s) are doing manual operations (load, unload, inspect, and deburr) and walking from machine to machine. The time to change tools and workholders (perform setup) is not shown.

Key :
DP = Drill press
L = Lathe
HM = Horizontal milling machine
VM = Vertical milling machine
→ Material flow
--- Operator's path
Ⓧ Operation sequence

Figure 2-2. Example of an interim manned cell.

Another example of lean manufacturing conversion (Sekine 1990) shows the marked improvement in productivity that cells can achieve. In some instances, functional job-shop or flow-line conversion is impractical. Therefore, flow lines and flow-line conversions are used. In Sekine's example, it is shown that at the same time manufacturing cells are being designed, flow lines using a conveyor are being reconfigured into U-shaped cells (Figure 1-9). The conversion allows these newly arrayed flow-line systems to operate on a one-piece flow basis. The operations

in an assembly cell are usually manual. An operator must stay at each workstation until a task is completed. As with manufacturing cells, long setup times typical in flow lines must be vigorously attacked and reduced so flow lines can be changed quickly from making one product to another. This makes them flexible and compatible with the manufacturing cells and subassembly and final assembly lines. Again, cells are designed to manufacture specific groups or families of parts. Hence, manufacturing and assembly cells are the first choice. In the U-shaped layout that was shown in Figure 1-9, Workers 2, 3, and 4 cover multiple operations. Notice that Workers 3 and 4 share Operation 7. Workers 1 and 2 are covering Operations 1, 11, and 12 using the rabbit chase (Suzaki 1987) method.

The need to line balance is necessary in the flow line, but is eliminated in the cellular design methodology. This is accomplished by using standing and walking workers who are capable of performing multiple operations.

Cells have many features that make them different from other manufacturing systems. Parts move from machine to machine and one at a time within the cell. Small, highly controlled batches move from cell to cell, from cell to subassembly, or sometimes straight to final assembly.

For material processing, machines are typically capable of completing a cycle initiated by a worker. These machines are called single-cycle automatics.

The U-shape layout puts the start and finish points of the cell next to each other. Every time an operator completes a walking trip around the cell, a part is completed. The cell is designed so cycle time is equal to or slightly less than that for final assembly. This is the necessary cycle or *takt* time. Machining time for each machine is less than the time it takes for an operator to complete a walking trip around the cell. Thus, the machining time can be altered without changing the production schedule, as long as the machining time stays within the confines of the cell's cycle time.

The cell is designed to make parts as demanded by downstream processes and operations. There is no overproduction allowed—a major form of manufacturing waste. Overproduction results in the need to store parts, transport them to storage and retrieve when needed, account for them, purchase baskets for storage, and acquire forklifts. This requires people and costs money, but adds no value. In assembly cells, cycle time may be throttled up or down by adding or removing workers.

In manufacturing cells, there is no need to balance the machining time for the machines and processes. It is necessary only that no machining time be greater than the required cycle time. The machining speeds and feeds can be relaxed to extend the tool life of cutting tools and reduce wear and tear on machines, as long as the machining time does not equal or exceed the cell's cycle time.

Fixtures on cell machines are designed to hold a family of parts, so rapid changeover from one part to another is possible within the parts family. Fixturing is designed with error proofing, or *poka-yoke* functions, in mind to prevent errors and stop defective parts from getting into the system. Fixtures are designed for correct and easy loading and unloading and do not allow defective parts to be loaded.

In some cells, *decouplers* are placed between processes, operations, or machines to provide flexibility, part transportation, inspection for defect prevention (poka-yoke), and quality control. The decoupler inspects a part for a critical dimension and feeds back adjustments to the machine to prevent it from making oversize parts as the process cutter wears. A process-delay decoupler delays the part so it can cool, heat, cure, or undergo whatever process is necessary for a time period greater than the cycle time required by the cell. Decouplers and flexible fixtures are vital parts of both manned and unmanned cells.

Step 2: Setup Reduction/Elimination

When cells are formed to make a family of parts, the problems of process and machine changeover from one part to another must be addressed. Therefore, everyone on the plant floor must be taught how to reduce setup time using single-minute exchange-of-die techniques. A setup-reduction team acts to facilitate the single-minute exchange-of-die process for production workers and foremen. The team demonstrates the methodology on a project; usually the plant's worst setup problem. Reducing setup time is critical to reducing lot size. Dr. Shigeo Shingo, father of the single-minute exchange-of-die system, designed its four stages to be sequential (Figure 2-3).

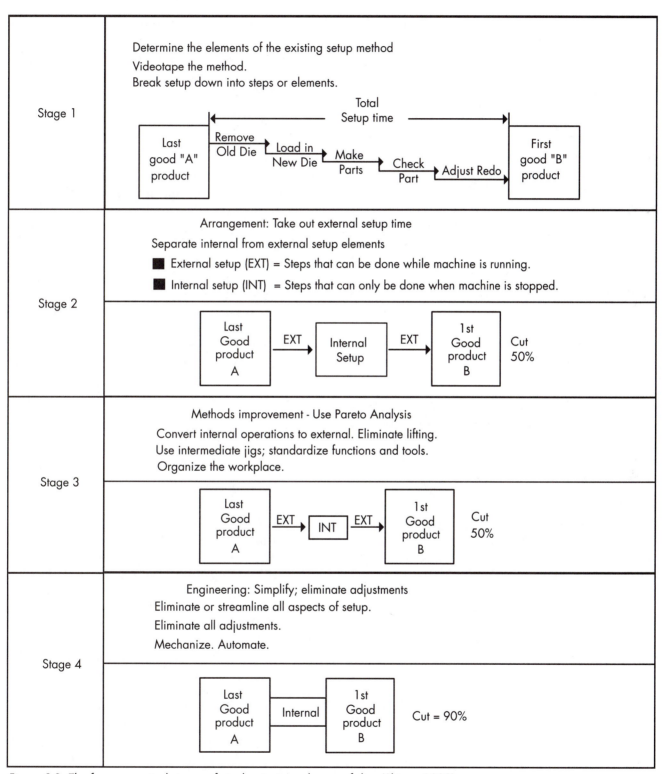

Figure 2-3. The four conceptual stages of single-minute exchange of dies (Shingo 1989).

The lean production approach to manufacturing means running small lots. This is impossible if machine setups take hours to accomplish. The economic order quantity (EOQ) formula determines the quantity to be manufactured to cost-justify a long and costly setup time. However, it is a faulty approach that accepts long setup times as a given. Setup times can be reduced, often drastically. This action results in a direct reduction in lot sizes.

Successful setup reduction is easily achieved when approached from a methods-engineering perspective. Much of the initial work in this area has been done through time-and-motion studies, as well as Shingo's single-minute techniques for the rapid exchange of dies. Setup-time reduction occurs in four stages. The initial stage determines what is being done for setup in the operation. The current setup operation is usually videotaped and everyone reviews the tape to determine its elemental steps. A detailed list of the process is compiled from the video.

The next stage is to separate setup activities on the list into two categories, internal and external. Internal elements are those done only when a machine is inoperative, while external elements are done while a machine is operative. This elemental division usually shortens lead time considerably.

The third and fourth stages focus on reducing internal time. The key is for workers to learn to reduce setup time by applying simple single-minute exchange-of-die principles. If a company must wait for setup-reduction workers to examine every process, a lean manufacturing system never will be achieved. Therefore, it is absolutely necessary that cellular design is at least concurrent with setup reduction, if not ahead of it.

In the last stages, it may be necessary to invest capital to lower setup time to less than a minute. Intermediate jigs and fixtures and duplicate workholders represent the typical kinds of hardware needed. In many cases, long setup times can be reduced to less than 15 seconds in relatively short order.

The similarities in part geometry and/or processes in the parts family allow setup time to be reduced or even eliminated. Initially, setup time should be less than 10 minutes. As the cell matures, the setup time is continually reduced. A final goal is to reduce setup time to around 10–15 seconds, commonly called *one-touch exchange of dies*.

Setup time for a cell should be reduced until it is equal or less than the typical manufacturing-cell cycle time of one or two minutes. This is usually accomplishable and provides significant initial reduction in lot size. The next goal is to reduce the setup time to less than manual time, or the time a worker needs to load, unload, inspect, deburr, etc., during a process. After each production setup, defect-free products should be made from the start. Ultimately, the ideal condition is to eliminate setup; this is called *no touch exchange of dies*.

In summary, a savings in setup time decreases lot size and increases the frequency of lots produced. The smaller the lot sizes, the lower the inventory a system is carrying, making for shorter throughput time and improving quality.

Step 3: Integrate Quality Control

A *multiprocess worker* is capable of operating more than one kind of process. A *multifunctional worker* can perform tasks other than operating processes or machines. A multifunctional worker is also an inspector who understands process capability, quality control, and process improvement. In lean production, every worker has the responsibility and authority to make a product right the first time and every time, and to stop an operation when something goes wrong. This line-stop authority for workers is critical to the success of lean production in a factory. While the integration of quality control into a manufacturing system markedly reduces defects and eliminates the need for inspectors, cells provide a natural environment for integration of quality control. The fundamental idea is to inspect to prevent a defect from occurring, and never allow a defective product to leave the manufacturing cell and get into the system.

When management and production workers trust each other, then and only then, is it possible to implement an integrated quality-control program.

Japan started on the road to superior quality by the visits of Dr. W. Edwards Deming in the late 1940s and early 1950s. The Japanese were desperate to learn about quality. The statistical quality-control techniques offered by Deming and others were readily accepted. Many Japanese believed that everyone in America used statistical process-control techniques. This, of course, was, and is not today, the case. However, the Japanese eagerly accepted quality-control concepts, and then they did something not even being done by American companies using statistical quality control. They taught factory workers quality techniques and methods. The Japanese even had a journal on the subject.

When every worker is responsible for quality and performs the seven basic tools of quality control (Figure 2-4), the number of inspectors on a factory floor is markedly reduced. Products failing to conform to specifications are immediately discovered because they are checked or used immediately.

Under the leadership of Vice President of Manufacturing Taiichi Ohno, a new idea took hold at Toyota. Ohno's ideas on quality were quite different in concept from the inspection philosophies of the time. First, every worker was an inspector responsible for quality at his/her workstation. Every worker on an assembly line could stop the line if they found something wrong. Everyone's attention was focused on problems delaying production. Problems were resolved first and permanently, so a line was not stopped again by them. Inspection to prevent defects from occurring, rather than inspecting to find defects after they had occurred, became the mode of operation in cells. Ultimately, the concept of *autonomation* evolved (see Step 9).

Through redesign, cells produce parts one at a time, like assembly lines. This is called *one-piece flow*. The process allows all production entities and internal customers to operate a *make-one, check-one, move-one-on* operation. The operator checks what a previous process produced to assure it is correct 100% of the time. Pull cords are installed on assembly lines to stop them if anything goes wrong. For example, if production is going too fast (according to the quantity needed for the day), or if workers find a safety hazard, then they are obligated to pull the cord and stop the line. Once a problem is discovered, it is rectified immediately. Meanwhile, other workers on the line who are stopped go about other required tasks such as maintaining equipment, changing tools, sweeping the floor, or practicing setups. A line does not move until a problem is solved. This is a fundamental difference between lean production and other manufacturing systems.

For manual work on assembly lines, a system for tracking defective work is called an *andon*. An andon is actually an electric light board that hangs high above conveyor assembly lines where everyone can see it. When everything goes according to plan, the board's lights are all green. When a worker on a line needs help, he or she can turn on a yellow light. Nearby multifunctional workers who have finished their tasks within an allotted cycle time see the yellow signal and move to assist the worker having a problem. If a problem cannot be solved within the cycle time, a red light comes on and the line stops automatically until it is solved. Music usually plays to let everyone know there is a line problem.

In most cases, red lights go off within 10 seconds. The next cycle begins when a green light comes on and all processes start at the same time. The name for this system is *yo-i-don*, which literally means "ready, set, go."

The stages on an assembly line are synchronized. Such systems are built through teamwork and a cooperative spirit among workers, fostered by a management philosophy based on harmony and trust. Contrast this with the way

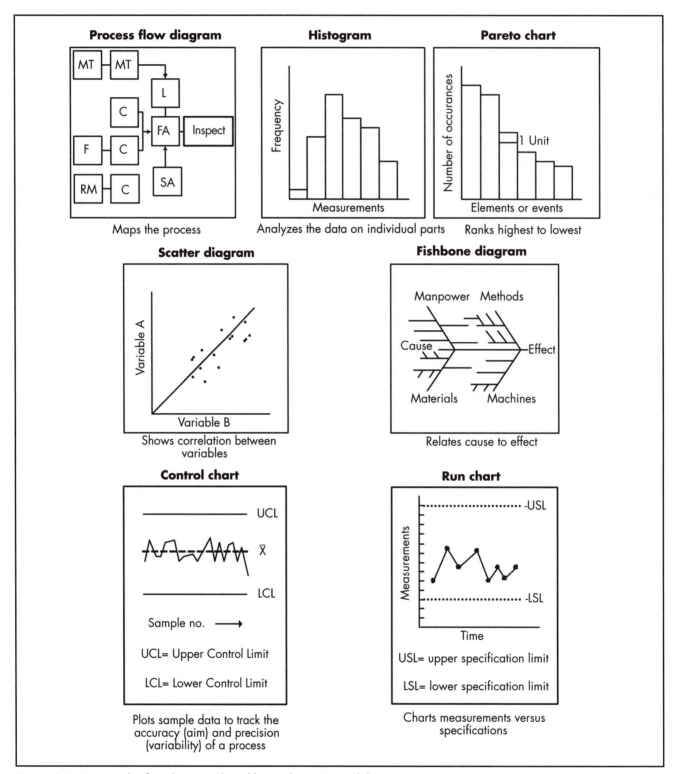

Figure 2-4. Seven tools of quality control used by workers to control the process.

things often operate in the functional job shop. How long does it take to find a problem, convince somebody that it is a problem, get it solved, and the solution implemented? How many defective parts are produced in the meantime? Line shutdowns in lean factories are encouraged to protect quality. Management must have confidence and trust in individual workers to give them line "stop" authority.

Step 4: Integrate Preventive Maintenance

Making machines operate reliably begins with the installation of an integrated preventive maintenance program that provides workers with training and the tools they need to maintain equipment properly. Excess processing capacity obtained by reducing setup times allows operators to reduce equipment speeds or feed, and to run at less-than-full capacity. Reducing pressure on workers and processes to produce a given quantity fosters a drive to produce perfect quality.

Multifunctional operators are trained to perform routine low-level process maintenance. Low-level tasks include adding lubricants, checking for wear and tear, replacing damaged nuts and bolts, routinely changing and tightening belts and bolts, and listening for telltale noises that signify pending failures. These and other tasks can do wonders for machine tool reliability, while giving workers a sense of pride in ownership. The maintenance department must instruct workers on performing these tasks and assist them with preparing routine checklists for process maintenance. Workers are also responsible for keeping their areas of the factory clean and neat. Thus, additional functions that are integrated into the lean manufacturing system are maintenance and housekeeping.

Typically, the following housekeeping rules are implemented:

- There is a place for everything and everything should be in its place. Everything

should be put away, so it is ready to use the next time.
- Each worker must be responsible for the cleanliness of the workplace and equipment. The 5s strategy is adopted—sort, straighten, shine, standardize, and sustain.

Naturally, processes still need attention from experts in the maintenance department, just as an aircraft is taken out of service periodically for engine overhaul and maintenance. This vital service must be carried out, but must not overtly impact production. One alternative is to switch to two eight-hour shifts separated by two four-hour time blocks for machine maintenance, tooling changes, restocking, long setups, overtime, early time, and other functions. This is called the 8-4-8-4 scheme.

Processes can decrease variability, but they must be reliable and dependable. Generally said, smaller machines are simpler and easier to maintain, and therefore, more reliable. Multiple copies of small machines add to the flexibility of the overall system as well. The linked-cell system permits certain machines in cells to be slowed and, like the long-distance runner, to run longer and easier without a breakdown. Many observers of the Just-in-time manufacturing system come away with the feeling that machines are "babied." In reality, they are being run at the pace required to meet takt time demand.

Advanced lean manufacturers build and modify their manufacturing process technology. It is what makes them unique from their competitors. In addition, they try to build equipment in multiple copies so that there are multiple sets producing similar products.

Suppose there is a manufacturing cell producing racks for a rack-and-pinion steering-gear assembly. It makes six different racks for the Honda Accord. In the same factory, a cell for Toyota makes racks for the Camry® and Avalon® models; the cell can make 10 different racks. The two rack cells are similar in design. In the event of a machine failure, a machine from another cell could be borrowed. Also, processing capacity and capability are replicated in proven increments. The manufacturing cell has an optimal design, and offers the security of dealing with a proven manufacturing process technology. Modifying existing equipment shortens the time needed to bring new technology on-line. Manufacturing on multiple versions of low-capacity machines retains worker expertise and permits a company to keep improving and mistake-proofing the process. In contrast to this approach is the typical job shop, where a new "super machine" is purchased and installed when product demand increases. Many companies mistakenly try to increase capacity by buying new, untried manufacturing technology that may take months, even years, to debug and make reliable.

Step 5: Level, Balance, Sequence, and Synchronize

The steps outlined here are the amalgamated experience of many companies that have Americanized and implemented some version of the Toyota production system. A basic tenet of lean production is that process flow defines machine layout where products having common or similar processes are grouped. Also, quick conveyance between cell processes is provided, along with a means to reduce setup time. The basic premise of the system is to produce the kind of product needed, in the quantities needed, and in the time needed.

The lean production system depends upon "smoothing" the manufacturing system. To eliminate variation or fluctuation in quantities in feeder processes, it is necessary to eliminate fluctuation in final assembly. This is also called *leveling* the final assembly process. It means the manufacturing engineer must level demand for subassemblies and components delivered from suppliers. An example to illustrate the basic idea follows. First, calculate the time it takes for daily demand

$$DD = \frac{MD}{D} \qquad (2\text{-}2)$$

where:

DD = daily demand for parts
MD = monthly demand for parts (forecast + customer orders)
D = number of days in each month

From this, cycle time (CT) can be found.

$$CT = \frac{1}{PR} \qquad (2\text{-}3)$$

where:
CT = cycle time, seconds

$$PR = \frac{DD}{Work\ hours\ per\ day}$$

This simple approach highlights the way lean production companies calculate cycle time. Life is simpler when the functional job shop is eliminated and a linked-cell system is installed.

Here is another example of how cycle time is determined for a mix of automobiles at final assembly. Suppose that the forecast requires 240 vehicles per day; and there are 480-production minutes available (60 minutes × 8 hours per day). Thus, every automobile cycle will equal 2.0 minutes (As defined earlier, cycle time for final assembly is called takt time.) Therefore, every 2.0 minutes an automobile rolls off the final assembly line. Suppose that the required production mix is as given in Table 2-1.

The sub-processes, including manufacturing and subassembly cells feeding a two-door fastback automobile, are controlled by this model's cycle time. Every 4.8 minutes the rear-deck-subassembly line produces a rear hatch for the fastback version. Every 4.8 minutes two doors for the fastback are made.

Every car, regardless of model type, has an engine. Engines are produced at a rate of one every 2.0 minutes (480 minutes/240 automobiles). Each engine needs four pistons. Therefore, every 2.0 minutes, four pistons are produced. Parts and assemblies are produced in minimum lot sizes and delivered to the next process controlled by *kanban*. Kanban is a physical production and inventory control system. It requires a minimum amount of in-process inventory, reducing inventory costs and releasing funds for other projects. Kanban is a major function in the lean production scheme and is discussed in detail in Step 6.

Balancing is making output from cells equal to the necessary demand for parts downstream. Parts, or components, are not made in sync with final assembly; only the daily quantity is the same. In essence, small lot sizes (made possible by setup reduction within cells), single-unit conveyance within cells, and standardized cycle time are keys to a smooth manufacturing system. Cycle time should be equal to takt time for final assembly; but, at the outset, simply matching the daily demand is sufficient. Ultimately, every part, sequence of assembly, operation, or subassembly takes the same amount of time to produce as the final assembly line takes to assemble the product.

For example, when an automobile body's painting is complete, an order for vehicle seats is issued to the seat suppliers. Seats are made in the same order as autos on the assembly line. They are made and delivered in the same amount of time as it takes the automobile to get from the paint station to the station where seats are installed. Hence, seat manufacturing is synchronized with automobile production. This is called *leveling, balancing,* and *synchronizing* the manufacturing system. Some subassemblies are shipped to final assembly in correctly sequenced lots in correct sequence to arrive for a specific auto at a predetermined time. The dashboard subassembly and other subassemblies may be produced in this manner. The minimum number of workers needed to produce one unit of output in the necessary cycle time is used.

Step 6: Integrate Production Control

People who work in production control schedule the manufacturing system. They determine where in the factory raw materials, purchased parts, and subassemblies go; when they should go there; and how many should go. In short, production-control workers determine where, when, and how many.

The production-control function is labor-intensive and many companies have tried to computerize the functions of this job with material-requirements-planning (MRP) software. Many companies experience disappointment and frustration using these computerized production control programs. The primary problem with software programs is that they are information systems, not control systems. Managers should use these systems to obtain information and control the system, not rely on them to carry out management's primary tasks of making good and timely decisions. There have been many problems resulting from a lack of discipline in the workforce. Workers often fail to update the MRP system at the proper time, or even at all. Thus, many times, managers make control judgments based upon incomplete or faulty information. The lean manufacturing approach is to redesign the

Table 2-1. Mixed model final assembly line example that determines model cycle time				
Quantity	Vehicle Mix for Line Model	Model Cycle Time (minutes)	Model Production (minutes)	Sequence (24 Vehicles)
50	Two-door coupe	9.6	100	TDC, TDF, TDF, FDS, FDW
100	Two-door fastback	4.8	200	TDC, TDF, TDF, FDW, FDW
25	Four-door sedan	18.2	50	TDC, TDF, TDF, TDS, TDW
65	Four-door wagon	7.7	130	TDC, TDF, TDF, FDW
240 vehicles / 8 hours		480/240 = 2 minutes per vehicle		

manufacturing system; that is, implement Steps 1–5, then introduce kanban methodology, which performs the production control function automatically.

Kanban is lean production's inventory and production-control subsystem. Production-control integration can be realized by using kanban to link cells, subassemblies, and final-assembly elements. The manufacturing system's layout must define the paths that parts follow throughout the plant. This process begins by connecting manufacturing cells, subassembly cells, and flow lines with kanban links. The need for routing sheets is eliminated and only final-assembly output is scheduled. The parts, the in-process inventory, flow within the structure. All cells, processes, subassemblies, and final assemblies are connected via kanban links, which pull parts and subassemblies to final assembly only in the quantities required. Kanban enables the integration of production control into the manufacturing system to form a linked-cell manufacturing system.

Kanban is a physical, visual-control system only good for lean production; it does not work for the job shop. Cells are linked by kanban, thus providing control over the route parts must take, control of the amount of material flowing between any two points, and information about when parts will be needed. There are many types of kanban: kanban squares, one-card kanban, two-card kanban, and many others. The most complex is the two-card kanban used in established lean production environments. There are two types of cards: *withdrawal* (or conveyance) *kanbans* and *production-ordering kanbans*. One can think of kanban as a link connecting the output point of one cell, with the input point of the next cell (see Figure 2-5). The kanban link uses carts or containers that hold a specific number of parts. Every cart in a kanban line has the same number of parts. Each cart has one withdrawal and one production-ordering kanban card.

Then the maximum inventory equals the number of carts multiplied by the number of parts in each cart.

The arrival of a production-ordering kanban card in the two-card or dual-card kanban system at the manufacturing cell initiates an order to make more parts to fill the cart. The withdrawal kanban cards tell the material handler where to take the parts. The link shown in Figure 2-5 has six carts and each cart holds 50 parts, so the maximum inventory is 300 parts.

The same link type connects subassembly cells to the final assembly. Other cells in a linked-cell system are similarly connected by a pull system for production control, as shown in Figure 2-6.

Step 7: Reduce Work-in-process (WIP)

Step 7 involves the integration of inventory control into the lean production system. Inventory in the system is held in highly controlled kanban links and is called *work-in-process*. Work-in-process inventory has been analogized to the water level in a river and its effect upon boat traffic (as shown in Figure 2-7). A high river level is analogous to a high level of inventory in the system. The high river level covers rocks in the riverbed and the boat can cruise safely. Rocks are equivalent to problems in the manufacturing system. Lower the river level (inventory) and rocks (problems) are exposed; thus endangering the boat (production system). The problems receive immediate attention when exposed in the lean production system.

The goal is to remove all rocks (problems), so a boat may travel safely (minimum inventory equals minimum inventory carrying costs). When all rocks are removed, a boat can run smoothly with a minimum water level. However, if there is no water and the river is dry, a boat will be useless. Thus, the notion of zero inventory is incorrect for any manufacturing system. While achieving zero defects is a proper objective, an inventory of zero is impossible. If there is no inventory, then there is nothing for workers to work on. The idea is to minimize the necessary work-in-process between cells. Kanban, used properly, will

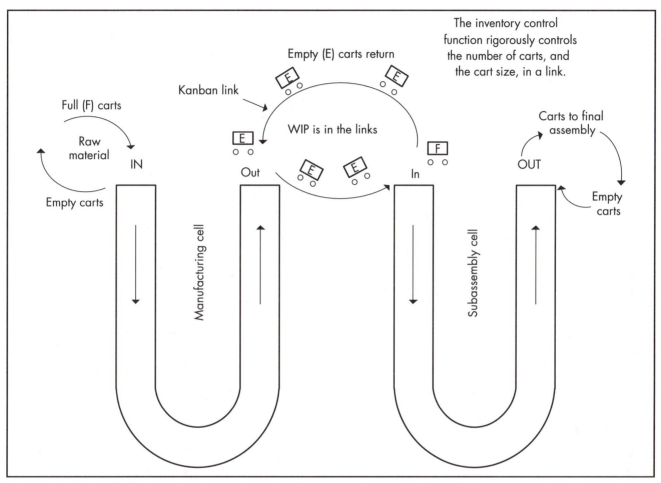

Figure 2-5. The arrival of an empty container at the manufacturing cell is the signal in the kanban system to produce more parts.

achieve the correct balance of inventory. Within a manufacturing cell, parts are already handled one at a time, just as they are in assembly lines. Therefore, cells should already be operating with minimum inventory. Buffer inventory in cells is a signal there are problems that should be addressed.

The level of work-in-process between the stand-alone process, cells, subassembly, and final assembly is actually controlled by foremen in various departments. Control is integrated and performed at the point of use. The following is an example of how the methodology works for a frame area.

Suppose there are 10 carts in the kanban link and each cart holds 20 parts. So, the maximum inventory in the frame area is 200 parts. The foreman goes to the stock area outside the cell and picks up the kanban cards (one withdrawal and one production-ordering), which takes one full cart of parts out of the system. The (maximum) inventory level is now nine carts, times 20 parts per cart, or 180 parts. The foreman waits until a problem appears. When it appears, the foreman immediately restores the kanban cards, which brings inventory to its previous level. The cause of the problem may or may not be identified by the restoration of inventory, but the problem condition is relaxed until a solution can be

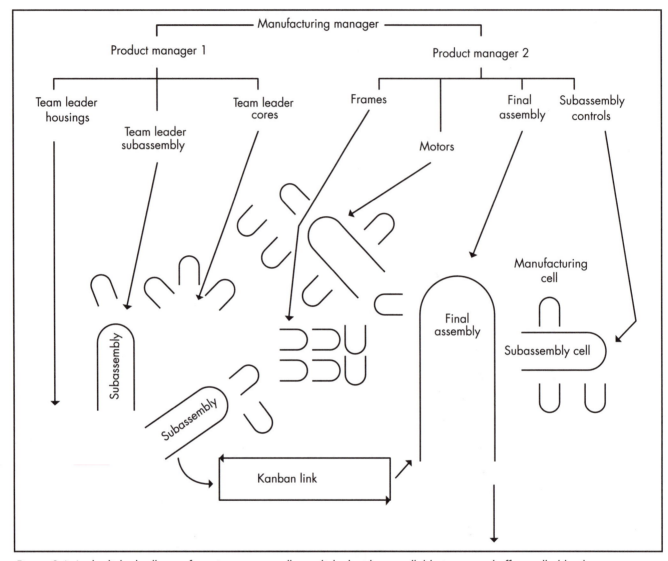

Figure 2-6. In the linked-cell manufacturing system, cells are linked with controllable inventory buffers called kanbans.

found. Then the cell team works at finding the root cause of the problem. Once the problem is solved, the foreman repeats this procedure. If no other problems arise, then the foreman tries to reduce inventory to 8 multiplied by 20, which is equal to 160 parts. This procedure is repeated daily in all kanban links in the factory. After a few months, the foreman in the frame area may be down to five carts, with 20 parts each. Over the next weekend, the system will be restored to 10 carts between the two points; but this time, each cart will hold only 10 parts, instead of the former 20. Thus, up to 100 parts are in the kanban link. If everything works smoothly with the new reduced work-in-process lot size, the foreman will then remove a cart to see what happens. More than likely, some setup times will need to be reduced. In this way, inventory in the linked-cell system is continually reduced, exposing problems. Problems are solved one by one in all areas of the factory. Teams work on exposing and solving problems. This is the method used

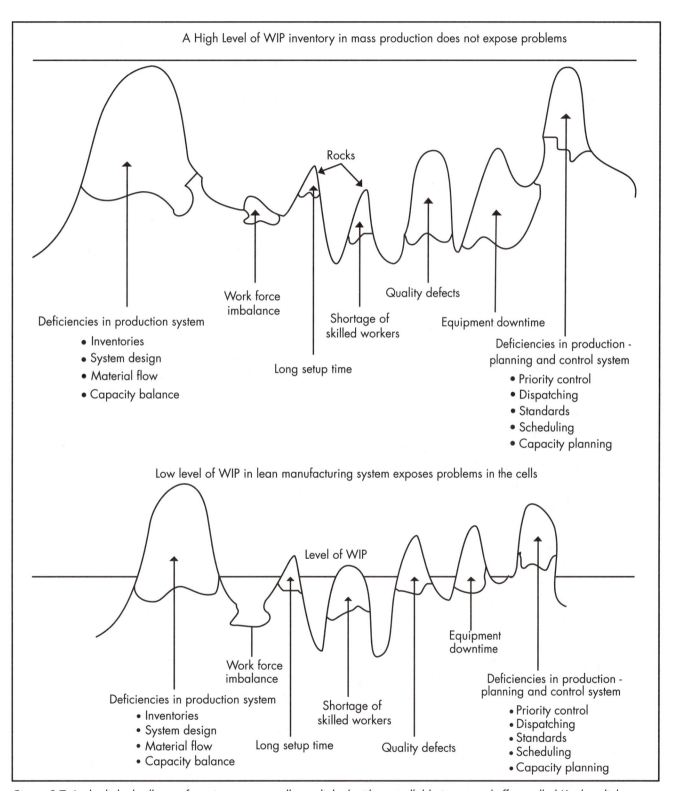

Figure 2-7. In the linked-cell manufacturing system, cells are linked with controllable inventory buffers called Kanban links.

for continuous improvement in the lean production factory.

The minimum level of inventory that can be achieved is a function of the quality level, probability of a machine breakdown, length of the setups, variability in the manual operation, number of workers in the cell, parts shortages, transportation distance, and other factors. It is determined that the minimum number of carts is three, and the minimum lot size is one. A very significant point is that inventory becomes a controllable independent variable, rather than an uncontrollable variable dependent on system-user demands.

Step 8: Integrate Suppliers

In lean production, one tries to reduce the number of suppliers and cultivate a single source for each purchased component or subassembly. This is a primary tenet of lean production. Vendors and suppliers are educated and encouraged to develop their own lean production systems for superior quality, low cost, and rapid on-time delivery of a product to the lean production factory. They must be able to deliver perfect parts to their customers when and where they are needed, and without incoming inspection. The linked-cell network ultimately should include every supplier. The goal is for suppliers to become remote cells in the linked-cell manufacturing system.

In the traditional job-shop environment, the purchasing department permits its vendors to make weekly, monthly, and semiannual deliveries with long lead times (weeks and months are common). A large safety stock is kept in case something goes wrong. Quantity variances are large. This, coupled with normal late and early deliveries, can cause the vendor supply situation to be chaotic. The situation leads to expediting, another form of manufacturing-system waste, since it does not add value to the product.

As a hedge against vendor problems in the functional job-shop manufacturing system, multiple sources are developed. Problems may occur because one vendor cannot handle all of the company's work. Normally the issue is the purchasing department's claim that pitting one vendor against another will give the company a competitive advantage and lower-cost parts. This may have a bit of truth in it, but the method is shortsighted in the long run.

The lean manufacturing system handles its vendor program differently. Just-in-time purchasing is a program of continual long-term improvements. The buyer and vendor work together to reduce lead times, lot sizes, and inventory levels. Thus, both companies become more competitive in the world marketplace because of this teaming relationship.

In the lean production environment, longer-term (18–24 months), flexible contracts are drawn up at the outset, with three-or four-week delivery lead times. The buyer supplies updated forecasts every month, which are good for 12 months, commits to long-term quality, and perhaps even promises to buy back excess materials. Exact delivery times are specified by midmonth for the next month. Frequent communication between the buyer and vendor is the norm. The kanban subsystem controls the material movement between the vendor and buyer. The vendor is considered a remote cell. Long-range forecasting encompasses six months to a year. As soon as the buyer sees a change, the vendor is informed. This knowledge gives the vendor better visibility, instead of a limited lead-time view. The vendor gets build-schedule stability and is not jerked up and down by the build schedule.

The lean manufacturing buyer moves toward fewer vendors, often going to local, sole sources. Frequent visits are made to the vendor by the lean production buyer, who may supply engineering aid (quality, automation, setup reduction, packaging, etc.) to help the vendor become more knowledgeable on how to deliver on time, the right quantity of parts that require no incoming inspection. This is true technology transfer. The vendors learn from the lean production customer. In this lean production system, the buyer and seller must build a bond of trust, be willing to work together to solve problems, and share cost savings.

The advantage of using a single source is that resources can be focused on selecting, developing, and monitoring one source, instead of many. When tooling dollars are concentrated in one source, money is saved. The higher volume should lead to lower costs. The vendor is now more inclined to go the extra mile or exceed expectations for the buyer. The buyer and vendor learn to trust one another, cultivating the relationship over time. An additional benefit to the lean production buyer is that quality is more consistent and easier to monitor when there is a single source.

Finally, there is the aspect of proprietary processes. Toyota, Honda, and other users of lean manufacturing have published little about their manufacturing and assembly cells. Unique processes exist that give companies like Toyota and Honda the edge in manufacturing strategies. They develop machine tools and the processes in-house, rather than buying them from a vendor. Lean manufacturers gain their competitive edge by developing unique manufacturing process technology in-house and keeping it locked in the cells.

Chapter 4 expands this concept of in-house development of machine tools with real examples. Table 2-2 summarizes the key points in managing the lean production plant. This list was obtained from the plant manager at a first-tier supplier to Toyota.

Step 9: Autonomation

Autonomation is defined as the autonomous control of quality and quantity. Generally, in the lean production factory this relates to stopping a line immediately when something goes wrong. Specifically, this means workers control the quality at the source, instead of using inspectors to find the problem. The workers in the lean factory inspect each other's work. This method is called *successive checking*. Taiichi Ohno, Toyota's former vice president of manufacturing, was convinced that Toyota had to raise its quality to superior levels to penetrate the world automotive market. He wanted every worker to be personally responsible for the quality of the piece part or product that he/she produced.

The need for automation simply reflects the gradual transition of the factory from manual to automated functions. Some people think of this as computer-integrated manufacturing. Others recognize that people are the most important and flexible resource in the company and see the computer as just another tool in the process, rather than the heart of the system. Hence, these companies are moving toward human-integrated manufacturing, where a creative, motivated work force is seen as the key to lean production.

Quite often, inspection devices are placed in machines or the factory uses source inspection to maintain quality. Other times, devices called *decouplers* are placed between machines or processes so the inspection may be performed automatically without stopping the process to do internal inspection. This attempt prevents the defect from occurring, rather than attempting to inspect after a part is made. Inspection by a machine can be faster, easier, and more repeatable than inspection by a human. This is called *in-process control inspection*.

Autonomation means inspection becomes part of the production process. It does not involve a separate location or person. Parts are 100% inspected by devices that either stop the process if a defect is found or correct it before the defect occurs. The latter requires an electronic feedback loop to the process controller. A machine may be set to shut off automatically when a problem arises. This function can prevent mass production of defective parts. The machine may also shut off automatically when the required volume parts have been produced; this prevents overproduction—a major and expensive form of waste. The prevention of overproduction is a vital function of the lean production inventory-control methodology.

Table 2-2. Managing the lean production system	
The lean production system is the basic philosophy and concepts used to guide production processes and their environment. The lean production system includes the linked-cell manufacturing system (cells linked by a kanban pull system), the 5-S philosophy, the seven tools of quality control, and other key organizational strategies.	
Lean Strategy	**Definition**
Kanban pull system (see Step 7)	Kanban uses a card system, standard container sizes, and pull versus push production to accomplish just-in-time production.
5S (seiri, seiton, seiketsu, seiso, shitsuke) (see Step 4)	The 5S strategy is used to sort, straighten, shine, standardize, and sustain the work environment.
Standard operation in manufacturing cells (see Step 1)	The manufacturing cells are used to combine people and processes. The components of standard operation include cycle time, work sequence, and standard stock on hand in the cells.
Morning meeting	A daily meeting is held for the purpose of sharing production and safety information, quite often by a quality circle.
Key points: process sheets	The process sheets, which are visually posted at each workstation, detail the work sequence and most critical points for performing the tasks.
Tooling parts: changeover and setup (see Step 2)	Machine setup is performed when an assembly line changes tooling to accommodate a different product.
Seven tools of quality control (see Step 3)	The seven tools to quality are Pareto diagrams, check sheets, histograms, cause-and-effect diagrams, run charts for individuals, control charts for samples, and scatter diagrams.
Production behavior	Rules include information on personal safety, safety equipment, clothing, restricted areas, vehicle safety, equipment safety, and housekeeping.
Visual management	Each line in the plant has a complete set of charts, graphs, or other devices, like andons, for reporting the status and progress of the area.

Step 10: Computer-integrated Manufacturing (CIM)

The factory floor manufacturing area is the heart of the production system. The production system includes and services the manufacturing system. The production system is the entire organization and includes manufacturing, engineering, accounting, marketing, production control, maintenance, and other areas. So, once the manufacturing system has been restructured into a Just-in-time manufacturing system and the critical control functions are well integrated, the company will find it expedient to restructure the rest of the company. This requires removing the functionality of the various departments and forming teams, often along product lines. It requires the implementation of concurrent engineering teams to decrease the time needed to bring new products to market. This movement is gaining strength in many companies and is being called *business process reengineering*. It is basically restructuring the production system to be as free of waste as the manufacturing system.

Shifting from one type of manufacturing system design to another affects product and tool design, engineering, production planning and control, inventories and their control, purchasing, quality control, inspection, the production workers, supervisors, middle managers, and top management. Such a conversion cannot take place overnight and must be viewed as a long-term transformation. Reorganization can be traumatic for the business arm of the company and it usually has a negative impact on worker morale.

However, Step 10 recognizes the company's need to reorganize and adopt lean production philosophies and methodologies. This effort often begins by forming product realization teams to bring new products to the marketplace faster. In the automotive industry, these groups are called *platform teams*. Platform teams are composed of people from design, engineering, manufacturing, marketing, sales, finance, etc. As the philosophy of team building spreads and the lean manufacturing system is implemented and established, it is only natural that the production system follows suit. Unfortunately, many companies are restructuring the business part of the company without having completed Steps 1–8 to convert the existing manufacturing system into a lean and productive one. Reengineering the production system, without simplifying and redesigning the manufacturing system, can lead to very difficult times for the enterprise.

The design of manufacturing process technology must be done early in the product development process. Manufacturing process technology within cells must be part of a well-designed, integrated system. Flexibility in the design of an integrated manufacturing system means it can readily accept new product designs, readily adapt to product design changes, and cope with volume fluctuations.

The critical control functions of production and inventory are designed right into the manufacturing system. Quality control and process reliability are tied to process technology and designed into the process.

Suppose a cell has six operations. The number two machine may have a workholding device that checks to make sure that the first machine produced the correct part geometry before it performs its processing steps. Sometimes the checking occurs in the part-holding transporting device, or the decoupler, between the first and second machines. The decoupler may simply check a dimension, or it may provide feedback to the first machine to make process corrections. The worker is critical in this process and handles every part and checks every process.

SUMMARY

In manufacturing cells, workers are considered to be the company's most important non-depreciable resource, a point of view not traditionally held in United States' factories where managers often think of labor as unstable and a costly input to the manufacturing system.

Information systems, or computers, are common on the factory floor in this modern age. However, these information systems cannot control the factory. They supply information for people to act upon in the decision-making process. People are much more flexible than computers. Therefore, in the lean manufacturing scheme, computers should be viewed as only a useful tool in the process.

Chapter 3
Manufacturing System Design

INTRODUCTION

Civilization was based upon manufacturing; and the basis of manufacturing is the manufacturing system. Looking back at history, one can see that strong and viable manufacturing bases of skilled craftsmen went hand in hand with high standards of living. People advanced because manufacturing sectors produced goods that were in demand. This demand stimulated commerce. When referring to ancient days, the phrase "industrial system" was used differently than it is used to describe today's modern industry. Nonetheless, the ancient manufacturing system, crude as it was, produced tools, weapons, cooking vessels, and clothing; all are products that helped nations advance to their present industrial bases. This was a slow process, beginning with the Stone Age. With the advent of the Stone Age, early man started making tools and weapons. Since this work was by hand, some Stone Age craftsmen were more skilled than others at making tools and weapons. Thus, a bartering system began for some of the more choice tools. This system started with the manufacture of stone items. Manufacturing began to grow; it improved slowly as workers' skills became more refined. This evolutionary process continued for centuries. It accelerated dramatically in the 1700s with the first industrial revolution and the advent of the concept of manufacturing system design. In short, manufacturing advanced with the development of the manufacturing system. The manufacturing system's role of advancing today's civilization cannot be overemphasized.

SYSTEM DESIGN TRENDS

In the modern world, significant changes are taking place in manufacturing system design. Changes have been fueled by the following trends:

- More companies serve global markets by making products for customers worldwide.
- As production of a variety of products increases, decreases in lot sizes and quantities result.
- Requirements for closer tolerances continue to increase. Requirements demand higher levels of accuracy, precision, and quality.
- An increasing variety of materials, especially composite materials with widely diverse properties, is leading to new manufacturing processes.
- Material costs, including costs for raw materials, components, subassemblies, material-handling processes, and energy continue to be major parts of total product costs. Direct labor continues to decrease and account for only 5-10% of total costs.
- Product reliability is increasing in response to excessive product liability lawsuits.
- The time between an initial design concept and a resulting product continues to shorten due to concurrent or simultaneous engineering.
- Ergonomics and worker safety continue to grow in importance as worker-compensation costs escalate and humanistic trends continue.

- Green manufacturing strategies continue to help protect the earth from further pollution.

These trends require the following types of manufacturing system responses:

- Continuous improvement, or continuous redesign and improvement of manufacturing systems, is an ongoing goal.
- Systems must produce superior products with reduced per-unit costs and on-time delivery in response to customer demands.
- All manufacturing costs can be reduced.
- Systems must be designed to offer flexibility and reliability. *Flexibility* refers to the ability to change rapidly with customers' demands, volume, product mix, and design changes. *Reliability* refers to systems' robustness; that is, the ability to produce high-quality products without breakdowns or quality problems.
- Redesigned systems capturing system processing into manufacturing cells need product design engineers with design envelopes that are readily visible, understandable, and adaptable to new product designs. The simpler, lean production system design is easily understood, controlled, and automated.

OPTIMIZATION OF THE MANUFACTURING SYSTEM

In general, a manufacturing system should be an integrated whole. The system should be composed of integrated subsystems, each interacting with the whole system. A system should have a number of objectives that optimize the whole process, as opposed to refining only portions of a system, such as certain processes or subsystems.

A system's daily operation requires information gathering, communication, and decision-making processes to be integrated. Answering questions such as: what, when, where, and how are critical to achieving a healthy company. These questions are related to the overall con-

trol of a system as well; for without control, there is no optimization.

Each company is unique, due to differences in subsystem combinations, people, product designs, and materials. Different interactions within social, political, and business environments also individualize each company's manufacturing, production, or service systems. In short, each company has its own set of problems. Clearly, there is a danger in grouping companies on a functional basis or calling them all *job shops*. However, the functional job shop is the most common design.

EVOLUTION OF FUNCTIONAL STRUCTURE

People invented and developed basic machine tools in the first industrial revolution. With these tools came the first levels of mechanization and automation. Factories developed along with manufacturing processes. These factories focused resources (materials, workers, and processes) at sites where power was available. For the most part, waterpower was used, explaining why early factories were placed near streams. Water turned waterwheels that drove overhead shafts running the length of factories. Belts from the main shafts powered machines on manufacturing process lines.

Grouping like machines that operated at approximately the same speeds was logical and expedient. Factories were laid out functionally, according to types of machines used. Machines were extensions of human capabilities or attributes. Machinists developed skills that were different from leather, iron, or foundry workers. Therefore, processes were divided according to the kinds of skills that were needed to operate particular processes.

When steam engines and, later, electric motors, replaced other types of power, early manufacturing systems achieved greater flexibility. Still, the functional arrangement persisted and became known as the *job shop*. As product complexity increased and the factory grew larger, separate functional departments evolved for product design, accounting, and marketing. Later in the scientific management era of F.W. Taylor and Frank and Lillian Gilbreth, departments for production planning, work scheduling, and methods improvements were added to help control the manufacturing system. These functions were initially developed for the job shop and were performed external to the factory floor. Taylor and Frank and Lillian Gilbreth are generally recognized as founders of the industrial engineering profession. Scientific management evolved to manage the factory, and systems for production control were developed.

SYSTEMS DEFINED

The word *system* abstractly defines a relatively complex assembly (or arrangement) of physical elements characterized by measurable parameters (Rubinstein 1995). This definition is quite appropriate for manufacturing systems (Figure 3-1). The important physical elements for all manufacturing systems are people, processes, and material holding and handling equipment. Raw materials and products are inputs, in-process materials, and outputs of the system. Some more common measurable parameters for manufacturing systems are throughput time and cycle time. *Cycle time* is the reciprocal of the production rate. If a system can make one vehicle per minute, the cycle time is equal to one minute/vehicle. *Throughput time* reflects the time that a product spends moving through the factory, while having value added to it via processing. *Work in process* reflects the volume of in-process inventory in the factory. The greater the volume of work in progress, the longer the throughput time. Cycle time, throughput time, and work-in-progress parameters for the manufacturing system are very different from those used for individual machines. These parameters are productivity measures during the implementation stages of lean manufacturing. An effective manufacturing system satisfies customers, both internal and external. Conflicts between these two groups of customers must be resolved.

To model and control the system:

- A system's boundaries or constraints must be defined.

- A system's behavior in response to excitations or disturbances from the environment must be predictable through system parameters.

In general, models describe how a system works or behaves. Mathematical models for control purposes generally require a theory or set of equations describing a system's boundaries and behaviors through input parameters. In short, if no theory exists, the model is not viable or robust and a system is uncontrollable. This is why 3D/virtual-reality simulation is such a great tool for factory design and analysis. The use of high-level simulation gives managers and engineers greater control. They visualize situations and then take immediate action on the factory floor.

Manufacturing systems are complex, thus difficult to model. Therefore, their design, analysis, and control are difficult processes as well. There are several reasons for this difficulty:

- System size and complexity inhibit modeling and control, due to implied-time expenditures.
- Systems are dynamic and unstable. The environment can change the system and vice versa.
- Relationships may be awkward to express in analytical terms, and interactions may be nonlinear. Thus, well-behaved functions often do not apply.
- Data or information may be difficult to secure, inaccurate, conflicting, missing, or too abundant to digest.
- Objectives may be difficult to define, particularly in systems that have an impact on social and political issues. Goals may conflict.
- The act of observing and trying to control a system changes the behavior of the system.
- Analysis and control algorithms for systems can be subject to errors of omission and commission. Some errors will be related to breakdowns or delays in feedback elements. This is because manufacturing systems include people in information loops.

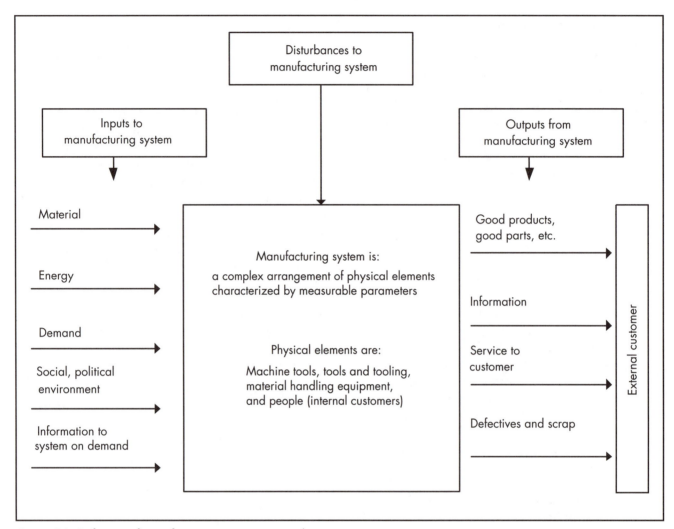

Figure 3-1. Definition of manufacturing-system inputs and outputs.

Because of these difficulties, the technique of digital simulation is not widely used for modeling and analysis of manufacturing systems. However, more companies are simulating portions of their factories.

MANUFACTURING VERSUS PRODUCTION SYSTEMS

In general terms, a manufacturing system inputs materials that can be measured by machines and people. Materials are processed and gain in value. Manufacturing system outputs may be either consumer goods or inputs to

some other process. These outputs are called *produced goods.*

The production system services the manufacturing system. An analogy would be the human heart, representing the manufacturing system. The manufacturing system (the heart) pumps blood (the material flow). The production system supplies oxygen and food and checks blood pressure, volume (work in process), and pulse rate (cycle time). Material-control functions are critical to performance of the manufacturing system. A linked-cell manufacturing system permits, even invites, integration of critical control functions. Continuing with the heart analogy, these critical control functions include:

- quality control (no blood pathogens or clogged arteries restricting material flow);
- production control (good blood pressure or movement in the system);
- inventory control (optimum blood supply or amount of work in process); and
- machine tool reliability (no blood clots and material flowing well).

Management cannot fully control all inputs into the manufacturing system. Manipulating controllable inputs or the system itself must counteract the effect of disturbances. For example, controlling material-availability problems such as shortages or demand fluctuations are both difficult tasks. National and international economic climates cause shifts in the business environment that can seriously change any of these inputs. All manufacturing systems differ in structure or physical arrangement. In addition, all manufacturing systems are serviced by a production system. Because the oldest and most common manufacturing system is the functionally organized job shop, most production systems are also functionally organized into departments. Walls usually separate people in functional areas from other areas. Thus, communication breakdowns are common. Also, long lags in feedback loops result in additional manufacturing system problems.

CLASSIFICATIONS OF MANUFACTURING SYSTEM DESIGNS

Five manufacturing system designs can be identified: the job shop, the project shop, continuous process the flow shop, and the linked-cell manufacturing system. The continuous process design deals primarily with liquids, powders, or gases (such as an oil refinery), rather than discrete parts. The other four manufacturing systems manufacture discrete parts. Figure 3-2 shows the four traditional systems and Figure 3-3 shows the linked-cell manufacturing system.

The Job Shop

The most common manufacturing system worldwide is the job shop. It is characterized by large varieties of components, general-purpose machines, and a functional layout (Figure 3-4). The job shop's distinguishing feature is that it can manufacture a wide variety of products as a result of manufacturing small, often one-of-a-kind, lot sizes. Job shop manufacturing is common for specific customer orders; but in truth, many job shops produce material to fill finished-goods inventories. Because job shops must perform a wide variety of manufacturing processes, general-purpose-manufacturing equipment is required. Workers must have relatively high skill levels to perform the range of different work assignments. Job shop products include space vehicles, aircraft equipment, machines, tools, all types of equipment, and a long list of other products. Distribution of the total factory capacity for a job shop is shown in Figure 3-5. The 6%-production fraction is equivalent to the 36% value shown earlier in Figure 1-13b, except that the calculation in Figure 3-5 assumes a theoretical 100% capacity that equals 365 days multiplied by 24 hours per day. Though depressing sounding, these figures clearly demonstrate that a productivity problem exists in making a manufacturing system (not individual processes) more productive. An obvious conclusion is that in order to make the manufacturing system more productive, one must redesign it.

In the job shop, machine tools are functionally grouped according to the general type of manufacturing process: lathes in one department, drill presses in another, plastic molding in still another, etc. This layout's advantage is its ability to produce a wide variety of products. Each different product or component requires its own unique sequence of operations so it can be routed through required departments in the proper order. Routing sheets are used to control movement of material through the factory. Most of the time forklifts and handcarts are used to move materials between machines.

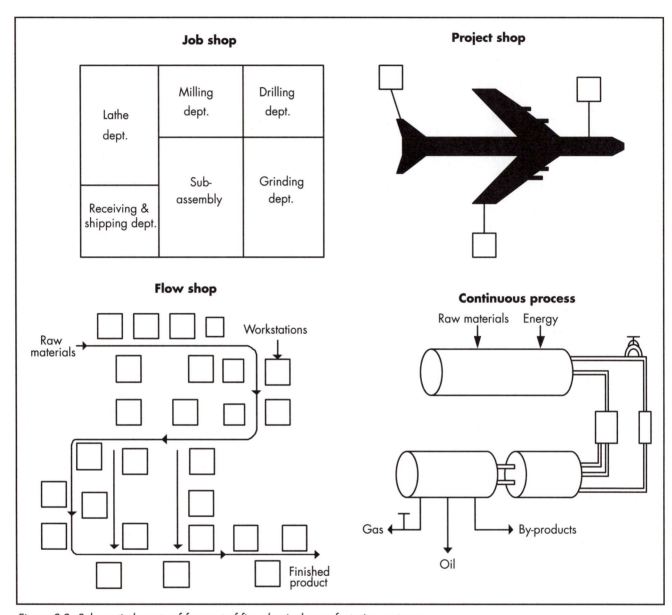

Figure 3-2. Schematic layouts of four out of five classical manufacturing systems.

If a company grows, the job shop often evolves into a production job shop. The production job shop is basically a large job shop with some flow lines and computer numerical control machines. The production job shop manufacturing system builds large volumes of products, but still builds in lots or batches, usually medium-sized lots of 50-200 units. An item may be produced only once, or it may be pro-duced at regular or irregular intervals. The purpose of batch production is to satisfy continuous customer demands for a product.

A job shop system's production rate can often exceed the customer demand rate. The job shop builds an inventory of Product A, and then changes to Product B to fill other orders. Changing products involves breaking down setups on many machines for Product A, and

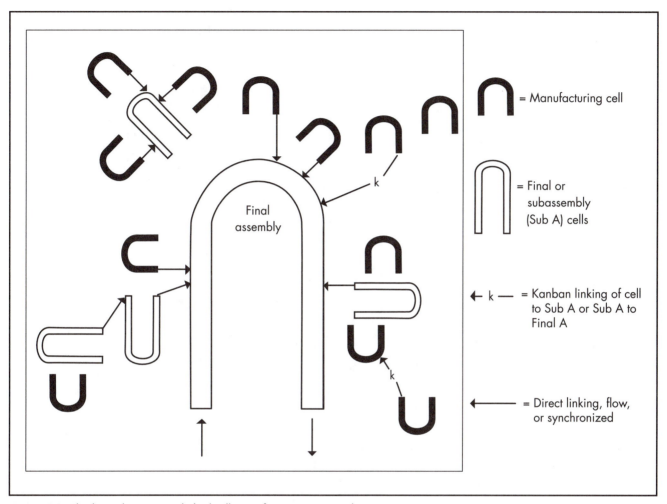

= Manufacturing cell

= Final or
subassembly
(Sub A) cells

← k ─ = Kanban linking of cell
to Sub A or Sub A to
Final A

← = Direct linking, flow,
or synchronized

Figure 3-3. The lean shop uses a linked-cell manufacturing system design.

resetting them for Product B. When stock for the first item is depleted, machines are set up again for Product A and inventory for Product A is replenished.

History has shown that manufacturing equipment can be designed for higher production rates. For example, automatic lathes capable of holding many cutting tools and automatically loading a new piece of stock are now used, rather than older, manual engine lathes. Machine tools are often equipped with specially designed workholding devices called *jigs and fixtures*, which increase process-output rates, precision, accuracy, and repeatability.

Industrial equipment, furniture, textbooks, and piece parts for many assembled consumer products (household appliances, lawn mowers, etc.) are made in production job shops. The production job shop system is sometimes called a machine shop, foundry, plastic molding factory, or pressworking shop. It is estimated that as many as 75% of all piece-part manufacturing is in lot sizes of 50 pieces or fewer. This estimation indicates that production job shops are an important segment of today's total manufacturing. Along with job and flow shops, the use of the production job shop is common in the United States.

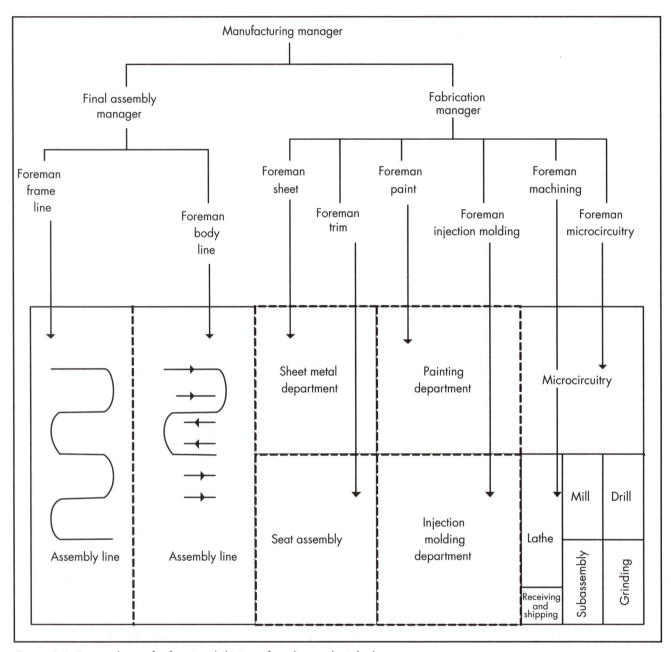

Figure 3-4. Factory layout for functional design referred to as the job shop.

Project Shops

The project shop is characterized by the immobility of the item being manufactured. In a typical project manufacturing system, a product must remain in a fixed position or location during manufacturing because of its size, weight, and/or the process it is undergoing. In the project shop, workers, machines, and materials travel to the manufacturing site. Bridges and dams are good examples of project shops in the construction industry. In the manufactur-

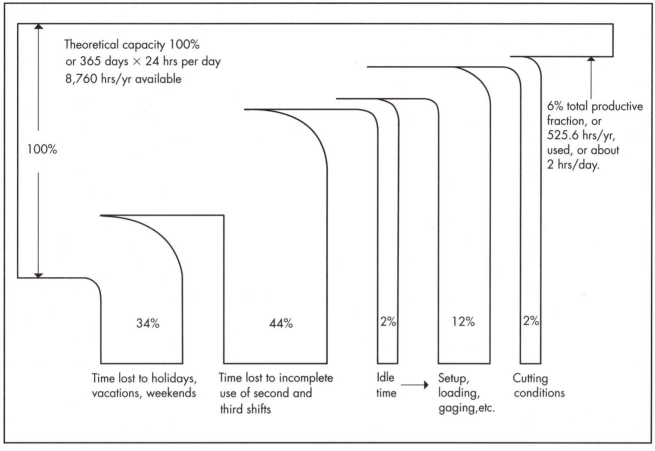

Figure 3-5. Distribution of total factory capacity of machine tools in a job shop.

ing industry, ships, locomotives, large-machine tools, and large airplanes are examples of project shops. The number of end items produced is usually not very large, but lot sizes of component parts going into the end item can vary from small to large. The job shop usually supplies parts and subassemblies to the project shop in small lots.

Fixed-position manufacturing, a variant of the project shop, is used for construction jobs such as buildings and roads, where the product is large and/or the site confined. Therefore, construction equipment and manpower go to it. When a job is complete, construction workers and equipment are removed from the manufacturing site. The project shop invariably has a job/flow shop manufacturing

system, making all components for the large, complex project; thus, it has a functional-production system.

Continuous Process

The continuous process system means that the product physically flows. Oil refineries, chemical processing plants, and food processing operations are examples of this system, which is sometimes called *continuous flow production* when referring to the manufacture of either high volumes of parts or of a single part. Beverage-canning operations or assembled products such as televisions are not continuous processes, but high-volume flow lines for discrete parts or assemblies. In continuous processes, products really flow because they are liquids, gases, or powders.

The continuous process is the most efficient, but least flexible manufacturing system. It usually has the leanest, simplest production system because this manufacturing system has the least work in process, making it easiest to control. In the main, these are Just-in-time manufacturing system designs, with small parts and very few workers. The continuous-flow process system might be ideal for lean production. These systems are designed and run by chemical engineers who are the manufacturing engineers for the chemical industry.

Flow Shops (Lines)

The flow shop has a product-oriented layout (see Figure 3-6). When volume gets large, espe-

cially in an assembly line, it is called *mass production*. These systems may have extremely high-production rates of typically 200,000-400,000 units per year in the automotive industry. Specialized equipment is dedicated to the manufacture of a particular product. People and machines create a flow line. One machine of each type is typical, except where duplicate machines are needed to balance the flow. The entire plant often is designed exclusively for production of a particular product, with special purpose, process equipment, rather than general purpose, the norm.

Investment costs of specialized machines and tools are high, as are the risks. Many production skills are transferred from operators to machines, resulting in lower levels of manual-labor skills than in a production job shop. Items flow through a sequence of operations by mate-

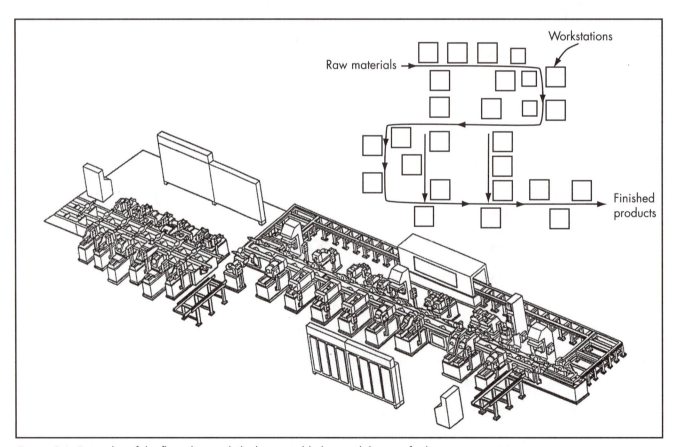

Figure 3-6. Examples of the flow shop include the assembly line and the transfer line.

rial-handling devices (conveyors, moving belts, transfer devices, etc.). Items move through operations one at a time.

All flow lines have the same inherent problem of line balancing. Total tasks required to assemble (or machine) a unit are divided into smaller tasks. This is the division-of-labor concept. Tasks are arranged so that the time a component or assembly spends at each station or location is fixed and equal (thus balanced). *Line balancing* means that the amount of work at each station is approximately the same to reduce idle time at the station. Lines are designed and set up to operate at the fastest possible speed, regardless of a system's needs. Flow shop layouts are typically either continuous or interrupted. A continuous flow line basically produces one complex item in great quantity and nothing else. A transfer line producing an engine block is a typical example. An interrupted flow line manufactures large lots, but periodically changes over to run similar (but different) components. Changing over a complex flow line may take hours or even days.

In a flow line manufacturing systems, facilities are arranged according to a product's sequence of operation. A line is organized by the processing sequence needed to make a single or regular mix of products. A hybrid form of the flow line produces a batch of products moving through clusters of workstations or processes organized by product flow. This is called *batch flow*. Garment or apparel manufacturing is traditionally done this way. For instance, a batch of shirts moves through a sequence of different sewing operations. Usually, setup times to change from one product to another are long, and often the process is complicated.

Most factories are mixtures of job shop and flow line systems. Demand for products can precipitate a shift from batch to high-volume production, and much of production is guided by that steady demand. Subassembly and final-assembly lines are further extensions of the flow line, with the former usually being more labor-intensive.

Since the advent of mass production, various approaches and techniques have led to development of machine tools that are highly effective in large-scale manufacturing. Their effectiveness is closely related to product-design standardization and the length of time permitted between design changes. A machine producing a part with a minimal amount of skilled labor can be developed if the part can be highly standardized. A part can then be manufactured in large quantities. An automatic screw machine (a complex lathe) is a good example of a machine for the manufacture of small parts. An automated-transfer machine that makes V-8 engine blocks (at a rate of 100 per hour) is an example of a super machine for mass production of large parts. Figure 3-6 is an example of a transfer machine. Transfer machines are specialized, expensive to design and build, and usually not capable of making another product. These machines must be operated for long periods of time to spread the cost of the initial investment-typically $20-40 million over many units. Although highly efficient, they exclusively make products in large volume. Desired design changes in a product must be avoided or delayed, because it would be too costly to scrap the machines. Such systems are clearly not flexible enough for product or process-design changes. Smaller versions of transfer machines developed for smaller-sized products made in large volumes are shown in Figure 3-7. They range in cost from $2-3 million.

The development of the numerical-control machine tool in the late 1950s and early 1960s permitted programmable control of the position of cutting tools in relationship to the workpiece. By the late 1960s, automatic tool changers had been added to the numerical-control machine, marking the birth of the machining center. Computers and workpiece changers were added next. Today, the computer-numerical-control machine tool is readily available to all manufacturers (Figure 3-8).

Products manufactured to meet demands of the free economy and today's mass-consumption markets must include changes in design

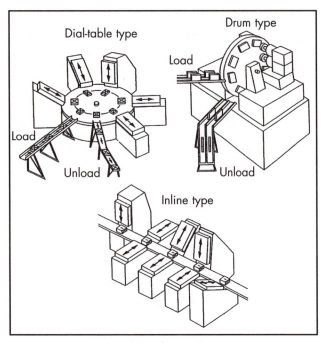

Figure 3-7. Examples of transfer machines.

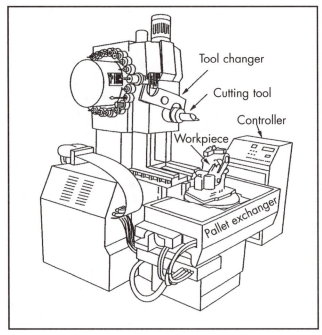

Figure 3-8. Computer-numerical-control machining center with many different operations performed in a single setup.

for improved product performance, as well as style. Therefore, hard-automation systems must be as flexible as possible, while retaining the ability to mass produce material. The recognition of this fact in the late 1960s lead to a coupling of the transfer line with the numerical-control machine and the flexible manufacturing system was born.

The primary components of the flexible manufacturing system are computer-numerical-control machine tools, material-handling systems, cutting tools, machine-workholding devices (pallets), and computer-control networks. Today, machine tools are computer numerical control, usually horizontal or vertical spindle-milling machines. The flexible manufacturing-system design (Figure 3-9) has eight four-axis, computer-numerical-control, machining centers, each equipped with a 90-cutter-tool magazine and a parts-pallet-changing system. The system designers claim to be capable of making more than 500 different parts. Such a system must be programmed and

scheduled for each part it produces. It can be as complex as the job shop it replaces.

The modern computer-numerical-control machine can be programmed to automatically change tools, workpieces, and cutting parameters. It seems logical that the versatile machine be joined with the transfer line to expand manufactured-part variety. Most flexible manufacturing system installations have a system manager supervising, primarily by monitoring the system. The system manager is responsible for supervising workers, including material handlers who perform loading/unloading tasks, a roving operator who presets tools and reacts to unscheduled machine stops, and a mechanical/hydraulic technician who repairs transfer devices, machines, workholders, and pallet changers.

Much has been written about flexible manufacturing systems and research continues. The systems are expensive to design and often require months or years to implement. They are complex to program, analyze, and control. By the end of the 1990s, it would appear that

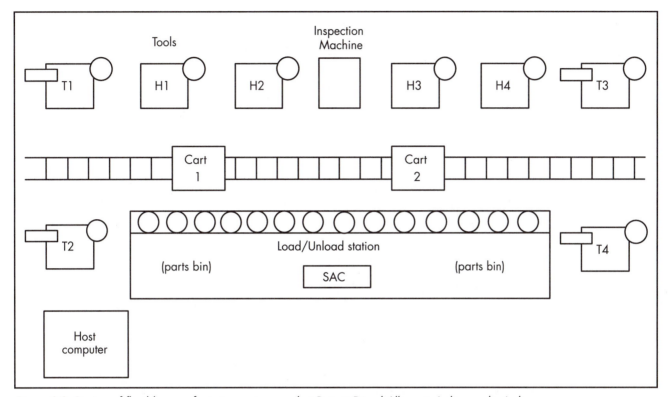

Figure 3-9. Design of flexible manufacturing system used at Detroit Diesel Allison in Indianapolis, Indiana.

fewer than 1,000 such systems world-wide. In the United States, most of these systems are found in large companies that can afford large capital outlays or that receive governmental backing, such as military defense contracts. The flexible manufacturing system represents the super-machine philosophy at its ultimate. Fundamentally, it is an attempt to blend the job shop's flexibility with productivity. Parts usually require two or three passes through a flexible manufacturing system. Fixturing in the flexible manufacturing system is costly and complex. The system's control computer must control the conveyor, maintain the computer numerical control library of programs, download these to the machines, handle scheduling of the system, track tool maintenance, track performance of the system, and print management reports. Not surprisingly, the system's software development often proves to be a major limiting factor.

Linked-cell Manufacturing System

The linked-cell manufacturing system is the newest manufacturing system. It is composed of manufacturing and assembly cells linked by a pull system for production control. In cells, operations and processes are grouped according to the manufacturing sequence needed to make a group of products or a product family. This design looks similar to a flow shop design, but is created for flexibility. The manufacturing cell often is configured in a U-shape, allowing workers to move from machine to machine with the shortest walking distance while loading and unloading parts. Figure 3-10 shows an example of a simple manned-manufacturing cell. Machines in a cell are usually single-cycle automatics, so they can complete a machining cycle untended, and have it turn off automatically when it is finished with a processing cycle. The cell usually includes processing needed for a finished part. Because machines in a cell are sin-

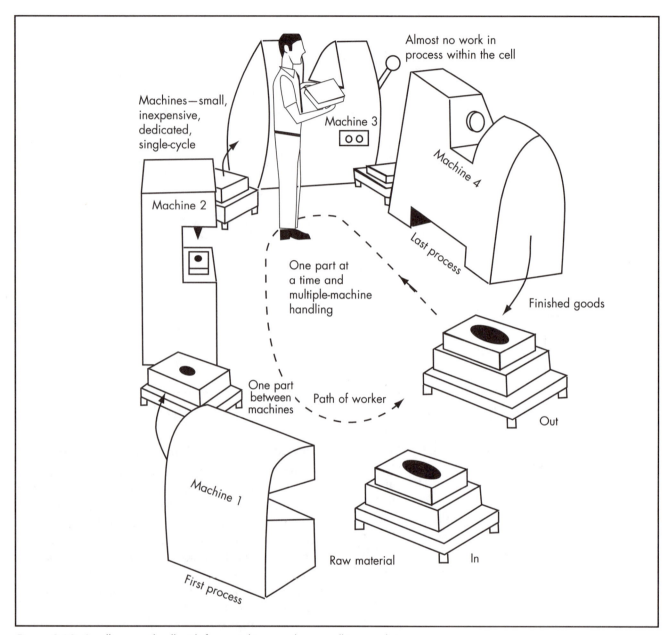

Figure 3-10. Small manned cell with four machines and one walking worker.

gle-cycle automatics, they can be making chips while an operator is doing other tasks in the cell. When an operator comes to a machine to unload a part, the machine completes a portion of the component and stops with its safety door open. The operator unloads and checks the part, loads a new part (which has just been unloaded and brought by the worker from the previous

machine), and starts the machine by hitting the walkaway switch. The analogy here is similar to what one does when preparing breakfast. One walks to the toaster with bread, loads the bread in, and hits a lever to start the toasting process. One does not stand there and watch, but walks away to get orange juice or make coffee. The toaster produces a signal once it completes its toasting cycle. When unloading the toaster, one checks to see if the bread has toasted properly. These rules are the basic operational rules for manned-manufacturing cells, or the *make-one, check-one, move-one-on* methodology.

STANDARDIZED WORK

Standardized work is a methodology for maintaining productivity, quality, and safety at high levels. It is a consistent framework for performing work at designated takt times. Standardized work illuminates opportunities for making improvements in work procedures.

There are three elements in structuring standardized work:

- takt time—the cycle time of final assembly;
- working sequence—dictates cell design; and
- standard in-cell stock—called stock-on-hand.

Takt time, as described earlier, should reflect the production rate of the final assembly line, which, in turn, reflects the pace of marketplace sales.

The *working sequence* is a series of steps that are the best ways to carry out a task. *Standard in-process stock* is the minimum number of workpieces needed to maintain a smooth flow of work.

Standardized work provides detailed, step-by-step guidelines for every job in the Toyota production system. Team leaders and their teams determine the most productive work sequence and make continuing improvements in that sequence. *Kaizen*, a form of continuous improvement, is useful to produce new patterns of standardized work. Figure 3-11 illustrates an example of a lean manufacturing cell where the takt time is 51.4 seconds (the work sequence and stock on hand are indicated). The work in the cell in Figure 3-11 is designed to have a cycle time that is slightly less than the manufacturing system takt time.

LINKED-CELL SYSTEMS

Manufacturing cells are key building blocks in linked-cell manufacturing systems. These systems are composed of directly or indirectly connected manufacturing cells. They utilize physical inventory and information control kanban for the linking process. Savvy manufacturing managers know they must examine the job shop system for redesign to improve productivity. Manufacturing companies are converting batch-oriented job shops into linked cells. One way to form a cell is by using group technology. Most lean companies, however, do not use this proven technology, preferring to simply form cells based on product families. There are two basic types of cells that feed final assembly: manufacturing cells, where most processes and machines are single-cycle automatics (i.e., complete the processing cycle untended); and assembly cells, where most, if not all, operations require an operator to be present to do tasks.

GROUP TECHNOLOGY

Most group technology methods often ignore the worker and simply find machines that will process groups of parts. Group technology is a philosophy of grouping similar parts into part families. Parts of similar size and geometry can often be processed by a single set of processes. A part family based on manufacturing-process type would have the same sequence of manufacturing processes. The set of processes is arrayed to form a cell. Thus, with group technology, job shops can be systematically restructured into production cells, with each cell specializing in a particular family of parts. The job shop shown in Figure 3-4 is redesigned into three cells to accommodate products that previously were manufactured in a job shop (Figure 3-12). Notice that no new machines are needed. Cellular conversion gives a marketing department an opportunity to find a new product line for excess processes and floor space freed by cellular conversions. The machines have at least the same utilization as in the job shop, but products spend far less time getting through processes. Parts are handled less, machine-setup time is shorter, in-process

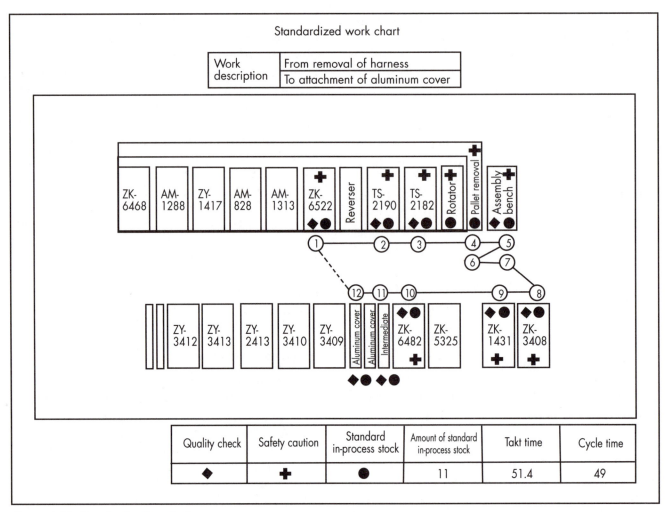

Figure 3-11. Standardized work chart.

inventory is lower, throughput time is greatly reduced, and workers are more effective.

The key points for manufacturing cells are:

- Machines are arranged in a process sequence.
- The cell is designed in a U-shape.
- One part at a time is made within a cell (one-piece flow).
- Workers attend to more than one process.
- Takt time dictates cell-production rate.
- Workers perform their jobs while standing and walking.
- Slower, smaller, dedicated, and less-expensive machines are used.

- Unique technology is often developed in-house.

Cells are typically manned, but unmanned cells are beginning to emerge with robots replacing workers. A robotic-cell design is shown in Figure 3-13 with one robot and three CNC machines. For the cell to operate autonomously, machines must have adaptive-control capabilities and use decouplers.

Cells are designed to manufacture specific groups or families of parts. Cells are linked either to each other or subassembly points by a pull system of material control called *kanban*. Kanban is the primary production and

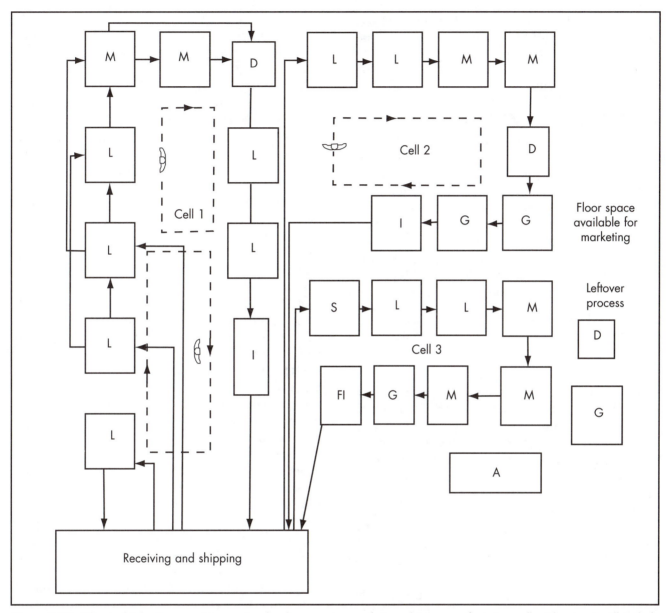

Figure 3-12. Classical job shop requiring system-level conversions redesigned into manufacturing cells. Chapter 4 will include additional details about Cell 3.

inventory control system for linked cells. Production control is one of the critical control functions in manufacturing system designs.

In addition to manufacturing cells, flow-shop elements within a factory are redesigned to make them operate like cells. To do this, long

setup times typical of flow lines must be vigorously attacked. It is imperative that flow lines be able to change over quickly from the manufacture of one product line to another. The need to line-balance a flow line every time it changes to another part must be eliminated or drastically reduced. This can be accomplished with decouplers. Both cells and flow lines make piece parts for subassembly and final-assembly lines. It is important for flow-line behavior to mimic manufacturing cells to optimize system flexibility and productivity.

DESIGNED FOR FLEXIBILITY

Flexibility is a premier design feature for lean production and cellular manufacturing systems. Once implemented, cellular systems can react quickly to changes in customer demand, product design, or product mix. Cells in a factory are linked directly to subassembly cells or lines. Cells and flow lines are on final assembly lines at the point of use, or they are connected by kanban links. This makes a factory product oriented and flexible in:

- its operation of equipment,
- changeover,
- process, and
- capacity or volume.

To effectively operate equipment in a lean environment, rapid tool change is a must. There should not be any adjustments, and automatic-error detection must take place. Changeover must be easy, with the speed of the setup and exchange of tooling and dies smooth and rapid.

Design criteria in process consideration looks at differences in operations and processes for different parts. It also looks at the ability to handle a different mix, a different order in the mix, and a different volume in the mix.

In a flexible, lean environment, the ability to increase or decrease production output, rate, and volume is significant.

COMPARING LEAN PRODUCTION TO OTHER SYSTEMS

Table 3-1 provides a brief comparison of lean manufacturing and the job shop philosophy. A popular idea a few years ago was to find the functional job shop system's bottlenecks or constraints and work to eliminate them. Part of this misguided idea was that material

queues were viewed as necessities that permitted downstream operations to continue, when there was actually a problem with the upstream or feeding operations. The linked-cell manufacturing system approach recognizes the job shop design as the fundamental problem. Better management by constraints only results in small improvements in productivity and quality in the job shop. It is the manufacturing system that must be redesigned.

Figure 3-14 summarizes manufacturing systems by comparing different methodologies based on production rates and flexibility, or the amount of different parts the system can handle. Project shops and continuous process systems are not shown. Cells provide a wide middle ground between job shops and dedicated mass-production flow lines. Figure 3-14 is derived from factory-floor data. It shows that the widely publicized flexible manufacturing system lies between the job shop and the transfer line. This is expected, since the flexible manufacturing system was developed from a merger of these two systems.

Like in a job shop, it is necessary to schedule parts and machines within a flexible manufacturing system. This function, however, makes flexible designs difficult to link to other manufacturing systems. The flexible system often becomes an island of automation within a job shop—a characteristic of super machines. Inventory accumulates in the flexible manufacturing system.

In contrast, manufacturing cells produce parts one at a time in a flexible manner. Cell capacity and cycle time can be quickly altered to respond to customer demands for change. For manufacturing cells, the cycle time does not depend on machining time.

Families of parts with similar designs, flexible-workholding devices, and tool changes in programmable machines allow rapid changeover from one component to another. Rapid changeover means quick or one-touch setup, often like flipping a light switch. Significant inventory reduction between cells is possible

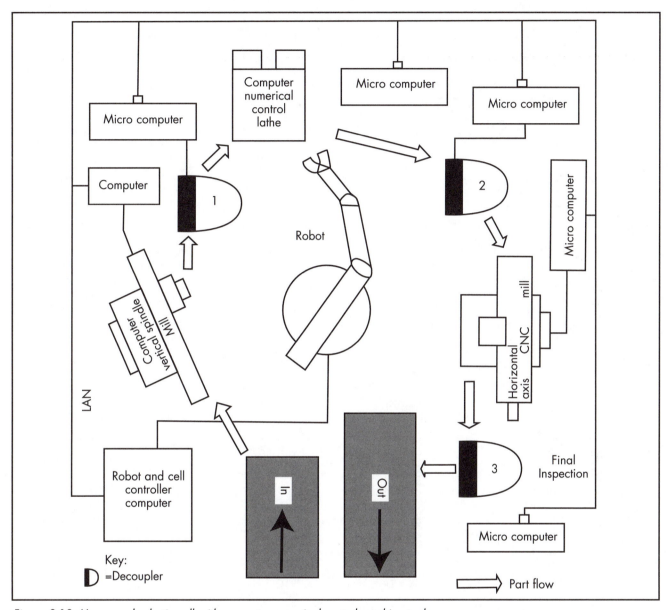

Figure 3-13. Unmanned robotic cell with computer-numerical-control machine tools.

with rapid changeover and when the inventory level can be directly controlled. The operator controls quality in a cell. Equipment is maintained routinely by the worker.

For robotic (automated) cells, robots typically load and unload parts using up to five computer numerical-control machine tools, but this number may be increased if robots become mobile. A machining center is similar to a cell consisting of one machine. However, a machining center is not a cell. It is not as flexible or productive as a real cell, which uses multiple, simple machines. A machining center cannot be considered a cell because there is no overlapping of machining times. Cellular layouts facilitate the integration of critical production functions, while maintain-

Table 3-1
How lean manufacturing philosophy differs from that of a typical US Company

Factors	Lean Manufacturing	Typical job shop / flow shop
Inventory	Inventory is wasteful. It hides problems. It is a liability. Every effort must be extended to minimize inventory.	Inventory is a necessary asset. It protects against forecast errors, machine problems, late vendor deliveries. More inventory is "safer" and necessary.
Lot sizes	Keep reducing lot sizes. The smallest quantity is desired for both manufactured and purchased parts.	Formulas. Keep revising the optimum lot size with some formula based on the trade-off between the cost of carrying inventories and the setup costs.
Setups	Eliminate/reduce them by extremely rapid changeover to minimize the impact. Fast changeover permits small lot sizes and allows a wide variety of parts to be made frequently.	Low priority. Maximum output is the usual goal. Rarely does similar thought and effort go into achieving quick changeover. Use EOQ to determine lot size.
Vendors	Procure from a single source. Vendors are remote cells, part of the team. Daily, multiple deliveries of active items are expected. The vendor takes care of the needs of the customer, and the customer treats the vendor as an extension of the factory.	Adversaries. Multiple sources are the rule, and it is typical to play suppliers against each other to get lower costs but multiple vendors increase the variability in the components.
Quality	Zero defects. If quality is not perfect, then improvements can be made. Continuous improvement in people and process is the goal.	It costs money to make high quality products. Tolerate some scrap. Track what the actual scrap has been and develop formula for predicting it. Plan extra quantity to cover scrap losses.
Equipment maintenance	Constant and effective. Machine breakdown and tool failure are eliminated or reduced by routine maintenance.	As required. Not critical because inventory is available.
Lead times	Keep them short. This simplifies the job of marketing, purchasing, and manufacturing as it reduces the need for expediting.	The longer the better. Most foremen and purchasing agents want more lead time, not less.
Workers	The internal customers are the experts. Changes are not made until consensus is reaches. Employee involvement is critical, especially in the design of the cells. Managers are coaches who serve workers in teams.	Engineers provide ideas and are the experts. Management is by edict. New systems are installed in spite of the workers, not thanks to the workers. Measurements are used to determine whether or not workers are doing as directed.
Cost reduction	Cost reduction comes by non-stop like water through the pipe type manufacturing, thus reducing the TPT.	Cost reduction comes by driving labor out of the product and by having high machine utilization.
Production control	Material should be "pulled" through the factory, using kanban.	Material should be coordinated by MRP and "pushed" out into the factory.
Overhead	Any function that does not directly add value to the product is waste.	Overhead functions are essential.
Accounting's view of labor	Labor is a fixed cost. The internal customers are one of the system's primary resources.	Labor is a variable cost.
Equipment maintenance	Machines are distance runners, slow but steady and always ready to run.	Machines are sprinters, and pulled hamstrings are to be expected.
Automation	Autonomation is valued because it facilitates consistent quality and prevents overproduction.	Automation is valued because it drives labor out of the product.
Expediting	Expediting is a manufacturing sin.	Expediting is a way of life.
Cleanliness	Housekeeping is everyone's responsibility.	Work means getting your hands dirty.
Evaluation (measurable parameters)	Multiple performance criteria based on cost, quality, on-time delivery, and flexibility.	Evaluation is based on quantified direct cost.

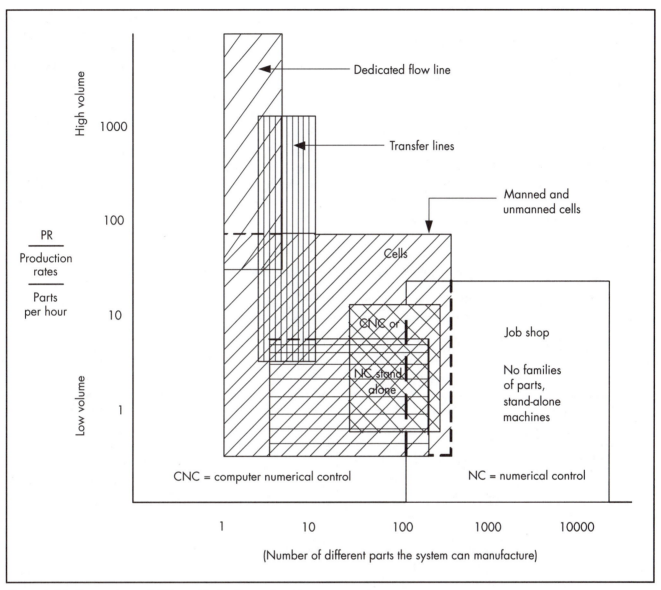

Figure 3-14. Comparison of different kinds of manufacturing systems.

ing flexibility and producing superior-quality products. For production workers, cells provide opportunities to perform more tasks and to experience a sense of overall job enrichment.

In the cell system, product designers easily see how parts are made, since all processes are arranged together. Designers can see future designs that can be produced in the cell. This is called *design for manufacturability*, an impor-

tant facet of lean manufacturing.

The linked-cell system is designed for one-piece flow. In essence, each piece of a final product is assembled with a single process, step, or operation. When something goes wrong with this system, it is easy to identify the problem and process. Problems can be quickly fixed. Make-one, check-one, and move-one-on is the operational watch-word for lean manufacturing system design.

SUMMARY

Every manufacturing system has certain control functions that must be carried out. Table 3-2 summarizes eight functions and lists techniques that both the lean production system and job shop use to aid these functions.

Regardless of the type of manufacturing system, the same control functions are performed for all. However, system tools used in lean manufacturing differ greatly from job shop tools. In the linked-cell system, many tools are manual or physical such as kanban cards, andon lights,

poka-yoke checks, and oral orders. In the job/flow shop factory under material requirements planning, the most important tool is the computer. If a system being computerized is well designed and robust, the computerized version will have a good chance of succeeding.

The following is an excerpt from the author's class notes: "A new manufacturing system design will result in another industrial revolution." With the design of the linked-cell system, aided by an environment of lean manufacturing, another industrial revolution appears to be well on its way.

Table 3-2
How eight manufacturing functions are controlled

Functions	Categories	L-CMS	Job shop/flow shop
How many to make per day	Families of products	Leveling the manufacturing system	Production plan-orders plus forecast
What mix of products to make each day	Finished goods for make-to-stock, customer orders for make-to-stock	Master production schedule	Master production schedule
Getting materials required to the right place at the right time	Components - both manufactured and purchased	Pull system WLK cards	Push system - material requirement planning (MRP)
Capacity of the system	Output for key work centers and vendors	Controlled by number of workers	Capacity requirement planning (CRP)
Executing capacity plans	Producing enough output to satisfy plans	Meet downstream needs	Input/output controls, route sheets
Executing material plans - manufactured items	Working on right priorities in factory	POK cards-pull system	Dispatching reports, route sheets
Executing material plans - purchased items	Bringing in right items from vendors at the right time	Kanban cards and unofficial orders	Purchasing reports, invoices
Feedback information	What cannot be executed due to problems	Immediate and automatic	Anticipated delay reports

Chapter 4
Axiomatic Design Principles

INTRODUCTION

The previous two chapters presented 10 steps for designing lean production, linked-cell manufacturing systems. The manner in which value is added to a product by a manufacturing system, along with the product's relationship to the marketplace, was also introduced. Well-designed products that perform can command higher prices on the world market and result in greater profitability for a company. Well-designed processes and systems result in lower manufacturing costs and superior-quality products, again increasing productivity and profitability. A poorly designed product cannot be manufactured well, even by the most expensive, sophisticated system. Conversely, a well-designed product cannot be manufactured well with a poorly designed manufacturing system.

System design, specifically the axiomatic-design approach, is an important subject in manufacturing systems. The material in this chapter was borrowed liberally from technical papers (Cochran and Dobbs 2001/2002).

Axiomatic design came to the author's attention in the late 1970s when he reviewed an ASME Transactions paper by Dr. Nam P. Suh. While the philosophy of Suh's work did not fully register at the time, it was recommended for publication. A few months later, the author solved a design problem by decoupling two functional requirements. He recognized that what Suh called "coupled" and "uncoupled," in reference to axiomatic design, was analogous to his own description of design of experiments.

How can a good manufacturing system design be distinguished from a bad one? The answer is to evaluate the production system design in terms of its achievement of the design objectives. To this end, a production system design decomposition is used. The basis for this decomposition approach is axiomatic design.

KEY CONCEPTS

Axiomatic design is the creation of synthesized solutions in the form of products, processes, or systems that satisfy perceived needs. This is done by mapping the *functional requirements* and *design parameters*. Functional requirements represent the goals of the design, or what one wants to achieve. Functional requirements are defined in the functional domain to satisfy the needs defined in the customer domain. *Design parameters* express how to satisfy the functional requirements. They are created in the physical domain to satisfy functional requirements. *Design domains* are shown in Figure 4-1.

The *customer domain* is where customer needs reside. These needs must be mapped in the functional domain, where they are translated into independent functional requirements. Functional requirements are then defined for a new design. Constraints appear after translating customer "wants" into functional requirements. These have to be obeyed during the entire design process. Constraints are linked to functional requirements, design parameters, and process variables. They are placed above the functional, physical, and process domains (Figure 4-1). Functional requirements are

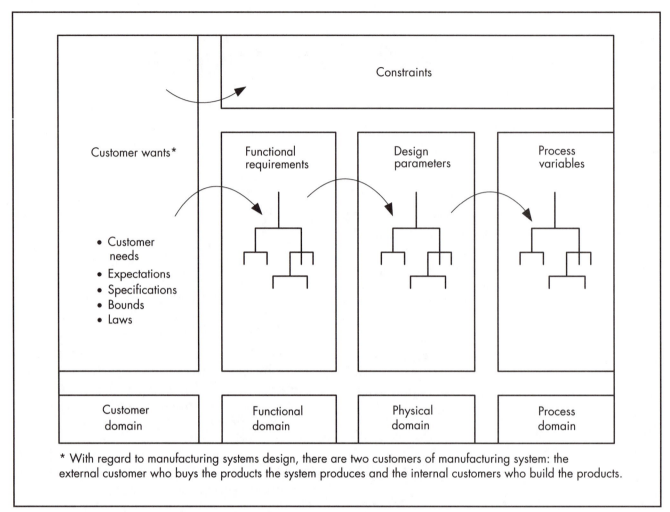

Figure 4-1. Designs can be represented in four domains (Suh 1990)

mapped to the physical domain; and design parameters are mapped to the process domain (in terms of process variables).

Design axioms have two fundamental characteristics:

- They cannot be proven.
- They are general truths; no violations or contrasting examples can be observed.

These characteristics suggest the use of a heuristic approach to develop the axioms. In this approach, an initial set of axioms is established and published. Axioms are then subjected to trial and evaluation in manufacturing situations. The extent that hypothetical axioms satisfy the requirement for true axioms is assessed by trial and error. Axioms are further analyzed, redefined, and refined, until the process converges on a set of comprehensive axioms. Here are two axioms, stated as directives rather than observations, applied to the design of manufacturing processes/systems, rather than products:

- Axiom 1 is the *independence axiom*. It maintains the independence of functional requirements.
- Axiom 2 is the *information axiom*. It minimizes the information content of a design.

DECOMPOSE THE PROBLEM

In most design tasks, it is necessary to decompose the problem. Figure 4-2 indicates the hierarchies in the functional, physical, and process domains. Development of the hierarchy is achieved by zigzagging between domains. After defining functional requirements for the top level, a design concept is generated. This results in the mapping or design decomposition process shown in Figure 4-2.

For mapping to be satisfied between domains, both axioms must be followed. Mapping between functional requirements and design parameters is described mathematically as a *vector*. The design matrix describes the relationship between functional requirements and design parameters.

$$FRs = (DM)(DPs) \qquad (4\text{-}1)$$

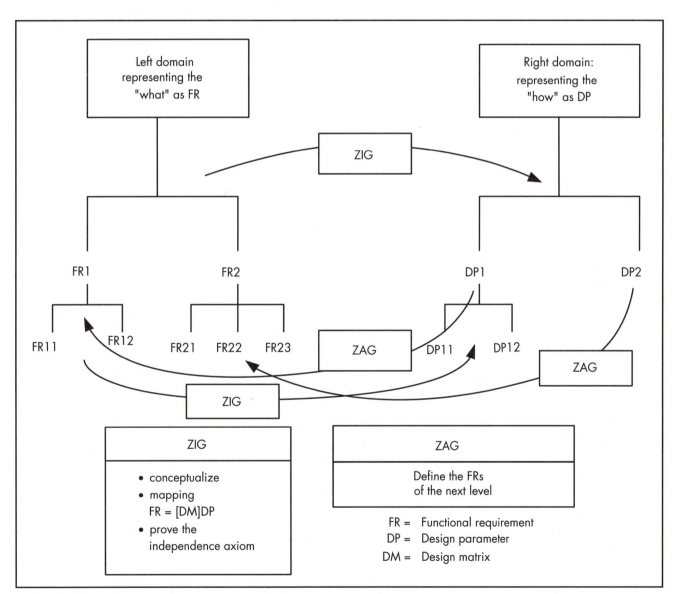

Figure 4-2. Zigzagging between domains results in design decomposition

where:

> *FRs* = functional requirements
> *DM* = design matrix
> *DPs* = design parameters
> *i* = 1 to number of machines in cell
> *j* = 1 to number of parts in family

An element in the design matrix, DM_{ij}, is given by:

$$DM_{ij} = \frac{\partial FR_i}{\partial DP_j} \qquad (4\text{-}2)$$

which is a constant in linear design.

To satisfy the independence axiom, the design matrix must be diagonal or triangular. The design of a diagonal matrix is called *uncoupled*, a triangular matrix, *decoupled*. Decoupled designs satisfy the independence axiom if parameters are implemented or set in a specific sequence. All other designs are coupled.

The second axiom, the information axiom, is defined as the probability of successfully achieving the functional requirements or design parameters.

$$I = \sum_{i=1}^{n} \left[\log 2 \frac{1}{P_i} \right] \qquad (4\text{-}3)$$

where:

> I = sum of the probabilities
>
> n = number of functional requirements of the total information content
>
> log = either the logarithm of Base 2 or the natural logarithm
>
> P_i = the probability of the design parameters satisfying the functional requirements

As the probability of the design parameters satisfying functional requirement decreases, information content needed in the design increases; thus it is inversely proportional. The simpler a system design, the less information needed to operate it.

Since there are *n* functional requirements of the total information content, *I* is the sum of the probabilities. The information axiom states that the design with the smallest *I* is the best design, since it requires the least amount of information to achieve the functional requirements of the design.

SAMPLE DESIGN

What are functional requirements? Examples can be found in the design of a supermarket. In the American supermarket, the material handler is a shopping cart; the shopper is the external customer. Internal customers are those who work in the supermarket—people who restock shelves, checkout clerks, etc. What functions should the grocery perform? Determination of the functional requirements is based on a designer's understanding of the perceived needs of customers, store owners, and workers. After considering the facts, a designer may arbitrarily decide that the functional requirements are:

- profitability (the store should make a reasonable profit while supplying provisions to customers at reasonable prices);
- accessibility (a user-friendly design should allow customers to easily get in and out of the store and access goods); and
- variety/selection (customers should be able to purchase desired brands and types of products).

Design parameters usually are measurable and represent the means by which functional requirements are achieved. Three design parameters may be:

- number of purchases per customer visit;
- times visited per customer; and
- number of products and different kinds (or brands) of an item.

The store designer may ask the following questions:

- How can the store and its elements be designed to satisfy the functional requirements?
- How should the store be laid out (arrangement of shelves, aisles, and cases, and stocking shelves with goods)?
- How should the shopping carts and checkout lines be designed to make the store profitable, usable, and desirable for external and internal customers?

Designers have no control over local product pricing or daily staffing, that is, how designs are actually used or misused. The same is true for products. Designers cannot control product misuse by customers. In summary, designers have no control over how design solutions are implemented.

Suppose a designer elects to design a store so customers have to walk the maximum distance, the full length of the store, to buy items most often purchased, such as milk and bread. The design may require that these items be placed at opposite corners in the back of the store to force customers to walk by and purchase the maximum number of products. The entrances and exits are at the same location, in the front of the store. Trucks bringing new stock are unloaded at the rear of the store.

The following questions should be asked:

- Does the design violate the functional requirements?
- Why did the designer place the produce section in the front right corner, near the entrance of the store? Is this layout because produce is one of the most perishable foods and the designer wanted to maximize exposure to it to increase turnover?

What if the designer installs multiple parallel checkout lines, automatic laser scanners, and shopping carts that are easily unloaded to minimize the time customers spend checking out? The following questions should be asked:

- How many checkout lines and carts should be in the store?

- Should carts be stored in the same place?

A typical supermarket design can be examined in terms of two axioms. The first axiom states that functional requirements must not be coupled by the proposed design. This is the case with the three functional requirements, which are independent. What about the design of a typical supermarket? Are functional requirements coupled by the typical design suggested? The placement of the milk and bread maximizes the walking distance for the customer in the store, and therefore maximizes time spent in the store. Thus, according to the first axiom, the typical supermarket design, which is not designed by functional requirements, may not be rational, since the two functional requirements are coupled by the customer action of taking the longest path to get the milk and bread. The designer for the typical supermarket uses another set of functional requirements, so that the suggested design is not coupled. If the two functional requirements are not coupled by a design, the design is an uncoupled one. Clearly, some functional requirements reflect what is desired in the layout or what the design needs to achieve.

The relationship between the functional requirements and measurable design parameters is established by the design. Design parameters represent the plan to achieve functional requirements through specific system designs. For the supermarket, measurable parameters may be throughput time and money spent per trip. This income can be tied to profit through cost. Thus, an equation can be written that ties the functional requirements to the design parameter(s).

Throughput time, for example, is a measurable design parameter for the second functional requirement. It is the sum of: walking time to get from the vehicle to the store, shopping time to collect the groceries, check-out time, and return time to the car.

$$\Sigma_{min} (W_T + S_T + C_T + R_T) = T_m \tag{4-4}$$

where:

W_T = walking time, minutes
S_T = shopping time, minutes
C_T = check-out time, minutes
R_T = return time to car, minutes
T_m = minimum total time, minutes

The second axiom states that, among designs for supermarkets that satisfy the first axiom, the simplest is the best. This is because it requires the least amount of information and operational instructions to run on a daily basis. Customers may dislike a supermarket if it is arranged (designed) in a complicated manner and has poor accessibility.

The typical supermarket design can be improved by decoupling its functional requirements. Suppose entrances and exits are at opposite ends of the store and a valet service is provided to bring customers' cars from the entrance to the exit, in time to load purchases after checking out. Customers would still have to walk by goods (maximizing exposure), while their time spent shopping would be minimized. Delivery trucks could come to the sides of the store, and in some cases, directly to the department being serviced. Another alternative might be to relocate checkout counters, entrances, and exits to other locations in the store. For instance, two or three entrances/exits on each side of the building would maximize customers' accessibility. Many local supermarkets have installed "self checkout" lines where customers scan items, get a total, pay, bag groceries, and leave the store. With this method, stores use less labor.

Designers strive to define manufacturing systems design objectives and then see how well they are met. At the Marysville, Ohio plant, where the top-selling Honda Accord® is assembled, Honda's manufacturing system is designed with the idea that there are two groups of customers, and customer satisfaction is the ultimate goal of every facet of the company. The customer satisfaction team includes product designers, salespeople, and manufac-turing engineers who are responsible for factory design.

Rich Tsukamoto, former president of Honda Engineering North America, stated, "The ultimate goal of the manufacturing system is to realize the necessary technologies, which will enable the system to produce products that satisfy the ultimate product customer." Manufacturing engineers are charged with the research and development of manufacturing processes and systems, which makes possible the effective manufacture of low-cost, high-quality products in a flexible way. There are two themes that manufacturing engineers must pursue to achieve the ultimate goal of developing technologies necessary to produce products that satisfy the customer.

The first theme is determining what the benchmark is for customer satisfaction related to manufacturing engineering services. It begins with the development of flexible equipment and a flexible manufacturing system. The manufacturing system should have the shortest throughput time. Thus, flexibility means a system can be reconfigured quickly to handle new product designs or design changes in existing products. This type of flexibility is important because it allows product engineers to concentrate as long as necessary on designs. This flexibility best satisfies customers, while allowing manufacturers to be on time with product introductions.

The second theme discussed by Tsukamoto is keeping Honda's costs competitive. The recent successes of Japanese companies can be credited to the constant improvement of their manufacturing systems. Continuous improvement really means continuously changing the manufacturing system design and continuously improving the processes. Simultaneous and continuous improvement of manufacturing processes and the innovation of manufacturing systems are keys to companies' survival.

Honda calls the internal customer the direct customer and the external customer the indirect customer. Or, put another way, Honda defines these customer types as:

- the internal customer, or the user of the Honda manufacturing system; and
- the external customer, or the buyer/user of the Honda product.

At Honda, the ultimate manufacturing engineering goal is to implement the necessary technologies to enable manufacturing products that satisfy the external customer, while recognizing internal customer needs. Honda's management does not imitate the manufacturing technologies of competitive companies. It does not believe it can make an exceptional product using the technology of other manufacturers. Therefore, Honda builds almost 100% of its manufacturing systems around in-house-built machines and equipment, thus arraying its manufacturing and assembly lines with unique process technology.

Today, Honda's manufacturing engineering group is responsible for in-house development, including the design and manufacture of:

- 100% of body welding systems, excluding conveyors;
- 100% of dies and molds used for stamping skin panels, major engine castings, instrument panels, and bumper fascia; and
- 100% of main machining lines for engine and transmission parts such as gears, cylinder blocks, heads, etc.

In addition to two plants in Marysville where the Accord® model and certain motorcycles are built, Honda also built a new plant in Ohio to produce Civic® automobiles and another to produce engines and transmissions. Its manufacturing engineering group provides 70% of new paint application equipment and 50% of automated assembly equipment for these new plants.

Today, the words "global" and "customer satisfaction" are clichés; everyone is looking for ways to become more productive and efficient. However, at the time Honda was formulating its company principles, industries in Japan were struggling to survive amidst the ruins of World War II. At the time, who

could have dreamed that any Japanese company would become an international manufacturing leader, a phoenix rising from the ashes of war?

The factors given in Table 4-1 are important for external customer satisfaction.

Table 4-1 Factors to achieve External Customer Satisfaction	
Factor	**Manufacturing Engineering Requirements**
Attractiveness	New Technology Flexibility Agility to meet changes
Quality	High accuracy Durability Reliability
Price / Cost	High operating efficiency Low investment / low first cost Constant improvement and innovation
Delivery	Mixed model production Rapid model startup

The factors (functional requirements) needed to satisfy internal customers, or the people who use the equipment, are given in Table 4-2. It shows how conflicts between two customers' priorities can occur on any factor. If all factors are equally weighted, manufacturing costs will rapidly get out of hand. Priorities must be established. This means that some factors cannot be fully implemented into every system. Fortunately, these factors are not of equal importance.

The biggest dilemmas for a manufacturing system are cost and quality. Regardless of how attractive products may be, or how first-class manufacturing systems are, products must sell at reasonable prices, while maintaining superior quality. Auto manufacturers' key priorities for achieving external customer satisfaction are minimizing initial costs, providing a car that offers a safe, comfortable ride, and produc-

Table 4-2
Factors to achieve customer satisfaction for the Internal Customer

Factor	Manufacturing Engineering Requirements
Safety in equipment	Meet (exceed) safety standards Function to prevent accidents
Reliability	Consistency Durability
Human Factors	Well-designed processes and operations Easy to operate Fail\safe design No dirty, dangerous or intensive work
Maintainability	Consider the technical level of production Design and layout considerations
Reflect Opinions	Listen to everyone Trim bureaucracy Stay in touch after start-up
Good Service	Technical support system Training manuals

ing a highly efficient (low-maintenance cost, good gas mileage) automobile.

In general, manufacturing systems and equipment, including material handling equipment, should be designed and developed with internal customer requirements as a priority. This is because these requirements have a more visible impact on manufacturing operations than those related to the customer using the final product. This is true even though manufacturing managers know the factors affecting external customers must be given the highest priority. This approach is preferred to the reverse approach of concurrent engineering espoused by many companies. The key to successful manufacturing is the development of equipment and systems, prioritizing factors that affect external customers, and then adapting equipment design to meet the highest-priority requirements of internal customers.

When manufacturing systems are being designed, the necessary criteria for each factor, priorities, and required work to achieve the priorities must be established. Using this design methodology, the best control of quality, work in process, inventory, and cost can be achieved while solving discrepancies between the requirements of the two customers.

CREATIVITY, FLEXIBILITY, CONTROLLABILITY, AND PRODUCTIVITY

Creativity, flexibility, controllability, and productivity in manufacturing systems summarize Honda's functional requirements to achieve outstanding technical competitiveness in the design of manufacturing systems. Flexibility means cultivating an agile capability that will enable a company to implement continuous innovation in processes, especially processes involving creativity and uniqueness. Companies should be able to incorporate new product changes into the operation of manufacturing systems, without the loss of production capacity. In other words, the next model of the Accord automobile is introduced into the manufacturing system while the previous model is being built.

The highest speed, or velocity, results from the shortest distance and lowest throughput time. This is achieved with the highest speed at each step, which reduces the number of machines so that the necessary product quantity (the daily demand) can be made with a single-serial system, that is, one-piece-flow everywhere. "Make-one, check-one, and move-one-on" is lean production methodology for the entire manufacturing system. Minimizing the number of steps in a process, while performing multiple functions at one step, reduces the quality problems associated with fixturing and parts handling. This also reduces the cost of processes and equipment, along with eliminating an investment in additional facilities for floor space. In addition, necessary changeover time is minimized.

Minimizing equipment size typically reduces cost and space required for the facility. Flexibility within these principal factory elements has implications beyond versatility and agility. It means that a system can adapt to changes in external customer demand in terms of volume (vehicles/month) or mix of products (more two-door and fewer four-door autos). Controllability refers to the critical control functions of production, inventory, quality control, and machine reliability. In other words, a system is designed to produce the right product at the right time, yet at a reasonable price. This begins the first step in the methodology outlined in the next section.

HONDA'S UNIQUENESS REQUIREMENT

Honda develops manufacturing equipment, processes, and systems by placing priority on factors that affect the external customer. The company adapts its manufacturing system design to meet the highest-priority requirements of its internal customers. Therefore, when Honda's managers and engineers plan a manufacturing system, they establish (in conjunction with the manufacturing department) the necessary criteria for each factor. Design and implementation teams set priorities and work to achieve those priorities by any means. By following this procedure, Honda tries to achieve the best possible control of quality, inventory, manufacturing, and cost, while solving discrepancies between customer requirements.

The uniqueness approach requires new methods and processes that are free from conventional thinking. Hence, Honda engineers and production workers struggle to develop manufacturing systems that meet the criteria and follow function and design requirements. The goal is to develop the shortest, most compact, and one-piece productive flow manufacturing system. As a system matures and inventory is continuously removed from the links, the system becomes increasingly compact. As processes are improved and quality goes from good to superior, the production rate at each step can be throttled up as required.

This reduces the number of different machines producing the same item and moves the company toward lean production. Ultimately, necessary daily quantities can be manufactured within a single-serial system with one-piece-flow. Duplicate machines are eventually eliminated to reduce product variability.

Honda's manufacturing engineers think a manufacturing system should have the following characteristics:

- highest speed at each step (fastest throughput time);
- a minimum number of steps in each process;
- one step, one machine (one-piece flow);
- multiple functions at one step, if no interaction; and
- minimum equipment size.

Process and System Design

Figure 4-3a shows a typical welding machine designed to hold four body panels (two sides, and one floor and roof) for spot welding. Honda engineers shrank the spot-welding process down to a small robot arm (Figure 4-3b). They mounted over 70 of these programmable arms on large box-like structures, which hold and simultaneously tack-weld the sheet metal for an Accord automobile body. Every Accord manufactured in the U.S. is welded on this one computer numerical control (CNC) machine. This ensures that every Accord body is identical. The machine can be changed from two- to four-door bodies in less than one minute. In the 1980s, Honda was making its Accord and Civic models on the same line. These were different-sized vehicles, so the same computer numerical control welding box could not accommodate both cars. A solution was found by designing and building two auto-welding boxes. The Accord box rapidly slid off the line before the Civic box slid on. Accord or Civic models could be welded using the same technology. In paint rooms, the same technology was introduced to interchange paint booths. Minimizing the number of steps and equipment sizes reduced costs

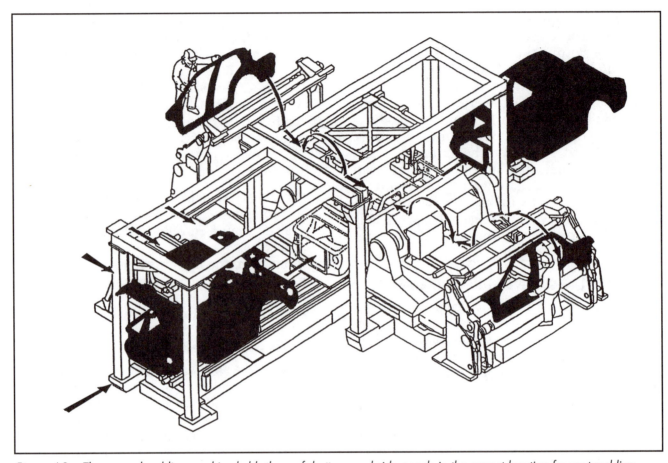

Figure 4-3a. The general welding machine holds the roof, bottom, and side panels in the correct location for spot welding.

and the required floor space. This is a typical example of where less part handling reduced quality problems.

Another example of unique process technology is found in a machine that integrates the processes of boring and honing (Figure 4-4). These processes usually occur sequentially. Combining them into one tool eliminates the variables caused by the fixturing of parts between two processes, as well as wasted transfer time. Honda has also developed a CNC gear-grinding machine that incorporates cubic boron nitride grinding wheels and induction-heat-treatment. This one-step, serial-gear-grinding machine is five times faster than conventional methods.

DESIGN PROCESS HIERARCHY

The discussion of supermarket design was restricted to the most important, first-order requirements of the system. The designer did not worry, for example, about the specific methods used by customers to traverse the store or where items were stored on shelves. This is always the case in design endeavors. That is, functional requirements and corresponding physical solutions can be decomposed and prioritized. It is fortunate that there is a hierarchy in design, in both functional and physical domains. It is fortunate as well that functional requirements can be decomposed. Because of this hierarchy, only a limited set of functional requirements need to be concurrently consid-

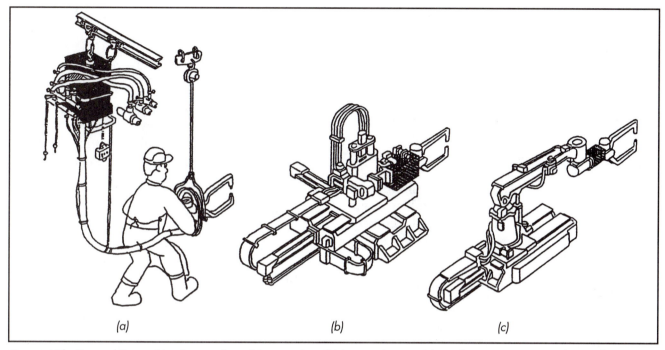

Figure 4-3b. Spotwelding at Honda went from (a) manual, to (b) large robots, to (c) small computer numerical control arms.

ered at one time; thus, immensely reducing the complexity of the design task.

The complexity of the design process increases rapidly as the number of requirements to be considered increases. Therefore, after establishing a set of functional requirements at a given level of the hierarchy, the designer must switch to the physical domain and establish a physical model or system that satisfies the specified functional requirements. Then, the designer goes back to the functional domain and establishes the next level of functional requirements. For example, in the case of the supermarket, one of the physical solutions for satisfying a functional requirement concerned the location of milk and bread. At the next level, the designer must decide how large to make the store and its respective shelving locations. The larger the store, the greater the selection, yet the customer spends more time getting their selection, which is less convenient.

A designer must recognize and take advantage of functional and physical hierarchies. A good designer can identify the most important

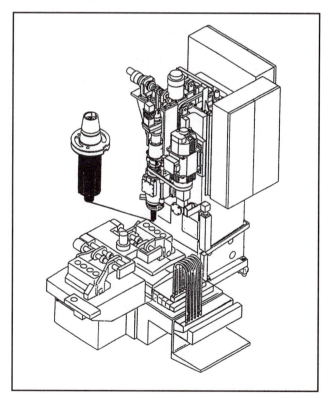

Figure 4-4. Boring and honing machine.

functional requirements at each level of the hierarchical tree by eliminating secondary factors from consideration. Uninformed designers often consider all functional requirements of all levels simultaneously, rather than making use of their hierarchical nature. With this approach, every design problem will appear to be too complex and formidable to solve.

FUNCTIONAL REQUIREMENTS

As noted, perceived needs for a product or process must be reduced to a set of independent functional requirements. Functional requirements and independence have specific meanings in the context of design axioms. Functional requirements are independent; that is, each functional requirement is independent of all other functional requirements. And, as such, each can be stated without consideration of any other functional requirement.

Functional requirements are *what* a designer wishes to achieve through a design. Design parameters state *how* a designer hopes to achieve them. Therefore, the best and most impartial method of defining functional requirements is in a *solution-neutral environment*. That is, functional requirements are defined without any preconceived physical solution in mind. Otherwise, functional requirements may simply reflect a designer's bias or the attributes of an existing design.

An acceptable set of functional requirements is not necessarily unique. For example, functional requirements for a supermarket are not unique to a supermarket. Also, another designer may choose a different set of functional requirements, depending upon his or her judgment of perceived needs for the supermarket, such as the need to eat. A designer is free to choose any arbitrary set of functional requirements as long as they are consistent with perceived needs. The physical solution will be different with a different set of functional requirements. However, the set of functional requirements must be consistent and minimal, in the sense that they are not redundant; that

is, all functional requirements must be independent from one another.

In summary:

- There is a hierarchy in both the functional and physical domains.
- There is correspondence between each level of the functional and physical hierarchies.
- To decompose functional requirements, a physical solution for each element at each level of the hierarchy must be conceived. That is, the complete FR hierarchical tree cannot be established by conceiving physical solutions at every corresponding level of the physical hierarchy. (Cochran et al 2000)

CONSTRAINTS

Constraints, in the context of axiomatic design, are defined as required limitations of acceptable solutions. They may be classified as either *input constraints*, which limit design specifications, and/or *system constraints*, which limit the manufacturing system. Input constraints usually are expressed as limitations on size, weight, materials, and cost, whereas system constraints are based on the capacity of machines, available skills for manufacturing, and even the laws of nature. A typical design constraint for a supermarket would be a store's size (square footage) or the number of checkout lines. An input constraint might be the number of pushcarts or maximum speed of electric carts in the store.

By definition, a constraint is different from a functional requirement. A constraint does not have to be independent of functional requirements and other design constraints. All functional requirements are independent of one another. In the supermarket example, profitability, accessibility, and variability, such as selection, are independent functional requirements. Therefore, the requirement that a functional requirement be satisfied should not in any manner compromise or affect the functional requirement. Time, a constraint, may be affected by any change in functional requirements.

ROLE OF INFORMATION

The world of design and manufacturing consists of the generation, transmission, conversion, and maintenance of information. The design process generates information in the form of drawings, layouts, equations, material selection, build schedules, operational instruction, etc. People on the factory floor need information to run machines, set processing conditions, control the flow of materials through the factory, and orchestrate the function of the entire manufacturing system. A simpler manufacturing system design requires less information to operate and maintain. The lean production system developed by Toyota and Honda is simpler. Therefore, it is easier to understand how the system works.

Two appropriate questions to ask are:

- Why is the information needed?
- What happens if there is not a sufficient amount of information?

The obvious answers are that without necessary information, the probability of achieving the desired output from a system is slim. It means that products manufactured without sufficient information may not arrive at the right place, time, and quality. This is a major problem for a manufacturer striving to attain lean manufacturing. Without the requisite information, the required knowledge for execution of a task is not available.

Information cannot exist without dimensional tolerancing. Consider the manufacture of an 18-in. (457.2-mm) rack bar. This is the nominal size and the most important piece of information in the dimension placed on the part drawing. But, the manufacturing process cannot make a part exactly that size, so a tolerance is applied by the designer to the nominal part drawing to reflect that fact. A designer can specify anything from 18 in. ±0.10 in. (457.2 mm ±2.5 mm) to 18 in. ±0.000001 in. (457.2 mm ±0.00003 mm). Thus, dimension and tolerance dictates the selection of different processes. Setup time, operation of the machine,

temperature control, etc., can be significantly different. For example, if a rod has to be cut within ±0.000006 in. (0.00015 mm), an ordinary hacksaw cannot be used to cut it to finished size because the rod cannot achieve that specific tolerance range. To achieve a specified tolerance, the rod may have to be carefully measured first, and then cut. An additional grinding operation also will be needed, requiring more processing information. In general, the amount of information required is much smaller when a tolerance is large, since the probability of success is larger.

DESIGN AXIOMS AND COROLLARIES

As stated in a previous section, the purpose of designing a product or process is to create a physical entity that satisfies functional requirements with the least expenditure of resources in the form of materials, energy, labor, and capital. To accomplish this goal, design decisions must be made rationally at every step of the decision-making process. Using axioms governing good design leads to effective decision making. In addition to axioms, corollaries and theorems can be developed, which also may be used in making design decisions more readily.

By definition, *axioms* are fundamental truths that are always observed to be valid and for which there are no contrasting examples or exceptions. They are deduced from a large number of observations by noting common truths that hold in all cases. Corollaries are a direct consequence of one or more of these axioms. From corollaries and axioms, theorems can be derived that can be used in making design decisions. Design rules, which apply to specific design/manufacturing situations, can be derived from these basic principles.

Axioms

Two design axioms govern good design practice, as briefly described in the introduction to this chapter. Axiom 1 deals with the relationship between functions (what the designer wants) and physical variables (how the designer hopes to achieve the functions). Axiom 2 deals with complexity. These axioms may be defined more fully as follows:

- Axiom 1 is the independence axiom; it maintains the independence of the functional requirements. Alternative statement 1: An optimal design always maintains the independence of functional requirements. Alternative statement 2: In an acceptable design, design parameters and functional requirements are related, so each functional requirement is satisfied independently without affecting other functional requirements.
- Axiom 2 is the information axiom; it minimizes information content. Alternative statement: The best design is a functionally uncoupled design that has minimal information content.

Axiom 1 states that the functional independence specified in the problem statement in the form of functional requirements must be maintained in the design of a solution. Axiom 2 states that, of designs that satisfy Axiom 1, the design with the minimum information content is best.

A design that satisfies Axiom 1 by maintaining functional independence is *uncoupled*. A design that renders functions interdependent is *functionally coupled* (and it violates Axiom 1). A coupled design is often decoupled by the addition of appropriate additional components. However, such a decoupled design may be inferior to an uncoupled system generated by complete redesign.

In Chapter 5, learning how to design manufacturing cells using existing equipment will be discussed. These cells are called *interim* because they are intermediate designs using machines that are not designed for cells. Interim designs are expedient, but not the final answer. They are certainly a coupled design. They can be decoupled through the addition of elements between machines called decouplers; or better, an uncoupled lean production cell can be designed.

Corollaries

Many corollaries are derived as a direct consequence of the two axioms of design. These corollaries may be more useful in making specific design decisions. Since they can be applied to actual situations more readily than the original axioms, they may even be referred to by the following design rules.

Corollary 1. This is the process of decoupling or separating parts or aspects of a solution when functional requirements are coupled or have become interdependent in the proposed designs. Functional independence must be ensured by decoupling, if the proposed design couples functional requirements. The cell design that uncouples the worker from machines and machining times from cycle times presents a demonstration of this corollary. Decoupling does not necessarily imply that a system has to be broken into two or more separate physical parts, or that a new element has to be added to an existing manufacturing system design. Functional decoupling may be achieved without physical separation. However, in many cases, physical decomposition may be the best way of solving the problem, such as when decouplers are added to manufacturing and assembly cells. Cells and decouplers are discussed in detail in Chapters 5 and 13.

Corollary 2. This is the process of minimizing the number of functional requirements and constraints. Maximum simplicity in the overall design, or the utmost simplicity in physical and functional characteristics, is the goal. For example, a minimum number of steps in each process should be used. Production problems and costs have a direct correlation to the complexity of the manufacturing system, and any effort made to simplify the system will result in significant savings. One of the best ways to simplify the system is to simplify the design of products themselves. As functional requirements and constraints increase, the system becomes more complex and information content increases. The conventional belief, that one system is better than another because it makes more than is necessary, is incorrect. A design should fulfill precise needs defined by functional requirements—no more or less. In a lean production system, the right amount is available at the proven place at the required time. Overproduction is not an advantage. Similarly, a process or system that fulfills more functions than specified will be more difficult to operate and maintain than one that meets only the stated functional requirements. Reliability also may decrease when a machine or system fulfills more functional requirements than the increased complexity required.

Corollary 3. This is the process of integrating design features into a single, physical process, device, or system when functional requirements can be independently satisfied in the proposed solution. The design should move toward the idea of a one-step process, or one machine with multiple operations at each step. In the lean production scheme, be cautious when considering multiple (serial) operations on one machine. The number of physical processes should be reduced through integration of parts, without coupling functional requirements. However, mere physical integration is not desirable if it increases information content or couples functional requirements. Good examples of physical integration consistent with Corollary 3 are found in the Honda plant that developed the boring-honing machine and shortened its engine transfer line from 16 to eight steps.

Corollary 4. This is the use of standardized or interchangeable processes and operations when they are consistent with functional requirements and constraints. Use standard parts, methods, operations, and routes to reduce inventory and minimize information required for material routing, manufacture, and assembly. Special parts should be minimized to decrease inventory costs and simplify inventory management, as per Corollary 3. Interchangeable parts allow for inventory reduction, as well as simplification of manufacturing and service operations; that is, they

reduce information content. They reduce it further if the design permits generous tolerances.

Corollary 5. This is the use of symmetrical shapes and/or arrangements consistent with the functional requirements and constraints. For example, right- and left-handed parts can be made together before separating them. Symmetrical parts require less information. They are typically easier to manufacture and orient in assembly. Not only should a shape be symmetrical wherever possible, hole locations and other features should minimize the information required during manufacture and use. Symmetrical parts promote symmetry in the manufacturing process.

Corollary 6. This is the use of the largest-allowable tolerance for products and their component parts when specifying functional requirements. Using the largest possible tolerances and finishes on parts reduces cost. Tolerances on surface roughness and dimensions play an important role in the final achievement of a simple manufacturing system. Reducing tolerances increases costs and the difficulty of manufacturing a product. More information is required to produce parts with tight tolerances. On the other hand, if a tolerance is too large (that is, too loose), errors in assembly accumulate, and other functional requirements cannot be satisfied. Therefore, tolerance specification should be made as large as possible, but should remain consistent with the likelihood of producing functionally acceptable parts. The correct tolerance band minimizes overall information content. When the tolerance band is too narrow, information content increases, since subsequent manufacturing processes require more information. Excess tolerances reduce reliability and, thus, increase the need for maintenance, which increases information content.

Corollary 7. An uncoupled design requires less information than coupled designs when satisfying a set of functional requirements. In lean manufacturing, most of inspection is carried out manually by operators when parts are produced in cells. In such a situation, the number of critical dimensions should be minimized. This corollary is a consequence of Axioms 1 and 2. Its implication is that if a designer proposes an uncoupled design that has more information content than a coupled design, the designer should return to the drawing board to develop another uncoupled or decoupled design with less information content. The linked-cell manufacturing system represents a system that can operate with minimal paperwork and information. It is the model for a paperless factory with a future.

SUMMARY

To get better, faster, and more competitive, a company needs to continually improve its manufacturing system design. The linked-cell manufacturing system is designed to automate the routine aspects of decision-making where possible and leave individuals free to solve problems to improve the system. To summarize the big picture:

- Design the manufacturing system with the characteristics of flexibility, uniqueness, efficiency (cost), and controllability (quality, materials, movement, and machines).
- Integrate critical control functions into the system including quality control, production control, inventory control, and machine-tool reliability.
- Integrate vendors (the supply chain).
- Design products that can be made in this system (reverse concurrent engineering).

Chapter 5
Manned Interim
Manufacturing and Assembly Cells

INTRODUCTION

A manufacturing company's success depends on its manufacturing-system design. The concept of the manufacturing-system design has been the fundamental driving force in the advancement of manufacturing, perhaps even civilization itself. For without this concept of manufacturing-system design, manufacturing would still be trapped in the intellectual darkness of the Middle Ages. The invention of the forerunner of the modern factory 200 years ago was the first system design. Periodically, a new design concept sweeps through the industrial world, igniting the fires of better and more productive manufacturing systems. These modern manufacturing systems are directly responsible for the improved standards of living in the world today.

For a manufacturing system to be successful, the design must satisfy the needs of its users, the company's internal customers. To do this, the system should ideally have the following factors in its design:

- safety—consistent with safety standards designed to prevent accidents—a fail-safe design;
- ergonomic—no dirty jobs, no heavy manual work, and no repetitive injuries;
- flexibility—easy for the user to change;
- reliability—consistent, repeatable, maintainable, and robust;
- involvement of employees—everyone has input and employee ideas are respected;
- good service—good support from engineering and technical staff, good training man-

uals, and good operating manuals/ instructions; and
- understandable—easy for each user to understand, control, and operate.

Products are ultimately in the hands of the external customer. To attain customer satisfaction, the manufacturing system must have the functional requirements of superior quality, competitive prices (that is, the lowest-unit cost), and on-time delivery. In addition, the manufacturing-system design must produce attractive products. Most important, the manufacturing system must be flexible; that is, it must be able to adapt rapidly to changes in customer demand. For instance, the customer may require more product, a different color mix, changes in the product design, and new models. This flexibility and adaptability are critical for a company to become leaner.

Basic, traditional types of manufacturing systems described earlier were job shops, flow shops, continuous process systems, and project shops. However, the newest design is the lean shop with its linked-cell design. This cellular-manufacturing system is the basic component of the lean-production philosophy and is composed of manufacturing and assembly cells linked by a pull system of inventory control. Design strategies for manufacturing systems are described in this chapter, but space does not permit detailed explanations of every method by which manufacturing cells may be formed. The main point to remember is that forming cells is an evolutionary project that restructures the factory floor.

LINKED-CELL MANUFACTURING SYSTEM

The lean production, linked-cell system is the newest manufacturing design. Figure 5-1 illustrates a linked-cell manufacturing system composed of manufacturing cells, subassembly cells, and final-assembly lines. Manufacturing cells make basic components for subassembly areas. Subassembly cells assemble units for final assembly. The basic building block of this system design is the manufacturing cell. The cell processes are grouped according to the sequence of processes and operations required to manufacture a group or family of parts or products (Figure 5-2). This arrangement functions much like that of the flow shop when parts move through the cell, one piece at a time. However, the manufacturing cell is designed for flexibility. It is typically arranged in a U-shape, so workers can move from machine to machine, loading and unloading parts, with the shortest walk distance. Machines in a cell are at least single-cycle automatics, so that they can complete the machining cycle untended, turning off automatically when finished. The cell usually includes processing needed for a complete part or subassembly.

Between each machine in Figure 5-2 is a decoupler holding one part, processed and inspected, and ready to be pulled into the next process. Decouplers in the manned cell help the worker inspect a part while permitting the worker to move in the opposite direction of the parts flow. One to four workers can operate the same cell, with output changing with the number of workers. Decouplers support material flow in the cell.

The first step in forming cells is to restructure portions of the archaic functional job shop by systematically converting it, in stages, into manned lean-production cells. Manufacturing and assembly cells can be linked directly to one another, subassembly cells, or flow lines. Perhaps more commonly, these upstream cells can be linked by the inventory-control pull system or by use of kanban.

INTERIM-CELL DESIGN EXAMPLE

Manufacturing cells produce parts one at a time using standing and walking workers. The cell in Figure 5-2 has seven machining operations and a final-inspection station. The cell produces a family of four parts, in this case, all pinions. Figure 5-3 illustrates a pinion to be machined of 430F stainless-steel barstock that is cold rolled and has a diameter of 1.78 in. ± 0.003 in. (45.2 mm ± 0.08 mm). When produced in a job shop, barstock is sawed to length, then turned on two numerically controlled turret lathes, followed by horizontal milling of the 4.75-in. (120.7-mm) step on the right end. These operations are followed by vertical milling of the end slot, and then a vertical mill drills and taps holes on the left end. Lastly, the 1.10-in. (27.9-mm) diameter is ground to size and finished on a cylindrical grinder. The operations are completed in a selected sequence as shown in Figure 5-4, which is a process-planning sheet developed for the job shop providing details for each operation. For example, the first turning operation is a roughing cut using a tungsten-carbide cutting tool. The length of cut for the turning operation is 16.50 in. (419.1 mm), plus 0.25 in. (6.4 mm) for approach. There are two roughing operations and one finish-grinding operation on the right end of the pinion.

The same family of parts can be manufactured in the lean-production cell shown in Figure 5-5(a-c). One to three workers man the cell. These workers are multifunctional and multiprocess. To be *multifunctional* means a worker can perform tasks related to setup, setup reduction, quality control, preventive maintenance, problem solving, and continuous improvement. To be *multiprocess* means a worker can operate various processes and/or carry out assembly tasks.

In Figure 5-5(a-c), each machine is at least a single-cycle automatic; that is, it can complete the machining cycle automatically, once it is initiated by the worker who activates a walk-

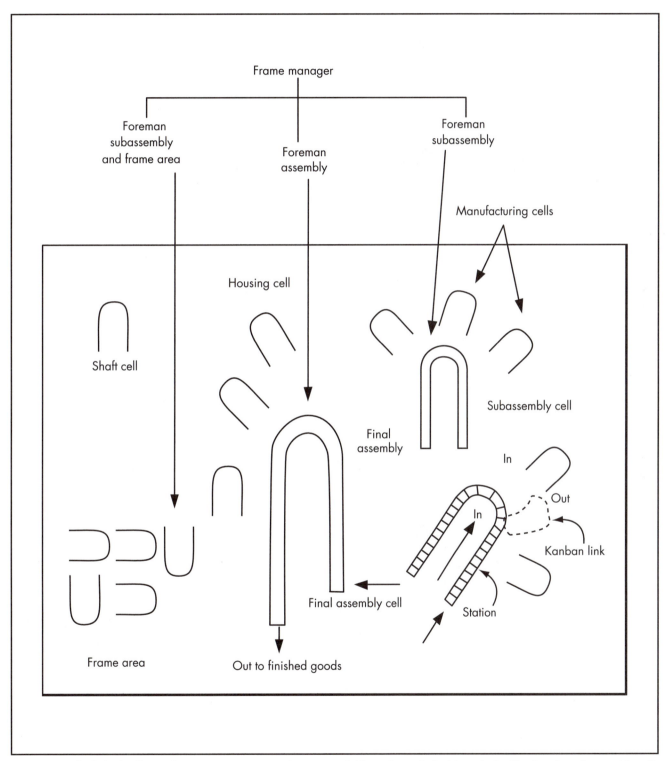

Figure 5-1. The linked-cell manufacturing system is product oriented. The cells are linked (see dashed line) to the subassembly cells or final assembly by kanban.

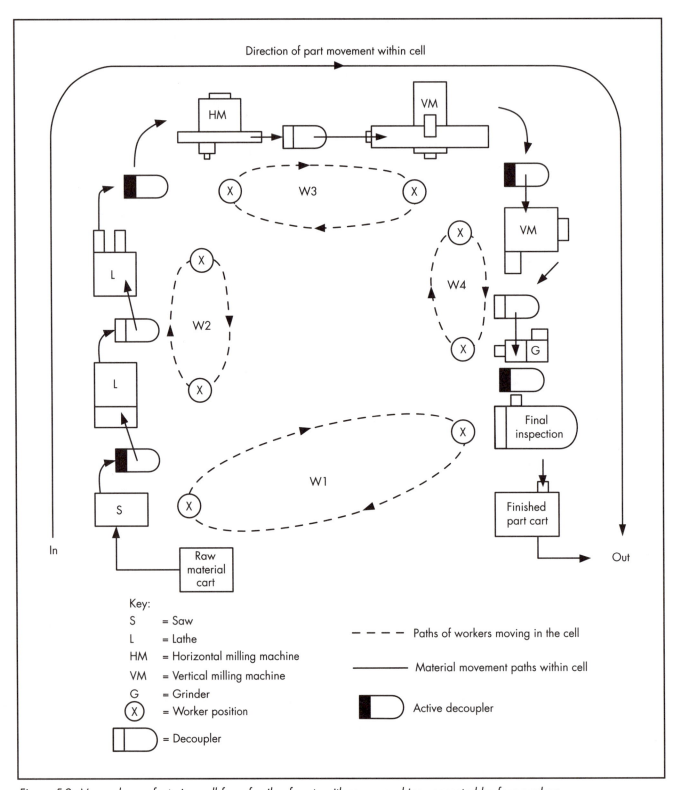

Figure 5-2. Manned manufacturing cell for a family of parts with seven machines operated by four workers.

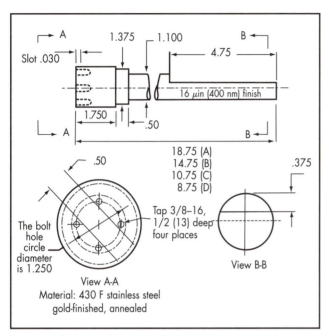

Figure 5-3. Pinion 101A, B, C, D.

away switch. Walk-away switches start the processing cycle and are typically located on the process, yet in the path of the worker walking toward the next cell process. This allows the worker a convenient and ergonomically correct method of starting the process. Figure 5-5(a-c) shows the same cell being operated by one, two, or three workers. This kind of cell is called an *interim-manufacturing cell*, because it uses machine tools that were initially designed for stand-alone applications in the job shop. When such equipment is grouped into U-shaped cells and properly modified, cells can be easily operated by one, two, three, or more, standing or walking workers. This cell is a good example of a less-than-full-capacity design that can be quickly modified for different parts in the product family, and to increase output by adding workers. The operator moves from machine to machine unloading, checking the part, loading the part from the previous process, and starting the machine via the walk-away switch. The decoupler in the two and three-worker cell serves to connect part flow between the work-

ers. Decouplers are placed between processes, operations, or machines to provide cell flexibility, quality control, production control, and process delay. The term *decoupler* is based on the first axiom of manufacturing design.

When machines are placed in the cell, a saw is added to cut bars to length. A second lathe is added to bring machining times under 45 seconds for all turning steps. In the cell, machining process times are in minutes, 0.30, 0.40, 0.40, 0.45, 0.45, 0.30, and 0.45; they begin with the saw and go around the cell to the grinder.

For turning cuts, process time equals the length of cut, plus the allowance/rpm multiplied by the feed rate. The final inspection machine is automatic and takes about 0.25 minutes to load in a part, depending on which component from the part family is being inspected (Table 5-1). The time for the inspection process is 0.30 minutes. Machining times given are for pinion number 101A from the part family. Part members in this family are different in length. Processing times are somewhat shorter for parts 101B, 101C, and 101D. Workers take about 0.25 minutes at each machine to perform various manual operations like unloading the machined part, checking the part, perhaps deburring, and loading the part from the previous machine. Workers spend about 0.05 minutes walking from machine to machine. The aisle between the machines is about 4-ft (1.2-m) wide.

Cycle time is calculated for a cell as follows:

$$C_T = (M_T \times O) + (W_T \times W_C) \qquad (5\text{-}1)$$

where:

C_T = cycle time, minutes
M_T = worker-manual time, minutes
O = number of operations
W_T = walk time, seconds
W_C = number of walk cycles

or,

$$\frac{1}{P_R} \qquad (5\text{-}2)$$

Part no.: 4943806 Part name: Pinion 101A		Order quantity: 1000 Lot requirement: 200			Material: 430F Stainless steel 1.780+0.003 in. cold finished, 12-ft bars 1000 pieces Unit material cost: $22.47			
Workstation	Operation number	Operation description	Setup hours	Cycle hour/100 units	Unit estimate	Labor rate	Labor + overhead rate	Cost for labor and overhead
Turret lathe	10	Face 0.015 Turn rough 1.45 Turn finish 1.110 Turn 1.735 Cut length: 18.75 Carbide tools	3.2 3.2	10.067 10.067	0.117 0.117	18.35 18.35	1.70 1.70	3.65 3.65
Vertical mill	20	End mill 0.50 slot ½ HSS end mill	1.8	2.850	0.088	19.65	1.85	3.2
Horizontal mill	30	Slab mill 4.75 x 3/8	1.3	1.500	0.022	19.64	1.80	0.78
NC turret lathe	40	Drill 3/8 holes–4x tap 3/8-16	0.66	5.245	0.056	17.40	2.15	2.10
Cylindrical grinder	50	Grind to 16 μ in finish 1.10	1.0	10.067	0.110	19.65	1.80	3.89
						Total cost for labor and overhead		17.27

Figure 5-4. Process-planning sheet for pinion 101A.

where:

P_R = production rate, parts/hour

Throughput time depends on cycle time and is calculated as follows:

$$T_T = C_T \times C \qquad (5\text{-}3)$$

where:

T_T = throughput time, minutes

C = number of cycles that the part was in the cell

Using Equation 5-1, the approximate cycle time for the cell shown in Figure 5-2 (manned by one worker) is:

C_T = (0.25 minutes × 8) + (3 seconds × 8) = 144 seconds/part = 2.4 minutes/part

Number of parts produced =

$$\frac{3,600 \text{ seconds/hour}}{72 \text{ seconds/part}} = 25 \text{ parts/hour}$$

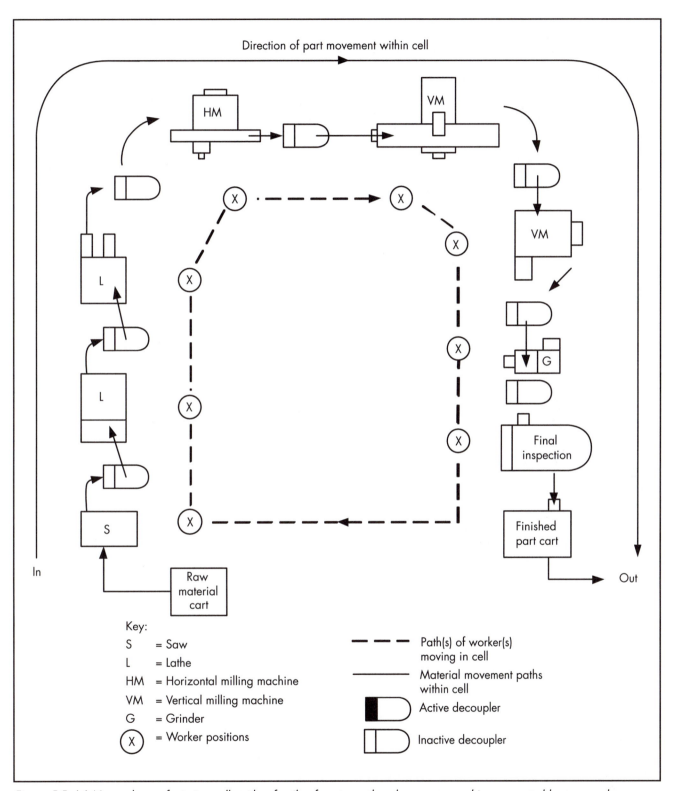

Figure 5-5. (a) Manned manufacturing cell, with a family of parts produced on seven machines operated by one worker.

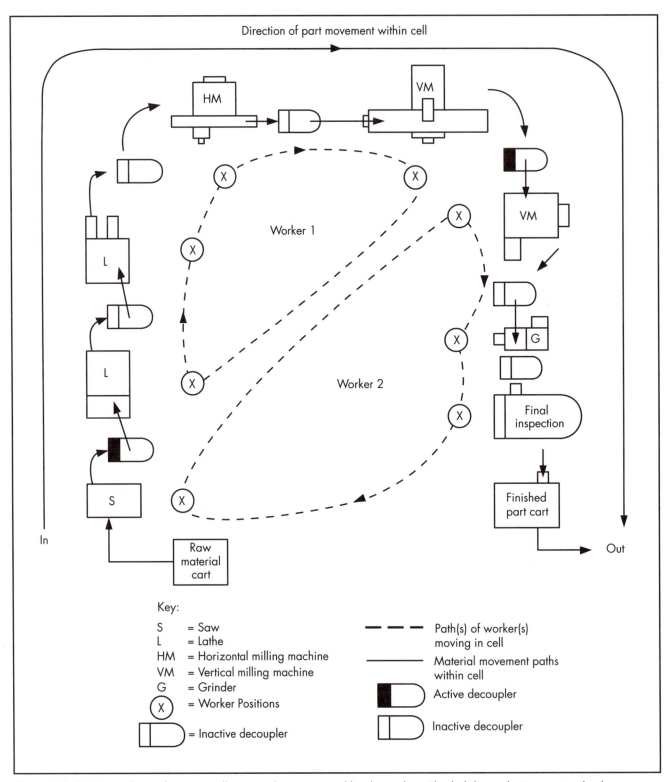

Figure 5-5. (b) Manned manufacturing cell, two workers connected by decouplers. Shaded decoupler is an active kanban square.

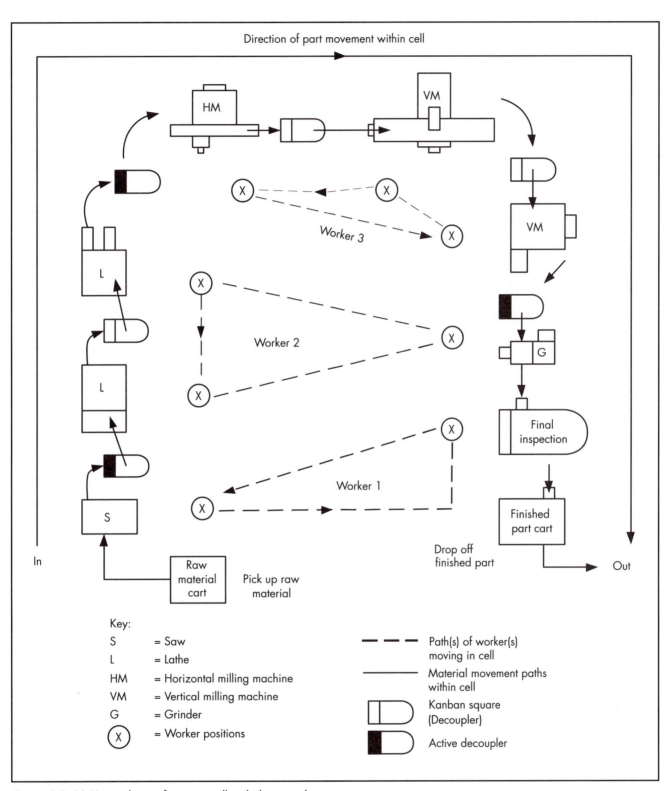

Figure 5-5. (c) Manned manufacturing cell with three workers.

Table 5–1
List of operations and respective times for manufacturing cell

Machine Tool	Operation or Process	Processing Time (minutes)	Operator manual time (minutes)	Walk time (minutes)
Saw	Cut bar to length	0.30	0.25	0.05
Lathe 1	Rough turn	0.40	0.25	0.05
Lathe 2	Finish turn	0.40	0.25	0.05
Horizontal mill	Mill step	0.45	0.25	0.05
Vertical mill 1	Mill slot	0.45	0.25	0.05
Vertical mill 2	Drill and tap holes	0.30	0.25	0.05
Surface grinder	Grind slot	0.45	0.25	0.05
Final inspect	Final inspection	0.25	0.25	0.05

The approximate throughput time for a part moving through a cell (using one worker) can be calculated using Equation 5-3:

T_T = 144 seconds/part × 8 transfers = 1,152 seconds/part or 19.2 minutes

What is the cycle time for the cell manned by two workers? Assume for the calculation that Worker 1 leaves a part in Decoupler 1, for Worker 2, who leaves a part in Decoupler 2 for Worker 1 and the workers take the path sketched in Figure 5-5(b).

So, the cell cycle time for two workers is:

C_T = (0.25 minutes × 4) + (3 seconds × 4) = 1 minute, 12 seconds/part = 72 seconds/part

Number of parts produced

$$= \frac{3{,}600 \text{ seconds/hour}}{72 \text{ seconds/part}} = 50 \text{ parts/hour}$$

The throughput time for the cell manned by two workers is:

T_T = 72 seconds/part × 10 transfers = 720 seconds or 12 minutes (approximately)

Note that two extra transfers are added for the two decouplers.

The cycle time for the cell manned by three workers is:

C_T = (0.25 minutes × 3) + (3 seconds × 3) = 54 seconds/part

Number of parts produced

$$= \frac{3{,}600 \text{ seconds/hour}}{54 \text{ seconds/part}} = 67 \text{ parts/hour}$$

What is the throughput time for the three-worker cell?

T_T = 54 seconds/part × 12 = 648 sec. per part or 10.8 minutes/part.

Suppose the machining time on the grinder must be increased to improve the surface finish. The new machining time is 50 seconds What is the impact of increasing the processing time on the cycle time for the cell with one, two, or three workers? There is no effect on cycle time, because all processing times are less than cycle times. What is the impact on throughput time for a cell? There is no effect on the throughput time, because the processing times are all less than the cycle time.

Suppose the manufacturing system needs more output from the cell. What should be recommended? As currently designed, what is the maximum hourly output from the cell, regardless of the number of workers; that is, what constrains output? Should the addition of a fourth worker be recommended? With four workers, each worker would do two operations and the cycle time would be about 36 seconds/part. Note: 0.45 × 60 < 36 sec/part.

A plot of the outputs (for one to four workers) should be linear (Figure 5-6). The concept of flexibility in manufacturing-system design is based on the ability to throttle up or down by the addition or subtraction of workers, with no changes to the actual process times required.

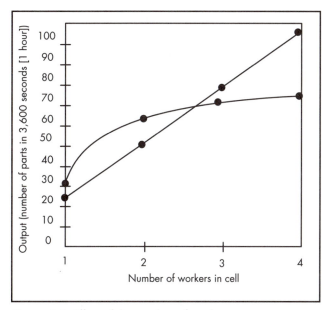

Figure 5-6. Effect of the number of workers on output.

In Figure 5-5(b), two workers can take different loops in the cell, but the cycle time and production rates remain about the same. This is how real cells should operate. Cell workers can adjust loops as necessary throughout the day. A cell can be run by up to four people to meet daily demand. Any or all of the staffing plans shown in Figures 5-2 through 5-5(c) can be used. Usually one operator controls input/output, helping to keep stock on hand within the cell under control. This operator also deals with changeover from one part to another.

The subassembly-flow lines and final-assembly lines within the plant are redesigned under lean-production methodologies to make system components operate on a one-piece-flow basis. To do this, long setup times typical in flow lines must be vigorously attacked and reduced so that they can be changed quickly from the manufacture of one product to another. Proper design and use of decouplers can simplify line balancing every time there is a change to the next part. Flow lines then become more flexible, lean, and compatible with cells. Both cells and flow lines make piece parts for subassembly cells and final-assembly lines. Resources within the sys-

tem that do not depreciate — direct labor and materials are fully utilized and minimized.

DECOUPLERS IN MANUFACTURING AND ASSEMBLY CELLS

Decouplers are placed between processes and manual operations to provide cell flexibility, quality control, production control, and process delay. Two axioms govern good design. Axiom 1 deals with the relationship between functions and physical variables, and Axiom 2 deals with the complexity of design:

- Axiom 1: maintains the independence of the functional requirements; and
- Axiom 2: minimizes the information content of the design.

Flexibility is the key functional requirement for the cell. Functionally, parts are processed one step at a time and pulled through the cell. The worker can walk either in a clockwise or counterclockwise direction; that is, with or against the part flow, without backtracking. When the worker walks in the opposite direction of the part flow, there is a problem.

Parts and information that move in an opposite direction of the worker's movement are an example of a coupled design. Adding extra components can decouple a coupled design. A decoupled design is inferior to an uncoupled design, a design that satisfies Axiom 1, because it requires additional information content. Axiom 1 states that the designer should decouple or separate parts or aspects of a solution if the functional requirements are coupled or become interdependent. Therefore, in a cell it is necessary to have one part between each successive process—the device that holds the one part is the decoupler—specifically, a production-control type of decoupler.

Decouplers reduce the dependency of one process or workstation on the next. In robotic cells, the decoupler replaces the functional capability of the workers. Decouplers in manned cells (Figure 5-2) serve to sustain part flow between workers. The decoupler permits different parts to pass one another within a cell. Decouplers can also provide functional quality control and process delay. A process-delay decoupler would delay part movement to allow the part to cool, heat, cure, etc., for longer than the required cycle time. Except for process delay, the decoupler does not act as a buffer. It holds only one part, completely processed to that point in the cell sequence.

WORK-IN-PROCESS VERSUS STOCK-ON-HAND

In Figure 5-5(b), parts arrive at the input side of the cell in a cart. A different cart connects the output side of the cell to the place where parts are to be used. Carts in the two-card-kanban system between cells are part of the withdrawal-kanban links.

Downstream cells and final-assembly lines are protected against problems in upstream cells by the presence of inventory in withdrawal-kanban links between cells. Material in cells is called *stock-on-hand*. Material between cells is work-in-process inventory.

Decouplers and fixtures that accommodate a variety of parts make flow lines more flexible and compatible with cells. Both cells and flow lines make piece parts and subassemblies for subassembly and final-assembly lines.

HOW AN ASSEMBLY CELL WORKS

The primary difference between manufacturing and assembly cells is that the processes and operations in assembly cells are usually entirely manual. That is, workers must stay at stations for the duration of a task. Workers cannot simply load parts into a machine, start the machine, and have it complete metal-cutting or heat-treating operations while the worker moves elsewhere in the cell.

The U-shaped-assembly cell shown in Figure 5-7(a) has eight stations and can be operated by one to four workers, depending on the required output for the cell. Kanban squares in the system pull material through the cell. These squares are production-control decouplers.

Suppose there is a worker at every station and the cell is operating at maximum capacity, but there is a serious problem. Balancing work at each station so each station-task time is equal is typically next to impossible to accomplish. Lean-production cells are designed to be operated at less-than-full-capacity. If there are two workers in a cell (Figure 5-7[b]), removal of material from the kanban square at Station 2 by Worker 2 (who is responsible for Stations 3 through 6) is a signal for the worker at Station 3 to attach the fan wire and install the fan. At this time, the worker at Station 3 removes material from the kanban square at Station 2, signaling Station 2 to install the printed circuit board. If the kanban square at the station has material in it, then the worker must wait until it is removed before beginning the next assembly. In this scheme, the operation times for Stations 3 through 6 are balanced with those in Stations 1, 2, 7, and 8.

Kanban squares are examples of a visual production-control system that is fast and accurate. Workers can easily see the signal and (when a part has been removed) quickly react to make one to replace the one that has been removed. The U-shaped-subassembly cell becomes part of the make-one, check-one, and move-one-on, serial-flow manufacturing system.

Suppose a company tries to operate at peak capacity using eight operators. The manual work at each station would need to be reconfigured to require the same amount of average time for each operator. This is called *line balancing*. Any variance would cause delays and disruptions in throughput times and production rates. Extensive redesign of the station or its hardware and methods would be required to achieve good line balance any time demand changes. This flow-line design greatly reduces flexibility.

A lean manufacturing cell design can be used to eliminate line balancing in the normal flow-line sense. Suppose a cell has only two workers. One worker performs the first, second, seventh, and eighth operations by walking from one station to the next. The other worker does the third,

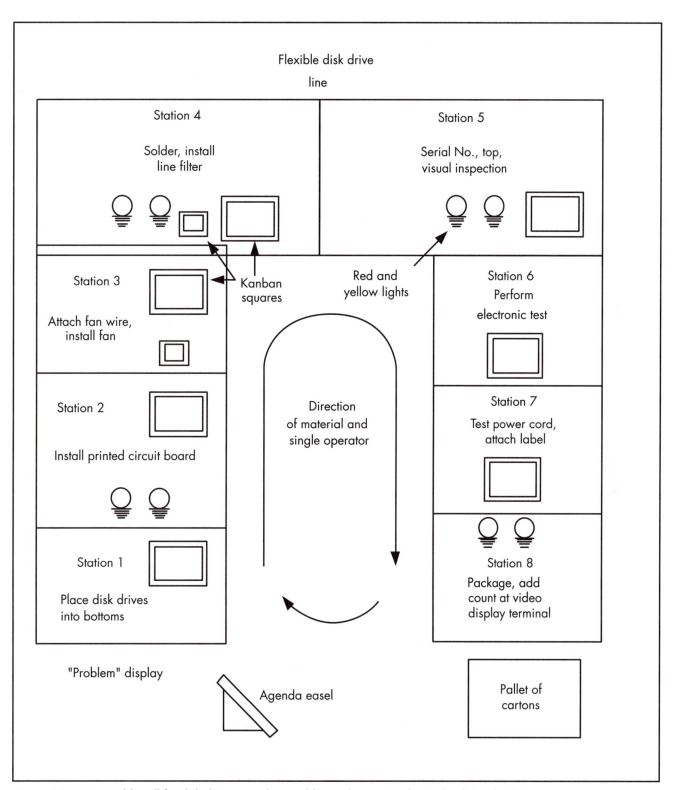

Figure 5-7. (a) Assembly cell for disk drives was designed by workers at Hewlett-Packard Greeley Division.

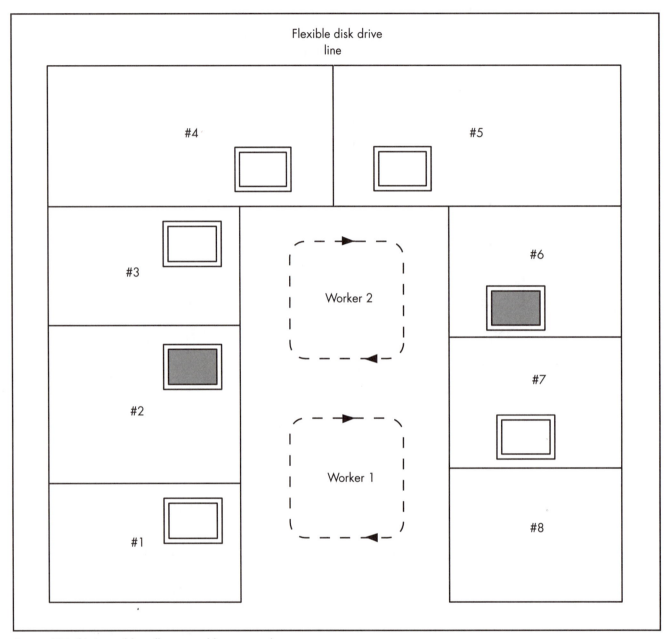

Figure 5-7. (b) Assembly cell operated by two workers.

fourth, fifth, and sixth operations. The two shaded decouplers illustrated in Figure 5-7(b) link the two workers. Only the total time it takes for workers to make half loops must be balanced. Obviously any two decouplers can be used to achieve this objective. Thus, one worker is responsible for three tasks, and the other, five tasks, to make the loop times balance. The foreman and workers can do this rebalancing quickly and almost naturally.

Alternatively, two workers could simply follow each other around the cell, with roughly half of the processes behind each other. Both workers perform all assembly tasks in sequence. This method is called the *rabbit chase* and eliminates the need to do precise line balancing for an entire cell or partial loops.

The rabbit chase is used in subassembly cells to allow all the workers to learn all the tasks in an assembly, so this frequently is how the cell is operated at the outset. Other staffing arrangements are used, after the initial learning period, where operators run groups of processes to achieve CT balance, as shown in Figures 5-5 and 5-7. The design accounts for the fact that operators will have different skill levels and will learn tasks at different rates. The U-shaped design provides the maximum flexibility to the worker for task allocation.

On the moving-assembly line, workers use red and yellow lights mounted above workstations to signal when they are having a problem (yellow) and may be delayed. The signal board is called an *andon*. Figure 5-8 shows an andon board for 10 workstations on an assembly line. As mentioned earlier, workers have the authority and responsibility to pull a line-stop cord if the system is having a problem. When a worker pulls a line-stop cord to indicate a problem, the andon light corresponding to that station is illuminated. Andon lamps also indicate the status of work on automatic- and manual-processing lines and cells. When a problem is severe enough to halt the flow, the worker turns on the red light. This stops the line and every worker on that line. When the problem is solved and the light is turned off, all operations on the assembly line begin together. Operations are synchronized that way. In the assembly cell, lights also indicate when there is a problem. Problems in the cell are documented and posted on the display board at Station 1. At the end of the shift, the day's problems are discussed and improvements suggested by line workers.

The assembly cell shown in Figure 5-7(a-b) can be operated by one worker when demand is slow, or as many as four workers when demand is at the maximum level. This is flexibility in output. The big difference between manufac-

Figure 5-8. Andon board.

turing and assembly cells is that the machines in manufacturing cells are usually single-cycle automatics, able to complete the process cycle unattended, unless it is a simple manual operation or a process like seam welding. In many subassembly and assembly cells, operations are typically manual and occasionally automated. Therefore, it is impossible for the worker to allow the process to run unattended.

Figure 5-9 shows another example of a conveyor line converted to a U-shaped line, with standing, walking workers. Notice the differences, not only in the manufacturing-system design, but also in worker duties and floor-space utilization. Workers 1 and 5 work in a rabbit-chase loop and control input and output points. Worker 2 covers part of Operation 2, plus all of Operations 3 and 4. Worker 3 carries out Operation 6 and shares Operation 7 with Worker 4, who is responsible for Operations 8 through 10. Workers 6, 7, and 8 are stationary. Notice the marked improvements in the measurable parameters with the U-shaped line. In particular, notice the 51% increase in production output, coupled with a 20% reduction in labor.

HOW A MANUFACTURING CELL WORKS

The cell shown in the upper-left corner of Figure 5-1 is designed to manufacture a family of shafts. A unique feature in its design gives the cell product flexibility. Machine-processing times are decoupled from cycle times, while products are built one at a time. Raw material for shafts arrives in carts. Figure 5-10 provides details. The cell consists of five machining processes and one final-inspection operation (required to produce the shaft family). The cycle time for the shaft cell is 110 seconds. This is the sum of the time the worker spends at each machine, plus the time spent walking from machine to machine. The worker in this example is walking counterclockwise in the opposite direction to part flow, unloading, checking the part, loading the part brought from the previous machine, and deburring. As the worker starts toward the next process, he presses a walk-away switch initiating the processing cycle.

The total machining time for a part is 280 seconds. The longest machining time is 180 seconds for Process 3; the shortest is 20 seconds for Process 4. The rule in lean manufacturing is:

$$M_T < C_T \qquad (5-4)$$

where:

M_T = machining time for number of machines, seconds

C_T = cycle time, seconds

In this case, except for the third machine, no machine delays the worker from cycling around the cell. Because Process 3, turn-bore, has a long machining time, 180 seconds, compared to the required cell-cycle time of 110 seconds, the third operation must be duplicated in the cell. Thus, turn-bore's machining time is 180/2 or 90 seconds average, again less than the required cell-cycle time of 110 seconds.

Machining times for other parts in a family can vary from part to part, because the length of cut will be different for different sizes of shafts. Machining times in Figure 5-10 are calculated from Equation 5-5 for Process 3A. Similar equations are used for other processes.

$$M_T = \frac{L + A}{F \times R} \qquad (5-5)$$

where:

L = length of cut, in. (mm)
A = allowance, in. (mm)
F = feed, in./minute (mm/minute)
R = revolutions per minute

As lengths of cut or feeds and speeds are varied between parts in the family of shafts, machining times are also varied.

The shaft cell in Figure 5-10 can change from one part to another without any rescheduling and cycle time is unaffected by change of parts. So, this cell design is representative of an uncoupled-system design. All machines in the cell can run unattended while an operator walks from machine to machine. At each machine, an operator performs various manual tasks such as unloading, inspecting, deburring, or loading parts. The time to change tools and perform setups is not shown. The cellular design relaxes the line-balancing problem, common to flow and transfer lines, while greatly enhancing manufacturing flexibility. The time it takes a worker to complete a walking loop around the cell controls production rate. This includes the required time to perform manual-manufacturing operations at each machine, but does not include

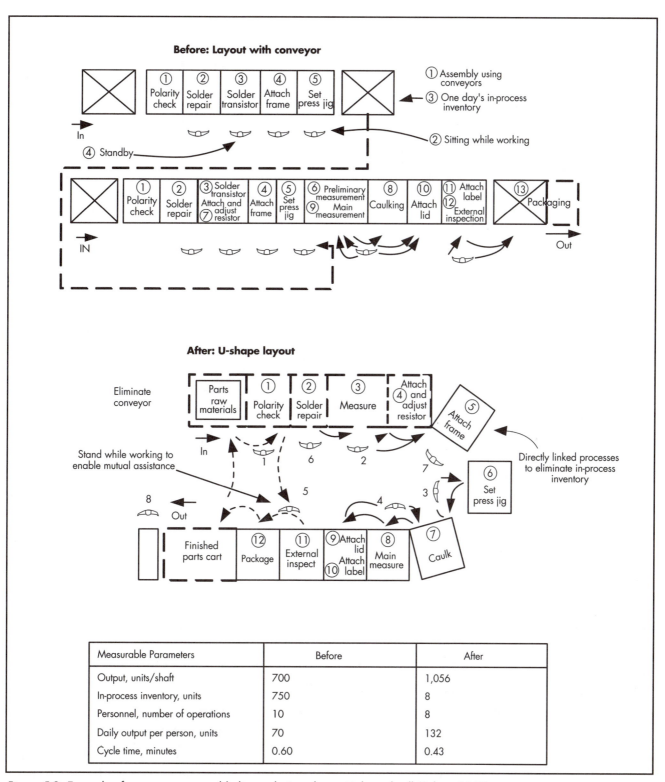

Figure 5-9. Example of a conveyor assembly line redesigned as a U-shaped cell (Sekine 1990).

Measurable Parameters	Before	After
Output, units/shaft	700	1,056
In-process inventory, units	750	8
Personnel, number of operations	10	8
Daily output per person, units	70	132
Cycle time, minutes	0.60	0.43

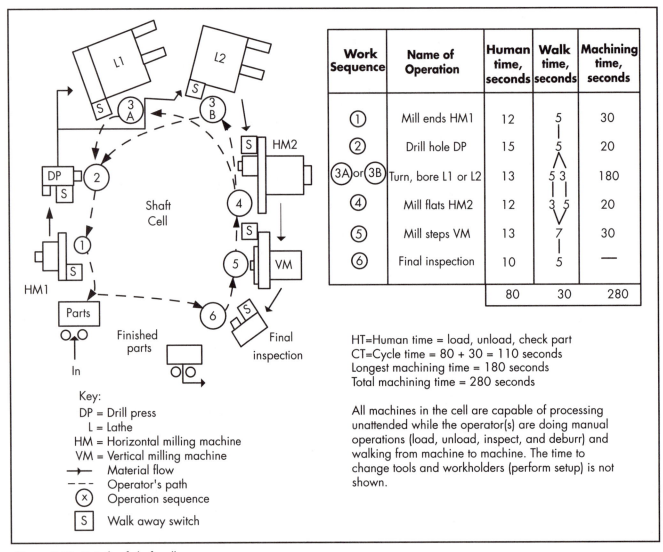

Work Sequence	Name of Operation	Human time, seconds	Walk time, seconds	Machining time, seconds
①	Mill ends HM1	12	5	30
②	Drill hole DP	15	5	20
③A or ③B	Turn, bore L1 or L2	13	5 3	180
④	Mill flats HM2	12	3 5	20
⑤	Mill steps VM	13	7	30
⑥	Final inspection	10	5	—
		80	30	280

HT = Human time = load, unload, check part
CT = Cycle time = 80 + 30 = 110 seconds
Longest machining time = 180 seconds
Total machining time = 280 seconds

All machines in the cell are capable of processing unattended while the operator(s) are doing manual operations (load, unload, inspect, and deburr) and walking from machine to machine. The time to change tools and workholders (perform setup) is not shown.

Figure 5-10. Details of shaft cell.

machine-processing times. Cycle time can be altered by adding or removing workers, or in some cases, fractions of a worker's time when two cells are close and a worker may be assigned to both cells.

In the cellular-manufacturing system there is no need to balance machining time for machines. It is only necessary that machining time is no greater than the required cycle time. Since machining time for turn-bore is greater than cycle time (180 > 110), the process is duplicated and the worker alternates machines

on each trip through the cell. Duplicated machines must do identical work. This may be checked with downstream decouplers, which inspect output from twin machines to ensure output is the same.

CYCLE TIME FOR A CELL BASED ON TAKT TIME

Requirements of the manufacturing system's takt time dictate the cycle time for a cell. Like all other cells in the plant, the shaft cell is designed to produce parts as needed, when needed by downstream processes, including assembly lines.

The demand rate for parts determines the cycle time according to the following calculations for takt time.

$$T = \frac{S_H \times S}{D_D} \qquad (5\text{-}6)$$

where:

T = takt time, minutes
S_H = one shift, minutes
S = number of shifts
D_D = daily demand for parts = monthly demand (forecast plus customer orders) ÷ number of days in a month

In the linked-cell factory, cells manufacture components for subassembly and final-assembly lines. A cell is designed to produce parts at exactly the rate a subassembly cell needs them, and no faster. Piece parts are produced at the rates needed by the cells. Cycle time ideally equals takt time, but this is difficult to do at the outset. In general, cycle time should equal takt time, or some multiple or division thereof.

An example from Honda, in Marysville, Ohio, is helpful. Suppose the factory is producing 300 automobiles per day. The body for each vehicle requires 24 different sheet-metal components. All 24 pieces of sheet metal are produced on one stand of presses. The presses stamp out 300 hoods, then dies are changed, and 300 roofs are stamped out. Dies are changed again, and 300 right-side-body panels are produced. It takes about 10 minutes to change dies. Presses produce parts every six seconds, 10 parts per minute, or 300 parts in half of an hour. Thus, a stand can produce the necessary daily quantity of sheet-metal parts every day (two eight-hour shifts). The daily-demand calculation is based on monthly demand. The required cycle time for presses is based on daily demand.

Honda relies on a mature lean-production system to prevent overproduction or underpro-duction of vehicle-body parts. Overproduction results in the need to store parts, transport them to storage, retrieve them, track them, additional paperwork, etc. It requires people and costs money; yet adds no value. Underproduction causes shortages of parts and stops the system.

ACHIEVING SUPERIOR QUALITY

This section examines cell-design detail that results in superior quality.

The cell operates on a make-one, check-one, move-one-on design concept. The piece of geometry created by machine HM1 (Figure 5-10) is checked before parts go to the drill press. The hole produced by the drill press is checked for size and location before the shaft goes to the lathes. Here, there is a problem. Two machines are trying to produce the same part geometry to meet the required production-cycle time. This is a problem to be solved by cell workers, engineers, and supervisors. At the outset, inspection and decouplers with automatic inspection may be used. Perhaps the best solution may be to divide the machining operation into rough and finish operations, with roughing work done on machine L1, and finish work on machine L2. The two lathes must be able to carry out their respective machining operations in less than 110 seconds. This may require upgrades in cutting tools, workholders, inspection tools, and even machine tools. It is at this point that the lean manufacturer will look at replacing store-bought machine tools with custom designed, in-house-built machines.

Some machining times are significantly less than the cycle time. As long as the machining time for a particular machine does not exceed the cycle time for a cell, machining speeds and feeds can be reduced, thereby extending cutting-tool life and wear and tear. The common relationship between cutting speeds and tool life is:

$$VT^m = C \qquad (5\text{-}7)$$

where:

V = cutting speed, in./min (mm/min)
T = tool life
M or C = empirical constants

Typical values for the exponent, M, are 0.14-0.40, so a modest reduction in speed results in a large increase in tool life. Also, this relaxation in cutting speed greatly reduces tool wear, which can improve surface finish. Dull tools cause cutting forces to increase. Increasing cutting forces can lead to chatter and vibration in the process. Tool wear can affect part specifications, hence quality. In short, when reliability of a process increases, the probability of a breakdown or production defect is reduced.

For cells, if the cutting process can be run a full eight-hour shift without changing any tools, quality is more controllable and consistent. No computer analysis is needed to find the process within a cell responsible for a bottleneck; it is the machine with the longest machining time. Everyone in a manufacturing system can see and understand how a cell functions, the process most likely to delay cycle time, and where critical resources need to be directed to obtain the greatest productivity gains. Therefore, in cellular manufacturing, the overall system design must be simple with built-in flexibility.

FLEXIBILITY IN CELL DESIGN

The key function-design requirement for a manufacturing or assembly cell is flexibility. Manufacturing cells should not be confused with flexible manufacturing systems. Cells are operationally different. Manufacturing cells have several types of flexibility, whereas, flexible manufacturing cells have little real flexibility.

Manufacturing flexibility considers:

- adaptability to change of product design;
- ability to reconfigure a manufacturing system or subsystem easily; and
- ability to adapt to product mix and volume change.

First, to be flexible, the process (or manufacturing subsystem) must be able to handle all product-design changes. Engineering-design changes are routine facts of life. This applies equally to new product designs. The latter is called *concurrent design* and reflects the ability of a company to bring new products to the market quickly.

Second, to be flexible, the manufacturing system must be able to reconfigure, that is, redesign, easily. The design should not be viewed as fixed and unchangeable, as is often the case in the job or flow shop. Design of a manufacturing system dictates material flow, and this must be done efficiently.

Third, to be flexible, an existing manufacturing system should be able to adapt to changes in the product mix, as well as existing volume, or changes in customer demand for the product. These are two different kinds of flexibility. The first type is volume or demand flexibility, where adding or subtracting workers changes production rates for a cell. This idea is in use at Wendy's® and many other fast-food restaurants, or manufacturing cells for hamburgers. At lunchtime, many fast-food workers are in a cell, so the production rate is high. By mid-afternoon, when business is slow and fewer workers are in a cell, there is a low production rate. Both production rates are carefully designed to meet customer demand in prescribed amounts of time, while maintaining quality. Manufacturing and assembly cells need to adapt monthly, or perhaps biweekly, to demand changes, rather than on a daily basis.

Presented here is another lean production, linked-cell, manufacturing-system design where flexibility is incorporated. Figure 5-11(a) shows a detail of the frame area from Figure 5-1. This area contains six manufacturing cells and one subassembly cell. All directly feed the mixed-model, final-assembly line. These seven manned cells are linked directly to a nearby cell by kanban or point of use. An example of this idea is a subassembly line directly linked via point of use in a final assembly line. Cell E is directly linked to Cell F. Cell D is feeding parts to Cell H, using kanban links. Cell H withdraws parts from Cell D as needed. In the linked-cell system, work-in-process between two cells is controlled by a withdrawal kanban, a function of the two-card-kanban system. The inventory within cells is called *stock-on-hand*. When cells are close to each other, they make a high percentage of perfect parts, with no machine breakdowns and virtually no setups. The kanban link often can be replaced with a direct link.

Figure 5-11(b) shows two different allocations of workers for a frame area. In the upper position, eight workers are tending machines in seven cells. The cycle time is 120 seconds, per unit. The next month, a longer cycle time is needed because demand has decreased. Six

workers are allocated to seven cells, resulting in a decrease in production rate and increase in cycle time to 165 seconds. Notice that all cells have the same cycle time. This cell system is well balanced. For a cycle time of 120 seconds, each worker is tending nine or 10 processes. Workers in these cells spend 10-15 seconds at a machine, and about five seconds walking to the next machine.

The frame-area foreman tries to allocate the minimum number of workers needed to keep the area running problem-free. Notice that some frame-area cells are completely operated by one worker. Other cells have two workers sharing tasks and machines, so only a part of the worker's time is used to operate a cell. If demand increases, more workers can be added

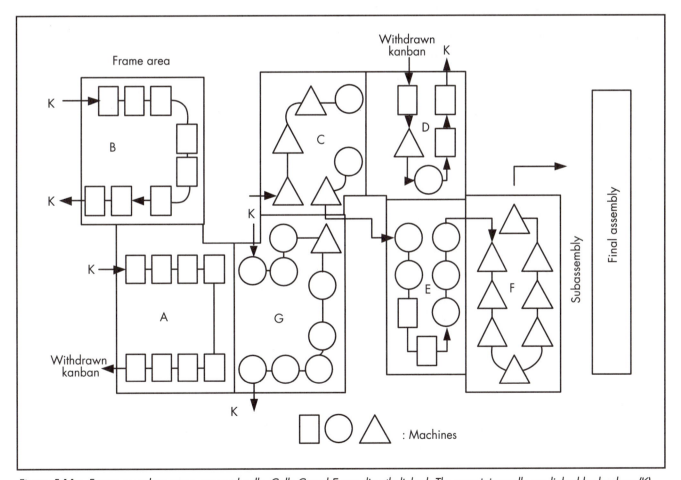

Figure 5-11a. Frame area has seven manned cells. Cells C and E are directly linked. The remaining cells are linked by kanban (K).

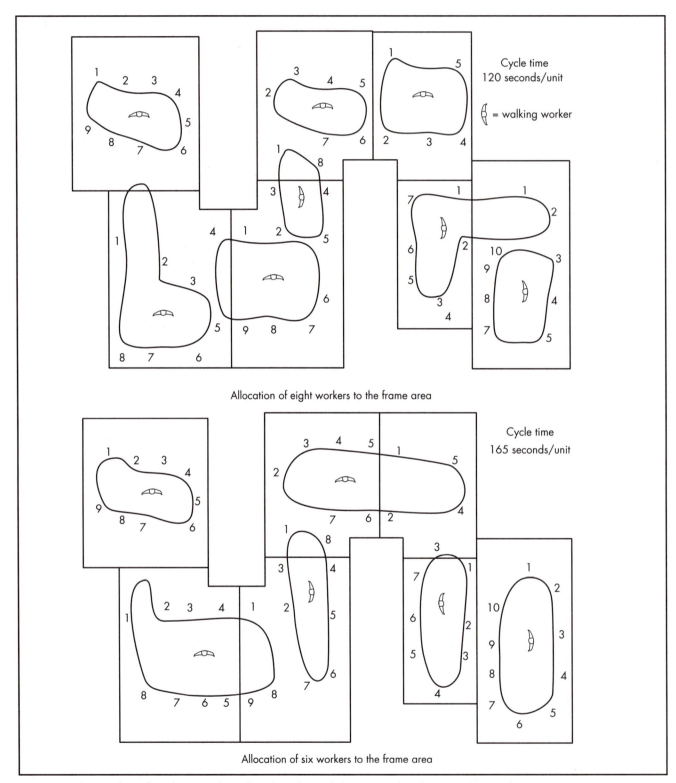

Figure 5-11b. Number of workers can be reduced as demand decreases, thereby increasing cycle time.

and two workers might be operating one cell. Decouplers between machines tie workpiece movements within a cell.

Manufacturing and assembly cells use walking workers, similar to fast-food restaurants with hamburger-manufacturing cells. These cells employ multifunctional workers who perform many tasks and duties, as well as operate different processes.

Changes in consumer desires may alter the product mix. Here is where the second major type of flexibility is generated. Cells make product families of various components and subassemblies. For example, consider a part family of four different parts. All four parts have the same sequence of processes. When parts differ in size (length of cut, for example), machining times differ because they depend on the length of the cut.

However, altering machining time will not disturb the cell's production rate, because the cell's cycle time is dictated by the time it takes a worker to carry out all manual tasks at each process and walk around the cell, not machine times. This is critical to cell function and design, but moreover, it is critical to the cell designer's fundamental understanding of cellular manufacturing. The cell design decouples the production rate for the cell from the processing rate of the machine tool. This is a primary concept of lean production, where the lives of personnel in production control get simpler. It also means that the mix of parts in the parts family can be changed without disturbing the production rate, as long as the cycle time is greater than machining time, and cell-setup time is reduced.

If the same set of parts is made in a computer-numerical-control (CNC) center, cycle time for each part will depend heavily on machining times, and parts of different sizes will have very different cycle times. This will result in different lot or batch times and lead to scheduling problems. Also, the cycle time in the machining center will be longer, because machining times are performed serially by one spindle, rather than overlapped by many spindles in several smaller machines. In the manufacturing cell, if machining time for one process is greater than the required-cycle time for the cell, the following alternatives are available:

- The process is duplicated, as shown in Figure 5-10, effectively splitting machine time in half. This is not an optimal solution, because it adds variability to part sizes.
- The process is accelerated to reduce machining time. There are many ways to accomplish this such as increasing depth of cut, feed rate, and cutting speed; but, they can all result in complications. For example, increasing cutting speed will result in decreased tool life, degraded quality, the need to make more cutting-tool changes, etc.
- The cell runs overtime at the same machining time, and the difference is absorbed in kanban links. This is usually only a temporary solution, but the easiest to implement.
- Some operations completed on a machine with the longest machining time are shifted to another machine with time available. This solution may not be technically possible.
- The product is redesigned.
- Finally, if product demand is so high that the capacity of the cell is exceeded, then the cell is cloned (replicated) to double capacity. Proven manufacturing capacity is, therefore, quickly doubled, and so is its flexibility. However, this process violates the concept of cellular manufacturing systems by producing the same component or subassembly in two cells.

When a cell is replicated, capacity is more than doubled. Suppose a cell is making two parts, A and B, and that demand has reached the point where the cell must be replicated. Now, one cell can make Part A and the other cell can make Part B, so cellular-manufacturing fundamentals are maintained. Setup between Parts A and B is eliminated, because each cell has become dedicated. However, if demand should decrease, one of the cells could go back to making both Parts A and B. Excess capacity is available to add new parts to cells. This leads to a condition called *less-than-full-capacity design*.

The cell also adapts to changes in product design for new or existing products. Cells can be designed for design-change flexibility. Twenty years ago, design of the manufacturing system was called *plant layout*. Today's textbooks call it *facility design*. All design work used to be done by industrial engineers when a new plant was being built, or it simply developed as the plant grew. Once the plant was laid out (designed), the job was considered to be complete.

Now the manufacturing system must be periodically redesigned, that is, the processes reconfigured to maintain flexibility, improve quality, reduce costs, decrease throughput time, and lower in-process inventory. To be flexible in the factory with a future, the manufacturing system and assembly cells must be easily redesigned. Equipment on the plant floor must be readily movable to restructure or relocate cells. Machines must be simple, programmable, and able to be mounted on air pallets or wheels. This is another good reason to purchase or build small process-specific machines. Power, water, and pneumatic connections must be mounted overhead on tracks for easy access. Equipment should not be bolted to the floor, unless absolutely necessary.

The product designer today knows the process capabilities for a family of parts, which are produced in a cell, so parts can be designed accordingly. This is truly designing for manufacturing.

HOW AND WHY CELLS ARE LINKED

At the outset, cells are linked by a pull system of material control, via the kanban inventory and production-control system. Within cells, parts move one at a time, from machine to machine, controlled by kanban squares and decouplers. One-piece-flow movement of parts eliminates queues and part-storage banks between processes, reduces material handling, and saves floor space. To optimize manufacturing with cells, setup time must be reduced, so rapid exchange of tooling and dies is important. Rapid exchange of tooling and dies is a highly effective technique for setup reduction and is Step 2 in the 10-step linked-cell strategy. Machines also must be improved to inform operators when something is going wrong, so that the problem can be quickly rectified. Therefore, foolproof methods must be implemented to prevent defects and machine breakdowns. These are Steps 3 and 4 of the lean-manufacturing strategy. Nevertheless, problems inevitably occur within cells, and buffers of inventory must protect the downstream processes and assembly areas from delays. Inventory buffers are between the cells; that is, within kanban links (Figure 5-12).

Parts move between cells in small lots of uniform size using kanban links. The inventory-buffer sizes between cells equal the number of parts in a container, multiplied by the number of containers in the link. The buffer size is controlled by the users of inventory, and minimized by controlling the number of containers in inventory links. Inventory buffers protect the downstream portion of the system against machine-tool breakdowns, defects, and delays occurring in upstream cells, remote cells (vendors), or transport systems. The critical functions of production and inventory control are integrated or infused into the manufacturing system as cells are linked to subassembly and final-assembly lines. The system is designed to call for subassemblies and component parts as needed (for example, when, how many, and where parts are to go). Users of this material-information system can directly control the inventory level.

Standard operation means that a system can meet customer demand with minimum labor, stock-on-hand, and work-in-process. There are three elements of a standard operation:

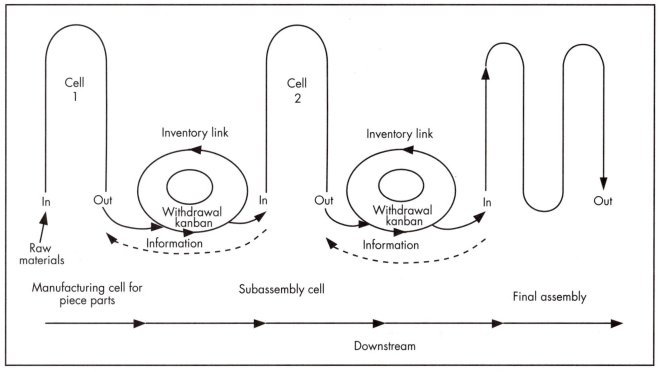

Figure 5-12. Cells are linked with controllable inventory buffers called kanban links.

- Takt time is calculated using Equation 5-6.
- There is a routine or sequence of operations needed to make the unit.
- There is a standard quantity of stock-on-hand in cells.

STANDARD OPERATIONS ROUTINE SHEET

The standard operations routine sheet (Figure 5-13) is used to plan the manufacture of one part in a family within a cell. The plan illustrates the relationship between manual operations performed by a worker, machining operations performed by a machine, and time spent by the worker walking from machine to machine. Manual operations include loading and unloading the machine, checking quality, deburring, removing chips, marking parts, and more.

The vertical column on the left of Figure 5-13 lists operations/processes on machines or stations. Details (drawings, photos, and instructions) on each operation are posted at the machines within a cell. The horizontal axis is time in seconds or minutes.

The cycle time for the cell is determined by the needs of the system for parts made by the cell. Figure 5-14 shows a standard-operations sheet for a small manned cell. Vertical columns have been filled in with operations. The layout schematic shows the path of workers or the sequence of operations. All processing times are less than two minutes.

Parts in a cell move from machine to machine, one at a time. For material processing, machines typically are capable of completing a machining cycle initiated by a worker. The U-shape puts the start and finish points of a cell next to each other. Every time the operator walks around the cell, a part is completed. As shown in Figure 5-14, machining processes overlap and need not be equal or balanced. The diagram reveals interference between the processing time (70 seconds), and the necessary cycle time (55 seconds). Total machining time is

Date:	Part No.:	Part Name:				Manual _____ Machine ----------- Walking
Takt Time:		Daily Neccesary Quantity				
Work Seq	Name of Operation	Time			Operation Time (" : Sec ; ' : Min)	
		Man	m/c	Walk	4 8 12 16 20 24 28 32 36 40 44 48 52 56 60	

Figure 5-13. Example of standard operation routine sheet used to plan work for a manufacturing cell.

10 minutes, 3 seconds. A numerically controlled machining center capable of performing machining operations could replace the cell. However, the part's cycle time will jump from two minutes to over 10 minutes, because combining processes on one machine prevents overlapping of machining times, which is called *parallel processing*. Adding additional workers can alter the cycle time for a cell.

DESIGN FOR CUSTOMERS

A cell has multi-process workers who can operate more than one kind of process or multiple versions of the same process. They also carry out inspection and machine-maintenance duties, making them multifunctional. Workers devise ways to eliminate setup time. Note that manufacturing and assembly cells eliminate the job-shop concept of one person/one machine; and thereby, increase worker productivity and utilization.

People who run processes are a company's most valuable asset. They, the users of the manufacturing system, are its internal customers. These users are often the company's most poorly used resources. Redesigning a manufacturing system into cells greatly assists in matching the skills of workers to positions in a manufacturing organization. The functional and production job shops' manufacturing systems must be restructured because they isolate people, restrict communications, and greatly increase feedback time on product-quality problems and other system concerns.

Changes will cause some conflicts between users of the manufacturing system and the ultimate customer of the system's products. The biggest dilemma is cost. However attractive a product or perfect a manufacturing system, the end product must sell at a reasonable price for the consumer. Generally speaking, the internal customer needs to dictate the design and development of a manufacturing system, even though factors affecting the external cus-

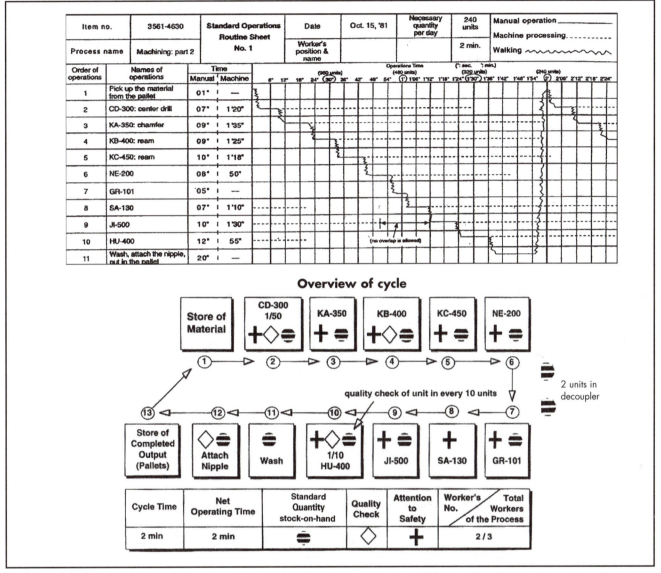

Figure 5-14. Example of a completed standard operation sheet for a manned cell. The overview of the cycle time is two minutes, stock-on-hand is 12 units (Courtesy of TRW/Koyo).

tomer (buyer of the product) are the highest priority. A system must be developed that places top priority on the factors affecting the final customer and adapts the system to meet the highest requirements of the internal customer (production worker). Resolving conflicts between these two customers requires a management environment where new ideas are free from conventional restrictions.

OTHER SYSTEM-DESIGN TOOLS

Most companies design their first cell by trial-and-error techniques. With the advent of newer languages and programs, *digital and high-level-graphic simulation* is gaining wider usage in the design and analysis of manufacturing systems.

Another technique being extensively researched is called *physical simulation*. This approach uses small robots, scaled-down models of machine tools, and mini-machines to emulate real-world systems. Mini-machines employ the same minicomputers and software as full-scale systems. In this methodology, the development of software needed to integrate hardware in the cell and design of cell-control logic (software) can be developed prior to installation of a full-scale system on the shop floor. Physical simulation is an ideal way to provide low-cost, hands-on education for workers in manufacturing systems. It is the best method to teach students what is required to integrate hardware with software. Unmanned cells and flexible-manufacturing systems can be simulated at reasonable costs.

GROUP TECHNOLOGY

Group technology offers a methodology for reorganization of the functional job-shop system, restructuring it into manufacturing cells. In a manufacturing facility, component parts of similar design, geometry, or manufacturing sequences are grouped into families. Machines can then be arrayed into groups or manufacturing cells to process the family of components. This manufacturing sequence defines the arrangement of machines and processes in the cell.

Looking back in time to the first manufacturing cells, there is no evidence to suggest that the Toyota production system designers even knew of or used group-technology methodology. There is no mention of group technology in Toyota literature. It would appear that early Toyota cells were formed using kanban. Processes were placed near each other to reduce movement of containers between processes and machines.

Finding families of parts is one of the first steps in converting a functional-job shop to a cellular-manufacturing system. There are a number of ways to accomplish this. Judgment methods using axiomatic-design principles are, of course, the easiest and least expensive, but also the least comprehensive. Eyeball techniques work for small manufacturers and restaurants, but not in large job shops where the number of components may approach 10,000, and the number of processes may reach 500 or more.

Consider the problem of a manufacturing engineer trying to justify the cost of a machining center that is computer numerically controlled. The manufacturing engineer uses experience and judgment to select as many high-cost, complex parts as possible to be machined. The engineer also performs an economic analysis to cost-justify the new machine. The manufacturing engineer determines that a family of component parts (or at least a partial family) will be produced on a machining center, which represents a type of cell (one machine). The same approach is valid for forming a manned cell of conventional machines.

PRODUCTION-FLOW ANALYSIS

Production-flow analysis uses the information available on route sheets. The idea is to sort through all the components and group them by matrix analysis, using product-routing information (Figure 5-15). This method is simple, inexpensive, and fast, but still more analytical than tacit judgment. Production-flow analysis is a valuable tool for system-reorganization problems. For example, it can be used for an up-front, or "before-the-fact" analysis, yielding some cost and benefit information. This gives decision makers information on what percentage of product will be made by cellular methods, what will be a good first cell to undertake, what other analysis methods will work best, and the amount of funds that may need to be invested in new equipment.

In short, production-flow analysis can greatly reduce the uncertainty of making a decision about reorganization of the factory floor. As part of this technique, an analysis of material flow of the entire factory is performed, laying the groundwork for the factory's new linked-cell layout. The use of production-flow analysis to identify elements of the first cell permits a

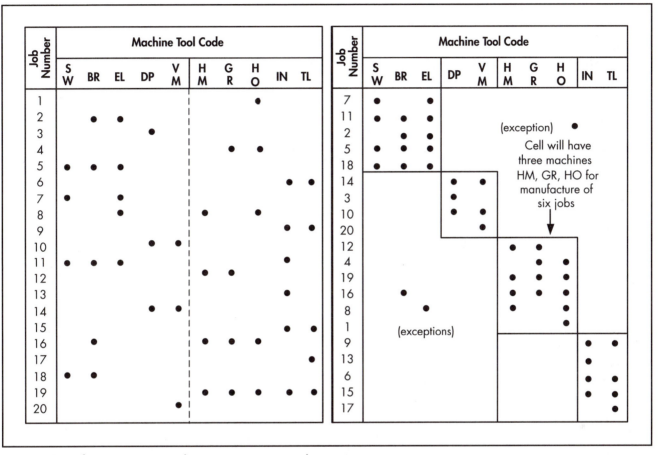

Figure 5-15. Information on route sheets suggests new product grouping.

CODING/CLASSIFICATION METHODS

company to implement that first cell without waiting until all parts in a plant have been coded by comprehensive-coding systems.

Many companies converting to a cellular system have used a *coding/classification* method, which is more comprehensive and time consuming than production-flow analysis. The coding classification system uses design codes, manufacturing codes, and codes that cover both design and manufacturing.

Classification sorts items into classes of families based on similarities. It uses a code to accomplish this goal. Coding is the assignment of symbols (letters, numbers, or both) to specif-

ic component elements, based on differences in shape, function, material, size, and manufacturing process.

No attempt to review coding/classification methods is made here. Coding/classification systems exist in bountiful numbers in published material and written information from consulting firms. Most coding/classification systems are computer compatible, so computer sorting of codes generates classes of parts families. The system does not find groups of machines. If a code is based on design data, errors in forming good manufacturing families will occur.

Whichever coding/classification system is selected, it should be tailored to a particular company and be as simple as possible, so that everyone understands it. It is not necessary for old part numbers to be discarded, but every component will have to be coded to find part families prior to the next step in the program. This coding procedure is costly and time-consuming, but most companies understand the need to perform this analysis.

OTHER METHODS

Other group-technology methods, including eyeball or tacit judgments, involve the following tasks.

- Find a key machine, declare all parts going to this machine a family, and move the machines needed to complete all parts in the family around the key machine. Often it will be prudent to off-load operations from the key machine to other machines within the cell.
- Build a cell around a common set of components like gears, splines, spindles, rotors, hubs, shafts, etc. There are natural families of parts that have the same or similar sequence of processes.
- Build a cell around a common set of processes. For example, the sequence of drilling, boring, reaming, keysetting, and chamfering holes is commonly used in manufacturing holes on parts.
- Build a cell around a set of parts to eliminate setups between parts. This is the approach used by Harley-Davidson®.
- Pick a product or products, then design a linked-cell system, beginning downstream with the final-assembly line (converting final assembly to a mixed model), moving upstream to subassembly, and finally, to component parts and vendors.

Part families do not all have the same material flow and, therefore, they require different designs (layouts). In some families, every part goes to every machine in exactly the same sequence. No machine is skipped, and no back flow is allowed. This is the purest form of a cellular system. Other families may require some components to skip some machines, and some machines to be duplicated. However, cellular back flow is still not allowed, except under extremely strict circumstances and it is rare even then. The strict and limited circumstances allowing the rare back-flow cell are during low-volume, high-process times, and with experienced cell workers.

The entire shop may not be able to convert to cells immediately. Thus, the manufacturing system will be a mix of job shop, flow line, and cells, evolving toward a perfect linked-cell system. Scheduling problems are created when in-process times for components made by cells are vastly different from those made under traditional job-shop conditions. However, as the volume of parts in the functional area decreases, the total system will become more productive and simpler.

PILOT CELLS

The formation of parts families leads to the cell design, but the design of cells is by no means automatic. It is the critical step in reorganization and must be carefully planned. Many companies begin with a pilot cell so that everyone can learn and understand how cells function. Companies should proceed with the development of manned cells, and not wait until every part has been coded. Many companies get started with coding and never form a cell.

The simplest approach is to select a logical product group and form a cell to manufacture it. Potential cell workers can assist in this and their inclusion in the implementation team should be mandatory. Only in this way will everyone learn how cells operate and how to reduce setup time on each machine and process. In the vast majority of cases, machines will not be used 100% of the time. For some machines, the utilization rate may not be what it was in the functional system. However, the system will be highly utilized and this should be kept in mind by the accounting department. The objective in manned cellular manufacturing is to fully utilize people, enlarging and enriching their jobs. In fact, one inherent result of a linked-cell system is that workers become multifunctional. That is, they learn to operate many machines and/or carry out many duties or tasks.

In the manned cellular system, a worker is decoupled from the machine so that the utility of the worker is no longer tied to the machine's utility. This means there will be fewer workers in the cell than machines and processes. In unmanned cells, utilization of equipment is more important because the most flexible element in the cells, the worker, has been removed and replaced by a robot and decouplers.

The manned cellular system provides the worker with a natural environment for job enlargement. Much greater job involvement enhances job-enrichment possibilities and clearly provides an ideal arrangement for improving quality. In the lean-production scheme for cellular manufacturing, part quality is checked between each step in the process.

BENEFIT OF CONVERSION

The lean-production strategy of simplifying the manufacturing system before applying automation avoids many risks and facilitates automation. Conversion to manned cellular systems results in significant cost savings over a two- to three-year period. Specifically, manufacturing companies report significant reductions in raw materials, in-process inventories, setup costs, quality costs, and costs of bringing new designs on line. However, this reorganization has a greater, immeasurable benefit. It prepares the way for automation. Progression from the functional shop to the factory with manned linked cells; and ultimately, robotic cells with computer control for the entire system, must be accomplished in logical, economically justified steps, each building from the previous stage. This results in computer-integrated manufacturing. The key is to integrate manufacturing first, then automate and computerize it.

Cellular manufacturing offers many advantages, including:

- Quality feedback between manufacturing and assembly operations is faster.
- Material handling is markedly reduced.
- Setup time is reduced or even eliminated.
- In-process monitoring, feedback, control of the inventory and quality are very greatly improved.
- A smoother, faster flow of products through operations is achieved.
- Cycle-time variability and line-balancing constraints are reduced.
- Implementation of automated manufacturing operations is easier.
- Process capability and reliability are markedly improved.

CONVERSION CONSTRAINTS

A major effort on the part of a business is required to undertake a conversion to linked cells. Constraints to cellular implementation are:

- Systems changes are inherently difficult to implement. Changing an entire manufacturing and production system is a huge job; therefore, it should be systematically completed. This change does require management- and worker-attitude changes, because it empowers workers to find problems and solve them.
- Companies spend freely for product innovation, but not for process innovation. It is easier to justify new hardware for an old manufacturing system, than to rearrange old hardware into a new linked-cell system. However, anyone with capital can buy the newest equipment, often creating another *island of automation*.
- Decision makers fear the unknown. They choose among several alternatives in the face of uncertainty. The greater the uncertainty, the more likely a "do-nothing" alternative will be selected, and the status quo maintained. While converting to cellular

manufacturing frees additional capacity via setup time saved and funds not tied up in inventory, such conversion requires an expenditure of funds for equipment modification, employee training (in quality, maintenance, and setup reduction), and many more items. The assumed long-term payback seems a high risk in the minds of decision makers. While in reality, cellular-manufacturing systems often pay back in months, not years.

- Decision makers use faulty criteria. Decisions should be based on the ability of the company to compete (attractiveness, cost, quality, reliability, and delivery time), rather than output or cost alone.

- Conversion to a linked-cell system represents a real threat to middle managers. Within the production system many functional areas that middle managers have been responsible for are shifted and integrated into the new manufacturing system. Also, the short-term perspective of financially oriented middle managers, versus the long-term nature of the program, results in a resistance to change. Changing a system design causes a change in the production system that services the manufacturing system.

- There is a lack of blue-collar involvement in the decision-making process of the company. Getting production workers involved in decisions is a significant change. Many managers and workers in old manufacturing systems have problems adjusting to this situation. Workers must be rewarded for ideas and suggestions. Bulletin boards can be used to post notes containing suggestions from workers. Suggestions must be recognized and a high percentage of good ideas implemented. It is vital to involve operators in the design of new cells. One idea advocates that manufacturing engineers allow workers to completely design the interim cell, even when they know they can do it better. Workers will take ownership of the cell design and work

to improve it. Another view strongly suggests that a worker volunteer to work at the side of a cell designer from start to finish. This is extremely important when designing the first cell in a factory. Lean-production proponents must stack the deck to insure that the first cell implementation is a huge success. Otherwise, it may take years before a company will consider implementing cellular manufacturing again—then it may be too late.

- Lack of top management leadership: factory leadership must have the courage to change. Leadership driven by top-level commitment is essential in changing the manufacturing-system design.

It is not known why some people make better leaders than others. It is known that that many tangible and intangible factors make people good leaders; it is also known that even good leaders make bad decisions. Dwight D. Eisenhower said, "It's easy to make decisions when you have all the facts." President Eisenhower fully realized that many times facts are missing or incomplete. Therefore, good leaders gather as much information as possible, then make decisions. Here are some facts and comments concerning leadership qualities:

- Good leaders have character and integrity — they inspire their followers to act as they do. (Batler 2003)

- Decisions that best benefit the group upset some people, but good leaders make these decisions anyway.

- Good leaders must be accessible and available to everyone; so flat, minimum levels in the production-system design are best.

- Good leaders are not pressured by accounting, and challenge experts and professionals by asking questions five times.

- Good leaders delegate, empower, and understand details.

- Even if things are not broken, good leaders ask how systems can be improved.

- Good leaders foster environments where the best people are attracted, retained, and encouraged to be creative.
- Good leaders pick people who are intelligent, have integrity, make good judgments, have energy, are balanced, are driven, and have the ability to anticipate.
- Good leaders have pizzazz, drive, expertise, charisma, and caring attitudes.
- Good leaders are willing to learn new skills, take on new responsibilities, and even reinvent their own positions.
- Good leaders are inspired to be the best.
- Good leaders can lead. They are lean-thinking, compelling, crisp, and clear.

Good leaders must have attitudes that are proactive. Leaders should not be afraid to spend part of each day on the factory floor running a process. Good leaders are in touch with manufacturing reality. They know what needs to happen strategically down the road and, they set things in motion for the future.

SUMMARY

Cells make parts one at a time using a flexible design. Cell capacity, or cell-cycle time, can be altered to respond to changes in customer demand. Cycle time is decoupled and does not depend on machining times.

Families of parts with similar designs, flexible-workholding devices, and tool changes in small, programmable machines allow rapid changeover from one component to another. Rapid changeover means quick or one-touch setup, often like flipping a light switch. Workers control quality in cells. They also perform routine maintenance on the equipment within cells.

Production and inventory control links define the paths materials take within the factory, and they are integrated. As quality improves, significant inventory reduction between cells is possible. Inventory levels can be directly controlled, reduced to minimum levels, and counted.

Most importantly, manufacturing systems must be designed to be flexible. The manufacturing system design must adapt to changes in customer demand and product design. Also, it must deliver quality products at the lowest possible cost, and with the shortest possible delivery time. Using linked-cell systems composed of manned manufacturing and assembly cells, linked with a pull system of production control, has proven to be the method to accomplish these objectives.

Chapter 6
Setup Reduction

INTRODUCTION

In a lean manufacturing class, the following exercise introduces students to rapid exchange of tooling and dies, including setup-reduction philosophy and techniques.

The class is led to a parking lot and a student is asked to drive a car up to the group and stop. The student is asked to change a rear tire while the class observes. Students are instructed to document tire-changing work, breaking the task down into elements, and timing each element. The procedure is videotaped. This changeover task usually takes 15-20 minutes, provided the student can find the necessary tools.

The class conducts the following simple analysis. Students are asked to re-examine the tire-change elements and determine which ones can be performed while the car is moving, and which can only be performed when it is stopped. The analysis results in the student performing the following tasks:

- removing the spare tire from trunk;
- finding the necessary tools needed to change the tire; and
- laying tools out in a logical array (good housekeeping practice is that there is a place for every tool and every tool should be in its place).

At this point, the student is asked to drive up to the area again. This time, the tire is changed and the student drives off in about half of the previous time. Back in the classroom, the discussion centers on how this task can be further improved, until a changeover time of 20 seconds or less is achieved. This is the time it takes a NASCAR racing team to change four tires, fuel a vehicle, clean the windshield, and give the driver a drink. This exercise teaches students how to perform many key steps in Dr. Shigeo Shingo's single-minute-exchange-of-dies (SMED) method.

SINGLE-MINUTE EXCHANGE OF DIES

Shingo was a member of the famous Japanese engineering and management team at Toyota Motor Company during its formative lean production years. He is considered the father of setup reduction and it was he who developed the single-minute-exchange-of-die methodology.

In lean manufacturing, discrete parts are mass-produced in small lots, sharply reducing work-in-process inventories. For small-lot production, equipment must be arranged in cells, so material moves easily and quickly from one process or operation to another. Within cells, one-piece flow is performed. Between cells, the kanban system controls small containers of parts. *Just-in-time* production means that a system has a serial-processing sequence and manufactures components as needed in required quantities, using small-lot production.

Successful small-lot production requires that setup time be eliminated, or at least drastically reduced. This action completely alters the economics of batch manufacturing. Workers, supervisors, and engineers must be involved and trained on the single-minute-exchange-of-dies method. A team implementing rapid exchange of tooling and dies trains workers to achieve a significant reduction in setup times and many other forms of waste.

The objective of single-minute exchange is to reduce setup time, simplify setup procedures, eliminate scrap and rework, and reduce inspection times. Indirectly, as setup time is decreased, operation frustration of the factory work force will decrease. The question becomes "Why haven't we done this before?" The most probable answer is that no one ever recognized the need. Under the archaic functional manufacturing system, setup was viewed as a given, something accepted. Setup time was measured or estimated and converted into a cost using the economic-order-quantity calculation. In the past, the most economical way to handle setup was to calculate it as a computed cost. Minimally, this was a suboptimal solution, inconsistent with the needs of the manufacturing system. Economic-order-quantity (EOQ) calculations ignore the costs of quality such as long delivery times, excessive material handling, and many other forms of waste.

ECONOMIC SETUP-REDUCTION TECHNIQUES

Almost without exception, every textbook on production, operations, or inventory planning and control presents calculations for computing economic order quantity. This is the quantity that balances the cost of holding inventory (caused by large-component quantities), against the cost of performing setup. The equation is usually given as:

$$\text{EOQ} = \sqrt{\frac{2SD}{ic}} \qquad (6\text{-}1)$$

where:

EOQ = economic order quantity
S = setup cost (or order cost)
D = continuous demand rate
i = interest rate
c = unit production cost

The conclusion drawn from this logic is that if setups are long and costly, then large lots will justify long setups. This analysis assumes that setup time is fixed and cannot be changed. Shingo and others have proven that setup time can be markedly reduced and, therefore, so can economic-order quantity.

Another way to approach the problem is to look at manufacturing costs. The calculation is based on the following equation in its most basic form:

$$T_C = F_C + (V_C \times Q) \qquad (6\text{-}2)$$

where:

T_C = total cost to produce part
F_C = fixed cost
V_C = variable cost per unit
Q = quantity to be built

Fixed cost includes costs that are insensitive to how many items are to be manufactured in a production run. Setup cost is an example of a fixed cost. *Setup cost* is calculated by multiplying time to complete the setup by the cost-per-unit time. *Cost-per-unit time* equals labor cost plus the cost of lost production time or stopping production during a changeover.

Variable cost is a unit cost composed of direct-labor cost per unit and material cost per unit. Figure 6-1 shows these costs plotted in classical fashion with linear relationships assumed. The plot shows that as the total quantity built increases, so does total cost.

If total cost is divided by quantity, Equation 6-2 becomes:

$$T_C/Q = F_C/Q + V_C \qquad (6\text{-}3)$$

This is expressed in terms of *cost per unit*. Recall that the lowest-unit cost is one of the "four horsemen" of lean production. Information plotted in Figure 6-1 is recast in Figure 6-2. This classical function is in many textbooks and journals, but does not accurately present how cost per unit varies with quantity for a given process. Note that variable cost is now the constant or horizontal line in Figure 6-2. So, at large quantities, total cost per unit approaches variable cost.

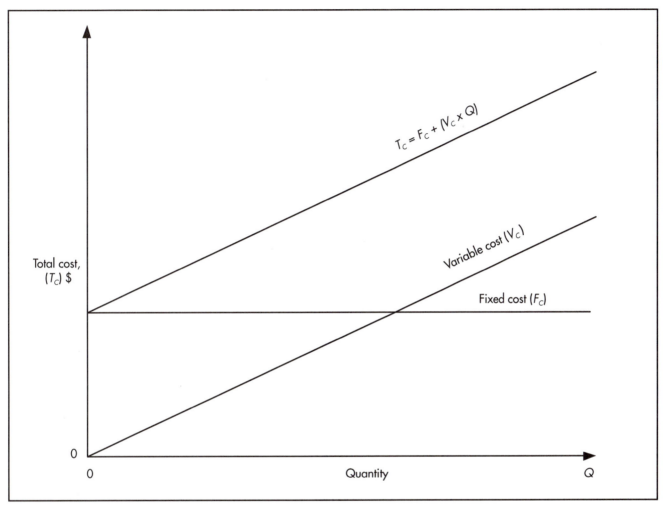

Figure 6-1. Total cost versus quantity.

This simple plot has been the driving force behind manufacturing/production system philosophies to mass produce in large lots and spread setup costs over many units. Figure 6-2 also reflects the basic economy-of-scale idea, but this plot does not extend to the right indefinitely. At some point, Q is large enough that the capacity of the process is exceeded and another process must be considered.

Figure 6-2 is a misrepresentation because, invariably, data is graphed on log-log paper for easy viewing and graphical analysis. The data, thus transformed, gives the reader a distorted impression that cost per unit changes gradually with quantity. The cost per unit does decrease with quantity, because fixed costs are spread over many units; but take another look.

Figure 6-3 shows Figure 6-2 as an undistorted, non-transformed relationship between cost per unit and quantity being built. When graphed on Cartesian coordinates, rather than log-log coordinates, the total cost per unit plunges rapidly toward variable cost-per-unit time. It then turns sharply and runs nearly parallel to the variable-cost line over much of the span of the build quantity. Cost per unit decreases while approaching variable cost per unit at its minimum. The change from rapidly

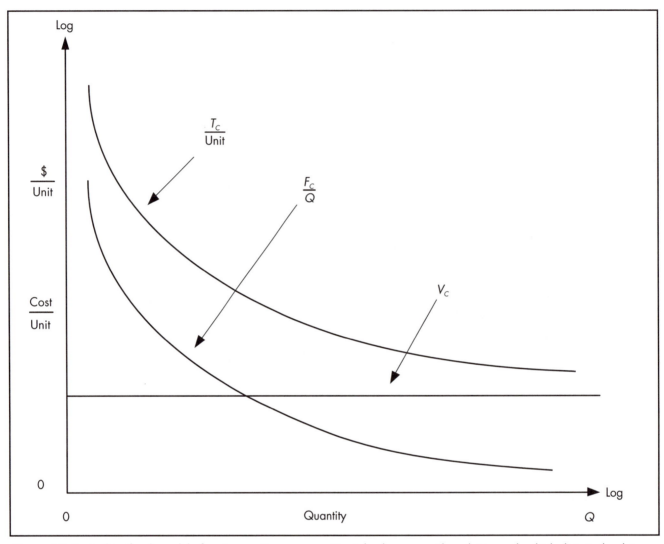

Figure 6-2. Typical textbook model of cost per unit versus quantity. A log-log or semi-log plot is used, which distorts the data.

changing cost per unit to slowly changing cost per unit occurs over a narrow range of quantities, Q_a to Q_b, the shaded area in Figure 6-3. From Q_b to Q_c, the rate of change in cost per unit is small compared to Q_a to Q_b.

To understand what happens to the economic picture when setup time, thus cost, is greatly reduced or eliminated, examine Figure 6-4. Total-cost function quickly equals variable-cost function. The dashed line in the plot depicts setup cost as greatly reduced, but not eliminat-

ed. Cost per unit is constant for all quantities when setup costs are eliminated. Therefore, manufacturers who use lean manufacturing strategies can build in small lots for basically the same unit cost as a company using mass strategies and who are building in large lots. Eliminating setups and changeover time will result in a competitive edge in flexibility.

In fact, building in small lots costs far less per unit. Quality improves because less inventory needs to be managed and stored. Layers of

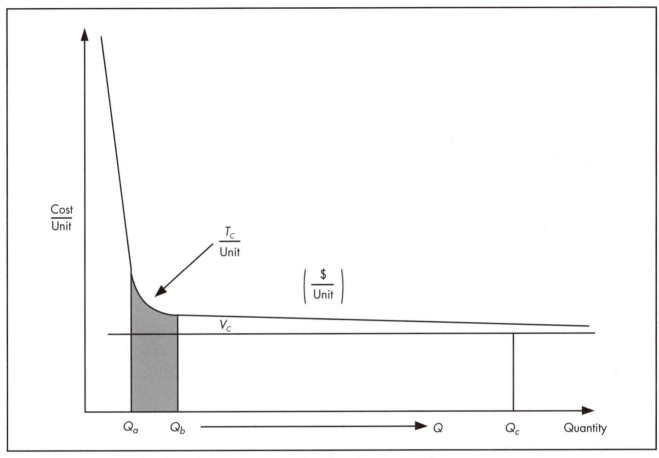

Figure 6-3. True picture of total cost/unit versus quantity plotted on Cartesian coordinates.

inventory are stripped to reveal problems, like lowering a river to expose rocks. Throughput time is greatly improved. Thus, the economics of setup elimination are persuasive.

CHANGING PROCESSES TO MEET CHANGING VOLUMES

In the traditional mass-manufacturing strategy, an increase in volume from customer demand dictates a shift to faster (higher) production-rate processes. Suppose there is an item that can be produced by an engine lathe, computer-numerical control (CNC) lathe, or six-spindle automatic. These processes are characterized by slow, medium, and fast production rates, respectively. As production rates increase, setup times also increase. However,

unit-labor costs decrease. Figure 6-5 shows the total cost per unit versus quantity (log-log plots for clarity) for the three different processes, any of which could manufacture the same item.

Production volume dictates which process to select in Figure 6-5. That is, cost-per-unit data determines the process to use for a given quantity. Three competing processes are examined on the basis of cost per unit. There is no minimum cost, only processes representing the lower-unit costs at different production quantities. Separating alternatives are break-even points or *break-even quantities*. These are quantities at which the cost per unit to build an item is equal for either of two processes. Thus, for cost per unit versus quantities, this classical approach determines quantities over which certain processes

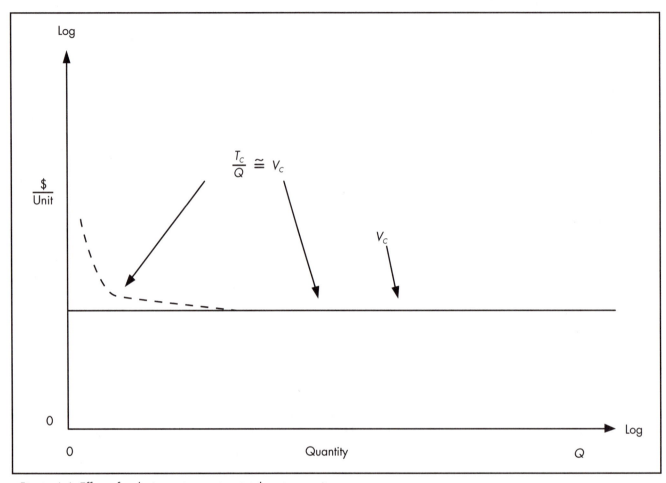

Figure 6-4. Effect of reducing setup cost on total cost per unit.

are more economical than other processes. The selection of the lowest-cost alternative is based on quantity that must be built to fill demand. If setup cost is accepted as a given, this is a valid, but suboptimal, approach.

In lean manufacturing, a different approach is taken to solving the problem. Setup time is reduced and products are built in the smallest-lot sizes possible. As unit cost approaches variable cost, material cost tends to dominate the variable cost per unit. The delightful news is that eliminating setup is not a complex, sophisticated undertaking. Setup reduction requires the knowledge of simple rules and the application of good operations and methods analysis, along with a bit of common sense. Clearly, this

could have been done long ago, but most companies failed to see the need.

Organizing to Eliminate Setup Time

Most setup problems are related to materials, manufacturing processes and systems, and management practices. Contrary to popular opinion, labor is usually a minor factor. Many companies use a team approach, rather than using individuals for setup-reduction efforts. The recommended approach combines a rapid-exchange-of-tooling-and-dies team and internal customers trained in single-minute-exchange-of-dies fundamentals (outlined in Chapter 1 and addressed completely by Shingo in his book on this subject [Shingo

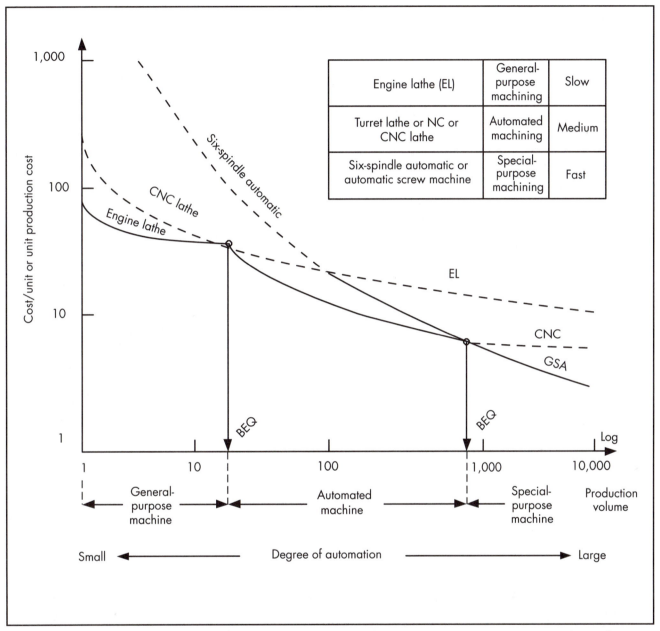

Engine lathe (EL)	General-purpose machining	Slow
Turret lathe or NC or CNC lathe	Automated machining	Medium
Six-spindle automatic or automatic screw machine	Special-purpose machining	Fast

Figure 6-5. Three different processes, any of which can be used to make the same item, are compared on the basis of cost per unit versus quality. The solid line represents minimum cost per unit.

1985]). The rapid-exchange-of-tooling-and-dies team tackles difficult setup problems, develops standard procedures, and trains operators in the single-minute-exchange-of-dies method. The following sequence of steps is recommended:

1. Select a full-time project leader who believes in lean-manufacturing philosophies and setup reduction.
2. Select a project team to do the work. The setup-improvement team usually includes some, or all, of the following people: a setup

operator, an industrial/manufacturing engineer, a design engineer, a toolmaker, a machine operator, a consultant (who has experience in setup reduction), a foreman or supervisor, a manager from the project area, and a union leader. Keep in mind that a team of four or five dedicated individuals is more nimble than a larger team.

3. Hold a series of informational meetings with managers, supervisors, foremen, and all workers, including the union committee. These meetings must emphasize that rapid exchange of tooling and dies results in faster, more frequent setups, and that workers are responsible for much of the effort. These meetings must explain:

   • what is to be done,
   • why it is to be done,
   • who is to do it, and
   • how it is to be done.

4. Suggestions should be very welcomed. The union should be advised and involved, and the union president invited to team meetings. This program should have nothing to hide. The sole motivation should be reducing setup time so manufacturing runs can be shortened, inventory and costs reduced, and productivity and quality improved.

5. Specific plant areas should be selected for pilot projects. These may be a collection of machines, processes, and operations organized into work cells or flow lines. As soon as machines have been arrayed into cells, setup problems can be addressed. Harley-Davidson formed cells specifically to reduce setup, so it was able to obtain immediate increases in capacity. A company's initial pilot project may have long setups, scheduling problems, large inventories (work-in-process), high-inventory values, or severe quality problems.

6. Once a team is trained in single-minute exchange of dies and setup operations, training of operators and setup personnel can begin. Single-minute exchange of dies

is simple and direct; everyone can do it. An attack on setups must be company-wide.

The Project Team

Regardless of team size or makeup, everyone must have a positive attitude, and be well trained in setup reduction and problem solving. The feeling that a job can be done better and less expensively is essential for success of this initial team, and for the project itself. It is important that factory workers not be neglected. Workers can be included on the team on a rotational basis. They know more than anyone about what it takes to eliminate setup time on their jobs. The proper atmosphere is also important. This should be a grass-roots program and shop-floor personnel should dominate it. It is not another engineering project. A key element is that the people who developed the existing setup should not be on the team to try to improve it, because they have vested interests. Problems with pride of authorship are best avoided. A fresh perspective is sometimes the best approach, particularly since everyone is a good critic, but few among them are creators.

An alternative to the team approach is doing most of work through existing channels. People in engineering and tool design review setups and try to invent solutions. This serves two purposes. It generates some high-quality ideas and introduces support areas to the idea of quick setups that can be applied to other work areas. However, this approach often fails to unearth many easy, low-cost, ready-to-implement solutions. Harley Davidson discovered that with a team approach, it reduced setup time from three hours to less than 12 minutes on the first machine line the team studied.

The temptation is to do other improvement tasks with the project team, including process improvement, changing the process sequence, quality standards, etc. This approach may be easiest to take, but it is not the most effective. The major objectives of the setup team should be development and implementation of solutions to reduce setup time and train workers and foremen in setup reduction. The team should spend time establishing objectives and obtainable goals, and avoid trying to solve problems encountered in areas other than those directly related to setup. The initial team must avoid trying to solve setup problems themselves, or it will run the risk of getting bogged down in one area.

To summarize, the role of the project team is to:

- train and involve operators, supervisors, and support personnel;
- gain experience from the worst setup projects;
- prepare plans and set priorities;
- determine installation timing;
- coordinate group efforts; and
- create and maintain the enthusiasm of everyone involved.

Motivation for Single-minute exchange of dies

The lean-production system is a serial-industrial process. The just-in-time concept means items are made when required, in quantities required, and as inexpensively as possible. Minimizing inventories, synchronizing manufacturing-system elements, and cellularizing upstream processes to minimize work-in-process are all steps in the lean manufacturing methodology.

It is important to stimulate the need for reducing setup-change time. Lean production uses *kanban*. Depending upon the type, kanban uses indicator cards or signs that, in addition to preventing overproduction and performing production-control functions, provide information on production and transactions. Kanban also acts as a tool for forcing the gradual improvement of the manufacturing system by reducing throughput time, creating fewer defects, and avoiding late deliveries. To function this way, the kanban must be located so that everyone can see the sequence, amount, and timing of work to be completed.

Over time, the number and size of the kanban decreases. In turn, this decrease reduces the system's work-in-process. Reducing lot size is fundamental to reducing work-in-process. Reducing setup times is fundamental to reducing lot sizes.

The basic approach to reducing setup times includes several key points.

- It is important to believe that drastically shortened setups are possible. Dramatic reductions can be accomplished by understanding that tooling change is not just a matter of removing one tool or die and attaching another. When setup time is reduced on one assembly line, managers and supervisors gain direct experience from improvements, making it easier to extend improvements laterally to other assembly-line operations.
- The setup process is simplified so that workers can perform it easily. Keeping setup changes away from machine operators merely creates a class of setup experts. Dealing with simplification of the setup process is a principal goal of setup improvement. Workers must be directly involved in the change process.
- Centering and locating adjustments should be eliminated. Adjustments depend on the right touch (or on luck), and are not repeatable. Differences show up when different people make these types of adjustments; even the same person may take varying times to make the same adjustment on different occasions. For these reasons, adjustments should be eliminated.
- A setup should allow defect-free products to be produced from the first piece on after changeover. There is no logic to speeding up a setup operation without knowing if quality products can be manufactured.

Total setup time is the time from the last good part of the previous setup to the first acceptable part in the new setup. Anything affecting that time frame is in the scope of a setup-reduction program (Figure 6-6). The typical industrial sequence is to set up the equipment or machine tool, run some parts, inspect

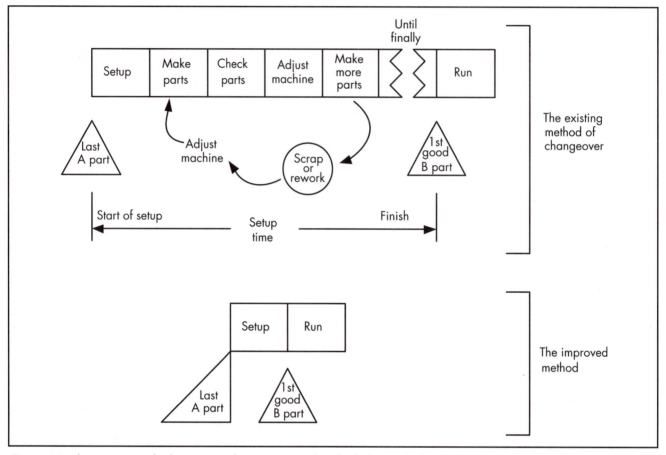

Figure 6-6. The existing method is converted to an improved method of setup by limiting unnecessary elements like adjustment.

those parts, adjust the machine, run another sample, measure, adjust, and so on, until an acceptable part is produced. This method generates scrap and rework and results in nonproductive time.

Functional Clamps

The use of functional clamps, instead of screw-type fasteners, should be highly encouraged. Screw-type fasteners should be replaced with dovetail grooves, pins, cams, wedges, etc. When use of screws is unavoidable, they should be turned no more than one full turn.

Intermediate Workholders

Workholding devices should be designed so that they appear the same to the machine tool

or process. This usually requires construction of an intermediate workholder such as jig or fixture plates to which the part workholder is attached. Jigs and fixtures are different, but plates are identical. The cassette tape for a videocassette recorder is an example of an intermediate workholder. Every cassette is treated the same by a videocassette recorder. Each one can be loaded and unloaded quickly with one handling. From the outside, every tape appears to be the same, but on the inside, every tape is different. Workholding devices, such as an intermediate jig, can help to quickly achieve one-touch setups.

A key to reducing setup time is eliminating adjustments. A significant difference exists between setting and adjusting. The channel selector sets the television to a channel. A house's thermostat sets the temperature. If settings can be manipulated, that tinkering or fine-tuning is called *adjusting*. Eliminate adjustments whenever possible. For example, it often takes a significant amount of time to change chucks (workholders) in a lathe. Figure 6-7 shows a solution where chucks of many different configurations are quickly mounted on

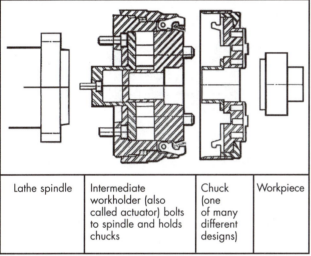

| Lathe spindle | Intermediate workholder (also called actuator) bolts to spindle and holds chucks | Chuck (one of many different designs) | Workpiece |

Figure 6-7. Example of intermediate workholder for lathe permitting rapid exchange of chucks. (Courtesy Sheffer Collet Co.)

an intermediate jig that remains attached to the lathe spindle.

To facilitate simpler tool-and-die exchanging procedures, the setup team should link one movement to another. This concept is shown in Figure 6-8.

Even though the number of setup man-hours may be unchanged, setup time can be cut by 50% when two workers instead of one perform changes. This is particularly appropriate when machines are large or change elements take a long time. Sequential setup changes should be made when numerous processes are involved.

Setup Flows Through Cell

A manufacturing cell that produces a family of parts must have processes changed over to produce each part within the family. Changeover is handled sequentially within a cell (Figure 6-9).

This example involves a cell with four processes making different parts. In manufacturing and assembly cells, as well as assembly lines, setup work begins at the head of the cell, or flow line, and moves through the cell one process ahead of the first unit of that particular part or model. Setup becomes an integral part of the cell operation. Setups in manufacturing cells are synchronized with those of final assembly as lot sizes are reduced along with setup times. As shown in Figure 6-9, when numerous processes are involved in the manufacturing cell of a family of parts, sequential setup changes are utilized. In the figure, a changeover from Part A to Part B is described for a cell with four processes. The worker is moving in the same direction as part flow and changes each machine over sequentially from Part A to Part B. After the worker has made four trips around the cell, the cell is making Part B exclusively. At the outset, setup times may be long compared to processing times that is, run times. Eventually setup times are reduced to less than the time a worker spends at each process.

The setup operation flows through a cell. Eventually, it should become one-touch-very quick, with one handling of the workholder. The setup change should allow production of defect-free products from the start. The first part produced after the setup is good. Ultimately, the ideal condition of eliminating setup between different parts will be achieved. However, dropping setup time to short intervals may be difficult in lathe operations. Turning usually requires a change in the workholder and tooling when parts are changed. There is no ideal setup change. If setup changes are necessary, they need to be performed with a one-touch motion.

Single-minute exchange of dies implies that setup time is a single-digit number of minutes (nine minutes and 59 seconds, or less). When setup time is reduced to less than one minute, it is called *one-touch exchange of dies*. Non-

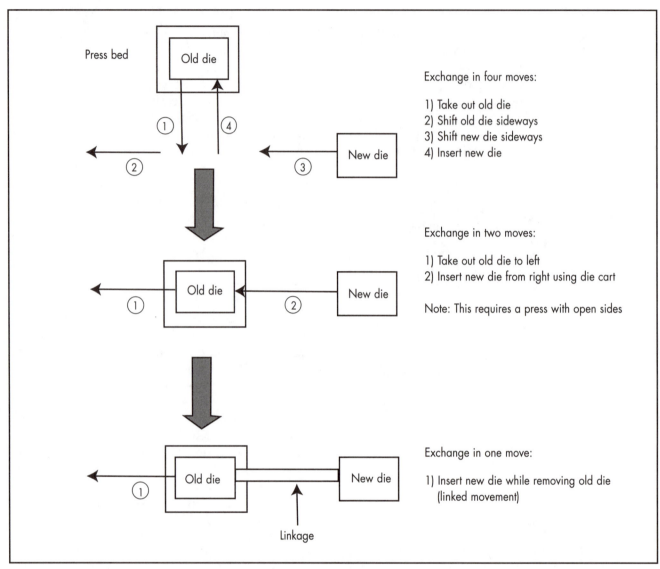

Figure 6-8. Simplifying tool and die exchanges by linking movements.

touch exchange of tooling and dies is automatic. (An example is a machine tool with an automatic tool or machine-pallet changer for parts.)

Rapid exchange of dies and tooling can reduce setup time from hours to minutes. This can be of remarkable benefit to the manufacturing organization. Reducing setup time increases available machinery capacity. However, additional process capacity should not be used to overproduce as this can lead to higher inventory costs and other detrimental effects on the manufacturing organization.

Basic Steps for Reducing Setup Time

The basic steps of a single-minute-exchange-of-dies, setup-time-reduction program are:

1. Determine the existing method.
2. Separate the internal from the external elements.
3. Convert the internal to external elements.

The flow through set-up process

Cycles through the cell	Four Processes in the cell			
	Machine 1	Machine 2	Machine 3	Machine 4
1	A	A	A	A
2	A (last A part)	A	A	A
3	Setup change	A (last A part)	A	A
4	B (first B part)	Setup change	A (last A part)	A
5	B	B (first B part)	Setup change	A (last A part)
6	B	B	B (first B part)	Setup change
7	B	B	B	B (first B part)
8	B	B	B	B

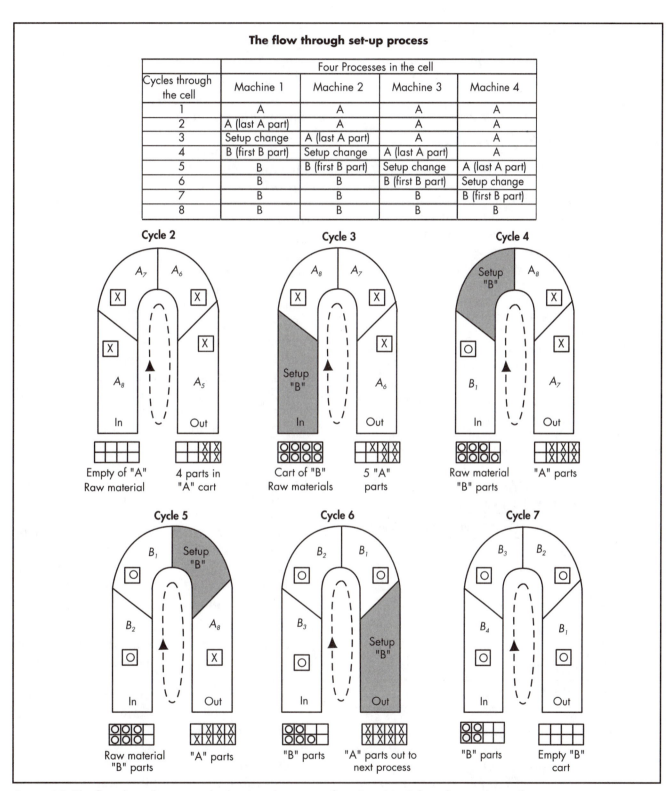

Figure 6-9. The flow through setup cycle showing changeover from Part A to B for a four-process cell.

4. Reduce or eliminate internal elements by continuously improving setup. Apply method analysis and practice doing setups. Eliminate adjustments. Abolish the setup itself.
5. Streamline external elements.

Determine the Existing Method

Operational analysis using motion and time studies can be used to determine the current setup procedure. The usual objective is to improve work methods, eliminate unnecessary motions, and arrange the necessary motions into the best sequence. A setup is broken into short elements and activities that consume the most time are noted. Problem-solving techniques can be applied separately to each particular activity to achieve the lowest-possible time.

Setup procedures are usually thought of as infinitely varied, depending on the type of operation and equipment being used. Yet, when procedures are broken into elements and analyzed from the single-minute-exchange-of-dies point of view, that setup operation includes a sequence of steps. The traditional setup time distribution is similar to that in Table 6-1.

Table 6-1
Steps in existing setup process

Operation	Proportion of time
Preparation after-process adjustment, and checking of raw material, dies, jigs, gages, cutting tools, etc.	30%
Removing and mounting new dies, etc., for next part	5%
Centering, dimensioning, and setting of other conditions	15%
Trial runs and adjustments	50%

Preparation, after-process adjustments, and checking of materials, tools, etc., ensure that parts and tools are where they should be and that they function properly. Checking includes the time period after setup is com-

pleted, when items like removed tooling and dies are returned to storage and the process is cleaned, etc.

Removing and mounting workholders, dies, tools, parts, etc., includes the removal of parts and tools after completion of processing. This also includes insertion of workholders, tooling, parts, and cutting tools for the next job.

Measurements and calibrations must be made prior to performing a production operation, such as centering, dimensioning, temperature, pressure, etc.

Trial runs and adjustments are made and checked against specifications after a test piece is machined. The greater the measurement and calibration accuracy in the prior step, the easier it will be to make the adjustments.

The frequency and length of test runs and adjustment procedures depend on the skills of the setup people. The greatest difficulties in a setup operation occur when adjusting equipment. The largest proportion of time associated with trial runs is derived from adjustment problems. So, manufacturers should seek to eliminate trial runs and adjustments from existing setups.

Because existing setups can be quite long, videotaping two or three setups is helpful for later review and analysis. When the worker, as a team member, reviews the videotape, waste in the existing setup will be revealed, even without carrying out an operations analysis. One would expect to find the following in a typical metal-stamping press:

- dies of different sizes and heights;
- different dies needing different shut heights on the press, making adjustments necessary;
- dies held with long, threaded bolts, often with stripped threads and badly worn or damaged heads;
- missing tools, nuts, and bolts needed for changeover;
- operators unable to locate tools or dies to be inserted;

- at least a two-person job to take an old die out and/or put a new die in the machine;
- in general, wasted motion and time;
- in general, nothing is standardized;
- 20-50% of time typically spent on adjusting (making a part, checking it, adjusting settings, and repeating), and 10% on locating and securing new tools or dies.

A motion analysis of the process using a stopwatch is the next best approach. Such an analysis, however, takes a great deal of time and skill. Another possibility is to use a work-sampling study. The problem with this option is that work samples are precise only where there is a great deal of repetition. Such a study may not be suitable when few actions are repeated. A third useful approach is to study conditions on the shop floor by interviewing workers and having them explain what they do in a step-by-step manner. Even though some consultants are advocates of an in-depth continuous-production analyses to improve setup, informal observation of the setup and a discussion with operators often suffices.

Separate the Internal From the External Elements

Internal, or mainline, elements refer to setup actions that require the machine to be stopped. *External,* or off-line, elements refer to actions that can be taken while a machine is running. The most important step in implementing single-minute exchange of dies is distinguishing between internal and external setup actions. Even though everyone usually agrees that preparation of dies and workholders, maintenance, and gathering of tools should not be done while processes are stopped, it is amazing to observe how often these practices still occur.

Mastering the distinction between internal and external setup actions is the most direct route to achieving single-minute exchange of dies. Internal and external elements must be rigorously separated. Once the process is stopped, the worker should never leave to handle any part of the external setup. As part of external setup, the die, tools, and materials should be ready for insertion into the process while it is still working on the first job. Any modifications or repairs to tooling or dies should be made in advance. In internal setup, only removal and insertion operations should occur. That is, operations must be done with the process stopped.

Lining up dies that are ready for insertion when the press stops can facilitate exchange of the old for the new die. To facilitate changeover, roller conveyors can be used for staging and changing dies, as shown in Figure 6-10.

A turntable cart (Figure 6-11) adds to the versatility of the exchange. Alternatively, the table may hold four to six small dies in designated locations, and dies can slide in and out. The entire table is on wheels so it can be rolled out of the way during a process run.

A typical die-exchange procedure is as follows (an actual method to be standardized and practiced):

1. Detach the old die from the machine's bolster plates.
2. Push table cart over to press and secure table next to press with brake or stopper.
3. Push old die onto table.
4. Rotate table and unload new die onto bolster.
5. Pull table away from press and attach new die to machine using the same set of bolts.

Figure 6-12 shows yet another approach to rapid die exchange in a small press. This approach uses a carousel conveyor, which is less expensive and has greater die capacity than the turntable cart, but is slightly less flexible. A cart services a group of presses and allows dies to be inserted in any order, as needed. A carousel conveyor is constructed around a particular press, and dies for the family of parts processed in this press are arranged on the carousel in order of use. The operator, as the first order of business, generally is responsible for getting the right dies in the right order for the day's production.

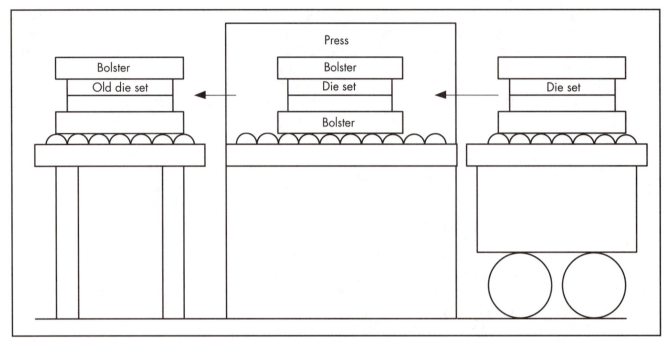

Figure 6-10. Roller conveyors used for staging and exchanging dies to reduce internal setup time.

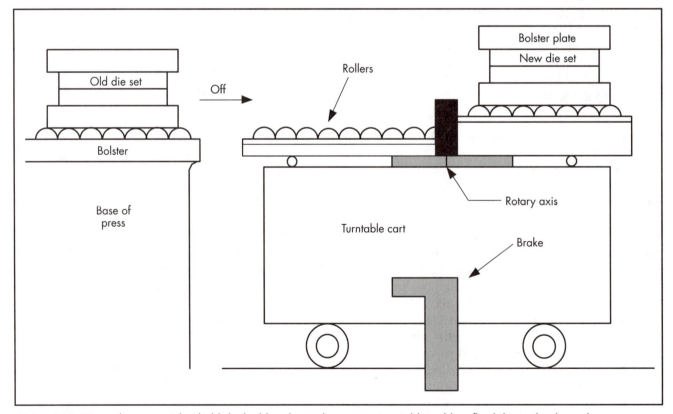

Figure 6-11. Die-exchange cart that holds both old and new dies on a rotary table, adding flexibility to the die-exchange process.

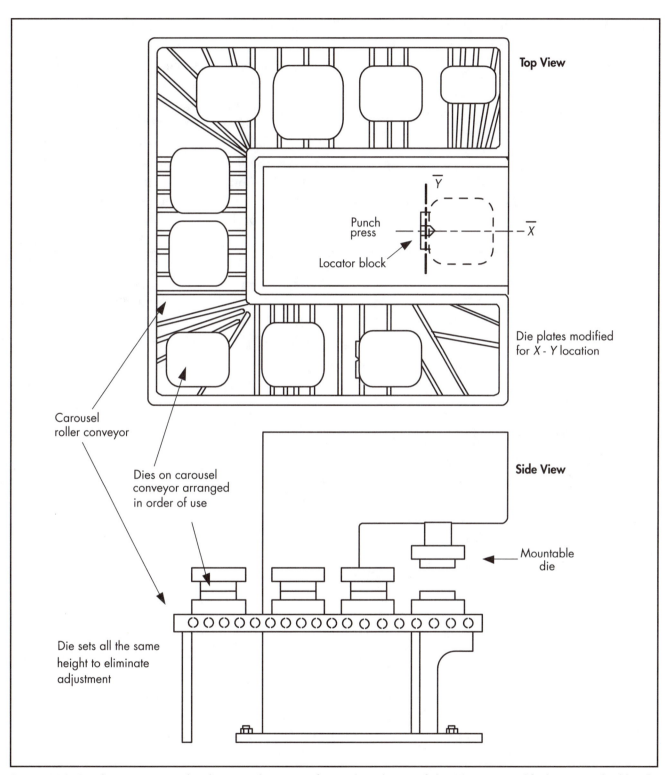

Top View

$\overline{Y}$

Punch
press

$\overline{X}$

Locator block

Die plates modified
for *X - Y* location

Carousel
roller conveyor

Side View

Dies on carousel
conveyor arranged
in order of use

Mountable
die

Die sets all the same
height to eliminate
adjustment

Figure 6-12. Punch press equipped with carousel conveyor for quick exchange of dies. Dies are modified to a standard height for quick location on the press bed (see Figure 6-14) and given a locator element.

Standardization of the height of dies going into a press and the length of bolts used to secure dies to the press bed greatly reduces the internal setup time (Figures 6-13 and 6-14). The methods shown in Figures 6-12 and 6-15 precisely locate dies every time. Adding female locator plates to the bottom bolster plate standardizes the die set. The male locator plate is permanently mounted on the bed of the machine (press). This locator establishes the *X-Y* position of every die set, every time a die is placed in the press.

The same idea can be applied to metal-cutting machines (Figure 6-16). Suppose a vertical milling machine is scheduled to process four jobs on four different fixtures. Each setup consists of removing the old fixture, then installing and aligning the new fixture to the spindle of the machine. Through redesign, four fixtures are mounted on a turntable and each is automatically aligned to the spindle when rotated into position. This is an example of one-touch exchange of dies.

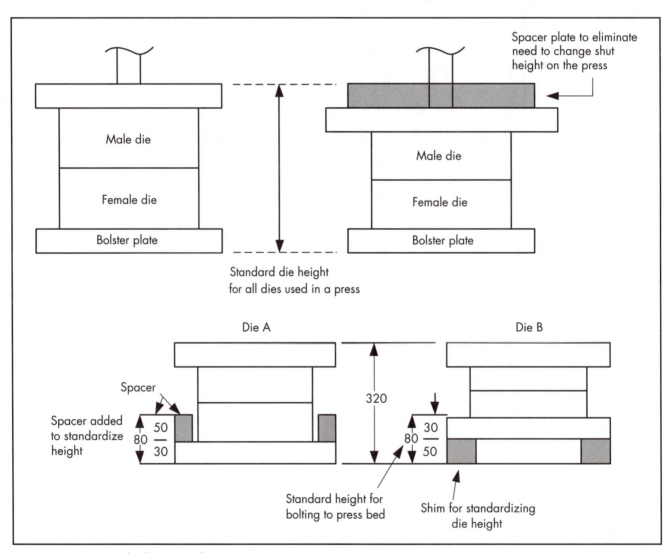

Figure 6-13. Die standardization techniques.

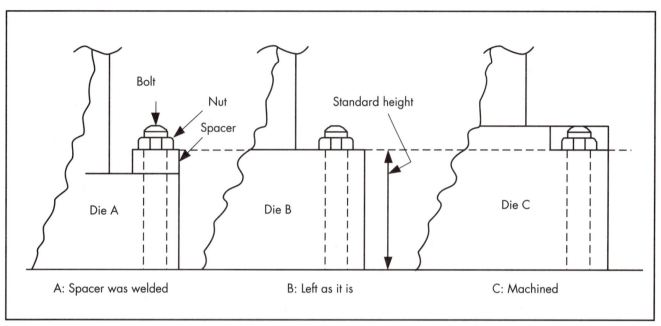

Figure 6-14. Standardizing the height of the base plate reduces the need for different bolt lengths.

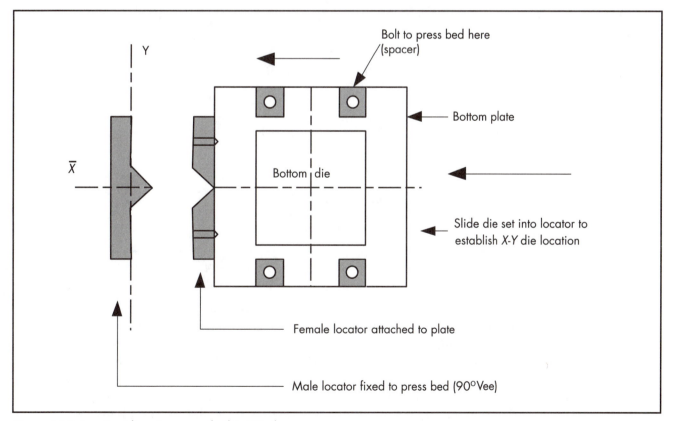

Figure 6-15. Locating die set on press bed in X-Y plane.

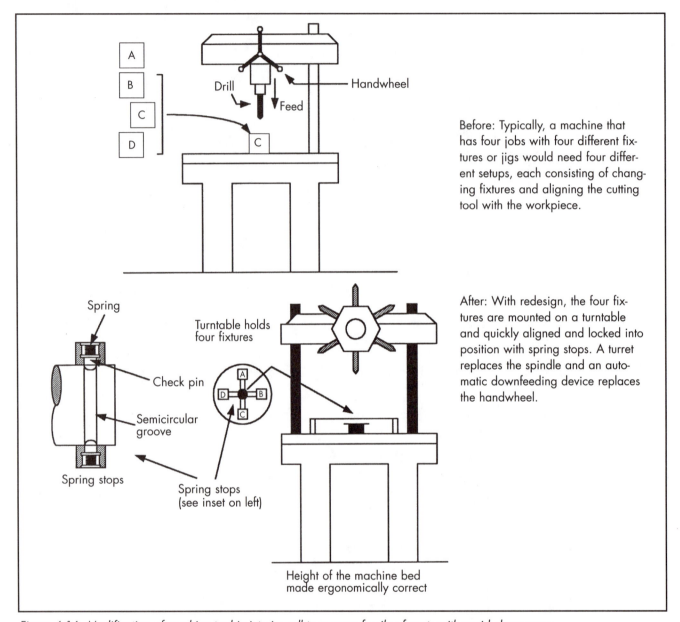

Before: Typically, a machine that has four jobs with four different fixtures or jigs would need four different setups, each consisting of changing fixtures and aligning the cutting tool with the workpiece.

After: With redesign, the four fixtures are mounted on a turntable and quickly aligned and locked into position with spring stops. A turret replaces the spindle and an automatic downfeeding device replaces the handwheel.

Figure 6-16. Modification of machine tool in interim cell to process family of parts with rapid changeover.

A higher-level solution might involve a turret mill with an oversized table. Remember that machines in cells process families of parts. Reducing the variety of parts coming to the machine permits the machine to be modified so that setup times can be eliminated. Figure 6-17 shows how setup was eliminated for four milling parts by permanently locating four fixtures (for four different parts) on one table. This is an example of no-touch exchange of dies.

Convert the Internal to External Elements

An important key to reducing setup time is converting internal setup operations to external operations. Chief among elements that can be readily shifted from internal to external are:

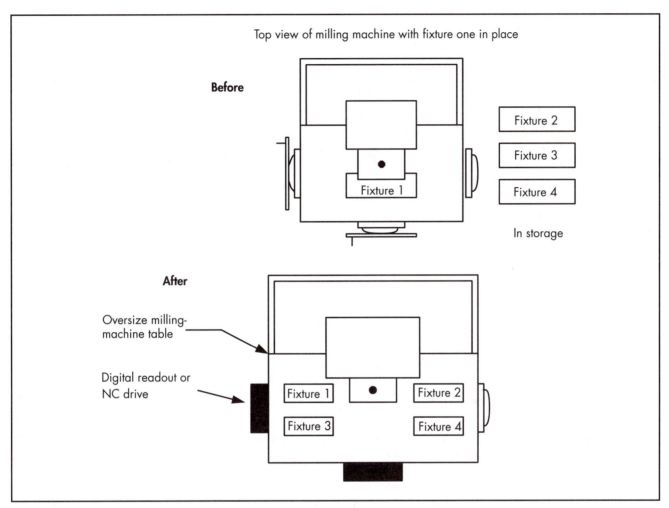

Figure 6-17. Top view of vertical-milling machine with four fixtures for four parts in family (no setup required).

- searching time (trying to find the correct die, looking for the right tools, carts, fixtures, nuts, bolts, etc.);
- waiting time (waiting for cranes, carts, skids, or instructions); and
- setting time (setting dies, tooling, fixtures, etc.).

If an activity can be safely carried out when the machine is running, then it can be shifted to an external setup. An example is the pre-heating of metal molds using waste heat of the furnace before inserting the molds into a die-casting machine. This means that trial shots, often needed to heat dies to the right opera-tional temperature, can be eliminated so the production run starts sooner. Temperature sensors on the dies tell the operator when they are at the right temperature for good molding.

External operations for preparing dies, tools, and materials should be routine and standardized. The internal die exchange also should be standardized, documented, and posted for workers to view. Workers should be instructed to practice setups during slack times to master and improve the routine method. The best setup times should be posted for all to see. While a defect-free exchange is the primary goal, it is important not to lose sight of safety during the process.

Reduce or Eliminate Internal Elements

Eliminating or reducing internal elements in the setup-time cycle directly affects setup time. In exchange of dies, the process of adjusting the shut height of the punch press often takes 50-70% of the internal setup time. This activity is considered essential to proper setup of the machine and often requires highly skilled personnel. However, standardizing press-shut height can eliminate the entire activity. Liners and permanent spacers are added to the die set so that altering the stroke of the machine is never necessary (Figures 6-13 and 6-14). If die sizes and shapes are completely standardized during the tool-design phase, the setup times are shortened tremendously at the outset. Standardization, however, can be an expensive long-range solution if started after the fact in a mature factory.

If the base plate is made the same size regardless of die size, then every die set will be located on the bolster plate in exactly the same position. This is another example of the intermediate-workholder concept. In this case, workholding devices are designed so they appear the same to the machine tool. This usually requires construction of intermediate jigs or fixture plates to which the jig or fixture is attached. Dies, jigs, or fixtures are different sizes, but plates are identical.

If the height of the base plates is standardized, the same fastening bolts, nuts, and tools can be used for dies (Figure 6-14). Bolts are the most popular fastening devices in tool-and-die mounting. A bolt fastens at the final turn of the nut and loosens at the first turn. Therefore, only a single turn of the nut is really required. There are many quick-acting fastener designs.

The intermediate-workholder concept can be applied to a cassette system that allows rapid setups by providing automatic-die location. An example is shown in Figure 6-18. Sizes of die-base plates must be standardized to fit into guide blocks. Figure 6-18 also illustrates a location device for die installation using a partial V-shaped element. This device locates the die-

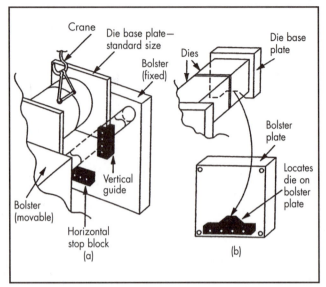

Figure 6-18. (a) Cassette system quickly locates die sets using guide blocks and stop block. (b) Die-location device with truncated location guide (Shingo 1981).

holder plate in two directions, without a need to standardize the size of the base plate. Such devices can be used in presses to locate dies on the bolster plate.

Power Clamps

Although hydraulically operated clamps have been used for many years, new devices and improved designs have increased their usefulness and capabilities (Figure 6-19). While manual-clamping methods may still provide low-cost alternatives, pneumatic and hydraulic power-clamping devices increase the potential of reducing internal setup time. New models offer improved seals and cylinder-bore finishes, extended guide plungers with positive stroke steps, leak-free fitting, and compact sizes that facilitate rapid clamping during setups. These developments allow fluid operating pressures to be increased from about 2,000 psi (13,790 kPa) to over 7,500 psi (51,711 kPa). This pressure increase permits smaller and more powerful clamps to be used.

Power clamping has four basic advantages over manual clamping.

139

Chapter 6: Setup Reduction

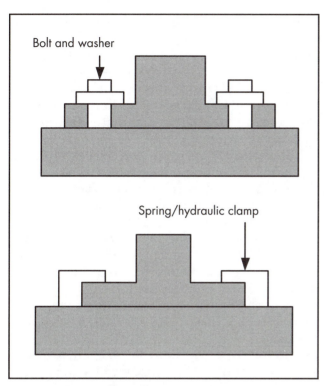

Figure 6-19. Spring-loaded, hydraulic, or pneumatic clamps for holding dies or fixtures in position to further reduce internal setup time.

1. Reduction of internal setup time—dies can be loaded and unloaded in less time than is usually needed with manual clamping. Obviously, more clamping points present a greater advantage. A single switch or lever can activate many clamps, either simultaneously or automatically, in a definite sequence.
2. Repeatability (quality)—the clamping force is constant from operator to operator, from shift to shift, and setup to setup. Operators may be bright and alert in the mornings, but tend to tire in the afternoons. This feature is important as the number of die exchanges increases (for example, as lot sizes decrease).
3. Maintainability—constant hydraulic/pneumatic pressure on the clamping device helps maintain secure gripping of the device, despite vibrations and impact.

4. Safety—operator safety is enhanced because fatigue is significantly reduced, and clamps that must fit into limited-clearance zones can be remotely activated.

Hydraulic Systems

Hydraulic systems are small and compact; leaks are visible; pressures are conveniently adjustable, as with air; and they are self-lubricating. But they also have limitations.

- They require more expensive pressurization and plumbing, rigid metal tubing, or relatively expensive high-pressure hoses.
- When leaks occur, they are messy.
- The relative high pressures make some people uneasy.

Pneumatic Clamps

Pneumatic clamps are simpler to apply than hydraulics; supply and adjustment are convenient; they are clean; and leaks are innocuous, other than a hissing noise. On the other hand, shop-air systems are typically in the 60-120 psi (414-827 kPa) range versus 2,000-3,000 psi (13,790-20,684 kPa) for hydraulic systems. Consequently, for a given clamping force, pneumatic cylinders must be larger, with the size ratio inversely proportional to the square root of the relative pressures. For example, with air at 100 psi (689 kPa) and oil at 2,000 psi (13,790 kPa), the minimum-size ratio would be 1 to 4.47 using standard-diameter cylinders, since the size ratio is inversely proportional to the square root of the pressure.

As far as safety is concerned, using oil at 3,000 psi (20,684 kPa), compared to air, at approximately 100 psi (689 kPa), is really not as dangerous as it might first appear. Air used at 3,000 psi (20,684 kPa) is compressed by a factor of over 200 (3,000 psi ÷ 14.8 psi atmospheric pressure). Volumetric compression is about 7%. An accidental line rupture would produce an explosion as air reverts to atmospheric pressure. By contrast, oil is relatively incompressible. At 3,000 psi (20,684 kPa), volumetric compression is only 1.5%. A line rupture would produce an oil shower (but that would be the worst of it). Figure 6-20 illustrates the use of power clamping in the exchange of large dies in a stand of presses.

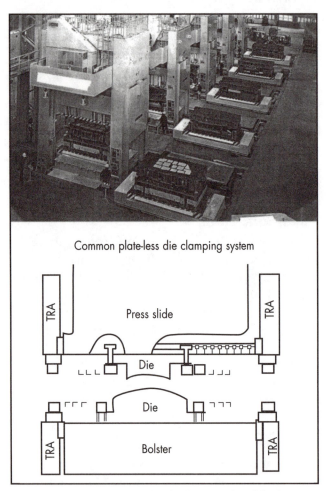

Figure 6-20. Large press stand (photograph) of five presses ready for quick-die change using automatic clamps driven by air cylinders. Entire die set can be changed out in 10 minutes.

Apply Methods Analysis

A less-expensive way to improve setup time is by applying methods analysis to examine the internal setup. Methods analysis techniques are the subject of many basic texts and handbooks. The secret is to teach these basic methods to operators so that everyone will seek ways to reduce setup time and improve the process. This is part of increasing operators' multifunctional abilities—the ability to do many tasks beyond "just run the machine and make parts." Methods analysis helps operators to eliminate unnecessary tooling movement, reduce manual effort, eliminate extraneous walking, etc.

Large punch presses or large molding machines have many attachment positions on all four sides. Setup actions for either machine can take one worker a long time. However, methods analysis can lead to development of parallel operations for two workers, eliminating wasteful movement and reducing internal setup time. Even though the total labor hours for setup do not change, the effective operating hours of the machine increase. Reducing setup time from one hour to 10 minutes means that the second worker would only be needed for 10 minutes during the internal exchange. Setup specialists perform many external setup operations and assist machine operators in setup actions.

Standardize Methods and Practice Setups

Dies, tooling, fixtures, part design, part specification, and methods are standardized. Once a standardized setup method has been achieved, workers must document it. This means that workers are asked to write down, step by step, the setup procedures for machines within a cell. Write-ups are compared to standards to see if workers are doing what should be done. Extra and missing steps become apparent. Some manufacturers have teams practice setups during slack periods to further reduce internal setup time.

Eliminating adjustments from the setup operation is a critical step in reducing internal time. Using spacers on die sets in a die setup eliminates the need for adjusting shut height on a press. Shut height is never changed for a family of dies. However, situations occur requiring that a machine be reset. Even then, there is a limited number of actual setting positions needed on most machines or operations, especially for manufacturing cells. Setting is an activity that should be viewed independently of adjustment. This can be accomplished by adjusting the machine's instrumentation as necessary to re-establish initial or previous setup conditions. This allows for setup without any trial and error. Digital readouts or limit switches, for example, expedite machine resetting without adjusting or fine-tuning. Setup conditions should be determined, recorded, and marked so they can be readily and accurately reproduced, time after time. Records of speed, feed, depth of cut, and other process settings should be posted along with data on temperature, pressure, and other functions. Step-function settings, like push buttons on an automobile radio, can also eliminate adjustment.

Molding machines typically require a different stroke for the knockout punch, depending on the die size being used. The machine's stroke is halted with a switch. To find exactly the right stroke position, an adjustment (movement of the limit switch) is necessary. A molding machine put into a cell environment requires only five positions for the limit switch. Instead of the one-limit switch, five-limit switches can be installed, one at each of five required positions. A simple electric circuit is installed to send electric current only to the limit switch that needs to be activated. As a result, the need to adjust the limit-switch position is eliminated (Figure 6-21). The mechanism is left alone, and only a function switch is changed to accomplish the change in setting.

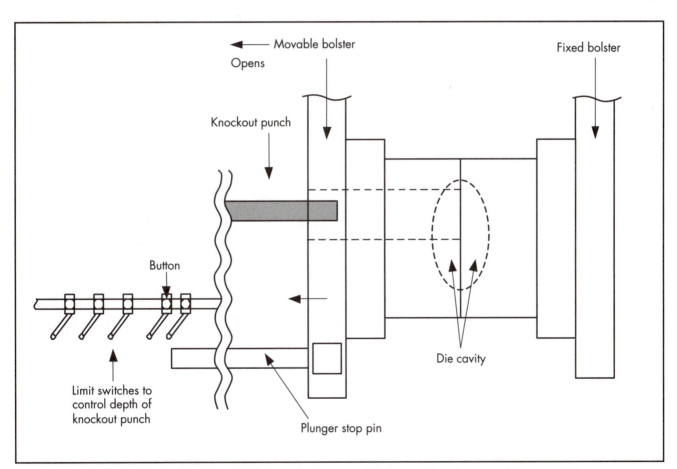

Figure 6-21. Installing limit switches at required positions eliminates knockout stroke adjustments (Shingo 1981).

No adjustment of the limit switch is needed because it has not moved.

In the machining cell for pinions described in Chapter 4, four different lengths of pinions are made on the same lathes. Each stopper automatically controls a cut's length. Previously, the position of the machine's stopper had to be changed and adjusted for each different shaft. To eliminate this adjustment, a rotary stopper with four different stops is used. The stopper is properly rotated to correspond to the shaft length during changeover. Figure 6-22 illustrates a schematic of the rotary stopper. In this way, adjustment is eliminated.

Machine-tool manufacturers usually do not know the applications of their products for a particular company, so they provide machines with continuously variable positional settings. Machines placed in cells, however, have limited applications, so the adjustment process is converted to steps, often with templates or digital readouts to accomplish settings without adjustment (Figure 6-23). Boring machines are often equipped with stops to produce the correct depth of cut on parts. A template can be

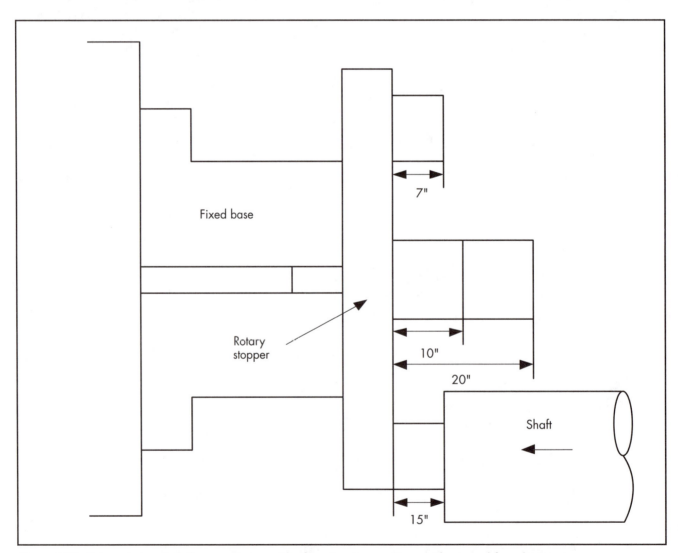

Figure 6-22. Rotary stopper in lathe operation provides four stopping positions, without need for adjustment.

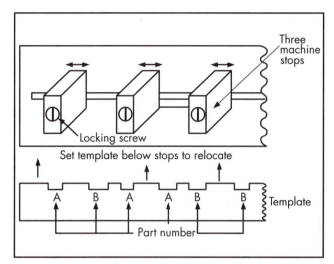

Figure 6-23. Template on boring machine speeds relocation of machine stops. Template is notched out for proper location by part number.

devised to quickly position stops for Part A, and relocate stops for Part B. This eliminates the "cut-and-try" aspect for the first Part B after changeover from Part A.

When the setting must be done with higher precision, eliminating adjustment may be difficult, unless a gage is used. This gage should be built-in with a magnified scale for quick, easy reading. Digital-readout scales showing the exact value are helpful.

Abolish Setup

The final approach to rapid exchange of tooling and dies is to abolish setup or automate it (this is usually an expensive solution). Several methods of abolishing setup have been suggested. Here are two additional methods:

- Redesign the product so it is uniform and uses the same part in various products.
- Produce various parts at the same time. This can be achieved through two methods.

In the first method, parts are processed in parallel, using less expensive, slower machines. For example, an arbor press, instead of a large-punch press, is placed in a welding cell to provide a simple bending function for components

prior to welding. Each worker operates a small arbor press and carries out welding jobs in the cell. This press has a small motor, but performs the same functions as a heavy, large punch press. If several presses of this kind are available, they can be used in parallel and dedicated to producing one type of part at a low cost. Multiple versions can be available to produce a limited variety of parts.

The second method uses the *set-of-parts system*. For example, in the single die of a punch press, two different shapes of Parts A and B are produced as a set, punched at the same time, and then separated. No changeover is ever needed. This requires that Parts A and B be used in the same quantities. Honda does this with doors, stamping the front left and right doors simultaneously.

For additional discussion and examples of eliminating setup time, refer to books on group technology that describe elimination of setup as a natural outgrowth of part-family formation.

SINGLE-MINUTE EXCHANGE OF DIES PHASES

Reduction or elimination of setup time is critical for converting any manufacturing system to a lean and flexible system. This effort is usually one of the first that a company is able to undertake. Results are immediate and obvious, but this does not mean that a setup-reduction program is a short-term project (Table 6-2).

Table 6-2
Setup reduction results at one company

Setup time	1976	1977	1980
60 minutes	30%	0	0
30–60 minutes	19%	0	0
20–30 minutes	26%	10%	3%
10–20 minutes	20%	12%	7%
5–10 minutes	5%	20%	12%
100 seconds–5 minutes	0	17%	16%
100 seconds	0	41%	62%

(Wantuck 1983)

Table 6-2 shows the result of a setup-reduction program at one company where it took four years to reduce setup time to less than 100 seconds for 62% of setups. Getting to this level of setup-time reduction typically comes in phases. The first phase requires little capital expenditure, and solutions can be achieved in a relatively short time. Reductions of 20-30% are typical. No analysis other than videotaping is required if everyone gets involved. This is a method involving workers. The objective is to improve setup incrementally, until it is eliminated or economically prohibited.

The second phase involves operation analysis, minor modifications to dies, tools, fixtures, machines, and procedures, and a modest expenditure. Again, benefits of 30-50% in setup-time reduction can be achieved in a relatively short period of time.

The third phase may involve methods analysis, design changes, and standardization of dies, tools, parts, machines, operations, and procedures. Large capital expenditures may be required, and complete conversion to rapid setups may take years to achieve. Benefits of 10-40% in setup-time reduction may be expected.

For manufacturing cells, setups of 10 minutes probably are achievable in the first phase, one minute in the second phase, and 10-20 seconds in the third phase, where machine tools are custom built for cells. The point to remember is that every time lot size is decreased (size of Container A), the need to reduce setup time will be felt. Setup is an interruption to the process. Work-in-process inventory between cells protects downstream processes from upstream problems. The goal is to develop a robust system of serial processes that are responsive to change.

SUMMARY

Here are some results that can be expected from setup reduction:

- small-lot production becomes possible;
- higher-inventory turnover;
- better use of manufacturing space;
- no stock-handling operations;
- no defective stock;
- no losses from product deterioration;
- mixed-model production;
- machine-production rate improves and production capacity expands;
- setup errors disappear, number of defective goods diminishes, and product quality improves;
- safer operations are possible;
- tool management improves;
- overall total setup time is reduced;
- setup-time reductions come at a low cost;
- workers no longer resent setup changes;
- need for special skills is eliminated as setup procedures become routine;
- flexibility improves and the system responds quickly to demand changes; and
- perceptual blind spots are eliminated.

Chapter 7
Integrated Quality Control

INTRODUCTION

Dennis Butt, a manager for Hewlett-Packard, Greeley Division, said, "In Just-in-time systems, quality is everybody's business" (Hall 1982). The cost of quality is the expense of doing things wrong (for example, making defects), plus the cost of finding defects, resolving problems, and reworking defects. Rework and its associated effort to correct problems is the so-called "hidden factory."

The real secret to securing good quality 100% of the time is when a critical aspect of a component is measured to prevent a defect from occurring. The cost of controlling quality is the expense of finding and reworking defective products. To achieve a high-quality level economically, a product needs to be designed so it can be manufactured without defects. Manufacturing systems must be designed to achieve superior quality at the least cost, and in a flexible manner. Flexibility usually means that a company designs and builds its own manufacturing equipment. It also means that a company understands that linked-cell manufacturing systems employing make-one, check-one, move-one-on methodologies are key to technological competitiveness.

Before the second world war, the quality of Japanese products was poor. Products were difficult to sell, even at extremely low prices. After World War II, the United States, one of the few countries with manufacturing facilities undamaged by war, prospered, fueled by the postwar economy. The U.S. was secure as a world leader in productivity and quality. As part of the Marshall Reconstruction Plan, a National Productivity Center was developed in Japan. Experts in statistical quality control, like W. Edwards Deming, Joseph Juran, and A. V. Feigenbaum went to Japan and aided Japanese industry by teaching statistical quality control methods. The Japanese took the advice of these experts especially seriously. They believed that everyone in the U.S. practiced statistical quality control. The Japanese not only acted on the advice, but also elaborated and improved it. They taught statistical quality control to their engineers and quality control departments. Later they expanded quality training programs to include managers and supervisors at all organizational levels. The seeds for total quality management programs were being sown.

The Japanese educated production workers in the fundamentals and techniques of process quality control. Thus, internal customers learned the now famous seven tools of quality. People who ran the processes learned how to control the quality of those processes. The primary message of total quality control was that the responsibility for the part quality rested with the workers who manufactured the part (Feigenbaum 1961). Japanese managers, production workers, and engineers became the best-trained, quality-control people. Training for total quality control encompassed all departments, including departments beyond manufacturing such as the lunchroom. All company functions, including product design and field service, improved. Because training was carried on at all levels, Japanese managers used the entire company's experience, especially that of the work force. Table 7-1 presents a brief history of quality control in Japan.

While most U.S. companies use statistical quality control, the Japanese developed many new methods of quality improvement and control. These methods depend less on sampling, statistics, and probabilistic approaches and more on self-checking and defect prevention, what is called *integrated quality control* in make-one, check-one, and move-one-on methodology. This chapter discusses the traditional methods of statistical process control, along with some of the more popular modern thinking.

Integration of quality control into the manufacturing system begins with giving workers responsibility and authority to make good products. This is key to attacking the source of defects in components. Inspect to prevent a defect from occurring, rather than finding a defect after a product has been made. This simple idea, in practice, however, is not always simple. It requires that a manufacturing system be changed to accommodate the techniques and methods of integrated quality control.

STATISTICAL QUALITY CONTROL

Statistical quality control began at Bell Telephone Laboratories in the 1920s. Since that time, its popularity grew across the globe as a multitude of industries began to use it. There are many different tools for statistical quality control. The two most popular techniques are acceptance sampling and control charts. Both methods use inductive statistics, which means that a small amount of data (a sample) is used to draw conclusions about a much larger, if not infinite, amount of data. This large amount of data is often called the *parent population*. The decisions based on the sample cannot be stated with absolute certainty. Therefore, uncertainties are encountered, calling for the mathematics of uncertainty, probability, and statistics.

The purpose of *acceptance sampling* is to draw a conclusion about a process by examining only a fraction of the process. Sampling inspection is needed when it is difficult, costly, or impossible to measure an entire population. For example, when making razor blades, the expense involved in observing every blade may be prohibitive. Alternatively, the required inspection processes may destroy a product.

Sampling inspection requires some decisions be made. One might ask, for example, "What is the maximum percentage of defective product that can be considered satisfactory?" That is, by definition, what level of defective product must be accepted? This defective-parts percentage is called the *acceptable quality level*. After determining how many samples must be taken to achieve a level of acceptance (or rejection), sampling inspection is carried out. Samples should offer true, unbiased representations of parent populations, but this depends on many factors, such as sample size and the way it is collected. Usually, it is difficult to obtain a truly unbiased sample of a population. For example, if inspectors draw parts from the top of each box of parts, operators quickly learn to put the best parts on top so the best work is inspected, and the entire lot accepted. But it is the acceptable quality level or the number of satisfactory defects that creates the most problems with sampling inspection. Today, in a world of high-quality competitiveness, defective products are absolutely unacceptable.

Control charts are used to track accuracy via statistical means. They also track precision (or variability) via the range or standard deviation of a process by plotting selected sample statistics. When a process produces products, no two are exactly alike because of variations in manufacturing processes, materials, and operator performance. Variability, whether large or small, is always present, and many sources can contribute to it. In 1924, W. A. Shewhart of Bell Telephone Laboratories developed statistical charts for process control (Shewhart 1931).

Table 7-1
Brief history of QC in Japan

Late 1940s	U.S. occupation forces showed the Japanese how to use statistical sampling tables (Military Standards).
1945–1950	Post-World War II — Japanese industry had to rebuild with only one resource, people. Quality of most Japanese product was poor.
1950	Deming invited to Japan, introduces SQC to design engineers and manufacturing engineers.
1953	End of Korean War — industry was rocked by the termination of U.S. military contracts. Japanese industry was reacquainted with the reality that Japan had few resources other than its people, and that they must develop manufactured goods for export to raise capital and the standard of living.
1953	Juran invited to Japan — introduces quality control to top and middle management.
1950s–1960s	Massive quality control training of Japanese executives and managers takes place.
1961	*Total Quality Control*, a book by A.V. Feigenbaum is published.
1962	Publication of Shop Floor Techniques began. Gemba and quality control techniques are taught to foremen.
1965	Total quality control started at Toyota and changed inspection focus to concentrate on the entire manufacturing process. Just-in-time marries up with total quality control at Toyota. Goes to all departments. Company-wide quality control implementation is everywhere — Objective-zero defects.
1966	*Quality Control to Expand a Company*, a Japanese book by H. Karatsu is published (often considered the bible of total quality control by the Japanese).
1960s–1970s	Total quality control concepts and techniques developed by trial and error on the shop floor.
1970	Quality control subcontractors offer services to small-to-medium companies.
1973	OPEC oil crisis — before crisis total quality control was stagnated. This is most apparent in the reduction of Deming Awards prior to the crisis. However, the crisis reignited the total quality control movement as a way for industry to stay competitive.
1975	Construction quality control — nonmanufacturing industry.
1980	White-collar quality control — service industry.
1990	Taguchi methods are widely used in America and Japan; Motorola introduces Six Sigma.
2000	Defects are measured in parts per million as Six Sigma concept spreads.

In traditional statistical-quality control, factors contributing to product variation are classified as causes that are inherent, random, or assignable. *Chance causes* are considered natural, consistent parts of a process. They are difficult to isolate or eliminate, or too small to worry about. Some examples of chance causes are variations in material chemistry or properties, measurement errors, machine vibrations, and variations in human performance. *Assignable causes* are events producing detectable changes in the behavior of a process that are measured by the accuracy or precision of the process. These changes are usually large in magnitude and controllable. Examples of assignable causes are tool change, tool wear, cutting tool chatter, temperature fluctuations, and pressure variations. When only chance causes are present, the process is considered to be under control. However, when assignable causes occur, the process must be analyzed to determine the source of the assignable error; the problem must be eliminated; and the process must be controlled.

Shewhart realized that it should be possible to determine when variations in product quality are a result of random chance or major process change (an assignable cause). He developed control charts for this purpose. There are several different types of control charts, but only charts for variable data are discussed here.

The X-bar chart monitors the process mean. The range (R) or standard deviation (S) chart monitors process variability. Control limits for both chart are usually set at three standard deviations above and below the process average. An example of X-bar and R charts, the most common types of control charts, are shown in Figure 7-1. In these charts, sample statistics (X-bar and R values) are plotted. The horizontal axis is time. Twenty-five samples of size five are plotted. Most values fall within the control limits, indicating a normal prevailing condition. Shewhart showed that sample data will be normally distributed, regardless of the population from which samples were drawn. If a point (for example, average of sample measurements) falls outside of the control limits, it is probably a result of an assignable cause. Another indication of an assignable cause is a run of seven points up or down. A run of eight points above or below a central line is another unlikely event, indicating that something about the process has changed. In Figure 7-1 this occurred, since samples 18-25 fall below the centerline X-bar, making it highly probable that the process mean has been shifted down.

The historical function of control charts has been to control the accuracy (aim), precision (variation), and stability (drift) of a process. However, people who run processes (users of manufacturing systems) traditionally have not used charts. Rather, people in quality control departments keep the charts. Inspectors used to be sent to the factory floor to gather sample data. The inspector's job became that of quality enforcer or process controller. In the past, production workers viewed their job responsibility as meeting production-rate standards, regardless of quality. Workers

thought if the product was bad, so what? It could be reworked or scrapped. Over the years, an adversarial relationship developed between the manufacturing and quality control departments.

In Figure 7-2, a decision about the parent population based on looking at only samples, can result in two types of errors, as well as two correct decisions:

- Type I or α error, viewing the process as bad, when it is not producing defects; or
- Type II or β error, viewing the process as good, when it is producing defects.

The standard control chart sets its control limits at three standard deviations. This means that the probability of making a Type I error is remote, while the probability of making a Type II error is usually quite large. The person who makes decisions about process quality is not the same as the person who runs the process. The decision maker determines error probabilities. If a sample indicates that a process is bad, the decision maker must take action; maybe even recommend stopping the process. If no problems are found, the decision maker makes an alpha error. This can make the decision maker look bad in the eyes of those who run the processes in the manufacturing system. On the other hand, a Type II error requires no action by the decision maker and, therefore, no blame is usually assigned. The "do nothing" decision shifts the blame for defects to production workers. Of course, the final customers and the company's reputation suffer when defective product is permitted to leave a process.

In manufacturing cells, workers are given tools to control the quality of processes. Workers use control charts to regulate processes. While some methods of inductive statistics do integrate workers into the quality control system, such methods do not guarantee zero (or even extremely low) defect rates. A common misconception about control charts is that they indicate what goes wrong in a process. Control charts should be used as

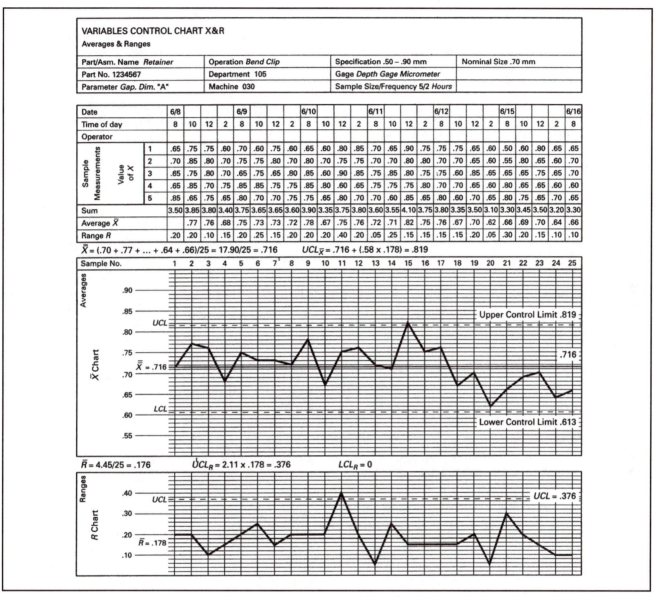

Figure 7-1. Example of X-bar and R charts, X-double bar = 0.738 and R-bar = 0.169.

detection devices to indicate when something goes wrong, but not what has gone wrong. If control charts are used incorrectly, they are a waste of time. For example, some companies actually collect data and then wait until the end of a shift to plot the points. By this time, it is too late to react to process trends and out-of-control points. This changes when workers maintain control charts.

Integrated Quality Control

Poor quality has meant the demise of more than one plan to implement lean production. Integrated quality control is sometimes called *total quality control* or *company-wide quality control*, because all departments in the company participate in quality control efforts, as do all types of employees. Dr. Richard Schonberger

	The decision maker took a sample and decided	
	Process not changed	**Process changed**
The truth was that the process had not changed.	No action as nothing is wrong.	Action is taken, but nothing is found to be wrong with the process; Type I—α error, decision maker is embarrassed.
The truth was that the process had changed.	No action but process is making more defects; Type II—β error.	Action is taken and problem is found in the process; decision maker looks good!

Figure 7-2. When the decision maker is not the person who runs the process, sampling can result in two types of errors in the decision about the quality of the products.

used the term *total quality control*. The idea is that, if a company takes care of quality, profit takes care of itself.

A total quality commitment for all production resources and levels of management is a requirement for integrated quality control. Every person must have an understanding of quality control, the methods used to obtain it, and the benefits. Large quality control departments are not the answer. Hiring more inspectors to work on quality checking is not the answer either. Actual control must be integrated into the manufacturing system. Integrated quality control is not a series of specialized techniques, but part of a manufacturing-based strategy that incorporates quality control at every level of an organization. Line personnel must be given the necessary training to carry out quality control functions. Eventually, integrated quality control is extended to include vendors, suppliers, and subcontractors to improve the quality of supplies and materials.

Quality Redefined

It must be cheaper to do a job right the first time. As Philip Crosby would say, quality is free, but it is not a gift (Crosby 1979). The cost of quality is the expense of doing things wrong, like allowing defects. Defects must be found and corrected and such improvements can cost money.

Genichi Taguchi provided another definition of *quality*: deviation from target (Taguchi 1987). By this definition, the cost of missing a process target at the optimal, which is the nominal position, is the driver to make the process better. Quality is a result of conformance to specifications or requirements. This means that the standards of conformance must be precisely stated. Failure to meet conformance standards costs money. The fastest and surest path to low-cost operations is to make a product right the first time, thereby eliminating rework and scrap. Figures on the amount of rework done in a typical factory are scary, and often range as high as 40%, meaning that 40% of what a company manufactures requires some rework. Some refer to this as the *hidden factory*.

Cellular Manufacturing Systems

Integrated-quality control goes hand in hand with the concepts of cellular manufacturing systems. Cell workers control quality in their cells. The rule is make-one, check-one, and move-one-on. The concept is simple: perform a step in a process; check the product to make sure that the step has been done correctly; and move on to the next step.

Between processes in a cell, devices can be added to assist workers in checking parts so defective products are not passed on. The checking of parts can be performed by manual or automatic operations. Automatic checking forms the basis for autonomation. This is an important concept, though the word is often confused with automation. *Autonomation* refers to autonomous control of both quality and quantities. For manned and unmanned cellular systems, this means that individual processes or devices between processes are equipped with sensors to detect:

- when sufficient product has been made (and not overproduced);
- when something has gone wrong with a process; and
- when something is changing that can eventually lead to a failure to meet product specifications (also called *defect prevention*).

Figure 7-3 shows the relationship between autonomation and lean manufacturing. Physically, sensors and devices, such as decouplers, are incorporated into machines to automatically check the critical aspects of parts at each stage of a process. Causes of defects are investigated immediately and corrective action is implemented.

Within a company, quality must be the responsibility of manufacturing workers. Their involvement is absolutely necessary. This means that the primary responsibility for quality is assigned to the people who make the product. These workers must develop improved habits and a desire for perfection; they must strive for zero defects. Quality depends on everyone's efforts, from sales, design, and purchasing workers, to those in manufacturing, shipping, and other departments. Changing a manufacturing system's design is critical to changing workers' attitudes. The effects of defective products on the linked-cell system cannot be ignored. Quality must be made a priority above output rates.

Control the Process

The Japanese term for defect prevention is *poka-yoke*. At every stage, a product must be checked; thus, every worker must be an inspector. Quality is controlled at the source. Production workers correct their own errors and there are no separate rework lines. This requires one-piece flow in cells and immediate feedback where problems occur on final assembly lines. This does not necessarily mean that workers inspect their own work. The next

worker can check work pulled from a previous worker or an automatic inspection device (placed between workers) can check quality characteristics. This is an example of one form of autonomation using decouplers.

Make Quality Easy to See

Display boards and highly visible charts are placed on the plant floor. Boards detail the quality factors being measured, the state of recent performance, current quality improvement projects, recent award winners for quality improvement, etc. Quality and its characteristics must be clearly and simply defined.

Insist on compliance to quality standards. Conformance to quality standards must come first, ahead of output.

Give workers authority. Workers must be able to stop a process when something goes wrong. Mechanized processes might have devices to do this automatically (in-process inspection). More refined systems may have the ability to adjust or even modify a process to correct a problem. A machine must be programmable. Equipping a machine or process to prevent defects from occurring is another form of poka-yoke. For inspection of finished goods, it should be a management mandate to check 100% of the attributes.

There should be a constant succession of projects for quality improvement in every work area. Continuous improvement should be a routine way of life and can be the work of quality circles. Quality circles are groups of workers who carry out process improvement projects, especially those affecting product quality.

Eliminate incoming inspection. An objective is to work toward elimination of the inspection of incoming goods. This requires a buyer to work closely with one vendor, to the exclusion of others. Ultimately, a vendor should be a lean manufacturer and an extension of a customer's system.

Eliminate setup time. The drive toward small lots requires elimination of setup time, which, in turn, makes it economical to reduce lot size. The concepts of economic order quantity

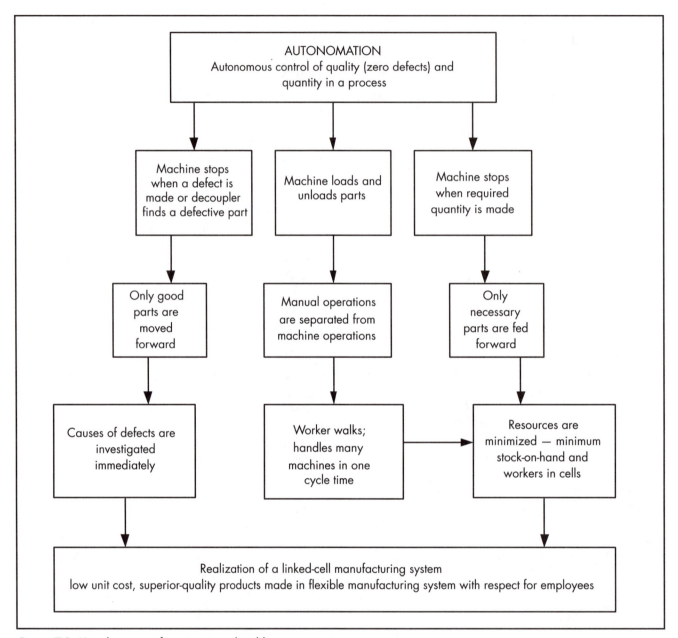

Figure 7-3. How lean manufacturing is realized by autonomation.

(EOQ) are limiting. The optimum lot size is one. This is readily achievable within cells. Obviously, between cells, the smaller a lot, the faster the feedback on quality. In addition, smaller lots makes problems easier to spot.

Keep the workplace clean. Good housekeeping is fundamental and absolutely necessary for a plant to improve quality and foster better work habits. Housekeeping is the responsibility of everyone, from the plant manager to the foremen and workers. Proper housekeeping is needed to improve and maintain safety in a manufacturing environment and to concurrently maintain pride and improve company morale. No one really wants to work in a dirty place. Obviously, a dirty workplace is a deterrent to superior quality performance in electronics fabrication, painting, and finishing areas, but also in other areas of a plant that must be well maintained.

Organize the workplace. Organization is important in areas where there are many loose tools and multiple components. The driving motto here is "a place for everything, everything in its place."

PROCESS ANALYSIS TOOLS AND TECHNIQUES

Table 7-2 lists some common tools of the integrated quality control methodology. Remember, in a pull system, quality and other problems can be exposed through deliberate removal of work-in-process inventory from kanban links. Therefore, inventory is a quality control device. That is, inventory is an independent control variable, rather than a dependent variable. Problems are discovered and analyzed using:

- control/run charts that track process behavior;
- process flow charts that define steps in the process;
- check sheets and histograms that analyze data from the processes;
- Pareto charts that identify the most important problems;
- scatter plots that locate correlations between factors; and
- cause and effect, sometimes called Ishikawa or fishbone diagrams, which determine the problem causing lack of quality.

In more recent years, Taguchi's design of experiments and statistical techniques are used to improve processes by reducing variation. Integrated quality techniques foster continuous improvement in the processes. Quality circles are used to find (and sometimes solve) problems. Widely implemented in the U.S.,

quality circles involve people and direct their attention to workplace problems.

Histograms and Run Charts

A *histogram* is a graphical representation of frequency distribution using rectangles with widths representing class intervals and areas proportional to corresponding frequencies. The *frequency histogram* is a type of diagram where data is grouped into cells (or intervals), with a notation made of the frequency of observations falling into each interval. When grouping, each observation within a cell is considered to have the same value (midpoint of cell).

Histograms are used in many ways in quality control including to:

- determine process capability (control tendency and dispersion);
- compare the process with specifications;
- suggest the shape of population (normal distribution versus skewed); and
- indicate discrepancies in data (such as gaps).

Frequency values usually are shown as vertical rectangles. Rectangle lengths are proportional to numerical values, while widths are proportional to class intervals. A histogram shows either absolute frequency (occurrence), or relative frequency (percentage). Histograms also may be cumulative. There are cumulative and relative cumulative frequencies.

There are several different types of histograms, with each type possessing its own advantage for different situations. Figure 7-4 shows frequency versus location for 45 measurements. One observes that the aim of the process is low, but data is within tolerances. Several disadvantages of the histogram include its inability to show trends and take the time factor into consideration. If data shown in the histogram spreads over time, it is called a *run chart* or *graph*.

A run chart (Figure 7-5) plots quality characteristics as a function of time. It provides general trends and a degree of variability. Run charts reveal information that a histogram

Table 7-2
Integrated quality control tools

Category	Concept
1. Organization	Production responsibility for quality — quality circles
2. Goals	Habit of improvement for everyone Perfection or zero defects — not a program, a goal
3. Basic principles	Process control and defect prevention, not detection Easy to see quality — quality on is display so buyers can see and inspect — easy to understand Insist on compliance Line stop when something goes wrong Correct your own errors 100% check; make one, check one, move one on Project by project improvements

4. Facilitating concepts	Quality control department as facilitator
	    Audit suppliers
	    Help in quality improvement projects
	    Train workers, supervisors, and suppliers
	Small lot sizes
	Housekeeping
	Less-than-full-capacity scheduling
	Check machines daily, use checklists
	Total preventative maintenance (see Chapter 8)
	8-4-8-4 two-shift scheduling

5. Process analysis tools and techniques	Expose problems, solve problems Defect prevention, poka-yokes for checking 100% of parts N=2, for checking first and last item in a lot Analysis tools Cause-and-effect diagrams (Fishbone or Ishikawa) Histograms, run charts, and check sheets Control charts (X-bar and R-charts) Scatter diagrams (X-Y correlation chart) Pareto charts Process flow charts Taguchi and design-of-experiments methods

cannot, such as certain trends over time or at certain times of the day.

Individual measurements, not samples, are taken at regular time intervals, and points are plotted on a connected-line graph as a function of time. The graph is then used to illustrate obvious trends in data. Run diagrams are necessary, at least for a short time, to identify the basic nature of a process. Inappropriate tools are sometimes used to analyze data. For example, a control chart or histogram might hide tool wear if frequent tool changes and adjustments are made between groups of observations. As a result, use of a run diagram (with 100% inspection, where feasible) should precede the use of control charts utilizing averages.

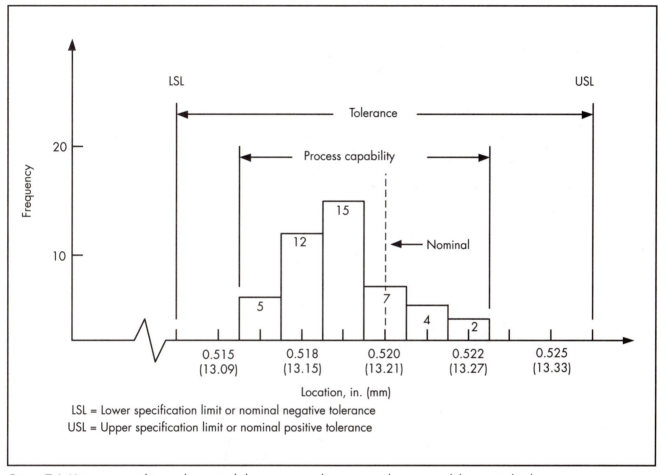

Figure 7-4. Histogram used in quality control shows process data versus tolerances and the nominal values.

Process Flow Chart

The first task in systems analysis should be the creation of a flow chart. A flow chart is a pictorial representation of a process, as well as of decisions and interconnectivity between steps and decisions. A flow chart provides excellent documentation of a process at a particular time and it shows the relationships between process steps.

Flow charts are constructed using easily recognized symbols to represent the type of processing performed. A flattened oval represents starting or stopping points of a process; diamonds represent decisions; and rectangles represent process steps. Lines connecting process steps end with arrows showing the direction of flow of parts or information.

Making a flow chart often leads to the discovery of omissions in a process. Flow charts point out steps that are believed to be taking place, but are not; or a sequence of operations that does not make sense when analyzed.

Figure 7-6 is an example of a flow chart. This example is complex, but it deals with the issue of what happens to component parts, subassemblies, etc., during manufacturing. Flow charts can be used for any process within an organization, from high-level-management processes to the process of shipping an order to a customer.

Example : The lengths of manufactured connecting rods are measured. Construct a run diagram to determine how the process is behaving. For 30 hours, measurements are made every 60 minutes in the order that the rods are produced.

First shift	35	40	27	30	30	34	26	31
Second shift	24	23	20	15	23	17	16	21
Third shift	15	13	28	8	20	9	5	11
Fourth shift	16	5	9	13	16	10		

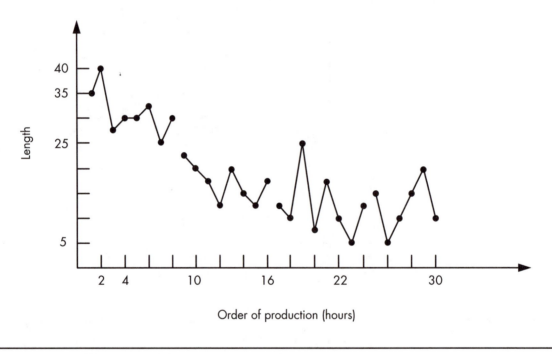

Figure 7-5. An example of a run chart or graph.

A few simple rules to follow when constructing a flow chart include:

- List the steps of the process.
- Use the simplest symbols possible.
- Make sure every feedback loop has an escape.
- Make certain every process has only one arrow proceeding outward. Otherwise, use a decision diamond.

Pareto Diagrams

Pareto diagrams are types of bar charts or histograms. They display the frequency that a particular phenomenon occurs relative to the occurrence of others. They help focus attention on the most frequently occurring problems and prioritize efforts toward problem solving. This type of diagram is styled after the Pareto principle. According to the Pareto

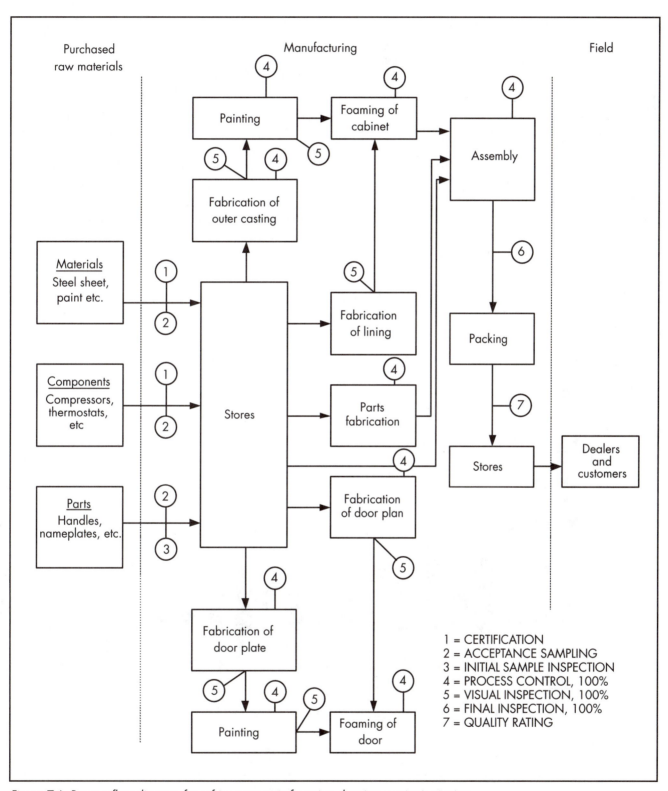

Figure 7-6. Process flow diagram for refrigerator manufacturing showing monitoring points.

principle, a minority of problems cause a majority of disturbances. A plot of this nature shows the biggest bang for the buck because when it corrects a few problems, there is an alleviation of a majority of disturbances. These few problems are areas where quality improvement must focus. A Pareto chart helps establish top priorities and is visually easy to understand. A Pareto analysis is also a simple process to perform. The only expertise that may be needed is in the area of data gathering. Figure 7-7 shows a Pareto analysis of the usage rate of various methods of total quality control reported by attendees at a quality control conference.

Cause-and-effect Diagrams

One effective method for improving quality is the *cause-and-effect diagram*, also knows as a *fishbone diagram* because of its structure. Initially developed by Kaoru Ishikawa in 1943, this diagram organizes theories about probable causes of problems. Listed on the main line of the fishbone diagram is a quality characteristic that needs to be improved or a quality problem that needs to be investigated. Fishbone, that is

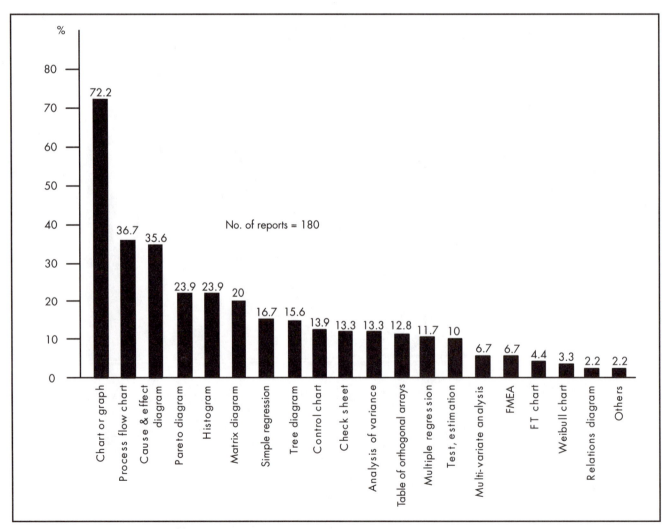

Figure 7-7. Usage rate of TQC methods and techniques reported at QC conference.

diagonal, lines are drawn from the main line. These lines organize the main factors that could be the cause of the problem (Figure 7-8). Branching from each factor are even more-detailed factors. Everyone taking part in making a diagram gains new knowledge of the process. When a diagram serves as a focus for a discussion, everyone knows the topic, and conversation does not stray. The diagram is often structured around four branches including machine tools or processes, workers, the method, and material being processed. Another version of the diagram is called the cause-and-effect diagram that includes the addition of cards. The effect is often tracked with a control chart (Figure 7-9). The possible causes of the defect or problem are written on index cards and inserted in slots in the charts.

Scatter Diagrams

The scatter diagram is a graphical representation that is helpful in identifying a correlation that may exist between a quality or productive-performance measure and a factor that might be driving that measure. Figure 7-10 shows the general structure commonly

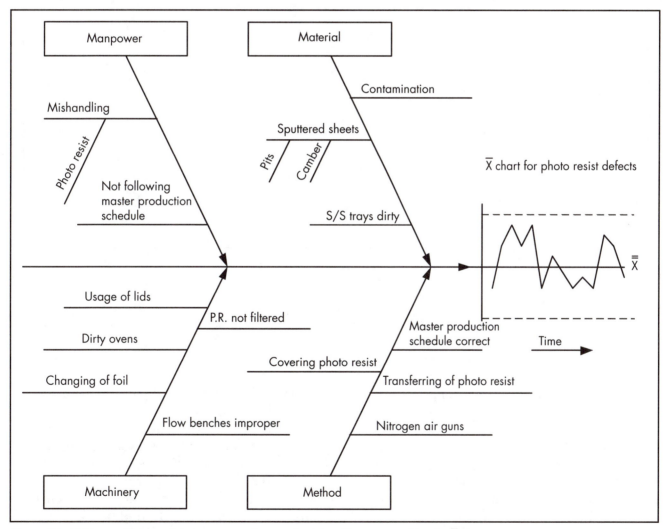

Figure 7-8. Fishbone diagram showing causes that produce the effect captured by the $\overline{X}$ chart.

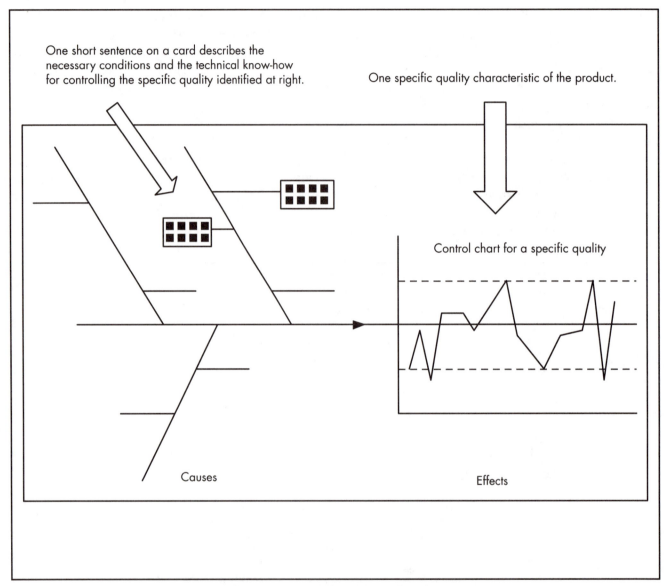

One short sentence on a card describes the necessary conditions and the technical know-how for controlling the specific quality identified at right.

One specific quality characteristic of the product.

Control chart for a specific quality

Causes

Effects

Figure 7-9. Basic structure of a cause-and-effect diagram with the addition of cards.

used for a scatter diagram, along with some typical patterns.

Check Sheets

Check sheets are used to record data on a process and determine problem areas. Their use follows the Pareto principle in that they are tools to help locate defects, symptoms of defects, and causes of defects. To determine

defects of each area, a tally of problems can be kept for each step of a process.

The check sheet (Figure 7-11) is also an excellent way to view data as it is being collected. It can be constructed using predetermined parameters based on experience with a cell or system. The appropriate interval is checked as data is collected. This often allows the central tendency and spread of data to be seen. Here

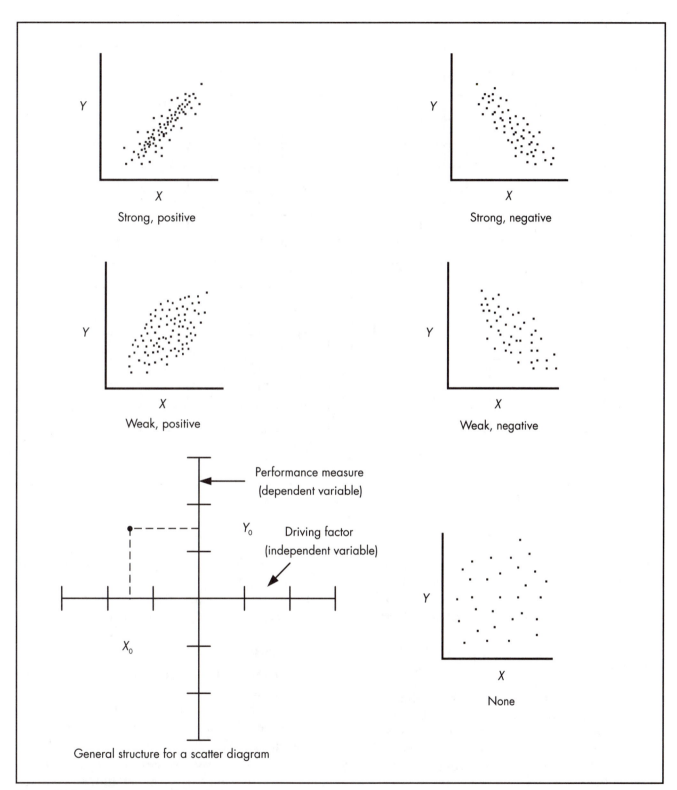

Figure 7-10. Typical patterns of correlation.

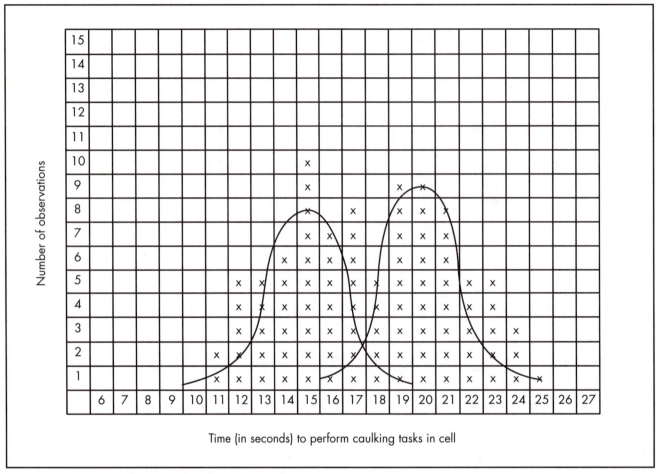

Figure 7-11. Example of a check sheet for gathering data on a process.

central tendency is defined as arithmetic mean, or more commonly, the average of the data. Check sheets provide basically the same information as a histogram, but they are easier to build (once they are formatted).

Suppose the operation time to perform caulking in a redesigned cell is being recorded. Why is the data bimodal? Looking carefully at the cell design, two workers share the operation. The data would suggest that the two workers do not caulk the same way, since there appears to be a five- or six-second difference in their average times to complete the task. Clearly, further study is needed to determine what is going on. For the next

check sheet, a different symbol would be used for each worker.

Figure 7-12 is an example of a check or observation sheet for data gathering.

X-bar and Range Charts

Variation occurs as a natural part of any manufacturing system and is an initial reason to be concerned with quality control. In a perfect world, processes would make multiple parts and each part would be identical. However, in the real world, differences occur and tracking these differences helps products meet customer needs. Two aspects of this

FACTORY FLOOR OBSERVATION SHEET

Date:		Operator Name (s):													
Process:		Part No:								Part Name:					
	Observation										Calculation			Remarks	
	1	2	3	4	5	6	7	8	9	10	Min	Max	Avg		

Figure 7-12. Sample check sheet.

process that are of concern are the *central tendency* (or where the process is centered), and *variability* (or spread of the process around the mean). Control charts, or more specifically, X-bar (mean) and range (R) charts have traditionally been two ways of tracking these conditions.

Variability is thought to consist of two types, that which is inherent in the process called random or chance cause, versus that which exhibits observable or detachable causes when acting on a process. These are traditionally called assignable causes. Random variation is a natural part of any process and is difficult to isolate. Assignable causes are

just the opposite in that they produce easily detectable changes in the output of a process. Efforts to eliminate assignable causes produce a good return.

Many types of control charts have been developed, but the X-bar and R charts are the ones used for variable data (that is, aspects of the process that are measured). Figure 7-13 shows an example of X-bar and R charts. A control chart statistically determines upper- and lower-control lines drawn on either side of a process average. These are upper- and lower-control limits. They help determine if a process is in control or if it has digressed to being out of control. There are many rules to judge the state

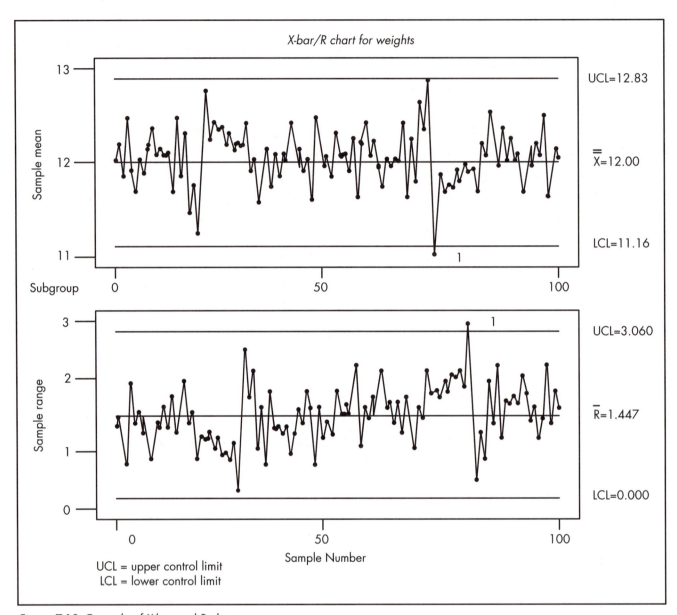

Figure 7-13. Example of X-bar and R charts.

of process control, but simply put, an operator looks for unnatural patterns in plotted points. The point marked with a "1" on a control chart indicates an out-of-control point, since it is natural to have 99.73% of points within upper- and lower-control limits. Together, the X-bar and *R* charts can be used to judge the centering of a variation in a process. Figure 7-14 presents a summary of the basics of X-bar and *R* charts.

Process Capability

A good process is repeatable; it makes parts within specifications or tolerances prescribed by design engineers. Designers specify nominal or desired sizes. Recognizing that no two products are identical, designers apply tolerances to desired sizes. Processes selected should produce all parts within desired tolerance ranges.

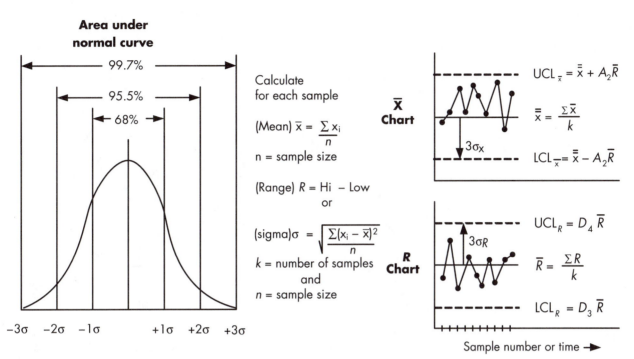

Area under normal curve

99.7%

95.5%

68%

$-3\sigma \quad -2\sigma \quad -1\sigma \quad +1\sigma \quad +2\sigma \quad +3\sigma$

Calculate for each sample

(Mean) $\bar{x} = \dfrac{\sum x_i}{n}$

n = sample size

(Range) $R = Hi - Low$
or

(sigma) $\sigma = \sqrt{\dfrac{\sum(x_i - \bar{x})^2}{n}}$

k = number of samples and

n = sample size

$\bar{X}$ Chart

$UCL_{\bar{x}} = \bar{\bar{x}} + A_2\bar{R}$

$\bar{\bar{x}} = \dfrac{\sum \bar{x}}{k}$

$3\sigma_x$

$LCL_{\bar{x}} = \bar{\bar{x}} - A_2\bar{R}$

R Chart

$UCL_R = D_4\bar{R}$

$3\sigma_R$

$\bar{R} = \dfrac{\sum R}{k}$

$LCL_R = D_3\bar{R}$

Sample number or time →

Calculate the average range $\bar{R}$ or the average $\bar{\sigma}$ and process average $\bar{X}$ after k samples

$$\bar{R} = \frac{R_1 + R_2 + R_3 + \ldots R_k}{k} \quad or \quad \bar{\sigma} = \frac{\sigma_1 + \sigma_2 + \cdots \sigma_k}{k}$$

$$\bar{\bar{X}} = \frac{\bar{X}_1 + \bar{X}_2 + \bar{X}_3 + \ldots X_k}{k}$$

$$UCL_{\bar{x}} = \bar{\bar{x}} + A_2\bar{R} = \bar{\bar{x}} + 3\sigma_{\bar{x}}$$

$$LCL_{\bar{x}} = \bar{\bar{x}} - A_2\bar{R} = \bar{\bar{x}} - 3\sigma_{\bar{x}}$$

$$UCL_R = D_4\bar{R}$$
$$LCL_R = D_3\bar{R}$$

Note: $\sigma' = \dfrac{\bar{R}}{d_2}$ or $\dfrac{\bar{\sigma}}{e_2}$

$$3\sigma_{\bar{x}} = 3\frac{\sigma'}{\sqrt{n}} = 3\frac{\bar{R}}{d_2\sqrt{n}}$$

so $3\sigma_{\bar{x}} = A_2\bar{R}$

Out of control

- Run — 7 points on one side of the central line
- Trend — 6 successive increasing or decreasing points
- Point outside the control limits

Sample Size	$\bar{X}$ Chart	R Chart		Estimate	σ'
(n)	A_2	D_3	D_4	d_2	c_2
2	1.88	0	3.27	1.13	0.56
3	1.02	0	2.57	1.69	0.72
4	0.73	0	2.28	2.06	0.8
5	0.58	0	2.11	2.33	0.84
6	0.48	0	2	2.53	0.87
7	0.42	0.08	1.92	2.7	0.89
8	0.37	0.14	1.86	2.85	0.9
9	0.34	0.18	1.82	2.97	0.91
10	0.31	0.22	1.78	3.08	0.92

Figure 7-14. Quality control chart calculations

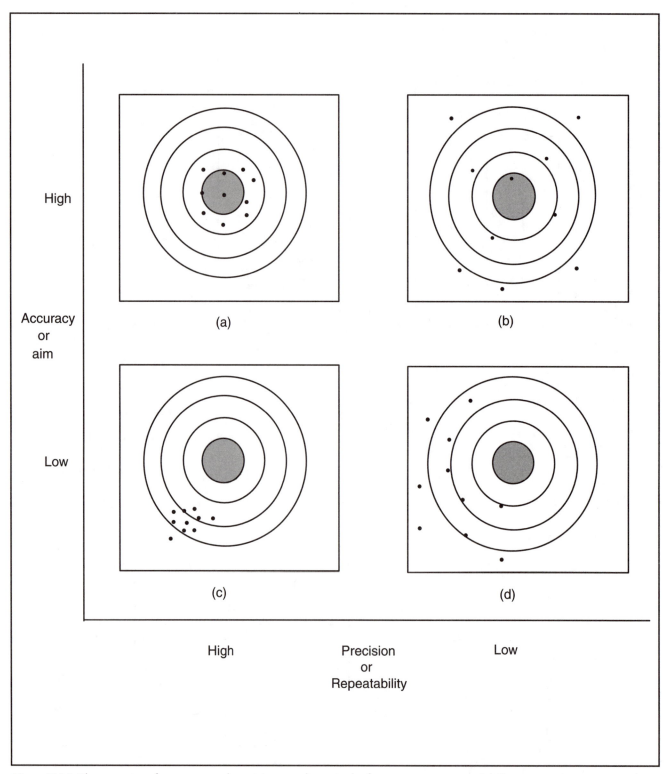

Figure 7-15. The concepts of accuracy and precision are shown in the four target outcomes: (a) The process is accurate and precise; (b) Accurate but not precise; (c) Not accurate but precise; (d) Neither accurate nor precise.

All manufacturing processes display some level of variability, referred to as *inherent capability* or *inherent uniformity*. For example, suppose that the task of shooting at a metal target is viewed as a process of putting holes in a piece of metal. The shooter may take 10 shots at a bull's eye. Thus, the shooter is the operator of the process. Figure 7-15 gives some possible outcomes. To measure *process capability*, that is, the ability to consistently hit a target, the target must be inspected after the shooting is finished. Thus, measuring process output determines the process capability of a manufacturing process. A product is examined to determine whether or not the process is what was specified in the design.

Process capability studies use statistical and analytical tools, similar to quality control studies, except that the process-capability results are directed at machines used in processing, rather than output or products from a process. Returning to a previous example, a process-capability study would be directed toward quantifying the inherent accuracy and precision in the shooting process. The quality control program would be designed to root out the problems that can cause defective products. Traditionally, the objective of quality control studies has been to find defects in a process. A progressive point of view is to inspect to prevent defects from occurring.

The *nature of the process* refers to both the variability (and inherent uniformity) and aim of a process. Thus, in the target shooting example, a perfect process would be capable of placing 10 shots directly in the middle of the bull's eye, one right on top of the other, leaving one hole after 10 rounds. The process would display no variability with perfect accuracy. Such a performance would be unusual in a real industrial process. Variability may have assignable causes and may be correctable if the cause can be found and eliminated. Variability where no cause can be assigned and where it cannot be eliminated, is inherent in the process and is therefore considered "nature."

Some examples of assignable causes of the variation in processes include multiple machines for the same components, operator blunders, defective materials, or progressive wear on the tools during machining. Sources of inherent variability in the process include the natural variation in material properties, operator variability, vibrations and chatter, and the wear of the sliding components in the machine, perhaps resulting in poorer machine operation. These kinds of variations, occurring naturally in processes, often display a random nature and cannot be eliminated. In quality control terms, these are referred to as chance causes. Sometimes, the causes of the variation cannot be eliminated because of cost. Almost every process has multiple causes of variability occurring simultaneously, so it is extremely difficult to separate the effects of the different sources of variability during analysis.

MAKING PROCESS CAPABILITY STUDIES

The objectives of a process-capability study are to determine the inherent nature of the process as compared to the desired specifications. The traditional approach is to examine the process output under normal conditions, or what is typically called *hands-off conditions*. The inputs, (materials, setups, cycle times, temperature, pressure, and operator, for example), are fixed or standardized. The process is allowed to run without adjustment while the output (the product or units or components) is documented carefully with respect to: (1) time, (2) source, and (3) order of production (Figure 7-16). A sufficient amount of data must be taken to ensure confidence in the statistical analysis, and then calculations outlined in Figure 7-17 can be done. The precision of the measurement system should exceed process capability by at least one order of magnitude.

Prior to data collection, these steps should be taken:

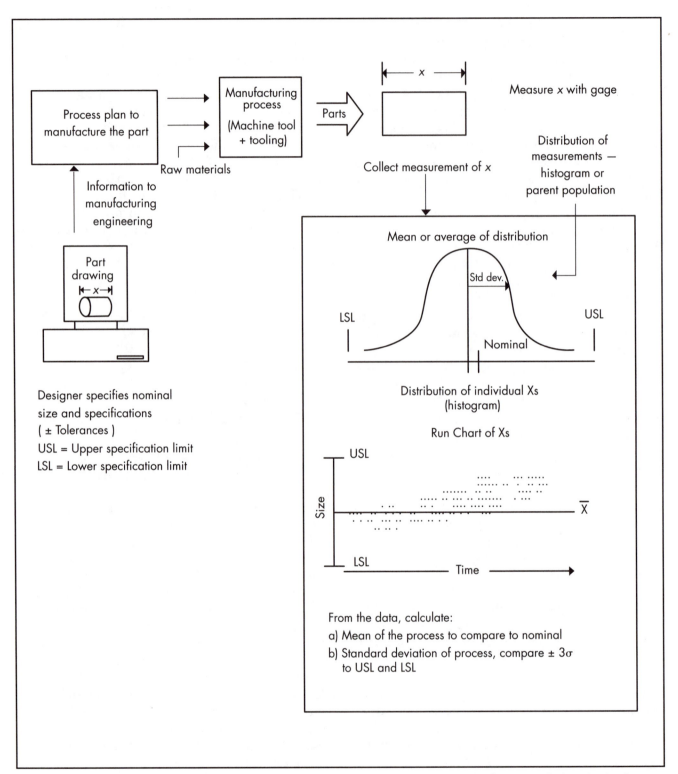

Figure 7-16. The process capability study compares the part as made by the process to the specifications called out by the designer. Histogram and run charts are commonly used.

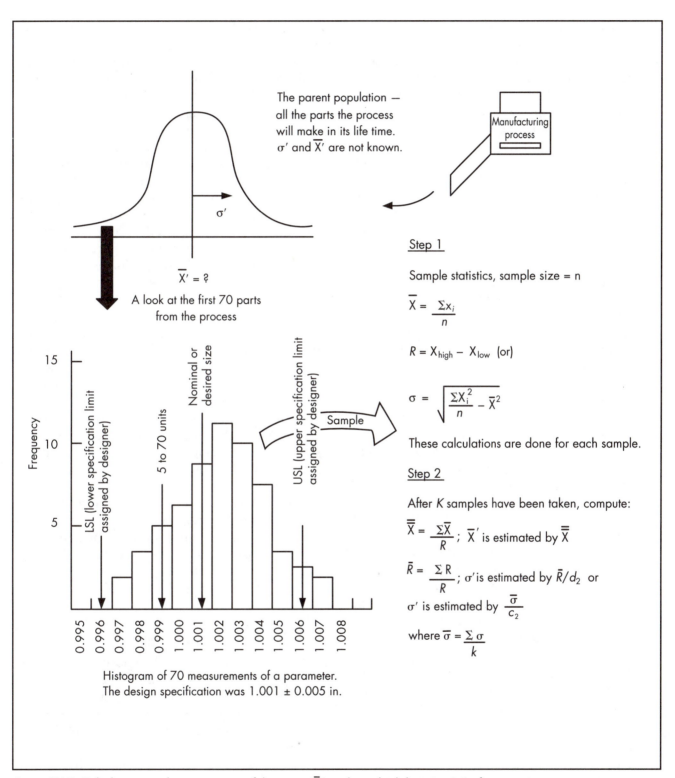

The parent population — all the parts the process will make in its life time. σ' and $\overline{X}'$ are not known.

σ'

$\overline{X}' = ?$

A look at the first 70 parts from the process

Manufacturing process

Sample

Histogram of 70 measurements of a parameter. The design specification was 1.001 ± 0.005 in.

Step 1

Sample statistics, sample size = n

$$\overline{X} = \frac{\Sigma x_i}{n}$$

$$R = X_{high} - X_{low} \text{ (or)}$$

$$\sigma = \sqrt{\frac{\Sigma X_i^2}{n} - \overline{X}^2}$$

These calculations are done for each sample.

Step 2

After K samples have been taken, compute:

$$\overline{\overline{X}} = \frac{\Sigma \overline{X}}{R} ; \ \overline{X}' \text{ is estimated by } \overline{\overline{X}}$$

$$\overline{R} = \frac{\Sigma R}{R} ; \ \sigma' \text{is estimated by } \overline{R}/d_2 \text{ or}$$

σ' is estimated by $\dfrac{\overline{\sigma}}{c_2}$

where $\overline{\sigma} = \dfrac{\Sigma \sigma}{k}$

Figure 7-17. Calculations to obtain estimates of the mean ($\overline{X}'$) and standard deviation (σ') of a process.

- Design a process capability experiment.
- Use normal or hands-off process conditions; specify machine settings for speed, feed, volume, pressure, material, temperature, operator, etc. This is the standard process capability study approach.
- Use specified combinations of input parameters that are believed to influence the quality characteristics being measured. Combinations should be run with an objective of selecting the best. For example, speed levels may be high, normal, and low, and operators may be fast or slow. This is the Taguchi or factorial approach.
- Define the inspection method and means; that is, procedure and instrumentation.
- Decide how many items are needed to perform statistical analysis. For a Taguchi approach, this means deciding how many replications are desired at each calibration level.
- For a standard process capability study, use homogeneous input materials and try to contrast these with normal, more variable input materials. For a Taguchi approach, material is an input variable specified at different levels: normal, homogeneous, and highly variable. If a material is not controllable, it is considered a noise factor.
- Data sheets must be designed to record date, time, source, order of production, and process parameters being used or measured while data is gathered. For a Taguchi method, this is usually a simplified experimental design, called an *orthogonal array*.
- Assuming that the standard process capability study approach is being used, the process is run and parts are made and measured. For a Taguchi experiment, the order of part making is randomized.

Assume that a designer specifies a part to be 1.001 in. ± 0.005 in. (2.54 cm ± 0.01 cm). After 70 units have been manufactured without any process adjustment, each unit is measured and the data recorded on a data sheet. A frequency distribution, or histogram (Figure 7-16), is developed. The histogram shows raw data and desired values, along with the upper- and lower-specification limits. These also are called *lower- and upper-tolerance limits*. Statistical data is used to estimate the mean and standard deviation of the distribution.

The mechanics of the statistical analysis are shown in Figure 7-16. The true mean of the parent population or distribution, designated $\overline{X}'$, is compared with the nominal value. The estimate of true standard deviation, designated σ', is used to determine how the process spread compares with the desired tolerance. The purpose of the analysis is to obtain estimates of $\overline{X}'$ and σ' values, the true process parameters, as they are not known. A sample size of five is used in this example, so $n = 5$. Fourteen groups of samples are drawn from the process, so $k = 14$. For each sample, the sample mean, $\overline{X}$ and sample range, R, are computed. For large samples ($n > 12$), the standard deviation of each sample should be computed rather than the range. Next, the average of sample averages, $\overline{\overline{X}}$, is computed. Sometimes the $\overline{\overline{X}}$ is called the *grand average*. This estimates the mean of the process, $\overline{X}'$. The standard deviation of the process, which is a measure of spread or variability of the process, is estimated from the average of sample ranges, the $\overline{R}$, or average of sample-standard deviation, $\overline{\sigma}$, using either:

$$\sigma' = \overline{R}/d_2 \qquad (7\text{-}1)$$

or

$$\sigma' = \overline{\sigma}/c_2 \qquad (7\text{-}2)$$

The factors d_2 and c_2 depend on the sample size, n, and are given in Figure 7-14. The process capability is defined by ±3 σ' or 6 σ'. Thus, $\overline{X}' \pm 3\sigma'$ defines the natural capability limits of the process, assuming the process is approximately normally distributed.

Note that a distinction is made between a sample and population. A *sample* is of a specified, limited size and is drawn from the population.

The *population* is the large source of items, which can include items a process produces under the conditions specified. The calculations assume that the population is normal or bell-shaped. Figure 7-14 showed a typical normal curve and the areas under the curve that standard deviation defines. Other distributions are possible, but the histogram in Figure 7-14 clearly suggested that a normal probability distribution can best describe the process. Now it remains for the process engineer and operator to combine their knowledge with results from the analysis to draw conclusions about the ability of the process to meet specifications.

Process capability studies can provide answers to these questions.

1. Does the process have the ability to meet specifications? To answer this, a process capability index, C_p, often is computed using the estimated σ' for the parent population.

$$C_p = \frac{USL - LSL}{6\sigma'} = \frac{T}{6\sigma'} \qquad (7\text{-}3)$$

where:

C_p = process capability index
T = tolerance spread
USL = upper specification limit
LSL = lower specification limit

A value of $C_p = 1.33$ is considered good.

2. Is the process well centered with respect to the desired nominal specification, the target? To answer this question, the deviation, Δ, from the target is calculated:

$$\Delta = \frac{estimated\,process\,mean - nominal}{\frac{1}{2}\,tolerance\,spread}$$
$$= \frac{\overline{X}' - N}{\frac{1}{2}\,(USL\text{-}LSL)} \qquad (7\text{-}4)$$

where:

Δ = deviation from target
$\overline{X}'$ = estimated process mean
N = nominal

The condition for not producing rejects is:

$$\overline{X}' - N + 3\sigma'\ 0.5(USL - LSL) \qquad (7\text{-}5)$$

Another capability index, C_{pk} that combines both factors is:

$$C_{pk} = \frac{\min.\ \left\{|USL - \overline{X}'1|, |LSL - \overline{X}'1|\right\}}{3\sigma'}$$

In Figure 7-18, the process capability almost equals the assigned tolerance spread, so if the process is not perfectly centered, defective products result. If this is the case, as shown in Figure 7-18, the process needs to be re-centered so the mean of the process distribution is at or near the nominal value. Most processes can be re-centered. Poor accuracy often is due to assignable causes, which can be eliminated.

MOTOROLA'S SIX SIGMA

To meet the challenge of both international and domestic competition, Motorola developed the six-sigma concept. The concept is shown in Figure 7-19 in terms of four-sigma and six-sigma capabilities. Most people do not know what sigma represents. Sigma represents a standard and it is a measure of variability, repeatability, or lack of precision in a process. Most explanations regarding six sigma use incorrect diagrams. Figure 7-19 shows the correct relationship between four sigma and six sigma. The distance between the upper- and lower-specification limits does not change (or increase) for a process to improve from four- to five- or six-sigma levels. However, variability, as measured by σ', is decreased through process improvements.

The Taguchi method incorporates the following general features:

- Quality is defined in relation to total loss to the consumer or society from less-than-perfect product quality. Methods include placing a monetary value on quality loss. Anything less than perfect is waste.

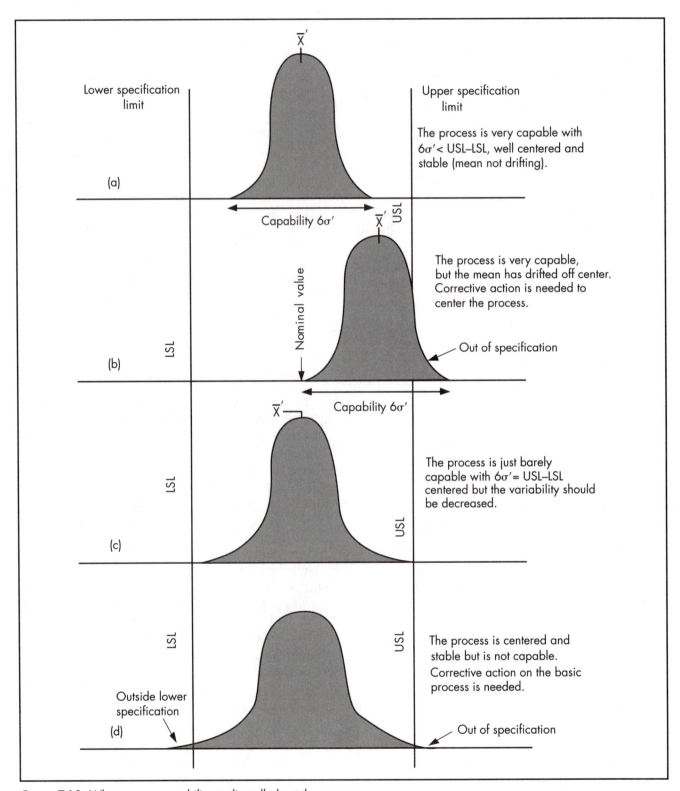

Figure 7-18. What process-capability studies tell about the process.

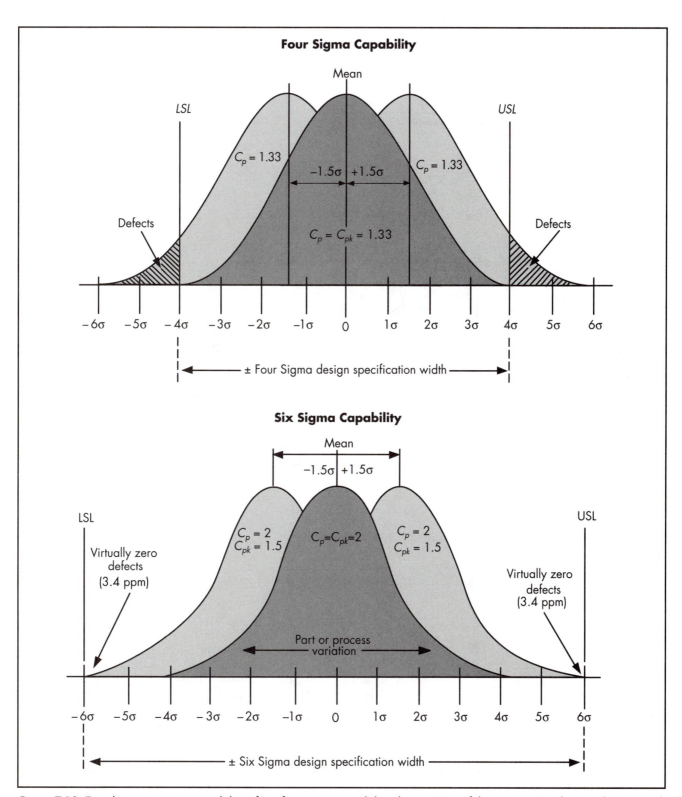

Figure 7-19. To achieve six sigma capabilities from four sigma capability, the precision of the process must be greatly improved.

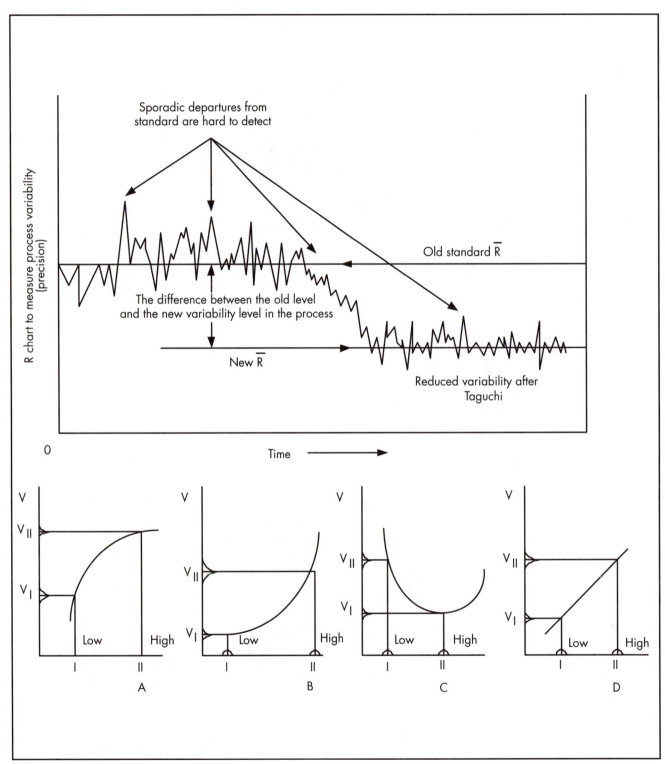

Figure 7-20. The use of Taguchi methods can reduce the inherent process variability as shown in the upper figure; factors A, B, C, and D versus process variable V shown in lower figure.

- In a competitive society, continuous quality improvement and cost reduction are necessary to stay in business.
- Continuous quality improvement requires continuous reduction in the variability of the product-performance characteristics. Taguchi methods can be an alternative approach to making a process capability study. The Taguchi approach uses a truncated experimental design. This is called an *orthogonal array*, and determines which process inputs have the greatest effect on process variability (for example, precision), and which have the least. Inputs with the greatest influence are set at levels that minimize their effect on process variability. As shown in Figure 7-20, factors A, B, C, and D have an effect on process variable, V. By selecting a high level of A and low levels of B, C, and D, the inherent variability of the process can be reduced. Those factors that have little effect on the process variable, V, are used to adjust or re-center the process aim. In other words, Taguchi methods seek to minimize or dampen the effect of the causes of variability and, thus, reduce total process variability.
- Engineering product designs and their manufacturing systems determine the quality and cost of a manufactured product.
- Exploiting the nonlinear, interactive effects of a process or product parameters on performance characteristics reduces the variability in product/process performance characteristics.
- Statistically planned design of experiments or Taguchi experiments determine the settings for processes and other parameters that reduce performance variation.
- Design and improvement of products and processes can make them robust, and thus insensitive to uncontrollable or difficult-to-control variations called *noise* by Taguchi.

The methods are more than just mechanical procedures. They infuse an overriding new philosophy into manufacturing management, basically making quality the primary issue in manufacturing. The manufacturing world is rapidly becoming aware that the consumer is the ultimate judge of quality. Continuous quality improvement toward perfect quality is the ultimate goal. Finally, it is recognized that ultimate quality and lowest cost of a manufactured product are determined to a large extent by engineered designs of the:

- product,
- manufacturing processes, and
- manufacturing system (integration of product and process).

There is a new understanding of quality stating that inherent process variability is not fixed. Exploiting the nonlinear effects of products and/or process parameters on the performance characteristics reduces the noise level of a process.

Future manufacturing management should include the following changes:

- continual training and massive implementation of statistical process control;
- use of statistical process control as an interim quality control measure until the full slate of quality control techniques are fully integrated into American manufacturing;
- training and implementation of Taguchi methods for process design and improvement of products and processes;
- concurrent engineering of products and processes to reduce time needed to bring new high-quality, low-cost designs to the marketplace; and
- attitude adjustment—making quality a primary consideration and the process of improvement continuous.

Teams and Quality Circles

Popular programs are built upon the concept of participatory management, such as quality circles, self-managed work teams, and task groups. These programs have been successful in many companies, but have failed miserably in others. The difference is often due to the manner in which management implements the program. Programs must be integrated and managed within the context of lean manufacturing-system strategies. For example, management asking an employee for a suggestion that it does not or cannot use defeats a suggestion system. Management must learn to trust employee ideas and decisions and move some decision making to the factory floor in tune with financial constraints.

The quality circle movement started in Japan in 1962 and grew rapidly. Quality circles employ or embrace participatory management principles. A quality circle is usually a group of employees within a department. Its organizational structure includes members, a team leader, a facilitator, frequently a manufacturing engineer, and a steering committee. Its main objectives are to:

- provide workers with chances to demonstrate their ideas;
- raise employee morale;
- develop worker knowledge and quality control techniques; and
- introduce problem solving methods.

Solutions to typical production-type problems provided by quality circles unify company-wide quality control activities and clarify managerial policies, while developing leadership and supervisory capabilities (Table 7-2).

Quality circles implemented in U.S. companies meet limited success if they are not part of lean-production strategies. It is possible for quality circles to work, but they must be encouraged and supported by management. Everyone must be taught the importance and benefits of integrated quality control.

Under lean-production philosophies, cell teams are vital resources for continuous improvement. Cell teams work together from initial cell startups. Properly designed cells have roughly 15 minutes set aside at the end of each shift to have cell-team meetings. These meetings discuss daily events and seek solutions to problems. This is real continuous process/system improvement enlisting entire cell teams and supports members when it is necessary.

POKA-YOKE

While many people do not believe that the goal of zero defects is possible to reach, many companies have achieved zero defects for a length of time or reduced their defect level to virtually zero using poka-yoke and source inspection.

Poka-yoke is a Japanese term for defect prevention. Poka-yoke devices and procedures are often devised for preserving the safety of operations. The idea is to develop a method, mechanism, or device that prevents the defect from occurring, rather than to find the defect after it has occurred. Poka-yokes can be attached to machines for automatic checks of products or parts in a process. They differ from source inspections in that they usually are attributes inspections. The poka-yoke device prevents production of bad parts. Some devices may automatically shut down a machine if a defect is produced, preventing production of an additional defective part. The poka-yoke system uses 100% inspection to guard against unavoidable human error. Figure 7-21 illustrates a poka-yoke device. This device ensures that the workers remember to apply labels to products, thus preventing defective products.

Poka-yoke devices work when physical detection is needed, but sensory detection methods must be used to check many items, such as surface finish on a bearing race or glass-plate flatness. For such problems, a system of self-checks and successive checks can be used.

Source inspection looks for errors before they become defects, and either stops the system, makes corrections, or automatically compensates or corrects for the error condition to prevent a defective item from being

**Table 7-2
Typical quality circle problems**

Product quality	Methods
Paperwork	Materials
Hardware	Software
Communication	Tooling
Service	Material handling
Processes	Delays
Scrap reduction	Cost reduction
Productivity	Maintenance

produced. The common term for source inspection in manufacturing processes is *adaptive control*.

There are two ways to look at source inspections: vertically and horizontally. Vertical source inspections try to control upstream processes that can be the source or cause of defects downstream. It is necessary to examine source processes as they may have much greater impact on quality than do the processes being examined. For example, consider steel bars that are cylindrically ground. After grinding, about 10% of the bars warp, that is, bend longitudinally and are

rejected. The grinding process is studied extensively and no cause is found. The problem is with the heat-treat process that precedes cylindrical grinding. About 10% of bars do not get a complete, uniform heating prior to quench. These bars lay close to the oven door. Next, it is found that the door is not properly sealed, resulting in a temperature gradient inside the oven affecting nearby bars. Quenching of bars induces a residual stress that is released by the grinding process and that causes the warping. Horizontal source inspections detect defect sources within the processes and then introduce corrections to keep from turning errors into defects.

If a worker inspects each part immediately after producing it, this is called *self-checking*. There is an immediate quality feedback to the worker. However, it would be difficult for many workers not to allow a certain degree of bias to creep into their inspections (whether they are aware of it or not), since they are inspecting their own work. Operators of downstream stations or processes can inspect parts produced

Before Improvement	**After Improvement**
The worker had to remove a label from a tape and place it on the product. The operation depended on the worker's vigilance.	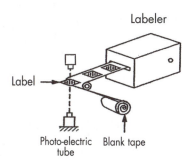 Labeler Label Photo-electric tube Blank tape
Comment: Label application failures were eliminated. Cost: $75	The tape fed out by the labeler turns sharply so that the labels detach and project out from the tape. This is detected by a photoelectric tube and, if the label is not removed and applied to the product within the cycle time of 20 seconds, a buzzer sounds and the conveyor stops.

Figure 7-21. Example of poka-yoke (Shingo 1986).

by upstream operators. If there is a problem with parts, defective items are immediately passed back to the workers at previous stations. Defects are verified there, and problems corrected. Action is immediately taken to prevent any more defective parts. While this is going on, lines are shut down.

For *successive checks* to be successful, several rules should be followed. All possible variables and attributes should not be measured. This would lead to errors and confusion from the possible information overload in the inspection process. The time involved to complete possible inspections would be excessive. Parts created by immediate upstream processes should be analyzed and checked for only one or two key points. Only the most important elements or perhaps the features more prone to error are inspected. Another important rule is that the immediate feedback of the discovery of a defect should lead to immediate action. For parts produced in an integrated production system, this is effective in preventing production of more defective parts. If a cell has only one or two workers, they are not in positions to directly check each other's work after each step. Decouplers can play a role here by providing automatic, successive checking of parts' critical features (before those parts proceed to the next processing step). Only perfect parts are pulled from one process to the next after passing the automatic-decoupler inspection.

Line Stop

Andon boards are important components of final assembly flow lines implementing lean manufacturing methodologies. *Andon boards* are pairs of yellow and red lights that hang above the workers on assembly lines. The boards tell everyone the status of the lines' processes. The numbers on the boards reflect the number of stations on the lines. Flowline workers can turn on yellow lights when assistance is needed, and nearby workers who are caught-up can assist. Yellow lights indicate

that lines can keep moving. However, if problem products reach the end of the work areas on moving assembly lines and the problems still have not been rectified, then red lights are lit. Red lights are only turned on if problems cannot be solved quickly and lines need to be stopped. When lines are stopped, engineers and supervisors rush to solve problems. When problems are solved, the red lights go off and everyone goes back to work. The line start up is synchronized and all workstations start at the same time.

Every worker should be given the authority to stop a production line to correct quality problems. In systems using poka-yoke or autonomation, devices may stop lines automatically. Assembly lines or manufacturing cells should be stopped immediately and started again only when necessary corrections have been made. Although stopping lines takes time and money, it is advantageous in the long run. Problems can be found immediately, and workers have more incentive to be attentive because they do not want to be responsible for stopping lines.

QUALITY CONTROL DEPARTMENT

The basic idea of integration is to shift functions that were formerly done in the staff organization (part of the production system) into the manufacturing system. The quality control department serves as a facilitator and acts to promote quality concepts throughout the plant. In addition, its staff educates and trains workers in statistical and process control techniques and provides engineering assistance on visual and automatic inspection installations. The quality control department's most important function is training the entire company in quality control.

Other important functions of the quality control department, outside of the company, are to audit vendors and provide technical assistance. A vendor's quality must be raised to a high enough level that the buyer will not need to inspect incoming materials, parts, or the subassemblies. A vendor must become an extension of the buyer's factory. Ultimately, each vendor must deliver perfect materials that need no incoming inspection. Note that this means the acceptable defect level of incoming material is zero %. The goal is perfection.

For many years, the common thought was that better quality would just cost too much. For mass production systems, this was true. To achieve the kinds of quality that Toyota, Honda, Sanyo, and many others have demonstrated, the job shop and functional production system must be phased out and replaced by an integrated quality function within a linked-cell manufacturing system.

Difficult, highly technical, and lengthy inspections can still be carried out in the quality control department. These types of quality control or technical inspections include total-performance checks, also called *end-item inspections*, chemical and X-ray analyses, destructive tests, or tests of long duration.

Making Quality Visible

Spotlighting of quality programs by visual display should occur throughout manufacturing facilities to make quality evident. These displays tell workers, managers, customers, and outside visitors about the quality factors being measured, the current quality-improvement projects, and who has won awards for quality. Examples of visible quality are signs showing quality improvements, framed quality awards presented to or by the company, and displays of high-precision-measuring equipment.

Displays have several benefits. In lean manufacturing, customers often visit a factory to inspect processes. They want measurable standards of quality. Highly visible indicators of quality, such as control charts and displays, should be posted in every department. Everyone is informed on current quality goals and the progress being made. Displays and quality awards are also effective ways to show the work force that a company is serious about quality.

SUMMARY

The decade 2000-2010 is bringing a gradual transition from statistical process control (as a primary means of quality management) to the more extensive implementation of statistical, experimental-design methods. These methods are being used to design and to constantly improve product and process quality. This is a natural evolution essential to continual improvement of processes, products, and services. Anything less is tantamount to stagnation and potential demise.

Although Taguchi methods have only recently been introduced in the U.S., they have been employed for many years in Japan. Taguchi methods were developed as a result of Japan's emphasis on quality, limited resources, and the urgent need to develop products rapidly. In elemental form, these methods allowed for design and production of products that are robust and insensitive to environmental disturbances (noise factors). Further, they are relatively easy to use and quick to produce positive results. They are the next logical step.

An example of the use of Taguchi techniques in a brewery follows. It was observed that there was quite a bit of variation in the bottle-filling machines. This situation led to bottles being overfilled to ensure that every bottle had the minimum volume. This large spread (or standard deviation) led to a high percentage of overfilled bottles. A Taguchi experiment was performed on one of the bottle-filling machines. Through analysis of data, new operational settings for the machine were derived, which reduced variability in the filling process. This allowed the average-fill height to be lowered and thus less beer went into each bottle. The savings on this one machine amounted to over $400,000 in the first year.

The whole idea of Taguchi methods is to continuously improve processes, which can result in decreasing variability in processes as shown in Figure 7-22. This requires time and hard work on the part of everyone.

Competition speeds the rate of innovation. Due to competition in the free market, there is reason to expect that proper use of Taguchi methods will force major improvements in both products and processes. Taguchi meth-ods are relatively easy to use and fit well into the trend toward lean manufacturing. They do not require extensive training and educa-tion in probabilities, statistics, or experimen-tal designs; so they can be quickly grasped and employed. Every engineer involved in process improvement should know how to run a Taguchi experiment to improve the process-es in their factories.

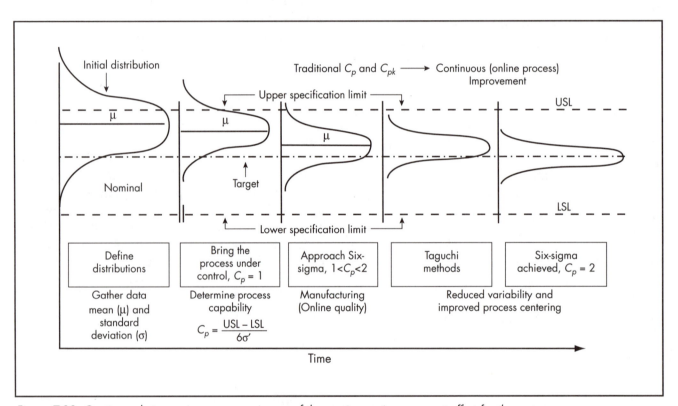

Figure 7-22. Continuously improving processes is part of the continuous improvement effort for the system.

Chapter 8
Integrated Reliability

INTRODUCTION

Time must be allotted in the manufacturing schedule for checking and maintaining equipment and for workers to discuss and resolve cell problems. Unless processes and workstations in the manufacturing system are properly designed and maintained, breakdowns will occur and disrupt product flow. Some manufacturing processes must run continuously; such processes already follow many of the lean manufacturing tenets. Typically, the problem with continuous processes is long setup time. There is a long period of changeover time when the system changes materials, dies, or tooling, or when maintenance is performed.

Workers and processes in a lean manufacturing system must be ready to produce what is needed when it is needed. This may not be possible if a system is running on a maximum output schedule. Processes and people operating on a tightly balanced system can never catch up if a time buffer is not planned. This time buffer is provided for catching up production or for maintenance. The key is to develop a less-than-full-capacity schedule for the cells that includes adequate time for maintenance. Repairs or maintenance made under pressure may not be accomplished properly, leading to further downtime for re-repair, tinkering, or adjusting.

ROLE OF MAINTENANCE

In large companies there is a need for designated mechanics but their role must change. If workers are doing a good job of trying to avoid emergency shut downs, the maintenance crews should be able to concentrate on more constructive tasks. There are some tasks, like the repair of complicated equipment, that workers cannot be expected to learn. These high-level maintenance tasks should be left to the specialists. If the number of maintenance employees has been reduced significantly due to a company's dedication to lean manufacturing, then those who are left should be able to troubleshoot and more fully utilize their diagnostic and technical skills. Maintenance personnel should be multi-skilled. They must be able to perform high-level electric and mechanical tasks as well as be trained in some process operating skills.

INTEGRATE PREVENTIVE MAINTENANCE

With integrated preventive maintenance, operators are required to become aware of their equipment behavior and its routine problems and to be active participants in the maintenance process. Chief among these problems is process drift—the loss of stability or accuracy. Therefore, there is clearly linkage between integrated preventive maintenance and integrated quality control. The quality control function lies not only in the quality control department, but also with workers on the factory floor. Getting the process centered on the statistical mean and then maintaining the aim or accuracy of the process is different from reducing the variance and then maintaining the process spread (variability or precision).

Preventive maintenance is designed to preserve and enhance equipment reliability. A correctly integrated preventive maintenance program provides a significant increase in production capability throughout the entire production system. The ideal preventive maintenance program prevents equipment failure.

People not exposed to preventive maintenance may question its value. Some believe that it costs more for regular downtime and maintenance than it costs to operate equipment until repair is absolutely necessary. However, not only the costs but also the long-term benefits and savings associated with integrated preventive maintenance should be compared. Without integrated preventive maintenance, the following costs are likely to occur:

- lost production time resulting from unscheduled equipment breakdown;
- variation in quality of products due to deteriorating equipment performance;
- decrease in service life of equipment;
- safety-related accidents due to equipment malfunction, and
- major equipment repairs and lost production time.

The long-term benefits to be considered include the following:

- If maintenance is a primary responsibility, operators are more familiar with equipment and potential problems.
- Processes are in better control and documented with machine and tool records, thus producing better quality.
- Quality, flexibility, safety, reliability, and production capabilities are improved.
- Reliable equipment permits inventory reduction.

Long-term effects and cost comparisons undoubtedly favor preventive maintenance. A carefully designed and properly integrated program requires a positive managerial attitude that will set the pace for success. Another preventive maintenance principle promotes the idea of performing housekeeping at an optimal level so no machine breakdowns occur.

Involve Internal Customers

In lean manufacturing, workers are responsible for machinery/equipment in a manufacturing cell. This philosophy encourages workers to take responsibility for maintenance, operation, and process performance. Workers should be trained to recognize machinery's optimal performance and to troubleshoot processes and equipment when performance changes are noticed. Regular lubrication and cleaning should be normal parts of operators' daily routines. If workers are responsible, they become more sensitive to the care and maintenance of machines, particularly if the performance of their particular machine reflects on their performance records.

Machine operators should be trained to observe their equipment and respond to these observations. If a piece of equipment needs special attention and an operator cannot perform the level of maintenance necessary, he or she should see that a proper maintenance specialist comes to the machine. Through preventive maintenance, production workers become more conscious of their performance and take pride in their work.

Cell workers must realize the importance of orderly and clean workplace processes. *Process drift* (for example, loss of stability, aim, or accuracy) is a problem that operators must detect. This problem is closely linked to integrated quality control and is something that workers should be able to identify. Housekeeping should be a ritual in daily job performance. Routine cleaning familiarizes an operator with the machine, thus making it easier to understand details involved in its operation.

Integrated preventive maintenance emphasizes the significance of executing totally correct procedures for operating equipment within a manufacturing cell. When a worker operates a manufacturing cell in an incorrect manner, irregularities in processes stand out. Problems are readily observed and may be prevented at earlier process stages. Keep this thought in mind—if a manufacturing process or system is not maintained or improved, then the process is degrading. (This is a layman's restatement of the second law of thermodynamics.) The manufacturing strategy is to design methods to properly train people to check processes.

Scheduling Preventive Maintenance

Scheduling preventive maintenance is a task typically assigned to a mechanical or industrial engineer. Production supervisors believe manufacturing processes should not be shut down simply for preventive maintenance, yet higher-level preventive maintenance must be performed on schedule by the maintenance department. For this reason, preventive maintenance should be flexible within certain limits. Scheduled preventive maintenance should occur between eight-hour shifts, in four-hour time blocks, or on weekends when necessary. However, this may be inconvenient for maintenance engineers and specialists. Processes can be used on an alternating basis when overhaul maintenance is required, and if extra processes are available. In this case, where a replacement machine is available, a machine can be removed from the cell and replaced with another, so the required overhaul can be carried out.

The manufacturing system's pace in an entire plant is synchronized to system takt time; and the system's needs determine production rates for specific processes or cells. Machines are not operated at maximum rates. Furthermore, an entire eight-hour shift is not scheduled unless it is required to meet daily production needs. Some amount of time (possibly 15 minutes) at the start and end of each shift is allotted for routine repair and maintenance. If an entire eight-hour shift is scheduled, this is a symptom of a serious problem and steps should immediately be taken to isolate and correct the situation. With regular scheduled maintenance, processes last longer and provide higher reliability. The idea is not to overtax processes, people, or tools. Workers are less likely to make mistakes and machines are

less likely to breakdown if they are not under pressure. In the manufacturing arena, steady and consistent performers win long-distance races, not necessarily the fastest performers.

Placing a time cushion at the end of each work shift, with a 7.5-hour shift, allows the manufacturing cell or flow line to stop for team meetings. The first 10 or 15 minutes of a shift are dedicated to maintenance checks, machine warm-up, lubrication, tool checks, etc. There is also additional flexibility to respond to changes in product demand because of the wider latitude it affords manufacturing and assembly cells. Thus, to increase the production rate, one needs only to add workers to cells and increase the process-operation rate when necessary.

4-8-4-8 Scheduling

Integrated preventive maintenance covers the maintenance of machine tools, workholding devices, cutting tools, and training of personnel. This function is integrated into the daily regimen of the factory floor. Low-level tasks are shifted from the maintenance department to lean production workers. Daily, workers prepare and use machine-tool checklists, much like the checklists that pilots use to check an aircraft before takeoff. No machines should crash during an eight-hour shift. Workers also are responsible for most routine machine-tool maintenance. The maintenance department still carries out major machine overhauls and takes lead roles in repairing major breakdowns.

For an integrated preventive maintenance program to operate effectively, the entire plant is run on a 4-8-4-8 schedule. The two four-hour time blocks between the two eight-hour work shifts allow for maintenance or unavoidably long setups. In addition, an eight-hour shift can begin early or run over when needed, without disrupting the next shift. Lean manufacturing systems are designed to be run at less-than-full-capacity to allow for breathing room to keep everything and everybody up and operating 100% of the time (see Table 8-1).

Operating machine tools, processes, and equipment at reduced speeds or with reduced

Table 8-1
Less than full capacity scheduling

Schedule	Meet it every day. Breakdowns and maintenance do not cause stoppages elsewhere.
Quality	Do not let schedule cause errors through haste.
Marketing	Output can be increased on short notice to fill a hot order; buys time to add workers if necessary.
Worker jobs	The operator's number one job is making parts—direct labor—but if there is no work (schedule is met) then the operator performs indirect labor. This is often mental; that is, thinking about improvements in quality, productivity, and equipment. Mental work may be the worker's most important contribution.
Automation	With automation, the worker may perform 100% indirect labor, for example, quality checker or trouble shooter. Lean production eases the transition from direct labor to indirect labor.

production rates further enhances machine and tool life. This is a foreign concept to most North American factories. The idea of less-than-full capacity operation suggests less-than-100% utilization. It is best to worry about effective personnel utilization and allow machine utilization to meet demand. However, manufacturers want machines to be ready to be used.

MANUFACTURING ENGINEERING

Manufacturing and mechanical engineers are responsible for designing, building, testing, and implementing manufacturing equipment. Maintainability also should be considered when designing or purchasing equipment. Simple, reliable equipment that can be easily maintained should be specified. In general, dedicated equipment can be built in-house better than it can be purchased. Many companies understand that it is not good strategy simply to imitate or copy manufacturing technology from another company and then expect to make an exceptional product. Companies must perform research and development on manufacturing technologies, as well as on manufacturing systems, to produce effective and cost-efficient products. However, effective, cost-efficient, manufacturing systems make research and development in manufacturing technology pay off. Once a lean production system is implemented, machines can be designed, built, and installed into manufacturing

cells. Companies who have adopted lean manufacturing find the following advantages.

- The cell and the processes within it are designed for the system so the cell operates on a make-one, check-one, and move-one-on basis, with processes meeting cycle time, and cycle time is equal to the system's takt time.
- The cell is flexible, allowing rapid changeover for existing products and rapid modification for new products or model changes.
- The cell has unique processing capabilities.
- The cell has maintainability, reliability, and durability.
- Equipment and methods are designed to prevent accidents (safety).
- The cell is easy for workers to operate; that is, it is ergonomically correct.

Equipment is designed and developed with the needs of internal customers as a priority, even though factors affecting external customers are the highest priority for manufacturing engineering. Although many plants lack expertise to build machines from scratch, most have expertise to modify equipment and give it unique capabilities. Equipment modification to prevent recurring breakdowns requires that management assign the highest priority to this work. The most skilled maintenance personnel must be given this task so breakdowns are eventually eliminated.

TOTAL PRODUCTIVE MAINTENANCE

The evolution of total productive maintenance is described as (Nakajima 1988):

- 1950s: preventive maintenance—establishing maintenance functions;
- 1960s: productive maintenance—recognizing the importance of reliability, maintenance, and economic efficiency in plant design;
- 1970s: total productive maintenance—achieving productive maintenance efficiency through a comprehensive system based on respect for individuals and total employee participation;
- 1980s: total productive maintenance evolves as an equipment management strategy involving all hands in a plant or facility in equipment or asset utilization. (Without total productive maintenance, corporate survival is questionable and it is a critical step in the lean strategy); and
- 1990s: integrated predictive maintenance is a key step in lean manufacturing's five pillars of total productive maintenance.

The Five Pillars

The five pillars of integrated preventive maintenance/total productive maintenance are (Nakajima 1988):

1. Eliminate the six big losses, and thereby improve equipment effectiveness. The six big losses are: Losses caused by equipment failure—breakdowns of machine tools, material handling devices, fixtures, etc.; losses caused by setup and adjustment failures—exchange of dies in molding machines and presses, and tooling exchanges in machine tools; speed losses, including idling and minor stoppages due to the abnormal operation of sensors, blockage of work on chutes, etc.; losses caused by reduced speed due to discrepan-

cies between the specified and actual speed of equipment; process defects due to scrap and rework; and reduced yield from machine start-up to stable production.

2. Develop an autonomous maintenance program. This means workers are involved in daily equipment maintenance. The seven steps of autonomous maintenance are:

- Initial cleaning: Clean to eliminate dust and dirt mainly on the body of the equipment; lubricate and tighten; discover problems and correct them.
- Countermeasures at the source of problems: Prevent the causes of dust, dirt, and spattering of liquids; re-engineer equipment parts that are hard to clean and lubricate; reduce the time required for cleaning and lubricating.
- Cleaning and lubrication standards: Establish standards to reduce the time spent cleaning, lubricating, and tightening (specify daily and periodic tasks).
- General inspection: Follow the instructions in the inspection manual. Quality circle members discover and correct minor equipment defects.
- Autonomous inspection: Develop and use autonomous inspection check sheets.
- Orderliness and tidiness: Standardize the individual workplace control categories; thoroughly systemize maintenance control.
- Establish inspection standards for cleaning and lubricating; follow cleaning and lubricating standards in the workplace; establish standards for recording data and standards for parts and tool maintenance.

3. Fully autonomous maintenance: Develop a company maintenance policy and goals for maintenance. Record the mean time between failures, analyze the results, and design countermeasures. These steps are based on the five basic principles of operations management. In the Japanese literature, they are known as the five Ss: *seiri,*

seiton, seiso, seiketsu, and *shitsuke.* A rough translation of the five Ss means organization, tidiness, purity, cleanliness, and discipline. Develop a scheduled maintenance program for the maintenance department. This usually is done in cooperation with industrial engineering.

4. Increase operator and maintenance personnel skill. The operators should discuss problems and solutions with the maintenance people at the time preventive maintenance work is done on their equipment. Part of the operator's job is to keep records on the performance of the equipment, so the operators must be observant or must learn to be observant.

5. Develop an equipment management program including a record of machine and tool use that notes how much they were used and who used them.

ZERO DOWNTIME

The goal of preventive maintenance is to eliminate machine breakdowns and associated problems, including tooling problems, process drift, and related incidents. In short, zero downtime results in 100% on-demand utilization. Fighting maintenance fires, a mode that most maintenance departments seem eternally caught in, does not ensure zero downtime. Preventive maintenance and its benefits cannot be realized without the efforts of the entire organization-workers, management, maintenance crews, and other support people. Operator involvement is critical.

LEAN PRODUCTION

When considering the maintenance component of the organization, the first focus should be on a preventive maintenance program. Without a good one, the equipment is never maintained at a level sufficient to ensure that the organization has assets capable of producing a world-class product or service.

In the lean system, total preventive maintenance's goal is to achieve preventive mainte-

nance through employee participation in maintenance activities. Employee involvement is key to successfully meeting customer requirements. As lean production builds high quality into the production process itself, rather than achieving it later through inspections and repairs, preventive maintenance catches trouble at the source, rather than letting anything go wrong and then fixing it.

The foundation of total preventive maintenance focuses on the partnerships between the manufacturing personnel, the maintenance department, manufacturing and design engineering, and other technical services to improve overall equipment effectiveness.

BENCHMARKING

Prior to the development of a total preventive maintenance plan, benchmarking or recording the current status of an organization is a good idea. This evaluation includes more than the maintenance organization. It should embrace all parts of the organization involved in manufacturing maintenance, design, and purchasing of the assets of the company. The most important benchmark for total preventive maintenance is the current state of the equipment, that is, percentage of uptime.

Benchmarking provides the starting point from which to calculate improvement. As such, it also provides the means to demonstrate progress, money savings, and that productivity is affected in a way that improves the bottom line. Benchmarking also shows the production/maintenance teams that they are making progress. This keeps interest and enthusiasm levels high.

Benchmarking involves documenting as much current equipment data as possible. From the current status it can be illustrated to management where the equipment was (in terms of productivity), where it is, and where the trend patterns are pointing.

A first step in benchmarking should be an analysis of the amount of additional capacity the company could get from its machinery if uptime improved. Such data might include quality records for the equipment, time data, maintenance downtime histories, setup times, and procedures. Other documentation might include photos of the physical condition of the equipment at program start (to compare with similar photos after total preventive maintenance implementation).

PILOT AREAS

Selecting a pilot area is an important step in the total preventive maintenance sequence. Rather than attempting to implement total preventive maintenance plant-wide from the start, most lean manufacturing companies start with a pilot cell or target pieces of equipment identified as critical to the manufacturing system.

PREDICTIVE MAINTENANCE

Implementing a predictive maintenance program, a basic function of the five pillars of preventive maintenance, is the next step established as a formal method for monitoring equipment and ensuring that wear trends are documented. In this way, equipment can be overhauled, with worn components changed, before a failure occurs. Figure 8-1 shows a typical inspection form for a hydraulic and pneumatic system. Such forms must be developed for belts, chains, and general equipment.

COMPUTERIZED MAINTENANCE MANAGEMENT SYSTEM

The organization's ability to improve its service of the equipment is followed by an increase in the amount of data available for performing failure and engineering analysis. This highlights the need for a computerized database for tracking and trending equipment histories, planned work, the preventive maintenance program, the maintenance of spare parts, the training and skill levels of the main-

Hydraulic Inspection	Item	OK	Needs Repair
Hydraulic pump	Proper oil flow?		
	Proper pressure?		
	Excessive noise?		
	Vibration?		
	Proper mounting?		
	Excessive heat?		
Intake filter	Clean?		
	Free oil flow?		
Directional control valves	Easy movement?		
	Proper oil flow?		
Relief valve	Proper pressure?		
	Excessive heat?		
Lines	Properly mounted?		
	Oil leaks?		
	Loose fittings?		
	Damaged piping?		
Pneumatic Inspection	**Item**	**OK**	**Needs Repair**
Compressor	Proper airflow?		
	Proper pressure?		
	Excessive noise?		
	Vibration?		
	Proper lubrication?		
	Excessive heat?		
Inlet filter	Clean?		
	Free airflow?		
Directional control valves	Easy movement?		
	Proper airflow?		
Muffler	Proper airflow?		
	Proper noise reduction?		
Lines	Properly mounted?		
	Air leaks?		
	Loose fittings?		
	Damaged piping?		

Figure 8-1. A typical inspection form for hydraulic and pneumatic systems.

tenance workers, etc. Systems commonly used for this task are called *computerized maintenance management systems*, a comprehensive relational database accessible to the entire organization.

CONTINUOUS IMPROVEMENT

As an integrated preventive maintenance program matures, it provides increased support to other advanced programs. As lean manufacturing implementation is embraced, processes operate when they are scheduled and produce at the rate they were designed to deliver. Integrated quality control is enhanced, since the equipment is stable and produces a quality product every time it operates. Employee involvement programs are matured, since most problems are related to the equipment. This makes the worker's responsibilities easier to meet and leads to more motivation to maximize their competitive strengths.

Standardization

The objective of standardization is to develop the daily routine so continuous improvement can occur. Clear standards are critical to continuous improvement. Without standards, internal customers have no goals by which to judge their work. Operations and methods fall back to the old ways. The result is continual fire fighting, not continual improvement.

Standards must be set and followed. For every deviation from the standard, the problem must be identified and eliminated. If possible, improve the standard so the same problem does not recur. As more jobs become standardized, there is less confusion. Training of new operators becomes easier, which is extremely important where people rotate jobs often and work on multiple machines. In short, standards make jobs easier.

Standard Work

Standard work or standard operation is a tool to achieve maximum performance with minimum waste. Standard work is composed of three elements:

1. Cycle time—the time between completion of the last component or product and completion of the next product.
2. Work-sequence—the sequence of work performed by the internal customer.
3. Stock-on-hand—the standard amount of work that is currently underway and necessary to conduct smooth operations.

Standard work is not simply something management demands and operators comply with. It is implemented to involve management and operators in the development process. Anyone should be able to follow the instructions of standard work. Toyota's goal is that a new operator should be able to master the standard work after three days of training on a process.

Combination tables. A standard work combination table displays the information at each work center in such a way that anyone can follow the instructions. The standard work combination table in Figure 8-2 shows the 12 operations in sequence and the walking time; manual time, such as unloading the part; checking and load times; the machine processing time; and the way these elements combine to produce the cycle time. This table is similar to the standard operations routine sheet, but the standard work combination table gives control to the team leader so work being conducted can be reviewed. The revision date on the standard worktable indicates at a glance how quickly improvement activities have taken place. But, even though visual control is useful, the standard work combination tables' main purpose is to further improvement.

Charts. An example of a standard work chart is shown in Figure 8-3. It has two functions. It allocates an operator's areas of responsibility within a work cell or line. Second, it serves to develop standard work based on cycle time.

Standard work can be pursued through the following steps:

1. Standardize current work practices with the assistance of engineers, team leaders, and workers.
2. Locate problem areas.
3. Solve the problem and develop new improved methods.
4. Implement the new methods.
5. If the new methods prove satisfactory, develop new standard work.

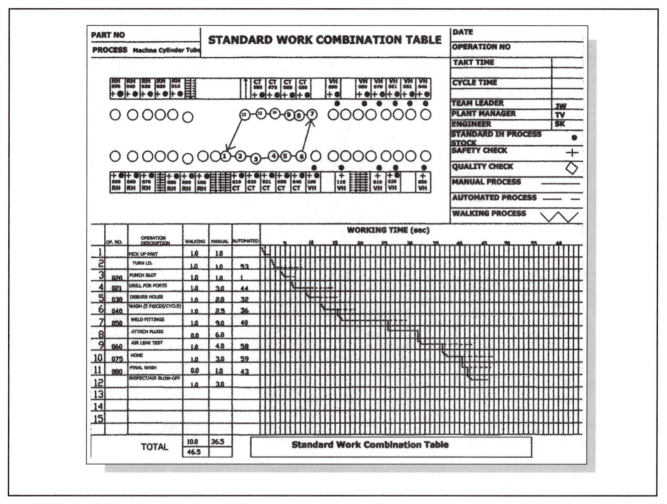

Figure 8-2. Standard work combination table.

6. Require workers to write the standard work combination tables with supervisory assistance.
7. Justify the process over again.

The development and improvement of standard work involves everyone, especially the line operators. It is said that Toyota practices improvement activities to reduce worker task time by as little as half a second. Standardization provides the foundation.

Employee Involvement

Machine failures are associated with the way people think and act. Machine operators, main-tenance crews, and other support people should be trained to understand how their roles interact; and thus, what they must do to support one another.

Operators should learn how to perform routine machine maintenance, be instructed in proper operating procedures, and develop an awareness of the signs associated with early machine deterioration. Maintenance people should learn how to assist production people with routine activities, readjustments, taking corrective actions, and increase maintenance skills. By involving every employee, zero machine trouble can be achieved. Employee

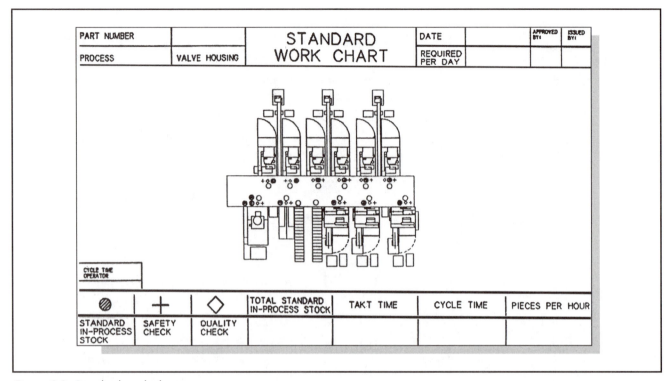

Figure 8-3. Standard work chart.

involvement ensures early detection and early correction of abnormal machine conditions.

Five-S

Toyota developed the Five-S strategy to describe in more detail what proper housekeeping means. The five Ss are:

1. *Seiri-sifting-organization:* Analyze what is available for the task, determine what is required to complete it, and discard what is unnecessary. Anything extra is wasteful. For example, having extra tools, materials, pencils, and paper is waste and should be eliminated.

2. *Seiton-sorting-arrangement:* Once the minimum requirement is determined, there must be "a place for everything and everything in its place." Assign a location for essential items. Make the workplace self-explanatory so everyone knows what goes where. Eliminate confusion and lost time associated with searching for items out of their proper place.

3. *Seiso-sweeping-cleaning:* Once the work site is organized and arrangements are completed, tools must be kept clean and easily obtainable so there is no fumbling or lost time. If something goes wrong, a backup tool should be available, in proper working condition, and stored exactly where it can be readily found.

4. *Seiketsu-spic-and-span-hygiene:* The working environment should be as clean as possible. Hygiene usually complements the other aspects of detailed housekeeping. Effective organization and work arrangement is reinforced by keeping the entire area as clean as possible, particularly the floor.

5. *Shitsuke-strict-discipline:* The other four Ss must be pursued with strict discipline. The rules must be followed and become part of the daily routine. It seems the fifth S is the

most difficult one to follow. Working areas, tooling, and processes begin as organized, arranged, and clean, but over time the workplace becomes messy and deteriorates. This is the second law of thermodynamics in action on the factory floor. All systems degrade with time unless maintained. Daily discipline greatly enhances the Five-S tool.

The Five Ss help to identify problem areas and waste. However, lean production depends on everyone's active involvement. Thus, every member of the factory must follow the Five S principles before results are noticed and sustained on a daily basis.

KAIZEN ACTIVITIES

Kaizen means continuous improvement. It is the constant search for ways to improve the current situation, involving all factory functions.

The Team Concept

In lean production, the team is a key vehicle through which continuous improvement is achieved. Usually a production team works on problems in its specified area of the factory. Along with the production workers, the team may include engineers, maintenance support, and adjunct members the team may need to solve a specific problem. There are two specific teams in lean production: first, there is the cell team made up of a specific cell's workers; second, there are teams composed of members from several cells or flow lines.

Anyone can make a suggestion for improvement. Some suggestions the various teams may implement without approval from anyone above it in the organization. The central point is to give the team the responsibility and the authority to make decisions.

The team leader for each area is the moderator. He or she has veto power over any suggestion. If problems are of a greater scale, the team calls on other teams or departments. The team may use the seven tools of quality (which will be discussed in the next chapter) to gather and present facts about the problem.

Team meetings usually occur during the set-aside time for each cell after the shift. In cases where the cell team needs to stay longer, they receive paid overtime.

Monthly Engineering Meetings

Monthly engineering meetings are a Kaizen activity. Usually manufacturing engineers present problems that they and the production team are attempting to solve. The seven tools of quality often are used in a specific problem presentation format. Here, the lead engineer makes the presentation to a group of engineers, management, and production team leaders. The presentation uses as many visual aids as possible.

After the presentation, the group is asked to suggest possible solutions. The engineer and the group select the options to try the next month. Through this exercise, the engineers and others in the group learn how to become problem solvers. This process is not intended to improve a person's presentation skills or writing skills. The idea is to teach everyone how to use analytical tools to systematically solve problems.

The Japanese demonstrate the ability to use Kaizen tools every day, not just for a presentation. They make it a habit to solve problems in a systematic way. As a result, a systematic, written history of the problem exists. These written histories, called "story boards," include the various implementations for improvement, and the current status of the situation. As with the other elements of lean production, it takes much practice and discipline for this process to become a daily problem-solving habit. The goal, however, is not simply to go through the motions of lean production. The goal is a new, more effective and challenging way of thinking and acting that leads to a lean manufacturing environment.

The Suggestion System

The suggestion system also involves everyone in the factory. It is another mechanism to involve everyone in the production process and to send the message that employees contribute through their minds, not just with their hands. If suggestions are not given through a team, they can be given through a formal cost-reduction program. Ideas are submitted to a cost reduction coordinator who in turn presents the idea to a cost-reduction team. If a production team can handle a suggestion, it will be given to them for review and implementation. If a detailed study is required, a cost-reduction team member is assigned to the project.

The suggestion system and, indeed, all Kaizen activities, encourage continuous improvement through employee involvement. It is a system designed to make improvements quickly without bureaucratic red tape. It is a system that underscores the principle that employees should be given the responsibility to suggest improvements and the authority to implement them.

RELIABILITY

An essential element in a lean manufacturing system is system reliability. Lean systems have serial, linked processes, and by definition, do not have redundant components or duplicated machinery. Therefore, every component must operate properly every time. To accomplish this goal of continuous availability, consider three different, but related areas. These are the hardware systems, the software systems, and the work force. Each system can be studied independently, but the greatest improvements are realized when the three are related.

First defined by *Webster's Dictionary*, *reliability* was originally, "the extent to which an experiment, test, or measuring procedure yields the same results on repeated trials." This definition evolved and now implies complete confidence in and reliance upon a system to the point that no alternate provisions are made. It now encompasses ideals such as consistency, repeatability, maintainability, and robustness. Analyzing a system requires that reliability be measured using some standardized method.

In every factory, different people possess different views of reliability. For example, the plant manager would view reliability as the relative frequency and severity of unanticipated events, and the consequence of the events. The area team leader might view it as the uptime versus the downtime of a process. The engineer would view reliability from the technical point of view with the classical "bathtub" plot of failures (see Figure 8-4).

Studies

Typically, when studying a system, both the number of faults and the time between faults are analyzed. The number of faults are observed in a system during a fixed time interval during which the machine is operational. The time between faults is a measure of the time from one fault occurrence to the next.

Defining a *fault* is a critical step in the process. Often faults are defined as those events that bring an entire process to a halt, but this definition is not the best. A better method of defining faults would be any event that was not anticipated. The concept is further explained in the software system discussion. The second step in the process is to record data and then statistically analyze it. The final step is to consider the faults in the system and try to relate the symptoms exhibited in their root causes. Asking "why" five times is a method to determine the underlying cause of a fault. Trying to fix it immediately is different than making changes based on the symptoms.

Hardware

Hardware systems are defined as those machines necessary to produce the product. These can be anything from a simple screwdriver to an automated welding machine on a factory floor. Identifying faults in hardware systems often is easy since when a machine fails it often has a direct and immediate effect on the

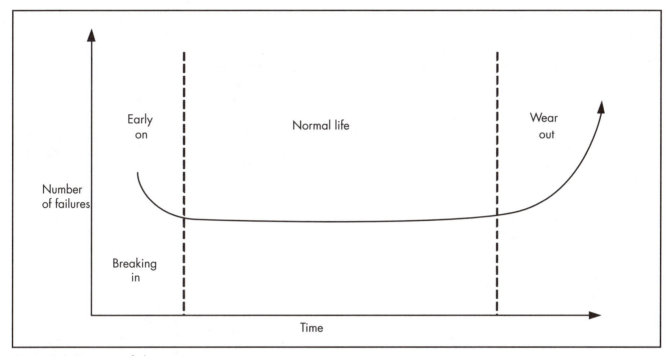

Figure 8-4. Equipment failures versus time.

product or process. Hardware systems can fail in many ways. The machine may fail completely and stop running or a period of operational unavailability due to corrective maintenance may take place. A component failure in the machine or a power failure may cause the machine to be down. The challenge in hardware reliability lies in the identification of the root causes. Difficulty arises because of the often complex relationships present in factories.

Before real improvements can be made to the hardware in a manufacturing cell, the shift from crisis management and reactive maintenance to planned maintenance and service must occur. This is essential and may seem intuitive, but a recent survey of over 70 manufacturing plants in a variety of industries revealed that over half of the maintenance work performed was reactive. That is, over half of the work done to keep machines running was done after the machine stopped running. It is then obvious that reliability of hardware is one of the areas in desperate need of improvement.

The best improvement to machine or hardware reliability is to decrease the number of machines that do the same jobs. In manufacturing cells, this means eliminating duplicate machinery. This may require switching to a two-shift usage of a machine. This transition's advantages are threefold. First, when an error is found, only one machine needs to be checked and corrected. The same is true of process improvements in that only one machine is required to be replaced or upgraded. The second advantage is that it is easier to identify the source of the error and the machine associated with the fault if there is only one source for each process. The third advantage is not a reliability improvement, but rather a general improvement to the process as it simplifies the paperwork required to identify the source of a fault once an error is found.

Slowing the process is another way to improve machine-tool reliability. This can be accomplished without considerable financial cost.

A third equipment reliability improvement is through the implementation of successive checks following each process step. Inspecting at each station allows identification and correction of the causes of errors, before other processes mask those causes.

To improve hardware systems, operators must possess detailed knowledge of equipment operation and be focused on process reliability. Lean manufacturers consistently better their competitors in hardware reliability. A lean manufacturer allows the operator, someone with the required level of knowledge, to be directly involved in hardware design development and improvement. This is in contrast to the manufacturer who has a "specialized" or "focused" study team making recommendations, since this group may not be able to acquire such knowledge.

Reliability requires the operator's involvement in equipment maintenance. Operators do not necessarily need to be able to repair every problem, but more frequently must be able to call upon an advanced technician when a more complex problem develops. Thus, maintenance should work with the operators to return the machine to its original condition. The goal should be to restore the equipment to a like-new condition, rather than just restoration of operational capability.

Software

Software includes data and logic programs that only control the machine tools and material handling devices, and programs for the collection, distribution, and analysis of data essential to the production process. Software may range from the code controlling an automated welder to the software routines reading inventory bar codes. Software should enhance and simplify processes and operations by doing the routine work. However, software is not flexible and has "bugs" in it. The bugs or faults in a software system arise from the errors in logic or the code, or program, and the faults of the computer hardware that interfaces it to the environment. Those errors directly relate to human errors made while creating the code or designing the system components. Frequently, this is due to some overlooked condition in the original software plan or an improperly analyzed operating environment.

When studying software reliability, it is important to track not only the system failures, but also its faults. This is important because while not every error requires the production process to completely halt, it may cause repeated effects and slow the system. To return to the bar code example, suppose tool parts are being scanned. If the system scans in a 2-in. (51-mm) drill bit as a 3-in. (76-mm) drill bit, this does not bring the system to a halt. It could result in surplus inventory, or cause a machine failure if the 3-in. (76-mm) tool crashes into the workpiece during rapid transverse. It could also cause a part defect, a hole 1 in. (25 mm) too deep. Therefore, it is important to track faults and not failures. However, just because the system does not "crash" does not mean it is error-free. Software errors can hide in code and appear long after the system goes into service.

An example of a frequently overlooked fault is wrong information and/or input to a system. A failed input device or incorrect input may be the cause. An input device failure could vary from a smeared lens on a bar-code reader to a worn cable on a keyboard. An inappropriate input could result from a mislabeled container. An inappropriate output or response occurs when the input to a system is correct, but the outputs are incorrect. This reveals an error in the code.

Code reliability is highly dependent on the time allowed between code development and its use in the field. Time must be allowed for review and testing. Obviously, the more the code can be reviewed, the more errors can be identified and corrected.

Software reliability depends on whether the user is creating the code, or simply modifying an existing code for another application. Suppose a program is used to scan bar codes. If the program has been used to scan bar codes in a painting facility, and now the user wants to scan bar codes in the tool area, the modified code possesses better reliability than a new one developed solely for the tool area. Because the software is at least a second-generation program, it has already undergone one complete round of program debugging, so it is already free of most errors that caused faults in the first generation of the code.

But remember this, computers are unreliable but humans are even more unreliable. Any system that depends on humans is unreliable.

Workers

Reliability depends on the internal customers (the workers) required during the production process who keep the process flowing continuously. Worker reliability has been frequently studied and theorized about. Every manager has their own theory on how to keep people on the job and productive.

Ed Adams, Production Machine Builders, LLC, Knoxville, TN, is a design/manufacturing engineer who designs machine tools, workholders, decouplers, poka-yoke devices, and more for manufacturing cells under contract from lean manufacturing vendors.

The following are Ed Adam's Five Ps for people in manufacturing systems.

1. Purpose—do my efforts complement the great task?
   - Make certain that everyone in the organization knows the purpose.
   - Be the best in the world at what we do.
   - Have a design, cost, and quality that permit us to pick our market.
2. Passion—how much am I really holding back?
   - Have a sincere, deep, and unrelenting desire to pursue the purpose.
   - Elevate the intensity, hours, and planning the amount and method.
   - Hire only those willing to do the same.
   - Be accountable for motivating and requiring others to do the same.
3. Pragmatism—could I explain it to my grandmother?

- Learn to use brains and not money.
- Eliminate waste—do not plan it forever, start today with a plan and be ready to improve it.
- Refuse to delegate work that does not add value.
- Stop useless reporting.
4. Participation—can I ask my subordinates for advice?
   - Ultimately, people are our only asset: with them, much can be done. Without them, nothing can be done. The contribution of others limits the effort of one individual.
   - People must be educated, trained, respected, and fairly paid.
   - Arrange responsibilities so individuals have an opportunity to make a meaningful contribution to the organization's success. Without this, self-respect suffers.
   - Use every employee in a humane and challenging manner. Everyone is paid to think and their thoughts are valuable.
5. Principles—is the daily routine predictable? (See Table 8-2.)
   - Standardize as much as possible (all activities). (See Table 8-3.)
   - Train involved personnel in those standard practices.
   - Rules are made to be broken.
   - Only break rules after good participative investigation.
   - Institutionalize continuous improvement.

Final rule—life is more important than work.

THE SECOND SHIFT

The less-than-full-capacity schedule calls for a second eight-hour shift. Perhaps one area that often can be improved in lean manufacturing systems is the use of shift work in the process. According to the Bureau of Labor Statistics, approximately 15.5 million Americans work nontraditionally; that is, either rotating or fixed shifts.

Table 8-2
Training, rewards, involvement, motivation for internal customer

	Tell all workers that part of their job is to make signs and manuals covering:
Job	What it is; how it is done
Machine tool	How to keep it running right and avoid failures
Team activities	Its successes, current performance, and concerns
	Results
	Workers and foremen have primary responsibility for job descriptions and training, rewards, involvement, and motivation. Personnel department has secondary responsibility.

The reasons to be concerned about shift work may not be obvious at first. Workers often report that they feel isolated from management and the rest of the organization on evening/night shifts. A major problem is that they experience a loss of contact with friends and family. Another reason that shift work is demanding: workers can only accomplish certain routine tasks during "normal" business hours. Examples of such tasks are routine automobile maintenance, most shopping, and doctor's visits. This causes most workers to return to daytime schedules on their days off, disrupting their physical well-being.

In addition, the number of routine tasks that must be completed does not vary depending on the amount of worker free time. This means that the worker must still do "X" hours of household chores, and "Y" hours of routine tasks each week no matter how much time is spent at work. Therefore, extra work hours add to fatigue and allow less time for rest.

The result of fatigue, if left uncorrected, is an increase in errors and safety violations on the job. The worker's ability to concentrate on tasks is significantly reduced. Sick days increase as the worker drains energy. In addition, home and family-oriented activities are missed, such as a child's school play or holiday events, and this can cause additional stress at home. These are only typical samples of the variables in the complex reliability equation.

Permanent shifts allow the person the opportunity to adjust to the nontraditional work schedule. Rotating shifts does not disrupt the traditional schedules except during brief periods. The second characteristic used to classify shift work is the speed and direction of the rotation. The rotation between shifts is said to be in a forward direction if a worker moves from the day shift to the evening shift. It is backwards if they move from nights to evenings, evenings to days, or days to nights; typical of a three-shift cycle. The *rotation speed* refers to the amount of time the worker has to adjust to the schedule shifts. This typically varies from a half day to half a week.

The third characteristic of shift work is the work-to-rest ratios. This is important when determining worker alertness. As the ratio increases, more work, less rest, alertness of the worker decreases.

The final distinguishing characteristic is how the worker views the shift. This means, do they see it as regular and/or predictable or sporadic? Workers typically adjust better to shift rotations when they can prepare for them.

Some ways to improve shift work are to avoid permanent night shifts and keep consecutive night shifts to a minimum. Avoid several days of shift work followed by four to seven day "mini-vacations." Try to plan free weekends and keep schedules regular and predictable. In addition, ensure good inter-shift communication by holding organizational and planning

Table 8-3
Housekeeping, station design, and cleanliness

Operator-centered
Tie to JIT implementation so reasons are clear and not perceived as harassment
Precise arrangement to: • Eliminate search time (human travel) • Cut material travel • Cut tool travel
Absolute cleanliness for: • Quality • Safety • Long machine and tool life • Making problems visible

meetings during all shifts, not just the day shift. The 4-8-4-8 schedule discussed earlier uses the four-hour shift break during the day for meetings, maintenance, etc.

TOTAL PRODUCTIVE MAINTENANCE IMPLEMENTATION

There are 12 steps involved in developing and implementing a total productive maintenance program (Nakajima 1988).

1. Announce top management's decision to introduce total preventive maintenance.
   • State the total preventive maintenance objective in the company newsletter.
   • Place articles on total preventive maintenance in the company newspaper.
2. Launch an educational campaign.
   • For managers, offer seminars/retreats according to level.
   • For general workers, provide slide presentations.
3. Create organizations to promote total preventive maintenance.
   • Form special committees at every level.
   • Establish central headquarters and assign staff.
4. Establish basic total preventive maintenance policies and goals.
   • Analyze existing conditions.

   • Set goals.
   • Predict results.
5. Formulate a master plan for total preventive maintenance development.
   • Prepare detailed implementation plans for the five foundational activities.
6. Hold total preventive maintenance kickoff.
   • Invite external customers, and affiliated and subcontracting companies.
7. Improve effectiveness of each piece of equipment.
   • Select model equipment. Form project teams.
8. Develop an autonomous maintenance program.
   • Promote the seven steps.
   • Build diagnostic skills and establish worker procedures for certification.
9. Develop a scheduled maintenance program for the maintenance department.
   • Include periodic and predictive maintenance.
   • Include management of spare parts, tools, blueprints, and schedules.
10. Conduct training to improve operator and maintenance skills.
    • Train leaders together.
    • Have leaders share information with group members.
11. Develop initial equipment management program.
    • Use total preventive maintenance design (maintenance prevention).
    • Use start-up equipment maintenance.
    • Use life-cycle cost analysis.
12. Perfect and raise total preventive maintenance implementation levels.
    • Evaluate for total preventive maintenance prize.
    • Set higher goals.

SUMMARY

Reliability encompasses three elements:

• Hardware—the machine tools that are necessary to produce the product.

- Software—the data and logic systems controlling the machine tools and collecting and distributing data essential to the control of the manufacturing system.
- Work force—the people required to actually operate the machinery within the manufacturing system.

Reliability is significant from three different viewpoints:

- Project managers—uptime versus down time;
- Plant managers—relative frequency and severity of unanticipated events; and
- Equipment manufacturer—financial cost, engineering effort, and reputation costs associated with a new technology.

Do's and Don'ts of Reliability

This is a list of do's and don'ts in the reliability area.

Do:
- understand failures caused by interactions;
- be aware of program timing;
- understand what customers expect;
- use common systems and methods;
- communicate with other engineers;
- track vendor performance;
- design for easy assembly;
- consider external influences; or
- regard reliability as a moving target.

Don't:
- invent during product development process;
- focus too narrowly and forget component interactions; or
- think a job is complete when everything is running smoothly.

Software Guidelines

Think about faults, rather than failures when considering the system's reliability. Faults can be wrong information, disconnected lines, system crashes, or inappropriate responses.

Work Force Guidelines

The following work force guidelines should be kept in mind:

- Avoid permanent (fixed or nonrotating) night shifts.
- Keep consecutive night shifts to a minimum.
- Plan free weekends.
- Keep schedules regular and predictable.
- Ensure good inter-shift communication.
- Do not hold meetings during day shifts only.

Support Routines

In a lean-production factory system, support routines reinforce the core principles of stability and continuous improvement through employee involvement. This is where machine and work routine standards lend to workplace and production-process stability. Preventive maintenance, or repairing machinery before a breakdown occurs, creates stable, predictable production environments. Likewise, the Five-S strategy for keeping the workplace clean, orderly, and ready smoothes the road to effective work.

And last, on the stable platform created by other support routines, continuous improvement activities and the suggestion system draw the minds and energies of the work force into the production process. Using active teams, employee suggestions, and systematic approaches to problem solving, allows continuous improvement through people.

The primary goal of preventive maintenance is to prevent failure of equipment before it would actually occur. The objective of total productive maintenance is to increase productivity, improve processes, increase the percentage of time equipment operates, and minimize the number of required steps by keeping an operation simple. This program requires heavy involvement from production workers.

Chapter 9
Refining Lean Production

The lean production system must be refined to bring it to maximum productivity. This refining entails leveling, balancing, and synchronizing. These functions must be carried out in the proper sequence.

Knowledge of the definitions of these terms is critical. They are key aspects of lean production manufacturing systems.

- *Leveling* smoothes production by making the final assembly a mixed model, thus creating a level demand for components.
- *Balancing* matches the quantity produced by cells and subassembly cells to leveled demand.
- *Synchronizing* matches the time to produce the component or subassembly to that required by the system. (This is also called *build to sequence* where the supplier builds components to match the sequence of the final assembly line.)
- *Sequencing* sends subassemblies (not made in sync) to final assembly in the order and in the build sequence.

LEVELING

Leveling is the process of planning and executing an even production schedule. In an ideal situation, a lean factory will produce an even distribution of products every hour, each shift. That is, every item should be manufactured the same way, every day. Balancing is setting the rate of production to match the rate of consumption. The principle behind leveling and balancing is simply to regulate final production output and final assembly to minimize demand spikes.

Final assembly should not pull products from upstream subassembly cells, manufacturing cells, or production processes in a manner that causes production to fluctuate or peak. Fluctuations cause production planners to set production rates on upstream processes at the maximum levels of demand spikes. This, of course, results in overproduction and excess inventory, or waste. On the other hand, it is desirable to have maximum flexibility in final assembly lines so a company can produce to dealer orders and not to stock. This means that a manufacturing system must be flexible. For example, suppose an order normally needs to be filled four weeks after it is received. If the actual manufacturing lead-time is two weeks, the system should be able to change over to meet the customer's desires and easily fill the order.

Smoothing Final Assembly

Lean manufacturing companies have yearly production plans that forecast how many items they plan to produce. A yearly plan includes a running two-month plan. Product types and quantities are forecasted two months before the delivery month in question. A detailed plan is formulated one month before manufacturing starts. The amount produced daily is the result of the monthly production plan. Leveling and balancing are important concepts incorporated into the daily schedule.

Leveling or smoothing tasks is based on average total daily production and the averaged quantity of each variety of products in this total. For example, suppose a final assembly line produces 10,000 vehicles monthly (as shown in Table 9-1). This would make it necessary to schedule and produce 500 automobiles a day and 10,000 in 20 days. The factory would work two eight-hour shifts per day, separated by two four-hour time blocks. Each shift would have 480 working minutes. Suppose that 300 variations (options) of these automobiles were being produced. It would be necessary to balance variations in the daily schedule. Continuing with the example, suppose that three major model types were being produced. The daily average quantities of each type and the sequence on the final assembly can be seen in Table 9-1. This is called a *mixed-model final assembly line*. There should not be any setup time between models in this situation. Workers on such lines need to make at least one of each model every day so they do not forget how to assemble each model.

The assembly line receives next month's schedule from the production control department in the latter part of the current month. Each model's daily average requirements are calculated. Once a manufacturing cell or process receives a monthly forecast of average daily usage of parts it makes, the process can adapt its operations to the new schedule. For example, the load on a machine may normally be set at 90% of capacity, and each worker may operate up to 10 processes. When demand is increased, temporary workers must be hired and each worker runs eight machines.

Machines that reach 100% utilization must be examined and work must be off-loaded to less-utilized machines. Work must be simplified and standardized so new operators are able to quickly achieve proficiency. Overtime can accommodate short-term increases. It can yield up to a 37.5% increase in production. Process improvements that net slack time can increase output if necessary.

When demand decreases, the steps necessary to correct for this decrease are considerably more difficult. Temporary workers must be moved or laid off in manufacturing areas. Cell cycle times must be increased, meaning each worker operates more machines. Also, cycle times on assembly lines must decrease, again reducing the number of required workers. Extra workers are transferred to other areas of the plant or work reduced schedules. An important goal of lean manufacturing is to operate the system with a minimum number of workers. On the other hand, it is not necessary to operate with a minimum number of processes. Having excess machine capacity means that when demand increases, only temporary workers are needed to effectively increase the production rate, and subsequently, the output.

Leveling the schedule is not usually easy. Suppose (as shown in Figure 9-1) there is an unbalanced monthly schedule, which is typical of the job shop. During the first week, suppose such a system produces about 100 units; the

Table 9-1
Mixed-model final assembly sequencing to level the system

Assembly Sequence
4DS, 2DS, 4DS, MV, 4DS, 2DS, 4DS, MV, 4DS, 2DS

Model	Monthly Demand	Daily Demand*	Takt Time
4-door sedan (4DS)	5,000	250	1.92 minutes
2-door sedan (2DS)	2,500	125	3.84 minutes
Minivan (MV)	2,500	125	3.84 minutes

Takt = $\frac{480 \text{ minutes} \times 2 \text{ shifts}}{500}$ = 1.92 minutes per vehicle

*Assuming 20 working days in the month

next week another 100; and the third week 200. So, the system must output 600 units in the fourth week, creating a classic end-of-the-month crisis where everything is a rushed order. To level such a schedule, the month can be divided into two parts. Next, two-week periods can be divided into one-week periods specifying daily quantities. Then, the actual production profile becomes nearly equivalent to the leveled schedule profile. Leveling a production schedule greatly improves the system's overall behavior.

Production Leveling

Heijunka is the Japanese term for production leveling and a defining goal of lean production. It is one of the central reasons for manufacturing stability. In some factories, production levels jump to peak capacities at times. At other times, production levels are at low volumes. Changes in production volumes are inefficient and result in waste. The more changes made in production volumes, the more waste created.

Waste is created because swings in production volume mean equipment is underutilized, thus wasting some of the machinery's capacity. This means that operators have lost the pace of their work, or the easy rhythm that lets them exert the least amount of effort over the least amount of time to complete a task. Swings in production mean that when production demand is at capacity, people must work overtime, raising a product's cost.

In a typical mass-production factory, goods are produced in as large a quantity as possible to reduce setups. If products cannot be shipped until the end of the month, excessive inventory must be accommodated. Double and triple handling is required and there is a risk of product damage or deterioration. If quality problems occur in the final assembly stage, parts will need to be reworked or scrapped according to the severity of the defect.

Leveling production for a given period develops steady material flow and, consequently, eliminates much waste. If each operator knows what to expect, he or she will be better able to control a production area. Production then becomes more manageable and process flow improvements become easier. In addition, when different products are produced in a mixed fashion every day, the finished goods inventory level is lowered. Leveled production also reduces the risk of overproduction.

Production smoothing allows people to focus on production activities without worrying about sudden changes in scheduling or expediting work. Combined with quick setups and manufacturing cells, leveling can improve line performance and reduce parts-shortage problems.

Advantages and Disadvantages

The following advantages can flow from leveled production:

- Highs and lows of the production process smooth out.
- There is inventory reduction.
- Transportation and handling costs reduce.
- Overall productivity increases in the factory due to waste elimination.
- Direct labor hours may decrease.
- Part suppliers are provided with leveled loads.
- The quality system is enhanced with successive checks and poka-yoke devices implemented to prevent defects.

The following disadvantages also may occur:

- Setup changeovers can be more frequent.
- Workers must be trained in multiple operations, routine maintenance, continuous improvement, and quality control.
- Jigs and fixtures must be redesigned to accommodate multipurpose use.

By keeping production volume constant, problems are more easily exposed and corrected. Lay the proper foundation, outlined in steps one through four (discussed in Chapter 2) before making radical changes in production scheduling. For example, first reduce setup times, rearrange the work layout into lean production cells to match product flow, increase

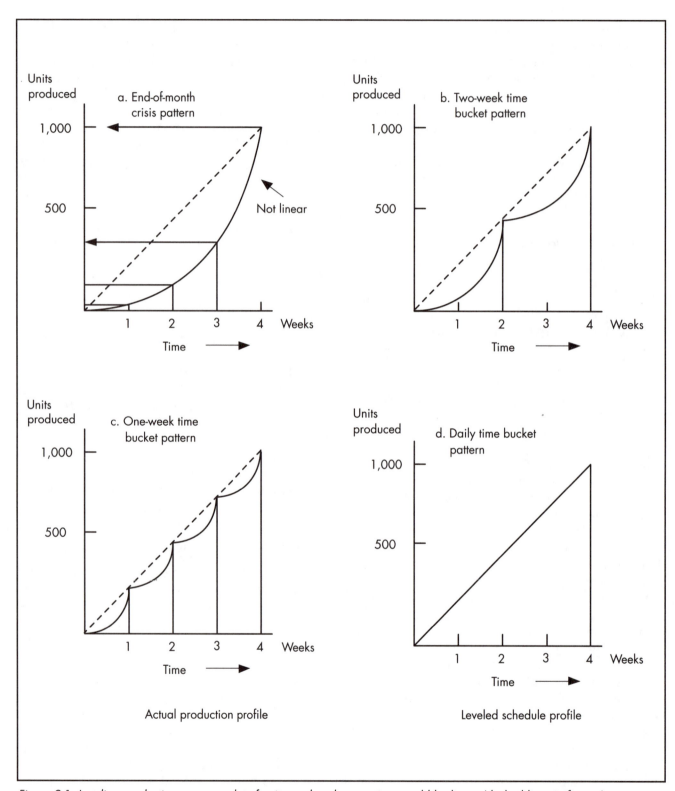

Figure 9-1. Leveling production means a plot of units produced versus time would be linear (dashed lines in figures).

cycle time stability, reduce scrap, and design poka-yoke devices into the process.

Workers first should be trained in principles, techniques, and lean production system tools. Their approach to manufacturing should have evolved to the point where they look for problems to be exposed. In short, successful product leveling needs to be built upon the foundations discussed in the previous chapters. If it is not, the results can easily be mass confusion.

MIXED MODEL FINAL ASSEMBLY

To perform leveled production as shown in Figure 9-1, a mixed-model assembly line must be created. The following are the steps for designing a mixed-model assembly line.

1. Determine cycle time
2. Compute a minimum number of processes.
3. Prepare a precedence diagram showing the relationships among elemental jobs.
4. Line balance (not the same as balancing the cells' production rates).
5. Determine the sequence schedule for introducing various products to the line.
6. Determine the length of the operations of each process.

Determine Cycle Time

In a cell, the cycle time is the number of minutes it takes for the product to complete a production cycle; that is, the total time it spends in the workstations and that cell's processes. In the final assembly, the cycle time is called the takt time. *Takt time* is determined by dividing the operating hours per day by the necessary output per day (the daily demand) and this sets the pace for the entire manufacturing system.

$$D_D = \frac{O_m}{M}$$ (9-1)

where:

D_D = necessary output per day
O_m = necessary output per month
M = number of operating days per month

$$C_t = \frac{H}{D_D}$$ (9-2)

where:

C_t = cycle time, minutes/part
H = number of operating minutes per day

$$T_t = \frac{1}{P_R}$$ (9-3)

where:

T_t = Takt time, minutes/part
P_R = production rate

The necessary output per month comes from the long-range forecast and actual orders. Once the cycle time is determined, production control develops standard operations for each of the multifunctional workers on the final assembly line. Standard operations are the best arrangement of man, materials, machines, and methods to produce the required amount of products efficiently. Standard operations are based on the product demand. As the demand changes, so do the standard operations and the takt times.

Takt time represents external customers' demand. It is important because it determines equipment requirements, work balance and flow, scheduling, staffing, and capital expenditures.

Preparing a Precedence Diagram

The third step in designing the mixed-model assembly line is the preparation of a precedence diagram. A *precedence diagram* shows the relationships among elemental jobs. This is simply identifying which job must go before another. The precedence relationship determines the sequence of operations on the final assembly line to allow for the proper product flow down the line.

Line Balancing

The fourth step is line balancing. Line balancing involves making the amount of work and, thus, the time it takes to perform the work (manual tasks at each station) as equal as possible (in terms of time). Task times must be less than the takt time. Generally speaking, the line-balancing problem has been solved using computer algorithms, which attempt to distribute the tasks to minimize the idle time at each station. The line balance can change if the product demand changes. When the line runs products that differ, then usually the standard operations, takt time, and line balance also change. That is the problem with mixed-model final assembly.

Determining the Sequence Schedule

The sequence schedule for introducing models to the mixed-model assembly line has two main goals. These are:

- Leveling the load (total assembly time) at each station within the line—this is still called "line balancing," but now planners and workers must deal with automobiles with two doors and with four doors coming down the same line.
- Keeping constant the rate at which each part on the line is consumed—this is referred to as "leveling demand" for subassemblies and components.

Not all product operations have the same or meet the takt time in mixed-model final assembly. Some may be shorter or longer than the takt time. If two products that exceed takt time are introduced to a line one after another, then a delay most likely occurs and the line eventually stops. For this reason, products with long takt times must be introduced to the line followed by short takt times. Workers assist each other across station boundaries. Workloads are smoothed such that each station finishes an operation at about the same takt time.

When mixed-model production occurs, inventory levels also are affected. That is, finished-goods inventory levels in the batch-production modes are higher than the levels of mixed-production modes (Figure 9-1).

Scheduling a mixed-model, final-assembly line to achieve good line balance is a key component of designing the entire production process. This requires great flexibility in the final assembly line at those stations that deal with different components or subassemblies on different models. Mixed-model final assemblies are beneficial because they reduce inventory, decrease the need for line changeover, and meet a variety of demand levels for multiple models.

After the calculation of monthly and daily schedules, determination of the daily sequence is critical. These schedules set the assembly order of various models through assembly lines. For example, a sequence may consist of vehicle Type A, then B, then A, then C, etc. This sequence schedule is communicated only to those stationed at the beginning of a final assembly line and not to any of the workers in upstream processes or subassembly lines. This is the most fundamental aspect of the linked-cell information system that differentiates it from other systems. The various upstream processes and subassembly lines receive only rough monthly forecasts. Supervisors of upstream processes must schedule their work forces on the basis of this rough monthly schedule. As a final assembly line builds a vehicle by pulling components from kanban stores near lines, the withdrawal kanban for these parts is detached and sent to specific upstream manufacturing or assembly cells. The withdrawal kanban then signals the upstream process to produce more components in exact quantities to be used and removed. Hence, the upstream processes do not need detailed production schedules. Kanban informs upstream processes of downstream needs as components are pulled toward final assembly.

Workers on final assembly lines must know only what type of vehicle they are building next. This information is provided to them from the central computer via a printer or computer monitor. Information about vehicle types being produced is transmitted to those at the start of the assembly line via a computer terminal. This terminal also provides labels for each vehicle. Information on labels instructs assembly line workers to build specific vehicles.

Major subassembly lines such as engine and transmission lines can also use this labeling system. Meanwhile, other subassembly cells, manufacturing cells, and processes use kanban to control production quantities and rates.

Obtaining the best sequence schedule of mixed-model, final-assembly production is a difficult task. The perfect model for sequencing entails keeping the speed and quantity of withdrawal constant for every component. That is, the system needs to have variation of consumed part quantities at final assembly held to a minimum; the consumption rate of each component part must be maintained as constant as possible. This is obviously impossible for complex assemblies, but an attempt to achieve such a status should be made.

LONG-RANGE FORECASTING

The Toyota production system is renowned for inventory turns of 70 or more per year, while being able to quickly respond to special customer orders. Toyota likes to call this an instant delivery system. It has a strong market-research program and forecasting methods to predict long-term demand for vehicles. These forecasts are highly reputed for their accuracy. How does Toyota do this? Does Toyota know something about long-range forecasting that the rest of world does not know? To understand the answers to these questions requires that understanding how the Toyota production system works.

Toyota produces a special-ordered vehicle in two days or less, but the production period for processing raw material to completion exceeds this time. The body, frame, and various other parts are already processed according to a fixed production plan, while painting and certain subassembly and final assembly processes take place over one or two days.

Toyota performs long-range forecasts and market surveys of over 60,000 people twice a year and investigates other trends every two months. As a result of this forecast methodology, Toyota constructs a monthly production plan that is fixed; it then breaks that plan into daily manufacturing orders. For example, deciding the quantity of vehicles to be produced in the month of March is finalized in early February. Precise daily schedules are planned and production is leveled to produce results such as making the same amount of every product every day. This daily schedule is only communicated to final assembly workers and information regarding specific demands for subassembly and component parts is communicated back from the same final assembly workers via their pull system of inventory control, known as *kanban*. In this way the forecast plan is converted to a production plan only for those orders received and accepted. In 1970, Toyota, under the leadership of Taiichi Ohno, invented a new kind of manufacturing system capable of producing large volumes of parts in small lots to make this work. Today, in contrast, the American system is a combination of the functional job shop and flow lines that produce large volumes with large lots and large amounts of inventory.

Many US companies are still using job shop systems slowly adopting lean production practices. Small-lot production requires that the job shop is eliminated and replaced with a linked-cell system where setup time between different products or component parts is eliminated and the final assembly line operates on a mixed-model schedule. Subassembly and component manufacturing are done in cellular manufacturing systems using multifunctional workers. Workers run numerous processes and are directly responsible for product quality and low-level maintenance of processes. Cells are linked to form a synchronized, integrated manufacturing system, which has as its ultimate goal the manufacturing of parts one at a time. Inventory levels are greatly reduced and manufacturing lead times are markedly shortened. This new system can quickly and easily respond to fluctuations in demand and allow for shorter long-range forecasting while increasing forecasting accuracy.

BALANCING

As the level of inventory in the factory shrinks and processes become more tightly linked, production rates become more closely coordinated. Ideally, the cycle time of each fabricated part and subassembly would be identical to the final assembly line's takt times. Balancing output of processes with final assembly carries over to balancing labor and processes. In a traditional factory, balancing entails shifting people and tasks along the assembly line. This creates a balanced flow line. In a lean production factory, balancing extends upstream to subassembly cells and component parts (the manufacturing cells).

As a production job shop converts to lean manufacturing, different types of machines are rearranged into manufacturing cells. The machines in these cells are arranged to process parts conveyed between them one piece at a time. Inventory between machines disappears when only one part flows between machines, which led some people to call this a zero inventory system. As pointed out in Chapters 6, 7, and 8, attention to machine setup time, quality, and total preventive maintenance (TPM) is essential.

Balancing Cells

The critical first stage of building a lean system is cellular manufacturing. Processes are placed near one another, usually in U-shaped designs as shown in Figure 9-2. Cells consist of small, simple pieces of equipment. Workers walk predetermined paths on precise time schedules. If possible, cells are designed so that cycle times match the takt times of final assembly lines. Output now can be balanced with assembly line needs. That is, cell output over short periods of time is matched to the rate of part use by subsequent operations and ultimately to final assembly. The kanban link between cycle and takt times absorbs any mismatching of cell production and usage rates by subassemblies or final assemblies. The fewer mismatches, the smaller the volumes are in kanban inventory links.

Suppose a cell is making two products, A and B, which a subassembly cell uses in equal quantities. Half of the time a cell is making Product A. While it is making Product A, there must be a sufficient amount of Product B in the kanban loop to meet subassembly demand for Product B, assuming there are no other problems in the manufacturing cell.

Different parts within the family produced by a cell may not require that the processes be utilized in the cell. Parts usually require different processing times, but parts made in one cell should require labor times in the same general range. This is a general requirement so different numbers of workers are not required to be in the cell for each different part in the family. This does not mean that total machining time between two parts must be balanced or equal because machining times are decoupled from the cycle time. The cycle time depends on the number of machines a worker visits on a trip around the cell.

Adding or subtracting workers changes the output rate from cells. That is, workers often cross product boundaries when they perform tasks on different parts during a single loop. However, during any fixed schedule period, the number of workers within a cell remains constant. When a scheduled period changes, personnel requirements may also change. Occasionally a cell is redesigned and the number of machines is changed. This causes the work pattern in the cell to change. These changes are necessary so cycle times of parts are matched with cell cycle times required by the new final assembly schedule.

Workers who perform only a single function, or experience only line balance problems with equipment fixed in place, may find that lean manufacturing's rebalancing is difficult to accept. Cells are designed with simple, single-cycle machines and equipment modified for flexibility. A properly trained operator should be able to operate and set up every machine in a cell. This is a goal but not a prerequisite for starting up a cell.

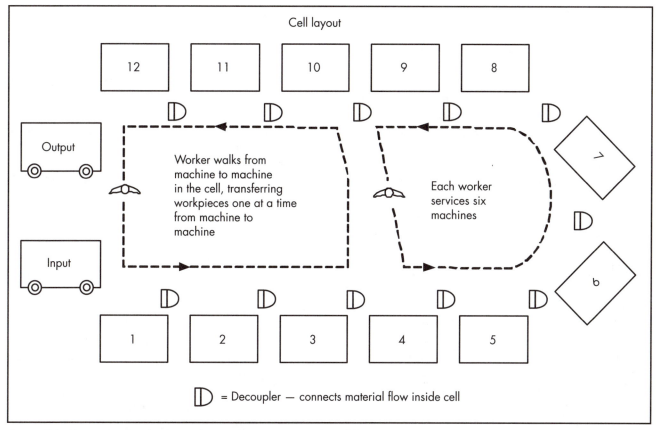

Figure 9-2. Manned cell with two workers making two parts, A and B.

Supervisors are responsible for maintaining data needed to determine how many workers are required for different cycle times in a cell. This job does not require large amounts of data, but rather a set of rules based on past performance, trial and error, and perhaps a calculation or two. The industrial engineering department can assist in solving complex balancing problems.

Balancing a cell is easier when the required cycle time is greater than 30 seconds. If the needed cycle time is less than 30 seconds, then replication of an existing cell should be considered, followed by a division of parts so the new cell is more dedicated. This requires twice as much equipment. However, since machines are simple, single-cycle automatics, this may not be a large capital investment.

Internal Customers

An important principle of lean manufacturing is that the internal customers can be the most important resource of a manufacturing organization, as well as one of the most limiting factors.

In the lean production factory, processes produce only the amount of product required. Lean design concentrates on worker utilization. Using processes to make more than is required violates the basic principles of lean production. Overproduction means that eventually inventory builds in a manufacturing system. This excess must be stored, tracked, and retrieved—all costly and wasteful operations. Frequently, these wasteful operations lead to the purchase of automatic storage-and-retrieval systems that require a maintenance person to keep running, a computer system to track, another worker to program the automatic storage, a retrieval-system computer, etc. This scenario is a total waste of valuable resources and it lowers an organization's ability to compete.

Lean production uses a minimum number of workers to achieve daily demands by balancing factory operations. Modifying a cycle by collecting cells into lines makes it easy to balance tasks among workers. Elements of work are shifted from one worker to another until operations are balanced. This may result in a situation in which a worker is no longer needed in the cell and can be assigned to another cell.

What can be done at full capacity if the production rate must be increased (and the cycle time lowered)? This situation presents a lack of flexibility at full capacity. One problem-solving approach would be to develop two cells with half the number of workers. This process doubles the cycle time while producing the necessary number of parts. For instance, five workers might be able to produce 57-58 parts per hour, just two or three less than the required 60. A little overtime would permit workers in cells to meet system-level requirements. Notice the objective of improvement is not to reduce cycle time. Changing cycle time only is necessary for meeting schedule changes dictated by final assembly. The objective is to minimize the amount of required labor while producing at a rate that yields parts needed for final production. Changes resulting only in excessive inventory stored in the manufacturing system are deceptive and really do not improve productivity.

The replication or duplication of the cell adds to variation in the product or parts a system produces. No two cells produce exactly the same parts. Two cells producing the same components violate the lean production concept of reducing variability. Usually, Cell A is dedicated to Product A and Cell B to Product B, while retaining the flexibility of doing Product A in Cell B, or visa versa should there be a decrease in demand.

Plant Balancing

The steps for balancing an entire factory are:

- balancing the rate of parts production to match the final assembly-line rate (overall cycle times are the inverse of production rates);
- adjusting work content and cycle times at each cell or station until times match system cycle times as nearly as possible; and
- trying to off-load work content of selected stations until selected stations are no longer needed.

The final assembly cycle time requirements should link subassembly cells and line areas. The notion that there are no storage areas on a factory floor is incorrect, however. The idea is to minimize material in these storage areas. The best places to minimize storage areas are near points of use and close enough to producing areas so operators have visual signals of part usage (Figure 9-3).

Linked and subassembly cells must be balanced to final-assembly cycle time. For example, if vehicles are assembled with a cycle time of 60 seconds, then steering gears and wheels should have cycle times of 60 seconds. Each vehicle needs one steering assembly, so steering assembly gears should have cycle times of 60 seconds as well.

In a factory, events rarely work out exactly as planned. Therefore, a continuous effort should be made to reduce deviations between the rate set by final assembly and the production rates of upstream elements. Real production improvement results from matching upstream processes closely to the rhythm set by the final assembly takt time.

Traditional line balancing refers to balancing the amount of work or labor at each station, regardless of cycle time. There is no attempt to achieve overall factory balance. In lean manufacturing, balancing the line or plant also refers to balancing material flow. The pull system of material control balances material flow. Material balance and labor balance are

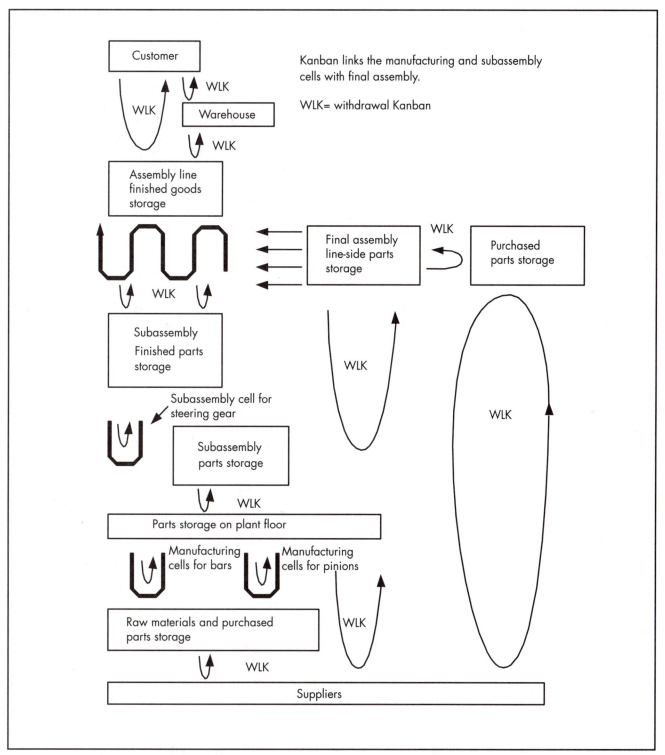

Figure 9-3. In the lean manufacturing system, manufacturing and assembly cells are linked to the final assembly area by kanban inventory links or storage areas.

dependent on each other. The primary indicator that labor is out of balance is an excess or shortage of material. The amount of work in process between cells results from unbalanced cycle times. The objective is to set cycle times as required by the schedule and then to shift tasks and operations accordingly. This results in less and less work for one worker, and eventually this worker can move to another area. It must be remembered that systems are designed to optimize labor content, as well as improve labor efficiency.

Plant balancing is a dynamic, ongoing process. Normally, a plant must be rebalanced whenever the production rate changes. The fear of losing line balance is the major reason for reluctance to stop a balanced assembly line once it is up and running. This is also true of an entire factory. There are countermeasures to this difficulty including:

- Visible signaling systems, like andon, allow a system to respond to temporary variations in part-usage rates and to changes in product mix.
- Flexibility built into cells permits a system to quickly adapt to requests for increased or decreased production rates or to changes in product mix.
- Less-than-full-capacity scheduling means keeping a little slack time, perhaps 20-30 minutes per shift at each cell, so a system can respond to variations from the planned schedule. This adds flexibility to a system.

Since a plant's schedule changes periodically, the operations also may have to change. Manufacturing cells and subassembly cells can usually continue working without rebalancing if the cycle times required do not vary more than about 10%. Cycle-time variations beyond 10% usually require rebalancing. Detailed planning for production must take this into account.

MANUFACTURING CELL TYPES

Manufacturing cells are developed according to three basic strategies: process, part geometry, or product. These strategies do not offer every available approach to cell formation, but rather, they offer techniques from which some benefits of cellular manufacturing can be quickly achieved. They result in grouping simple, flexible machines to meet required cycle times, while eliminating inventory, floor space, transportation distance, and quality problems. Cells can compete with multi-station, high-speed automatic equipment because they can be set up and debugged quickly, therefore offering manufacturing flexibility.

Process Cells

Process cells are useful when geometric information about parts is not available or when parts appear to be geometrically dissimilar. This method assists in defining cells when an understanding of the manufacturing processes is limited.

Geometric data is unnecessary to create cells based on processes. Parts produced by one key process are selected and then a cell is built around that process. Current routings are examined to find key machine tools and select candidate parts with common routings. Cells then are developed for the part families.

Part Geometry Cells

Part geometry cells are used when geometric information is available, associated manufacturing processes are well known, and parts look the same or similar. In other words, geometry-based cells group parts based on common geometric characteristics. With process cells, current production data is used to examine routings. However, new routings are then developed for target part groups based on part-feature analyses. Consideration is given to group tooling, machine loading, parts, and usage.

Product Cells

Product-focused cells are mini-factories dedicated to producing a product such as an assembly, a subassembly, or a finished primary part. These cells are intended to minimize inventory and may be cells that link to assembly lines in support of Just-in-time manufacturing. A bill of materials details component parts that are going into the subassembly where a common routing is developed for the component parts. Many times a factory within a factory results when incorporating both process and geometry-based cells, both of which are focused on a common assembly family.

SYNCHRONIZATION

Synchronization, refers to the process of timing movement of material between portions of the assembly line and major subassemblies. Even when material quantities have been leveled and balanced, unnecessary storage of in-process material can occur between unsynchronized operations. However, once operations are leveled, synchronization is just a matter of efficient, integrated scheduling. Leveling must precede synchronization because it helps eliminate process delays that make synchronization difficult.

Subassemblies that are synchronized for final assembly in the automobile industry are large items such as seats, panels, headliners, cockpits, doors, and engines. These subassemblies are all specific to certain vehicle models. They are made in sequence with the final assembly and delivered to designated workstations on the final assembly line at the same time as the vehicle needing that subassembly. Only the best lean manufacturers can accomplish synchronization, since any subassembly-line failure can also stop a final assembly line. Conversely, if final assembly is stopped, then synchronized subassembly cells and lines also must stop so elements stay in sync. Production processes that have stopped must restart together.

Yo-i-don Synchronization

Yo-i-don in Japanese means, ready, set, go. It is the name given to a method of synchronizing startup of manual manufacturing processes or operations. This method is not used with a

mechanical transportation mechanism such as a conveyor line. In these situations, the final assembly line would pace the line doing the door assembly. So, suppose the left front door comes off a vehicle at Station 26, goes by overhead conveyor to the door subassembly line, and gets fully stuffed with components (windows, door handles, speakers, etc.). It would then return to the final assembly line at Station 110, where the door would be reinstalled on the same car body from which it was earlier removed. Thus, the door line must be kept in sync with the final assembly line.

The yo-i-don method is used in body welding. Operations for the body may be divided into three primary processes such as underbody, side body, and top body (Figure 9-4). The underbody and side-body processes in Figure 9-4 can be divided into six processes and three sub-processes, U_1-U_6 and S_1-S_3, respectively. The top sides and bottom pieces come together at B_1.

Suppose a final assembly line is producing one unit per minute for the system takt time or factory cycle time. Operations at each of the subassembly, processing, and main assembly areas must be completed in one minute or some

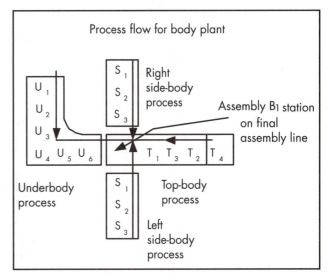

Figure 9-4. Synchronization of body parts in spot-welding lines.

multiple of one minute. Since each car needs a body, the car-body welding area produces one body every minute. Workers in each area must complete tasks and pass weldments to subsequent workstations at the end of prescribed one-minute-cycle times.

After completing assigned tasks and passing the weldment downstream, each operator presses a job completion button. This button turns on a green light on the andon, indicating that a certain task has been completed (Figure 9-5). (The *andon* is a signal board that hangs over the workplace.) At the end of each cycle, a red light illuminates if there are any incomplete tasks. When this happens, adjacent workers and supervisors provide assistance. The entire line comes to a halt when a red andon light illuminates. When an incomplete task has been completed, the red light is turned off and the process cycle starts again, with all processes beginning in sync. This method synchronizes plant operations by getting them all to start together in each cycle. The andon board is called the "bingo board" in some factories.

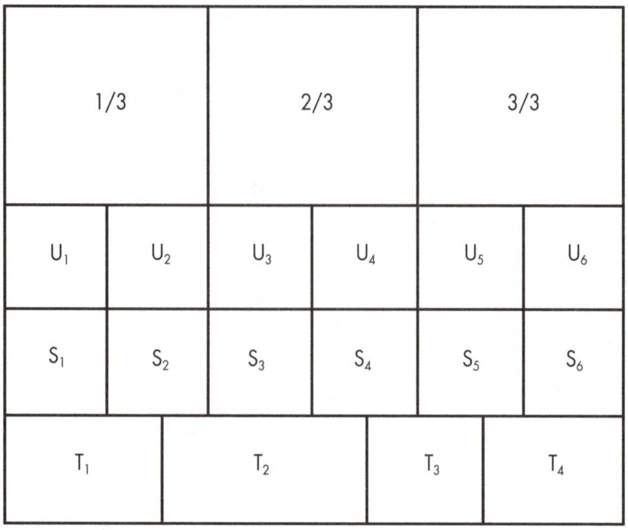

Standard Operations

Standard operations are designed to allow manufacturing areas and assembly cells to use a minimum number of workers. The first goal of standard operations is to achieve high productivity through efficient work. This means working without wasted motions. The *standard operations routine* is a standardized order in which each worker performs various tasks. Each worker is expected to write down operations, and this listing is compared with the standard operations routine. This procedure helps ensure that new workers are performing the correct steps in the correct sequence. A standardized operations routine sheet is used for this purpose.

Standard operations' second goal is to achieve a balance among operations and processes in compliance with the final assembly cycle time. Product quantity in a given period determines final assembly cycle time.

Figure 9-5. Andon for the body shop—a signal board indicating progress at each stage of the system.

Therefore, the cycle time concept should be incorporated into standard operations.

With the use of cams, micro-switches, and similar devices, different types of machines can be synchronized to the same production rate by the following methods:

- At completion of each machining cycle, the machine is stopped automatically and its components and attachments are returned to the start position.
- If there is space to hold a finished workpiece on the output side of a process (the downstream decoupler), the workpiece can be automatically ejected from machine to decoupler. If an empty place is not available, the machine must wait until space is available. An empty decoupler provides a signal to the upstream machine to make another part.
- When an unprocessed workpiece is available in an upstream decoupler, it is automatically fed to the machine, using guides to position it without human assistance.
- When an unprocessed workpiece is located and clamped into the machine, the next machining cycle is started.

Leveling quantities and synchronizing processes can significantly reduce delays, thus greatly reducing manufacturing throughput time. For example, using one-piece flow to eliminate lot delays for two serial processes reduces throughput time. The multiplier effect of eliminating process delays and lot delays with one-piece part movement in cells may improve throughput time to 98% if 10 processes are involved.

The final goal of leveling is achieving a minimum quantity of material as the standard quantity of work in process. In other words, only the minimal part quantities necessary to complete standard operations are kept on hand. This goal forces elimination of excessive work-in-process inventories in links. Therefore, standard operations must consist of cycle time, standard-operating routines, and minimum quantities of material. Concurrently, the elimination of accidents, breakdowns, and defects is also a major component of standard operations.

SUMMARY

Lean production and manufacturing systems have evolved from the strategies of successful factories. Lean principles are based on linked-cell manufacturing systems. Taiichi Ohno, Vice President of manufacturing for Toyota created the linked-cell system, but he never gave it a name. He simply referred to it as the Toyota production system. Toyota brought the strategy to the US and it has since been implemented in many forms.

Leveling and balancing are important features in lean manufacturing. Leveling smooths the daily production schedule so the demand for subassemblies and components is the same everyday— same volume and mix. Balancing means the upstream elements produce the necessary daily quantities. Similarly, when leveling and balancing are applied to lean manufacturing cells, they regulate and may reduce the labor content. Synchronizing the system matches the production rates of subassembly processes to the rhythm of final assembly. These subsystems produce goods in the same sequence and at the same rate as the final assembly.

A factory without production smoothing is often consumed by excess inventory and/or starved for parts. Upstream processes can experience inventory overflow due to bottlenecks, while downstream processes can wither away waiting for stock to arrive. The proper application of leveling and balancing will remedy these situations and provide key building blocks for a successful factory.

Chapter 10
Production and Inventory Control

Production control strives to answer the following scheduling questions:

- Where is material needed?
- When is it needed?
- How much is required?
- How does it get there?

Inventory control strives to determine the material levels throughout the factory using mathematical models to try to minimize the costs of materials versus the storage cost. This chapter discusses the integration of production and inventory control functions into the lean production and management system.

The traditional method for production and inventory control evolved out of the work of F. W. Taylor, Henry Gantt, and Frank Gilbreth, the first industrial engineers who developed planning and scheduling strategies for the job shop. The methodology they developed is called a *push system* because it pushes material through a plant according to a master production schedule and material requirements planning (Figure 10-1). These documents use forecasted demands and economic order quantity calculations to schedule the manufacture of a product, usually in large lots. Basically, computer algorithms determine dates for raw material purchasing and for delivery to the customer. Super-fast equipment is inserted between large work-in-process inventories to help deliver goods on time. Inventory in the plant is difficult to control because the control tools are of a planning nature, with little or no ability to actually manipulate or control inventory.

KANBAN

The lean method of production and inventory control uses a pull system known as kanban (meaning signal or card in Japanese) that responds to demand by delivering parts and products only as they are needed, or *Just-in-time*. In this manner, the downstream customer, either internal or external, pulls parts from an upstream supplier only as needed and controls materials used in production. This is accomplished by returning empty containers to suppliers. The arrival of empty containers at the point of production is a signal to make more parts.

Kanban links that connect work cells contain a specific number of containers that hold precise quantities of parts. Each container has a kanban card where the amount of inventory in a link is recorded. Users can manipulate the inventory level simply by changing the number of containers.

Kanban was originally conceived at Toyota Motor Company as part of the Toyota production system. Some people equate kanban with Toyota's production system; however, this is not accurate. The Toyota system is where inventory and production are managed and controlled by kanban. The Just-in-time philosophy at Toyota led to the development of kanban as a method to control material movement in a system, while minimizing inventory levels.

Since kanban was designed with Just-in-time objectives in mind, it requires a lean manufacturing system to be truly effective. Companies today cannot expect a newly implemented kanban system to deliver dramatic

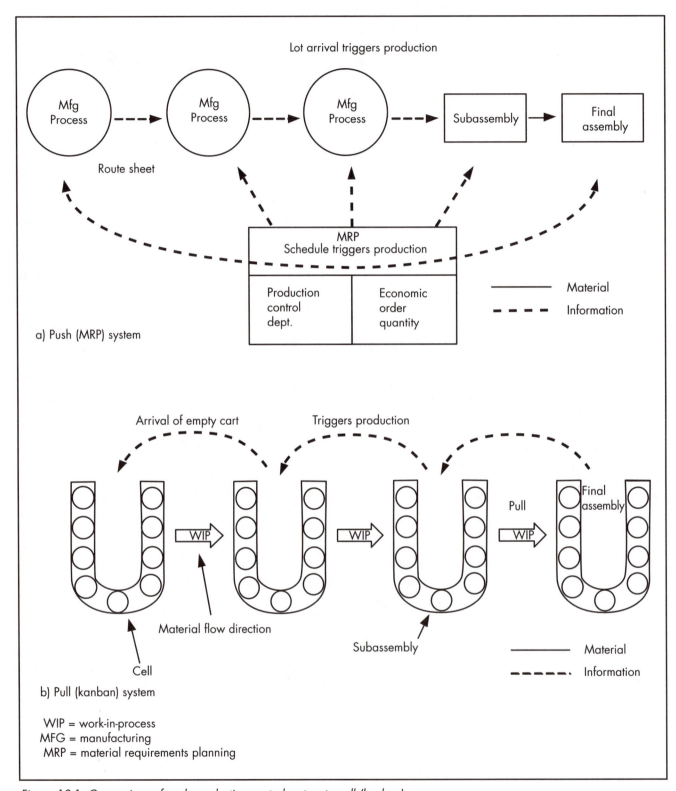

Figure 10-1. Comparison of push production control system to pull (kanban).

results in traditional job-shop environments. However, companies that have completed the first five steps of a redesign of the manufacturing system according to the *integrated manufacturing production system*, another term for lean production's cellular manufacturing subsystem, are adequately prepared to implement a kanban system. So, the prerequisites of implementing a pull system are:

- quality control with total preventive maintenance;
- setup time reduction;
- leveled and balanced production;
- manufacturing and assembly cells; and
- standardized work.

Toyota is not the only company to implement a pull system using kanban cards to control production and inventory. Many foreign and domestic companies have jumped on the kanban bandwagon. Some companies have developed hybrids of the push-and-pull system that outperform the popular kanban system. Many companies have experienced tremendous success in reducing inventories along while shortening delivery times. Of course, along with the ever-increasing popularity of the kanban subsystem, comes criticism of kanban performance. However, in almost every case, kanban criticism has risen from environments that have not yet embraced the prerequisites of lean manufacturing. Such companies have failed to take the necessary steps to redesign their manufacturing systems. To those who think that lean manufacturing is nothing more than a kanban system, take note of the following quote (Shingo 1981): "Now you might think that the Toyota Motor Company is just a company wearing a tight suit (referring to kanban), and you want to buy such a suit for your company. However, if you only buy the kanban subsystem, you soon discover that this suit will not fit your obese, fat body (your present manufacturing system) and chaos soon results."

How Does Kanban Work?

The kanban system, being a pull system, has the unique aspect of being an information network that flows backward from the external customer, through the manufacturing system, and ultimately to the company's suppliers. The system is simple to implement and use. It may consist of rectangular cards (kanbans) that are attached to specially designed containers. Each container is specifically designed for one part type and holds a precise quantity of parts. Containers in a link have the same capacities, and a specific number of these containers are placed into what is known as a *kanban link*. The link allows containers to move in a circuit, linking the two work cells. Kanbans create a manual, physical system that every worker on the factory floor can easily understand. This allows workers to develop trust in the system; trust is necessary for any system to flourish.

When Harley-Davidson implemented lean manufacturing in the early 1980s, they reduced the number of people working in the production-inventory control area from nine to three. The kanban pull system is integrated, meaning that it functions within the manufacturing system calling for parts as needed almost automatically. The route sheet has been eliminated but there is no confusion about:

- where the parts need to go,
- when to make the parts, and
- how many to make.

This information is built into the system. The kanban system is unique in that control information moves in the opposite direction of material movement. That is, downstream elements directly control upstream production rates.

The following are important distinctions to be made about materials in the linked-cell manufacturing system:

- Material within a cell is called *stock-on-hand*.
- Material between cells in the links is *work-in-process inventory*.

- *Zero inventory* means there is no inventory in the manufacturing cells.

Kanban System Types

There are many production- and inventory-control systems that claim to fall under the kanban heading. Often, any type of system using the pulling of parts and material is called kanban. In this chapter, however, three systems are examined. The first is known as the dual-card system, which requires two types of kanban cards, a withdrawal kanban and a production-ordering kanban. The second system, single-card kanban, is similar to the dual-card system but does not use the production-ordering card. Finally, a hybrid of push and pull systems is examined. This system, known as constant work-in-process, is not a kanban system, but has similar functions and even uses kanban cards.

Single-card System

The single-card kanban system is simpler though similar in function to the dual-card system. It is actually a combination of push-and-pull production-control strategies. The manufacturing portion of the system is based on a push philosophy. A daily schedule is assigned to each cell, and production follows this daily schedule rather than waiting for the signal from a production-ordering kanban.

A withdrawal kanban (Figure 10-2) is used to pull the parts from the upstream cell only as needed by the downstream cell. This is the only kanban needed, and it circulates between the upstream stock point and the downstream cell. No input stock points are needed, since withdrawn containers are delivered directly to the downstream cell, as demand requires. The containers move in links according to the following pattern: full containers from first cell to stock point, from stock point to second cell, and finally, empty containers from second cell back to first cell. There is accumulation of containers only at the output of upstream cells.

More specifically, the single-card system (Figure 10-3) functions according to the following steps:

1. The withdrawal kanban from a container just emptied at the downstream cell is placed on that cell's kanban collection box.
2. A withdrawal kanban is taken from the downstream withdrawal collection box for delivery to the upstream cell as a full container from the upstream stock point arrives with a withdrawal kanban from a previous cycle attached.
3. Empty containers are then delivered to the upstream cell to wait refilling according to that cell's daily production schedule.
4. Finally, the withdrawal kanban is attached to a full container in the upstream stock point to await delivery on the next cycle.

Although the single-card kanban system borrows some features from the traditional push system, it is still based solidly in the lean revolution philosophy. The containers, for example, are part-specific, have a standard capacity, and are found in specific numbers within the links. In addition, the cells are designed with quick setups in mind, allowing small lot sizes to be delivered in each container. This allows for the control of inventory at the downstream point of use. However, inventory is allowed to build at the upstream stock point due to the scheduled production there.

One advantage the single-card system provides is simple implementation, since there is only one kanban to learn and understand. Once this system is mastered, a dual-card system often is developed. Thus, the single-card system is often an intermediary step.

The single-card system helps to relieve clutter and confusion around the downstream input area, as the need for an input stock point is eliminated. Most importantly, though, it can be implemented even if a completely operational lean system is not in place. This feature has made the single-card system attractive to companies struggling to move from a job-shop

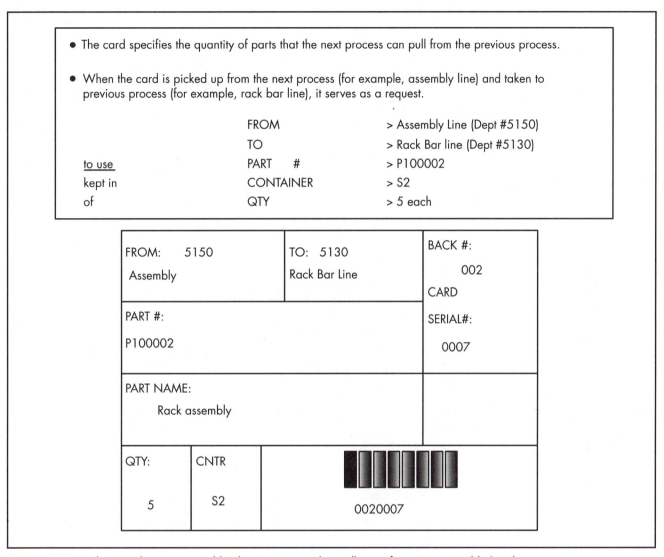

- The card specifies the quantity of parts that the next process can pull from the previous process.

- When the card is picked up from the next process (for example, assembly line) and taken to previous process (for example, rack bar line), it serves as a request.

	FROM	> Assembly Line (Dept #5150)
	TO	> Rack Bar line (Dept #5130)
to use	PART #	> P100002
kept in	CONTAINER	> S2
of	QTY	> 5 each

FROM: 5150 Assembly	TO: 5130 Rack Bar Line	BACK #: 002 CARD
PART #: P100002		SERIAL#: 0007
PART NAME: Rack assembly		
QTY: 5	CNTR S2	0020007

Figure 10-2. Kanban card in a one card kanban system,used to pull parts for use in assembly/production.

environment to a linked-cell manufacturing system.

The single-card kanban rules are outlined in Figure 10-4.

Dual-card System

A kanban card usually is a rectangular-shaped card enclosed in a vinyl packet and attached to a container of parts. Typically, the cards are made of plastic so they are reusable. The containers are designed for each component type and hold a precise (usually equal) quantity of that part number. The two types of kanban cards in a dual-card kanban system are:

1. the production order that signals an upstream cell or process to produce a certain part; and
2. a withdrawal kanban that serves to link two cells or processes.

Figures 10-5 and Figure 10-6 show examples of these two kanbans.

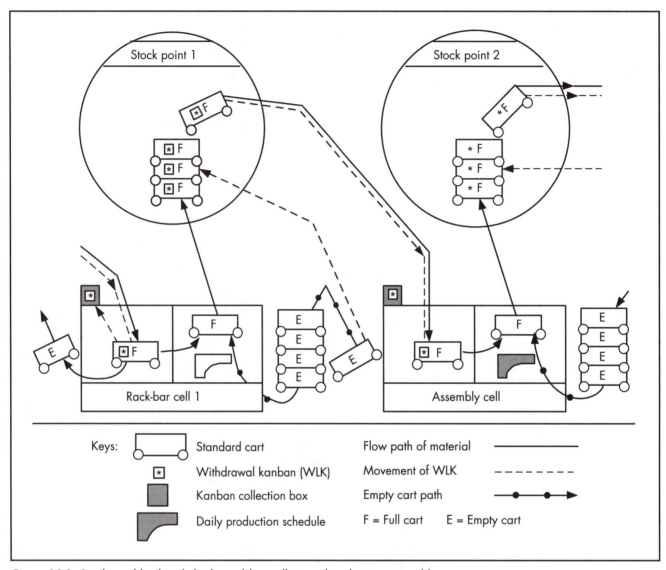

Figure 10-3. Single-card kanban links the rack-bar cells to rack-and-pinion assembly.

There is precisely one production-ordering kanban and one withdrawal kanban for each container. They identify the part number, container capacity, the previous cell, the next cell or process, and other information. A withdrawal kanban specifies the type and part quantity that a downstream process can withdraw from the upstream process. A production-ordering kanban specifies the part type and quantity that the next cell or process must produce. This system's beauty is that it is simple and visual and the users understand how it works. Therefore, the workers trust the system.

The container and kanban flow patterns for two cells are shown in Figure 10-7. In this example, Cell 1 supplies parts to Cell 2 as well as to other cells in the plant. Cell 1 is serviced by Stock-point M and Cell 2 is serviced by Stock-point N.

Standard-size carts or containers move material between the cells. Each container holds an identical number of parts. The carts or

KANBAN RULES
Single card kanban

1) Parts are transported in a specified number of containers and in specified quantities.

2) All parts in a container must be same.

3) All parts in a container must be of good quality.

4) A full container should have the exact number of parts as specified on the kanban card.

5) A kanban card must accompany every full container.

6) Containers must be stored only in designated areas.

7) Kanban cards and containers must be picked up and delivered between departments by a mail person.

8) Parts must be made or delivered only when requested by a kanban card.

9) As soon as the first part is removed from a full container, the kanban card must be immediately removed and placed in the return post.

10) The team leader should be immediately informed of any discrepancies in the kanban system.

Figure 10-4. Rules for single-card kanban.

Store Shelf no. N Item back no.	Preceding process
Item no. Serial # of part	Rack bar cell
Item name Rack bar	
Car Type Camry	Subsequent process
Box capacity / a / Box type / Issued no. 3 of 11	Rack-pinion assembly

Figure 10-5. An example of a withdrawl kanban for manufacture of rack bars.

Store Shelf no. M Item back no.	Rack cell
Item no. Serial # of part	
Item name Rack bar	
Car Type Camry	

Figure 10-6. An example of production-ordering kanban for manufacturing rack bars.

containers move in a link or on a circuit from Cell 1 to its stock point, then to the stock point of the next process. The material then moves into Cell 2 for processing. Empty carts return to Cell 1 for refilling. In summary, the withdrawal kanbans (WLKs) circulate between the output side of Cell 1 and the input side of Cell 2, just as they did in the single-card kanban system.

Production ordering kanbans (POKs) move between the stock point for Cell 1 and the supplying work cell. For each container, there is one POK and one WLK. Basically, the empty container is the signal to the manufacturing cell to make only enough parts to refill that cart. Partially full containers are not allowed. The system works as follows:

1. Starting at stock-point N, a full container of parts is moved into Cell 2. The WLK is detached from the container and placed in the kanban collection box for stock-point N.

2. The most recently emptied container in Cell 2 is transported back to stock point N where a WLK is attached.

3. The WLK and the empty container return to Stock-point M. (Stock-point N and M are not usually side by side; they may be in different parts of the plant or in entirely different buildings.) The WLK is detached from the empty container and attached to a full container of parts. The full container with the WLK is returned to Stock-point N. (This is the withdrawal of material from the upstream cell by the downstream cell or assembly area.)

4. A POK is attached to the full container (the one just removed from Stock-point M). This was detached from the full container and placed in the collection box for

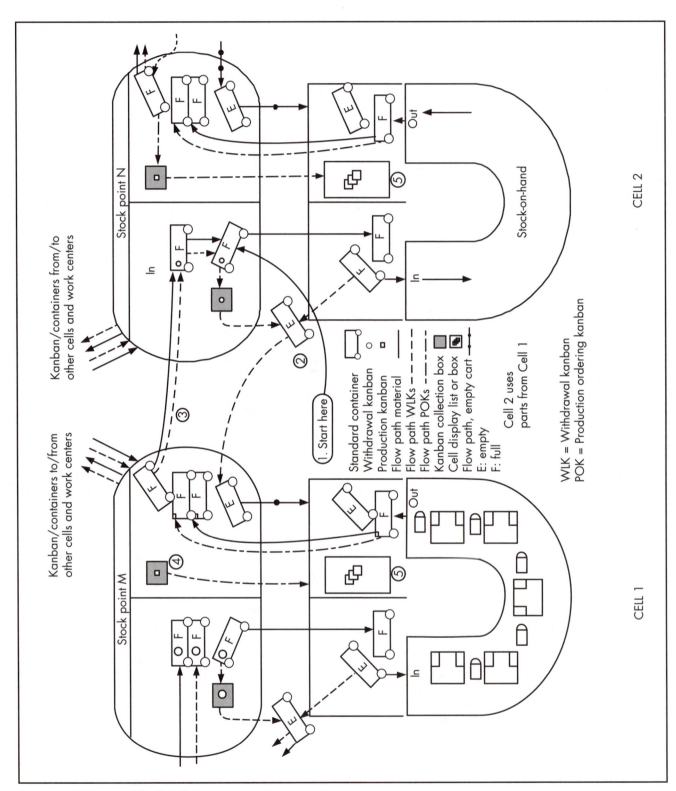

Figure 10-7. Dual-card kanban flows.

Cell 1. Then, (and only then), can the container be removed from the Stock-point M and transported to Stock-point N.

5. Periodically, POKs are removed from the collection box and placed in the dispatch box for Cell 1. These POKs become the dispatch list for Cell 1, controlling the order parts are manufactured in the cell. These jobs are performed in the original order that POKs were received at Stock-point M.

6. The parts that are produced in Cell 1 are placed in the empty containers taken from Stock-point M. The POK is attached to each container after it is filled. The container then returns to Stock-point M to be withdrawn by a downstream process when needed.

This sequence is repeated many times during the day. Parts are produced as needed, that is, as withdrawn from the upstream cell. Cell 1 may produce parts for cells or assembly lines other than Cell 2. Other users operate in exactly the same manner. The carts usually are color-coded to prevent confusion.

Rule 1. The downstream cell or process should withdraw the needed products from the upstream cell or process according to the information provided on the WLK (the needed quantity at the necessary time). This is the realization of Just-in-time: parts should be withdrawn as they are needed, not before they are needed, and not in larger quantities than needed. The key points for enforcing this rule are as follows.

- Any withdrawal without a WLK is prohibited. This prevents a large accumulation of excess inventory at the stock point supplying the downstream process (Stock-point N in Figure 10-7). The number of kanbans in the system is tightly controlled. (This will be discussed later as part of inventory control.) The withdrawal of any parts without a WLK undermines the kanban information system's control element.

- Any withdrawal greater than the number of kanbans should be prohibited. This is

necessary as the withdrawal of any parts without a WLK undermines the kanban information system's control element.

- A kanban (either WLK or POK) should be attached to the physical product, or its container, or should reside in a collection box. This key point eliminates the possibility of any unaccounted inventory in the system. If the number of kanbans in the system and the number of parts per container are strictly controlled, the amount of in-plant inventory can be determined and monitored at any time. This is the backbone of the kanban information system.

Rule 2. The upstream process should produce products in quantities withdrawn by the downstream process or cell, according to the information provided by the POK. This is the complement of Rule 1. If parts are withdrawn Just-in-time, then, by complying with Rule 2, the parts are produced Just-in-time. This is the cornerstone of cellular manufacturing using the lean production philosophy. The main points of this rule are:

- Production greater than the number of kanbans must be prohibited. This prevents a large accumulation of excess inventory at the stock point for the upstream process (Stock-point M in Figure 10-7) and eliminates the possibility of unaccounted inventory in the system.

- When the upstream process produces various kinds of parts, manufacturing should follow the ordinal sequence in which each kind of kanban has been delivered. This helps ensure that each type of part is ready and available at the upstream process stock points whenever needed at the downstream processes or cells.

Rule 3. Defective products should never be conveyed to the downstream process. If there is a defect, the line or cell should stop and immediately try to determine what corrective action should be taken.

One hundred percent quality control is necessary to achieve a truly effective kanban system. Based upon Rule 1 and Rule 2, the parts are produced and withdrawn in the necessary quantities at the necessary times. If a defective part is sent to a downstream process, then that operation must stop since there is no extra inventory in the WLK loop to replace the defective part. In practice, the amount of inventory in the kanban link reflects the probability of a defect occurring in the upstream cell or process. Thus, downstream processes are not delayed unless the entire inventory in the link is used. If this happens, then each upstream process is stopped until the defective item is reworked, replaced, and the problem corrected. The practice of integrated quality control and autonomation in a lean production system enforces this rule.

Rule 4. The number of kanbans can be gradually reduced to improve the processes and reduce waste. This rule conveys the fact that inventory can be an independent control variable. The number of kanbans in the system at any time controls the work-in-process inventory level. This number is initially the result of a management decision. Many companies opt for setting the initial inventory level in the link at about half of the existing level when the pull system is implemented. The initial number of kanbans can be computed by:

$$K = \frac{D_D \times L + S_S}{a} \qquad (10\text{-}1)$$

where:

K = number of kanbans or number of carts (K also equals the number of POKs or the number of WLKs)

D_D = expected demand for parts, per day

L = lead time, that is, processing time + delay time + lot delay and process delay + conveyance time

a = container capacity, a fixed amount, usually about 10% of daily demand

S_S = safety stock, usually 10% or less of $D_D \times L$

The maximum inventory level (M) is expressed as:

$$M = aK = D_D \times L + S_S \qquad (10\text{-}2)$$

The demand for parts is usually the daily demand, leveled, or averaged over a daily or shift amount, from the monthly demand. The lead time takes into account the time needed to process a container of parts, including the time to:

- change over the cell;
- process other items in the family; and
- convey a container to the usage point, plus any delay times.

Delay times include lot delay and process delay. Lot delay takes into account the fact that the first part produced cannot be conveyed to the next cell or assembly line until the last item in the lot is produced. Smaller lots reduce the lot delay time. Process delay accounts for stoppages due to machine tool failures, broken tools, defective parts, and other manufacturing problems. Process delay also includes delays in the throughput time in the cell for processing time greater than the cell cycle time. For example, suppose heat treatment requires 10 minutes in a cell with a one-minute cycle time. The process delay is 10 minutes.

Suppose the cell is making a family of four parts: A, B, C, and D. Obviously, there must be enough carts or containers in the loop of Part A so that downstream processes do not run out of them while the cell is making Parts B, C, or D. This is a form of process delay that adds to the work-in-process inventory and is a tradeoff for flexibility. By designing the cell to be able to make a family of parts, a delay time for each member of the part family is added.

Honda, in Marysville, Ohio, where the Accord® is built, has one stand of large presses that stamp out the sheet metal body parts for the four-door models. This stand of presses manufactures 24 different sheet metal body parts in runs of 300 parts. This is one-day's supply of each part.

The presses are changed over in about 10 minutes for each different part. Obviously, enough parts must be stamped out to last until the next quantity of those specific parts is stamped. Honda is constantly working to reduce the time required to change over these large presses from one part to another because this permits them to further reduce the run size.

Looking back at Equations 10-1 and 10-2, if lead-time, L, is relatively small and the demand per unit time, D_D, is relatively constant, then the policy variable for safety stock can be small, resulting in a smaller inventory level. Therefore, the number of kanbans can be smaller. In practice, this policy variable is expected to approach zero (as will be discussed later). Eliminating setup times reduces lead times.

As volume increases, more cells can become duplicated and dedicated. The inventory level between the cells can be further reduced. The smoothing of demand is achieved by smoothing production in the subsequent processes, as was discussed in Chapter 9.

Rule 5. If there is no kanban card, there is no manufacturing and no transfer of parts. The WLK card, as a production control device, should be attached to the carts or containers unless they are in transit within the cell to order production. This rule reveals the visual control nature of the kanban card. The key manufacturing information is readily at hand. The removal of the kanban card prevents a cart from being transported and used.

Rule 6. Kanbans should be used to adapt to only small fluctuations in demand (fine-tune production by kanban).

Flexibility means the system can respond to changes in demand. There are three cases where kanban can be used to fine-tune production, thus giving the system flexibility with respect to changes in demand.

- The first case is the result of product-mix changes of the final-assembly delivery dates, and of small changes in quantities.

There is no change in the daily total-production load. The production schedule only need be revised for final assembly—the schedule for the upstream processes is revised automatically by transferring the kanbans.

- The second case is the result of small, short-term fluctuations in the daily-production load, although the monthly total load remains the same. Only the frequency of kanban movement increases or decreases. The number of kanbans tends to be fixed despite demand variation.
- The third case is the result of seasonal changes in demand or of increases and decreases in monthly demand. The number of kanbans in the system must be recomputed (increased or decreased) and the production lines rearranged (the cycle time must be recomputed and the number of workers in the cells changed accordingly).

These rules must be followed for the kanban system to be an effective management information system that also controls the level of work-in-process.

Kanban Limitations

Kanban, as described in this chapter, is a relatively simple manual information system. Limitations for its use are as follows.

- Goods must be produced in whole discrete units. Obviously, kanban is not applicable to continuous-process industries such as oil refineries and breweries.
- Kanban should be a subsystem of an linked-cell manufacturing system, using Just-in-time philosophy. The use of a kanban system without the lean production philosophy makes little sense. Rules 1 and 2, regulating the use of kanban, require the manufacture and withdrawal of the necessary parts in necessary quantities at the necessary time.
- The prerequisites for linked-cell manufacturing systems, such as the design of the manufacturing system, standardization of

operations within cells, and smoothing of production must be implemented before an effective pull system can be implemented.

- The parts included in the kanban system should be used every day (high-use parts). Kanban provides that at least one full container of a given part number is available. There is not much inventory float if the contents of the full container are used up the same day they are produced.

Special Kanbans

A modified version of the WLK is used to reorder raw materials (Figure 10-8). Parts are withdrawn from the lot of 500, in containers of 100. When the stack of containers reaches the material requisition kanban, this kanban is used to requisition a coil of steel for the process (Press #10 preceded by shear). When the signal kanban is revealed, it is taken to the kanban post at press #10 and placed in the queue next to the material-requisition kanban. These two kanbans combine to instruct the workers at Press #10 to make 500 steel sheets in quantities of 100. The kanbans are reinserted in the stack of containers as shown. Table 10-1 lists some additional types of special kanbans.

Material-ordering kanbans are a special kind of withdrawal card. Material-ordering kanbans often are used to get material from vendors. An example of how these kanbans are used is shown in Figure 10-9. The information on the card is similar to what is needed on a withdrawal card except that the card has detachable pieces that go to the user's accounts-receivable department as shown in Figure 10-10. A two-trailer-truck system is shown.

Here is how the material-ordering kanban works:

1. At 8 a.m., a truck delivers material-ordering kanbans and empty containers to the vendor in a trailer.
2. Upon arrival at the vendor, the truck driver hands the material-ordering kanbans to the vendor's store worker. The driver picks up a trailer loaded with parts produced to the requirement of material-ordering kanbans brought at 8 p.m. the night before. The driver returns to the user's company and delivers the parts to the correct location within the plant.
3. At 8 p.m., the empty trailer is returned to the vendor. More material-ordering kanbans are given to the vendor and the full trailer is taken back to the plant. One day's supply is carried in two trailers.
4. If the trailers can be rapidly loaded and unloaded, only one trailer is necessary. Many material-transporting companies already have developed such systems.

CONSTANT WORK-IN-PROCESS

The constant work-in-process system focuses on maintaining a constant level of work-in-process over the entire manufacturing system. Work-in-process at any point within the system is allowed to fluctuate freely. Sometimes described as a single-kanban cell encompassing every machine in the plant, a constant work-in-process system is actually a push/pull hybrid. The system is not a kanban system. However, the constant work-in-process system has been a popular topic in recent literature. For this reason, the constant work-in-process system will be examined in similar fashion to the kanban systems previously discussed in this chapter.

The constant work-in-process system tries to control WIP like kanban but fails to make use of the demand-prompted pulling of material between cells. When a container of products leaves final assembly for the external customer, this signals the introduction of a new container of raw material at the beginning of the manufacturing system. Once the material is introduced, production continues without waiting for withdrawal from the downstream cells. When this product leaves final assembly, a new batch of raw material is introduced to take its place in the system. Thus, a pull system exists between the final-product-shipping

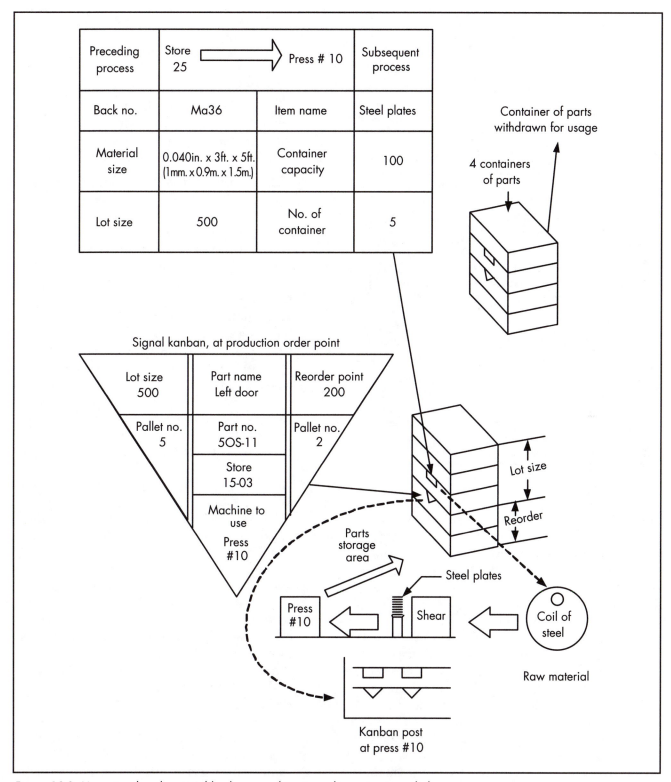

Figure 10-8. How signal and material kanbans combine to make parts as needed.

Table 10-1
Special types of kanban

Vendor kanban	This type of withdrawal kanban is used specifically to request delivery of parts from a subcontracted supplier. Delivery times, receiving gate, and daily frequency of deliveries are indicated on a vendor kanban.
Emergency or special kanban	This type of kanban is issued temporarily for defective work, extra insertions, or spurts in demand. Both MOK and POK exist. These kanbans are issued only for extraordinary reasons and are collected immediately after usage.
Signal kanban	This type of kanban is used for lot manufacture in job-order oriented production. It is a triangular form that is attached to a pallet or stack of containers at the reorder point. This kanban is removed and placed at the dispatching post to signal the need for the manufacture of additional parts.
Material kanban	This kanban is used in conjunction with the signal kanban. This material kanban is set higher than that of the signal kanban so that the material requirements will be fulfilled before manufacture of the desired part begins.

station and the first station in the plant. However, the rest of the time material is pushed through the system.

Though the constant work-in-process system is not a kanban system, it uses cards taken from containers of products leaving final assembly. These cards are attached to containers introduced to the beginning of the system. The cards are like route sheets. They follow the products through the manufacturing and assembly process, with the material, until final assembly is completed (Figure 10-11). At this point, the product is shipped to the customer, and the card returns to the beginning to be attached to a new container and start through the production process again. The containers are of standard size, although they are not part-specific like those in the kanban system. The number of con-

tainers in the system is maintained at a fixed level, creating a constant level of work-in-process inventory in the system.

Advantages

Some advantages associated with using the constant work-in-process system, rather than the typical kanban system for controlling production and inventory, include the following:

- There is no blocking. The buffers between the stations can conceivably hold the entire inventory of the system, so it is not necessary to stop and wait on the downstream cell to ask for a container. The station only stops producing if the raw materials upstream are disrupted—a pure push system.
- It is simple to control. Although the kanban system can be easily understood, the constant work-in-process system is an even simpler way to control inventory. The only variable is the total work-in-process in the system. With kanban, not only is the total work-in-process a variable to be controlled, but the work-in-process between each cell is controlled independently.
- The constant work-in-process system works well with a large variety of parts. With a kanban system, at least one container of every part produced in the plant must be held in work-in-process. If the number of parts is large, then the amount of work-in-process can easily become excessive even if only one or two containers of each part type is available. Since the constant work-in-process system containers are not part-specific, there is no need to have one for every part type in the system. So, the total number of containers, and thus the work-in-process, is not affected by the number of part types the system is capable of producing.
- Unbalanced lines can be handled well. A true kanban system has difficultly functioning in a facility that has not balanced the processes with the final-assembly

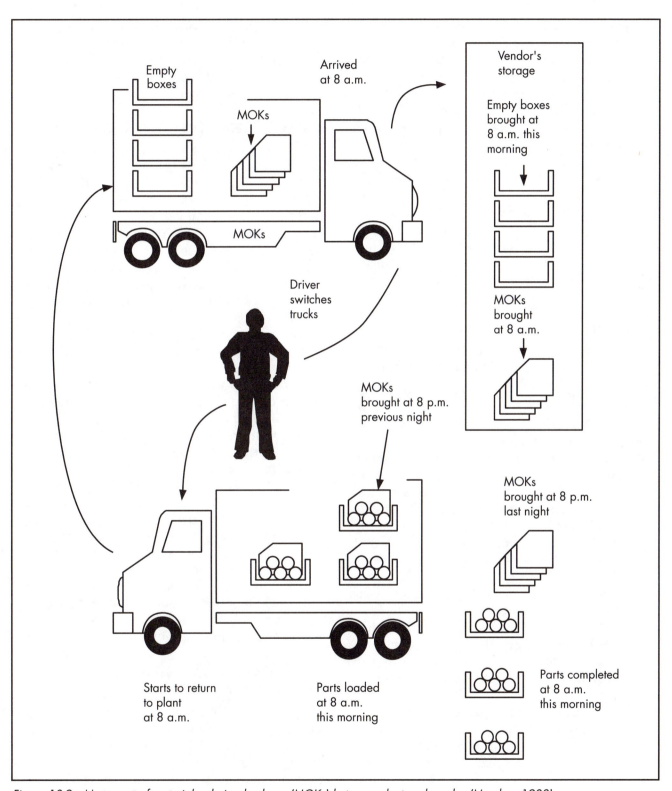

Figure 10-9. Movement of material-ordering kanbans (MOKs) between plant and vendor (Monden, 1983).

cycle times. There is always some cell preventing the other cell from producing due to its slower cycle. However, the individual cells in a constant work-in-process system are not subject to withdrawal from downstream. Thus, the slow cell in an unbalanced line does not prevent other cells from functioning.

- Bottlenecks near the end of the line are not devastating. If a cell near the final assembly in a constant work-in-process system experiences delays, this does not necessarily affect every upstream cell. They are still receiving raw materials from upstream, so they are able to continue production due to the pushing of material through the system.

Limitations

There are some drawbacks to the constant work-in-process system. Some of these include:

- Constant work-in-process is inferior to kanban if the final-assembly lines are balanced. Much of this chapter has been devoted to the contention that if the first five steps of lean production have been implemented (of which the fifth step involves leveling, balancing and synchronizing), then a kanban system will provide optimal control of production and inventory. Constant work-in-process cannot match kanban's performance under these conditions.
- Performance is poor if bottlenecks occur near the beginning. This is due to the fact that material is pushed from its introduction through the system to final assembly; a bottleneck at the start of this process can really delay the subsequent cells' production.
- A constant work-in-process system can experience routing problems. Since the parts are pushed through the factory, a routing sequence must be set. This is not a problem if the parts travel to the same cells. However, if some parts do not require

certain processes, then a routing-control methodology may be required. This is reminiscent of the traditional material-requirements-planning system (push system) in the job shop.

INTEGRATED INVENTORY CONTROL

The most powerful analogy presented in Japanese literature is the now-famous "rocks in the river" (Figure 10-12) (Shingo 1981). In this simple analogy, rocks are equated to problems and the river is inventory material moving through the plant. The river's level is equivalent to the work-in-process inventory flowing through the factory, just as the river flows between its banks. When the river level is high, the rocks, which represent hazards to safe navigation, are covered. Table 10-2 lists problems in the workplace and traditional solutions.

Now it may be asked, "Isn't that good? Hasn't inventory traditionally been used to circumvent the problems of poor quality, machine-tool breakdowns, long setup times, parts shortages, and other deficiencies in the manufacturing or production systems?" This is true, but there are errors in this thinking. Covering the problems is the wrong approach. Inventories are wasteful and expensive to carry. The greater the inventory in the system, the longer the throughput time. Low-cost, high-quality manufacturing never is achieved when work-in-process levels are high. In addition, the inventory, if not controlled, suddenly may drop because of factors outside of the company's control, revealing some problem in the system at the most inopportune time and throwing the entire plant into disarray.

INVENTORY: AN INDEPENDENT CONTROL VARIABLE

Lean production philosophy alters the nature of inventory completely, changing it from a dependent variable in the classical push system to an independent control variable in the pull system. Taking the rocks in the river analogy a step further, the river's volume of flow represents

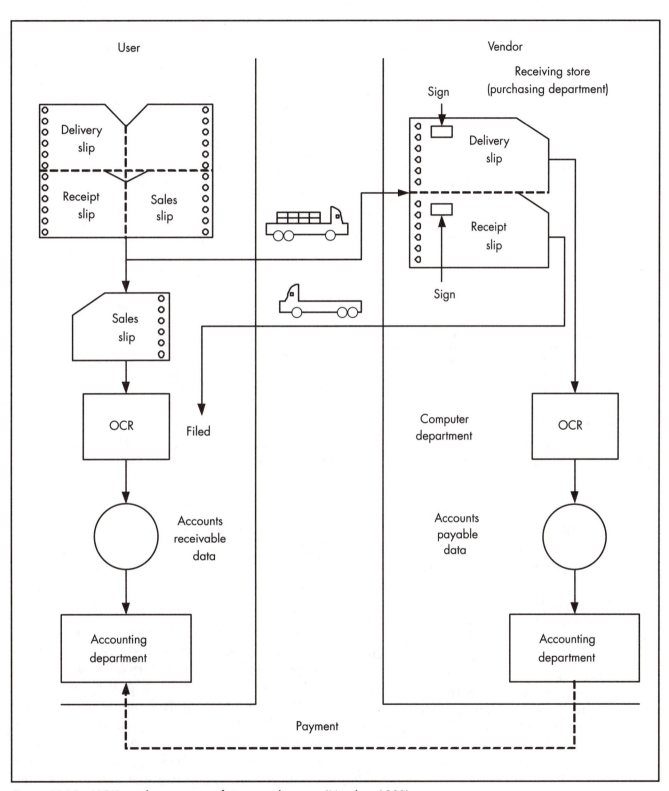

Figure 10-10. MOK voucher movement for two truck system (Monden, 1983).

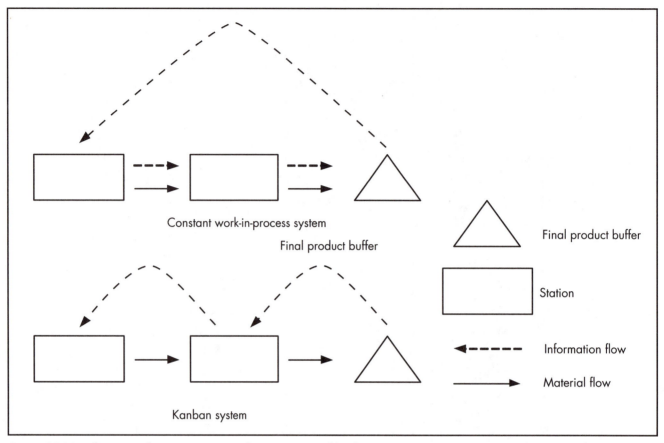

Figure 10-11. Information flow in constant work-in-progress and kanban systems.

capacity. The river's flow can be compared to the materials that flow in continuous-processing manufacturing systems such as chemical plants and refineries. Continuous-processing manufacturing systems represent the ideal in terms of efficient manufacturing with the minimum work-in-process. Therefore, they represent the vision of lean manufacturing except they are not typically flexible. To make discrete parts flow like water, setup time and lot sizes must be reduced and defective products and machine breakdowns eliminated in the system. Inventory flow rate is an independent variable that can be described as follows:

$$F_R = D \times W \times V \qquad (10\text{-}3)$$

where:

F_R = flow rate, ft³/min (m³/min)
D = amount of work-in-process
W = number of manufacturing systems (number of final assembly lines)
V = distance materials travel through the system ÷ throughput time

In classical manufacturing systems, concentration has been on the production rate with little regard for the inventory level. In a linked-cell manufacturing system, the amount of work-in-process is controlled. That is, inventory levels are deliberately raised or lowered, even though lowering the inventory level exposes problems. When this happens, the inventory is temporarily restored to ease customer discomfort or the company's discomfort

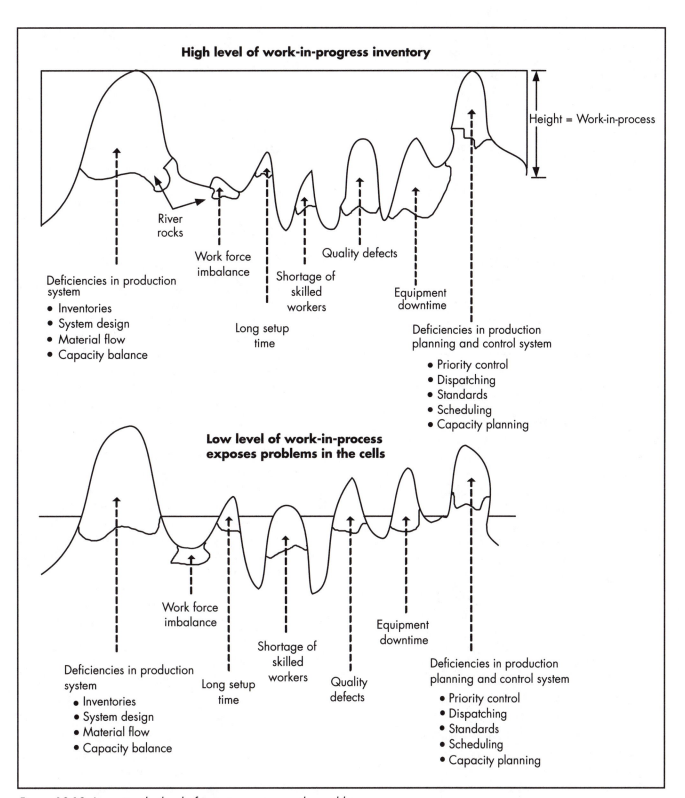

Figure 10-12. Lowering the level of inventory uncovers the problems.

Table 10-2
Problems and solutions in the workplace

Problems in the workplace (rocks in the river)
  Machine failure (waiting for repair)
  Bad raw materials (poor incoming quality)
  Tool failure (fractured, work, or missing tools)
  Workers absent or late
  Changeover from one part to another
  Waiting for parts
  Waiting for material handling
  Waiting for inspection/setup/or maintenance

Typical solutions in the job shop
  Lots of inventory and buffer stock
  Backup machines or material-handling equipment
  Supermachines (large and expensive automation)
  Extra tools and materials
  Extra repair parts
  Extra workers (expeditors and dispatchers)
  Elaborate information systems (computerized)
  Robotize and automate (expensive)

and the problem is attacked and eliminated. The rocks are removed from the river.

Kanban controls the inventory level. It allows for specific amounts of inventory to be added or extracted from the flow. Altering the production rate or the number of workers in the manufacturing cells can change the flow rate. The production rate in units per hour is the inverse of the cycle time in hours per unit. Other means are used to control cycle time. These include varying the number of workers in a manufacturing or assembly cell. More workers lower the cycle time and thus increase the production rate.

Returning to the analogy, the river level never can be lowered completely to the riverbed, because the work-in-process flow stops completely. There is no such condition as zero inventory. A certain minimum amount of inventory must be in the system. The analogy's power is that as more rocks are removed, the lower the river level that can be run safely, without interruption. In the same way, the work-in-process level between cells reflects the progress in removing setup time, eliminating

defective products, eliminating machine breakdowns, and standardizing the cycle times, that is, eliminating system variability. The nearer the system gets to perfection, the lower the work-in-process level can be while flowing smoothly.

Using Dual-card Kanban Systems

Dual-card kanban systems have a unique productivity improvement feature not found in either push systems or single-card kanban systems. Foremen or supervisors have the authority to remove kanban from the system to reduce inventory and thus expose problems. To do this, they do not have to remove the container from the system; they simply gather a pair of kanban cards from a full container. The container cannot be moved without a kanban card attached to it. Even though workers and foremen are upset when the removal of inventory from the system causes schedule delays, it gives them a chance to uncover problems in the upstream cells. The inventory can be released by reinstating the cards. Meanwhile, the newly discovered problem can be corrected. Once a solution is implemented, the inventory level can be lowered again; thus another round of problem solving begins. This cycle is repeated throughout the factory. Productivity and quality are improved while inventory and its associated costs are lowered. This feature makes the dual-card kanban system particularly effective.

The dual-card system is extremely effective for small-lot mass production of complex assembly items where there is the potential for delays caused by the compound effects of:

- large number of parts (wide variety);
- variable usage of the parts; and
- multiple stages of manufacture/assembly.

To avoid running out of parts when delays occur, huge buffer stocks normally are carried in the mass system. However, in lean manufacturing, the dual-card pull system signals the manufacture of each part number to match the up-and-down output rate of downstream production stages. The inventory between the cells is continually reduced by the removal of carts. Referring back to Figure 10-7, suppose the system begins with 11 carts (K) between the two cells. Suppose each cart holds 20 parts (a). The maximum inventory between the two cells is therefore 220 parts (11 × 20). The removal of a cart lowers the maximum inventory level to 200 parts. If no problems occur, another cart is removed. The process continues until finally no carts can be removed without serious delays occurring due to lack of available parts. Suppose this occurs until there are six carts remaining. This number often depends on how close one cell is to another and on the length of setup times between different parts.

Now the number of parts in each cart can be cut in half. The new amount of parts is now 10 and the number of carts is restored to 11 (11 × 10 = 110). Thus, the inventory level is similar, but the frequency of lot production is increased. The flow is smoother because smaller lots produce smaller demand spikes in the system. The setup reduction problem becomes immediately apparent since cutting the lot size increases the setup frequency. So now setup for that particular process is attacked to reduce or eliminate it. Once setup time has been reduced, another cycle of removing kanban cards can again reduce inventory levels. This cycle is implemented across the factory and is part of lean production's continuous-process-improvement philosophy.

The dual-card kanban system is integrated because it is carried out entirely by the people who run the manufacturing system. Eventually the users get the inventory level as low as possible without causing major disruptions to the manufacturing system. The system will require upgrading and automation to go to the next level. If factory management decides to go in that direction, this kind of automation usually is easy to justify.

Kanban Pull System Compared to Material Requirements Planning

In this section, various features of the pull system are compared to material-requirements planning (MRP), inventory levels, and production philosophy. The pull system is compared to the push system.

At its initialization, kanban should be a manual information system utilizing cards. This helps familiarize everyone with the system. The capital investment in a kanban subsystem is small compared to the costs of changing the manufacturing system. Material-requirements planning, on the other hand, is a computer-based system. Because the existing manufacturing system and MRP are so complex, MRP is not manageable without computer assistance. The capital investment in an MRP system is extensive. In 2002, the cost of a full-blown MRP installation is estimated to be between $500,000 and several million dollars. This includes labor, software, hardware, and training for system development.

Material-requirements-planning systems are known for taking a long time to implement. A materials manager who had just spent two years implementing his company's material-requirements-planning program was asked how many people were employed at his company. He responded that there were 500 workers and 200 others. He was then asked how many of these people understood the material requirements planning system. After a long pause, he estimated three. *How can any system function when only three people understand how it is supposed to work?* People will not trust a system they do not understand. Material is the lifeblood of the manufacturing system; not understanding how it is controlled is bad business.

A material-requirements planning system uses built-in economic-order-quantity calculations. Therefore, quantities vary considerably. It is better to have fixed small quantities and vary the frequency of ordering parts. The material-requirements-planning system was developed for planning in the job shop, not for control of the materials moving through the plant.

A dual-card kanban subsystem is truly a pull system of parts ordering and control. The ordinal production schedule is issued only to the starting point on the final assembly line and not for any other process. The transfer of parts and withdrawal kanbans linking the processes in the system determines the production schedule for each preceding process. Therefore, the parts are actually pulled through from the final assembly line to the start of the system.

The single-card kanban subsystem is a combination push-and-pull parts-ordering system. The manufacturing aspect in a single-card kanban subsystem is a push system because parts are produced according to a daily production schedule rather than for immediate needs as in the dual-card kanban subsystem. Coupled with this push system for manufacturing is a pull system for deliveries. Parts are delivered using withdrawal kanbans only as the downstream processes need them.

Material-requirements planning is a push system of parts ordering and planning; there is no real control function. A push system is simply a schedule-based system in which a multi-period schedule of future demands for the company's products is prepared. The computer breaks down the schedule for manufacturing and develops a production schedule for each work center based upon the master schedule. Then the parts are delivered throughout the system without regard to the immediate need. The connection between the planned schedule and reality may not exist.

Companies using pull kanban systems have less delay or lead time between parts manufacture and use, so they have only hours or minutes worth of material in inventory. A material-requirements-planning system carries days', weeks', or months' worth of material in inventory because the parts are produced to cover the demand for a week or longer.

A kanban information system is a logical element in a lean manufacturing system. The elimination of setup time makes small lot sizes economical. Making lots equal in size or as small as possible plus redesigning the manufacturing system are integral parts of the pull system.

A material-requirements-planning system produces parts in large lot sizes to cover the demand of a single time period. This system has not adopted the concept of small economical lot sizes through eliminating setup time and streamlining the operation. In material-planning systems, lot sizes vary considerably, so production cannot be smoothed.

The ease of associating requirements for parts with the schedule of end products is the crucial factor of information-system selection. Figure 10-13 shows the relationship between the ease of associating the requirements and the type of information system used. This affects inventory-level size, as discussed earlier.

The major distinguishing factor between the pull system and the material-requirements-planning system is the ability of the pull system to accurately associate the component-part requirements with the end-product schedule. The dual-card kanban system completes this accurate association because it manufactures and withdraws parts according to the system's need. Production control is truly integrated into the manufacturing system. The material-requirements-planning system does not have a high degree of association or integration with error introduced into the part requirements as a result of changes in the end-product schedule. Although material-requirements-planning systems correctly calculate the part requirements by precisely associating them with the master schedule of end products, long lead times and large lot sizes erode the close association between the part requirements and the end-product schedules. The way to make material-requirements planning into a truly effective information system is to reduce inherent error in its part-requirement calculation. However, if the setup time is reduced to make material-requirements planning more effective, it is not needed for material control in lean production systems, since pull systems are more productive.

SUPPLY-CHAIN MANAGEMENT

There is currently much activity in supply-chain management. However, unless lean production is achieved, a company does not have a

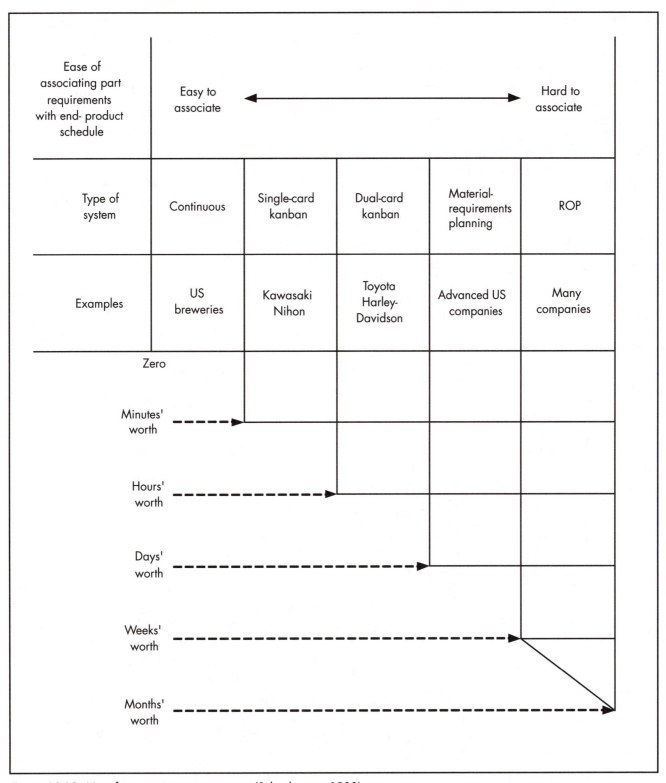

Figure 10-13. Manufacturing inventory systems (Schonberger, 1982).

chain of linked suppliers. It has a network of suppliers. Perhaps this strategy should be called supplier network management. As part of the last two steps in building a lean production system, the production system consisting of product design, manufacturing, sales, marketing, distribution, and purchasing must be in order. This requires an integrated internal manufacturing system, and the selection of the best vendors to be the sole component or subassembly sources.

THE PAPERLESS FACTORY OF THE FUTURE

Manufacturing systems have their dinosaurs. The production job shop, with its manufacturing system kept afloat by the ingenuity of people and by oceans of inventory, is one of those dinosaurs. Clearly the time has come for the invention of a new manufacturing system. What motivated Taiichi Ohno, then vice-president of Toyota, to develop this system, and why does the system have the characteristics that it does?

After World War II, Japan was known as a nation that made poor quality, low-tech, and inexpensive products. Yet, the Japanese government wanted to develop full employment in their country through industrialization. To do this, they needed to learn how to build quality products—products other nations would buy. The Japanese felt that the United States knew how to build these products, so they learned about quality control from Deming and Juran. Initially US quality gurus taught quality control techniques to the engineers and managers. Then the Japanese did something quite different, something not done in the US factories. Most surprisingly, the workers were taught quality-control techniques. Next, the workers were given the responsibility for quality and the authority to stop the processes if something went wrong. Toyota and its suppliers began to develop early versions of linked-cell manufacturing systems for the manufacture of part families. In these early cells, they learned to

eliminate setup and work together to eliminate defective parts. The workers became skilled so they could operate different processes. Make-one, check-one, and move-one-on became the operational standard. But these events do not totally explain why this unique system evolved. This question probably lies in the nature of the Japanese language.

As a language, Japanese is difficult to use for written communication. The classical, large mass-production system requires a sophisticated information system to deal with the complexity of the manufacturing system and its interfaces with the production system. Since Ohno could not change the Japanese language, he had to find a way to simplify the manufacturing and production systems to eliminate the need for written communication. Thus he replaced it with visual or automatic signals. He began to eliminate all kinds of unnecessary functions. In contrast, manufacturers in the United States tried to computerize and optimize these functions.

Management by Sight

The objective of management by sight or visual control is to provide an easy method to exercise control of the plant and provide quick feedback by simply using one's eyes to view the status of operations. Whenever an abnormal condition exists, the system provides a signal requiring that timely corrective action be taken. Management by sight calls for signals to be actively changing and, therefore, providing up-to-date information. Visual control causes employees to get out into the plant on a regular basis to exercise control. Anyone at any time can go to the shop floor and view the conditions. When successful, fewer reports must be sent through the organization, thereby reducing paper flow. There are two kinds of management by sight: information on displays, and workplace organization through the shop.

Information on Display

For visually displayed information to be effective in controlling plant operations, it must be updated continuously and be flexible, able to change with daily operations. Some items displayed in the plant using the lean system include:

- cleanliness control boards;
- control charts;
- job-training charts;
- housekeeping evaluations;
- machine checklists;
- one-point lessons;
- Poka-yoke maps/sheets;
- production charts;
- scrap-tally sheets;
- setup charts;
- standard-work-combination tables and production-capacity sheets, and
- team kaizen projects.

Workplace Organization Through the Shop

Items on the factory floor should be properly identified so abnormal conditions can quickly be seen.

Visual Control at Standard Operations

Items such as gages, meters, and valves can be marked to indicate normal operating conditions.

- Color coding can be used for gaging and meters, while valves may be tagged to indicate the normal position.
- The responsible person's name and telephone number may be posted so anyone finding a problem can immediately report it.
- When equipment is moved from one plant to another, visual preparation ensures installation can be completed quickly and easily at the point of destination.

Visual control should be made a part of every employee's daily operations so everyone can be involved in spotting abnormal conditions.

Visual identification can and should extend to areas related to maintenance throughout the plant, and not only to equipment.

When people store tools wherever they wish, the obvious result is confusion, frustration, and lost time. Good housekeeping procedures should be developed and followed. For example, if a tool is missing at the end of the day, everyone should be made aware of it and be involved in finding it. Management by sight highlights abnormal conditions. Some tools and techniques to accomplish this are: taped areas, tool display boards with proper identifications, and color coding to increase the visual control. With this control methodology, operating, housekeeping and workplace organization are more efficiently monitored and controlled.

The same principles apply with identification of any area where inventory, machines, equipment, containers and scrap bins are kept:

- If these areas are taped, color coded or partitioned off, they can become useful tools in determining problem areas.
- The idea is simple: a place for everything, and everything in its place.
- If the scrap tub is missing from a machine, it is quickly noticeable because an empty area is taped on the floor.
- A forklift parked in an area unidentified is not located in the proper position.
- Work-in-process containers found in an unidentified area belong in another location in the factory.
- If inventory is missing, or too much is in the designated location, there should be a visual flag signaling that there may be a problem.

Even if a trash can is mislocated, it will be noticed. Management by sight forces thought about the location and function of the items located in the shop.

Items conveying information either by their mechanical or electrical function include the following:

- Andon boards—used by operators to signal the occurrence of a problem—lights to signal that assistance is needed.
- Scrap bins—red metal bins divided into days of the week. An attached scrap tally sheet keeps a one-month history of the reasons for and quantities of scrap.
- Clean stands—yellow stands designed to hold one piece of product and indicate when the cleaning solution in the parts washer should be changed. After washing, the part is put on display along with the results of the cleanliness check. Upon reaching a specified unacceptable cleanliness level, the solution is changed before unacceptable parts reach assembly.
- First, middle, last-part examples—high-quality samples of each machined part are taken near the start, middle and finish of each shift. The parts are displayed to show the quality status at the point of inspection.

Visual control enables factory operations to be more tightly linked with improved communication and better problem-solving routines. It is another set of techniques underscoring the driving force of continual improvement in the lean production system. Management by sight also reinforces another central theme of lean production in the factory: for effective management, employee and team involvement are critical.

Line-stop Concept

Line stop is a fundamental lean production factory-control technique. It refers to stopping the production line when a problem occurs, identifying the problem, and then resolving the problem so it will not recur, thus regaining flow as soon as possible. The Japanese refer to the concept of line stop as jidoka. It means literally to make machines intelligent; that is, capable of determining if a line should be stopped. The objective of line stop is to give operators the authority to stop the process any time a problem occurs. However, it is difficult to implement. It takes discipline to respond to problems quickly. And it takes commitment from top management to shut down machines and the production line if necessary to find and permanently resolve problems.

Machines and Line Operations

The line stop concept applies to machines and line operations. Process-indicator lights assist the worker in detecting abnormal occurrences. On the line, the operator pushes a trouble button to get the attention of the team leader. If the problem can be solved within workstation cycle time, the line will keep moving; if not, the line will stop.

An andon light normally signals the occurrence. A yellow light may be used when requesting assistance with a problem, and a red light for stopping the line if the problem cannot be resolved quickly. Buzzers or music often are used in conjunction with the andon lights to enhance visibility. In brief, line stop is one more technique encouraging continuous improvement. Line stops should not be feared, but encouraged to expose and then resolve problems.

Other Control Techniques

Many other techniques and tools help in the planning and control of a lean production factory system.

Hourly Check

In addition to poka-yoke devices to spot and prevent defects, hourly checks of the product further eliminate the possibility of passing defective work to the next downstream process. A buzzer sounds once per hour to trigger 100% inspection of critical processing dimensions. Every part is 100% visually inspected. The hourly check reinforces the previous efforts of the quality system and pinpoints problems at their source.

Sample Size

When workers are not checking parts in the lean manufacturing cells, the quality control personnel carry out sampling inspection on the first, middle, and last part of each shift. These parts are taken from the line and examined in the inspection lab to ensure that specifications are met. The pieces are then put on display to show that quality parts are being produced by that shift.

If problems are discovered, details are relayed to the production line for corrective action. First, middle, and last piece inspection also helps determine when a problem occurred. If a problem was found on the last-piece inspection at the end of the shift, but not found earlier in the shift, the first two pieces can be re-analyzed to ensure that the problem only occurred near the shift's end. The imperfect parts then can be isolated for corrective action.

Various documents also help control the process.

- Control charts or statistical process control (SPC) sheets are put on display for reference, especially by the operators. Control charts and run charts (discussed in Chapter 7) ensure specifications will be met by detailing the particular operation. At the same time, they give the operator a sense of the patterns of process development and point out the effects of machine adjustments.
- Check sheets are another tool used in lean production. The most common is the machine checklist that aids operators in the correct startup procedures for the machines. Check sheets also are displayed for and provide help with maintenance when the machines are down. They can be used in any function and enhance the properly established procedures or rules.
- Process sheet or standard operation sheets are the most common control tools. They provide the necessary information for the machining or assembly of a part. For example, they outline speeds and feeds, material, sequence of operations, operator safety, tooling and gaging information, part number, and part name. A part drawing also is included. Standard

operation sheets are positioned above each operation and provide stability and standardize the process so specifications can be met consistently. They are also used to train new operators. Leave nothing to chance or memory. Make it easy to train and retrain the operators and prevent them from making errors.

SUMMARY

Control techniques serve as some of the tools workers can use to keep the production process moving toward its goal of stability and continuous improvement. Production leveling and the kanban card system keep production and inventory predictable, controllable and, thus, stable. Other techniques and aids help workers monitor the operations and spot problems in the line or defects in the products. Once highlighted, the troubles on the line or imperfections in the results should be tackled immediately and at the site. Monitoring and trouble-spotting tools include: management by sight, line stop and other techniques such as hourly checks; first, middle, and last inspection; display and control sheets, check sheets, and process documentation.

The Toyota system was created by trial-and-error processes within an environment where the language would not permit a written communication system (information system) that could control a large, complex manufacturing system. So Toyota developed a manufacturing system that was simple to operate and control with a simple information system, one now known as *kanban*. A pull system of production and inventory control, kanban uses visual cards for information transfer and control. The manufacturing system is redesigned so only the final assembly line must be scheduled. In fact, the long-range goal of the system is to eliminate the need for kanban by directly linking the processes. This means that the output from each cell goes to only one customer. Note that this defines what the cell or process is to make. Moreover, one of the system's operational characteristics is the gradual elimination of its primary information document, kanban cards and the resulting work-in-process inventory reduction. Thus, the proper path to obtain the paperless factory of the future is evident. It is critical to eliminate the manufacturing system of mass production using the job shop and replace it with cellular manufacturing systems linked via the kanban subsystem.

In conclusion, the kanban system accurately associates the part requirements with the end-product schedule. Part usage and manufacturing in the upstream processes determine the need of the end-product assemblies through the transfer of withdrawal and production kanban cards or carts. These parts are manufactured Just-in-time for the necessary products, in the necessary quantities, at the necessary time.

The lean manufacturing system, being manual at the outset, is easily understood by its users, something that cannot be said for many of the computerized systems used in the job shop. Employees understand how their actions influence the entire system and that they can make the system better.

Large lot sizes, long lead times, and changes in the schedule make it difficult for an MRP system to accurately associate the part requirements with the end-product schedule. The inexpensive kanban system can achieve better estimates of part requirements than computer based material requirements planning systems. The capital investment saved is better spent on implementing lean manufacturing to improve quality, lower costs, reduce inventory, and facilitate an inventory control system. The most expensive system is not necessarily the best.

Chapter 11
Making the Vendors Lean

INTRODUCTION

In the lean production system, vendors are integrated into a program of continuous, long-term improvement. Companies and vendors work together to reduce lead times, lot sizes, unit costs, and inventory levels, while improving quality. Vendors and customer companies become more competitive in the world marketplace.

When a company implements a lean manufacturing system, the system must be extended to the company's vendors. This requires that the company develop a program to educate and encourage suppliers to develop products of superior quality, at the lowest possible cost, on time, and with designed-in flexibility. Vendors essentially become remote cells that supply materials and subassemblies, which are withdrawn just as they are pulled from cells within the plant.

The archaic job-shop system and the lean production system each treat vendors in different manners. Some component or subassembly suppliers within the automobile industry actually build to sequence. Johnson Controls, Inc., a vehicle seat maker, is a good example. The company receives a signal from the final assembly area of the customer factory when a certain automobile model of a particular color exits the paint department. Johnson has two to four hours, depending on the customer plant and the current takt time, to build a set of seats and deliver them in sequence with the automaker's final-assembly process. Only world class suppliers can accomplish this feat.

LEAD TIME AND EXPEDITING

Most suppliers build to the daily demand and part mix; items are fed in sequence with the final assembly or they are stored line-side and picked as needed. In the mass-production system, the purchasing function has these characteristics:

- multi-sourcing (many vendors for the same item);
- weekly, monthly, and semiannual deliveries;
- long lead times (weeks or even months);
- large safety stocks;
- quantity variances;
- late/early delivery times;
- inspection of incoming materials;
- inconsistent packaging, and
- expediting of equipment or materials.

Lead time reflects the amount of time between ordering a component and when it arrives so that it arrives on time at the point of use (see Figure 11-1). Expediting is called for when the component has not arrived on time, was lost, or is defective. It must be hand carried through the manufacturing system. Someone must search for the lot and get it moving within the system. Expediting is one of the great wastes of the mass-production system.

Mass-production companies use multiple sources for the following reasons:

- as a hedge against vendor problems (strikes, defects, or late deliveries);
- because one vendor cannot handle all of the work; or

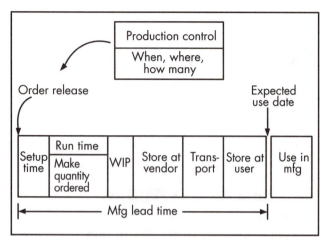

Figure 11-1. Manufacturing lead time is how far in advance you must release an order to the supplier such that it arrives when you need it.

- because vendors are competing with each other over the price.

LEAN SUPPLY CHAIN

It is interesting to contrast this with lean manufacturing. Lean purchasing in the lean-manufacturing system has the following characteristics:

- single sourcing with long-term contracts;
- less safety stock;
- specified quantities;
- on-time deliveries;
- daily, weekly, and quarterly deliveries;
- it bypasses incoming quality inspections because it is all perfect (zero defects);
- standard packaging; and
- less expediting.

Single Sourcing

There has been a considerable amount of discussion in the literature concerning supply-chain management and technology transfer. In lean manufacturing, technology transfer happens when a company shares its lean production knowledge and experience with vendors on a one-to-one basis. The company cannot afford to have multiple suppliers for the same components or subassemblies. Therefore, lean manu-

facturers focus on sole sourcing each component or subassembly. For lean automobile manufacturers, the final assembly plant may have only 200-400 suppliers, with each supplier becoming a lean and Just-in-time vendor to the company. The strategy of single sourcing is to maintain the proprietary aspects of lean production. In the case of the rack-bar cell described earlier, only one vendor should know how the cell processes racks using different gear-teeth angles.

When single sourcing, a company selects the best vendor to be the sole source for each part, component, or subassembly. This reduces variability between parts, thereby improving quality, since all parts are coming from the same manufacturing process or system. This is a key part of lean-production methodology. At every process step, there is only one source, one manufacturing process, and one set of tooling. This approach replaces the strategy of multiple vendors competing against each other. The adversarial relationship between the vendor and customer is eliminated because they become partners. When something goes wrong in this scenario, it is easier to identify the source of the problem.

Single-source advantages include the following:

- The buyer's resources can be focused on electing, developing, and monitoring one source, rather than many.
- Volume buying is more frequent, leading to lower costs.
- Vendors are more inclined to do special favors for customers, because customers are considered large accounts.
- Tooling dollars are concentrated at one source, rather than many. This saves money.
- It is easier to control and monitor product for superior quality.

Long-term Contracts

A company and a supplier develop contracts of 18-24 months in duration. This enables the vendor to take a long-range view and plan ahead. (Contracts with short lead times are renegotiated every six to 12 months.) Under these agreements:

- The lean company supplies updated forecasts every month (good for 12 months).
- The lean company commits to building a long-term quantity and to eventual excess-material buyout.
- Delivery is specified by mid-month for the next month.

Advantages of a long-term contract include the following:

- It builds schedule stability. There is no jerking up and down of a vendor's schedule, and there are smooth increases and decreases.
- There is better and more frequent communication between the buyer and vendor.
- There is better visibility. The vendor sees one year's worth of forecasted needs as soon as the company sees it, instead of viewing a limited lead-time view.
- There is less paperwork. There are fewer (possibly none) change orders to run through the system. This is good for the company and vendor.
- Inventory is reduced, initially at the lean company and later at the vendor, as lead time is reduced.

Frequent Deliveries

In some systems, frequent deliveries are critical. A vendor is expected to deliver materials to a company hourly, daily, or weekly, depending on the type of part or subassembly. Most parts can be categorized according to the purchasing department's "ABC" analysis. "A" parts are critical, high-cost parts, and there is usually one per product. For vehicles, this would be the engine, transmission, seat sets, steering gear, dashboard, etc. "C" parts are low cost, but numerous. "B" parts are somewhere between these two, but critical for different reasons. For example, many companies classify bulky parts such as packaging materials and sheet metal as "B" parts. They

may not be expensive, but they take up space and/or require expensive tooling.

100% Good Quality

If a supplier is taught how to implement cellular manufacturing so it can deliver the correct quantities on time, and with 100%-good quality, then an incoming inspection by the buyer is unnecessary. In short, vendors seek to become Just-in-time suppliers that carry out lean-production methods, while striving for zero defects.

Engineering Aid to Vendors

Often vendors are small companies that are unable to afford engineering expertise in manufacturing and quality areas. Here, vendors and customers must work together to improve vendors' manufacturing processes, productivity levels, and quality standards. Customers should visit vendors' plants at least annually, more often if there are problems. Vendors should visit customers to see how components are used in products.

Local Sourcing

While it is not absolutely necessary or even possible for suppliers to be geographically close to customers, the closer suppliers are to customers or companies, the easier it is to provide them with daily deliveries. Every day that material spends being transported adds to the level of inventory.

Freight Consolidation Programs

Materials from suppliers can be consolidated on one truck for transportation to customers. If a company has three suppliers in the same area who deliver daily, one truck and driver can pick up daily from each supplier and deliver to that customer.

Standard Packaging

Containers for parts being delivered to a lean company may be standardized by container size and number of parts (lot size). Half-full containers are never sent. Since the number of containers and items in the containers are easily seen, everyone knows the amount of available inventory. It is therefore unlikely that a lean company will run out of critical components, even if they are sole-source components. Naturally, the supplier must take precautions to ensure that it never shuts the lean company down due to a lack of parts or subassemblies.

Take for example, at Johnson Controls International, the supplier of seats for the Toyota Camry assembly plant in Lexington, Kentucky, there is a location in the plant called "the lock-up." This area contains a 24-hour supply of seats for the Camry. The seats are stored behind a large fence. Only the plant manager has a key to this area.

THE PLANT TRIP

A true understanding of lean manufacturing requires a visit to the vendor's facility to understand the supply chain. So, through a plant trip to see two suppliers of the same component, a comparison of two suppliers is possible at the component level. This is the level where the lean system builds parts using lean-manufacturing cells and the mass system uses large job shops (see Figure 11-2). For instance, one vendor may supply Toyota Camry parts and the other General Motors parts.

Lean Manufacturing Cells

Lean manufacturing cells are different from the interim manufacturing cells described in Chapter 5. Interim cells, designed with machine tools originally used in a job shop, are the predictors for true lean cells. In a true lean manufacturing system, manufacturing and equipment must be designed, built, tested, and implemented into manufacturing cells. This includes machine tools and processes, tooling such as workholders, cutting tools, and material-handling devices, especially decouplers. Simple, reliable equipment that can be easily maintained should be specified. In general, flexible, dedicated equipment that can be built in-house is better than if it is

purchased and modified for the needs of a cell. Many companies understand that it is not a good strategy to simply imitate or copy manufacturing-process technology from another company, and then to expect to make an exceptional product using the same technology that a competitor uses. When process technology is purchased from outside vendors, unique aspects are quickly lost. The lean company must carry out research and development on manufacturing technologies as well as manufacturing systems to produce competitive and cost-efficient products. Effective, cost-efficient manufacturing is the result of research and development in manufacturing process technology.

Advantages of in-house-built Equipment

There are unique advantages to an in-house-built equipment strategy:

- flexibility—rapid tooling changeover, rapid modification for new products, and less-than-full-capacity design;
- build exactly what is needed;
- maintainability, reliability, and durability are built into the machine tools; and
- ability to accommodate the needs of the existing cell and system single cycle automatics. Process delay can be specified if needed; poka-yokes can be used; equipment can be specified so it is easy to load, unload, and operate (walk-away switch and fail safe operation); make one, check one, move on methodology can be used; it is economical to build in quality; equipment is designed to produced single units, not batches.

Flexibility

Flexibility is built in when a process and its applicable tooling are adaptable to many types of products. It requires rapid changeover of jigs, fixtures, and tooling for existing products and rapid modification for new designs. The processes have excess capacity. This means that they can run faster if needed, but are designed for operating at less-than-full capacity.

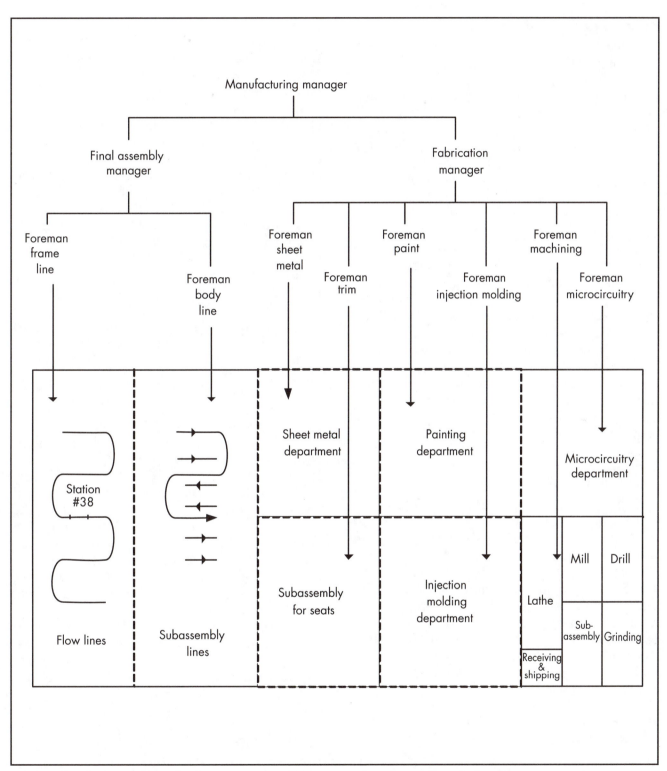

Figure 11-2. The factory layout for the mass production system is a flow shop with a job shop that segregates the process into departments (above) and further functionalizes the departments in functional groups (below).

Build Exactly What is Needed

Building only what is needed means a company is not paying for unused capabilities or options.

A machine may have unique capabilities that the competition does not have and cannot get access to through equipment vendors. When purchasing equipment from vendors, purchasers may be paying for capabilities the competition can get for free (from the vendor). For example, in the lean cell example described later in this chapter, a broaching machine produces gear teeth on a rack bar. The angle these teeth make with the bar varies for different types of racks. Although the broaching process makes gear teeth in racks, job shop broaching machines are not acceptable for the cell due to their large size and long changeover times. So for the cell, a unique machine tool for broaching must be designed and built.

Equipment should allow an operator to stand and walk. It should be of an appropriate height that allows an operator to easily perform tasks standing and to then move to the next machine in a step or two. The design of each process has a narrow footprint.

Maintainability, Reliability, and Durability

Equipment should be easy to maintain (oil, clean, changeover, replace worn parts, and with standardized fasteners). Many cells at lean production vendors are similar to each other. The sole-source company has the volume and expertise to get business from many other companies, making essentially the same components or subassemblies for different original equipment manufacturers (OEMs). The vendors build manufacturing cells for each OEM. Most equipment can be interchanged between cells in emergencies.

Accommodating the Needs of Cells and Systems

It is necessary to design and build machines, material handling equipment (decouplers), and tooling for the needs of the cell and the system.

Each process in a cell is a step in the component production process, with a process time that is less than the needed cycle time. Machines are typically single cycle automatics, but may have the capacity for process delay. An example of process delay would be the process of induction heat treatment that takes four minutes in a cell operating with a cycle time of one minute. Induction heat treatment has a capacity for four units. Each unit gets four minutes of heat treating, with one unit being output every minute.

Accidents. Equipment should be failsafe, or designed to prevent accidents. Some machines have walk-away switches so they begin processing after being loaded by a worker who is moving toward the next process. The start button is located on the exit side of the machine.

Ergonomics. Equipment should be designed so that it is easy to operate, load, and unload. Toyota ergonomic specialists recommend unloading with the left hand and loading with the right hand, while walking right to left.

Single units. Equipment should be designed to process single units, not batches. Small footprint, low-cost equipment is best. Machining or processing times should be modified so they are less than the cycle time. Cycle time is the production-allotted time in which one unit should be produced. Machine time is related to the machine parameters selected. This approach often reduces the cutting speed, thereby increasing tool life and reducing downtime for tool changes. This approach also reduces equipment stoppages, lengthens the life of equipment, and may improve quality.

Self-inspection devices. Equipment should have self-inspection devices such as sensors, poka-yokes, and counters to promote autonomation. Autonomation is the means to control quantity (do not overproduce) and quality (no defects). It is not the same thing as automation. Often a machine is equipped to count the number of items produced and prevent defects from occurring.

Movable equipment. Equipment should be movable. It should be equipped with casters or wheels, flexible pipes, and flexible wiring. There should be no fixed conveyor lines.

Self-cleaning. Equipment should be self-cleaning; automatically disposing of its own chips and production waste.

Profitability. Lastly, equipment should be profitable at any reasonable production volume. Equipment that needs millions of units to be profitable should be avoided. Otherwise, once production volume even slightly exceeds the maximum capacity that the machine can build, it would be necessary to purchase another one. The new machine would not be profitable until it approached full utilization. This may result in schedulers of equipment dividing volume into two machines, making neither one profitable.

Cell equipment is designed and developed with a priority on internal customer factors, even though factors affecting the external customer are ultimately the highest priority of manufacturing engineering. Although many factories lack the expertise to build machines from scratch, most have the expertise to modify equipment for unique capabilities. However, this is the interim cell approach, not the lean cell approach.

Case Studies

In the early 1980s, *Japanese Manufacturing Techniques* (Schonberger 1982) made Americans think about Just-in-time/total quality control as a way to make low-cost, superior-quality goods in manufacturing systems with short throughput times. The system was flexible. Then in 1991, *The Machine That Changed the World* (Womack 1991) told readers more about a new manufacturing system that everyone (including the Toyota inventors of it) now refers to as the lean production system. This knowledge helped manufacturers make productivity and quality gains that were significant.

Figure 11-3 contrasts the design of an assembly plant to explain the differences between lean and mass production. Illustrated is an automobile-assembly plant where a vehicle is being assembled. In one station, the steering gear is being installed (Figure 11-4). The vehicle spends one minute at this station (one of 150-450 stations), while a worker installs the steering gear. The steering-gear assembly is shown in Figure 11-5. A worker is able to perform every variation of the assembly of the steering gear, including right- and left-hand drives. The steering gears are made in another state and transported daily to the assembly plant in boxes of 10 or 20. They are delivered hourly to the point of use on the assembly line. The kanban system controls this process. The gear assembly plant makes gears at a daily rate that is equal to what the assembly plant consumes. The steering gear contains a rack-and-pinion subassembly, which is the critical element in the steering gear.

Figure 11-6 shows a portion of a plant where rack bars are made for American automobile-steering gears. Steel bars are sawed into lengths and moved in tote boxes to lathes where drilling, turning, grooving, facing, and threading are performed. Each lathe performs the needed operations for a rack bar. The bars are then carted to the broaches, which cut teeth in the rack. Next, the bar is heat-treated, again in large batches, with a quench-and-temper process. Then it is sent for magnetic-particle inspection for cracks. Next, it is straightened. When the bar returns from the inspection process, it is finish ground and ready for subassembly into the rack-and-pinion gear. The throughput time may be weeks.

As a system design, the job shop still exists. Figure 11-6 is simply a modern-day version where large volumes of goods are produced in batches of 50-200 pieces. This modified functional manufacturing system is a production job shop. The design groups processes functionally, but in this case, it has removed the walls between processes. Materials move from left to right through two acres of the plant floor. Parts must leave the plant for crack detection after quench and tempering and bar straightening. In this design, it is impossible for workers to move a part from machine to machine (or operation), one component at a time. The manufacturing system design prevents one-piece flow.

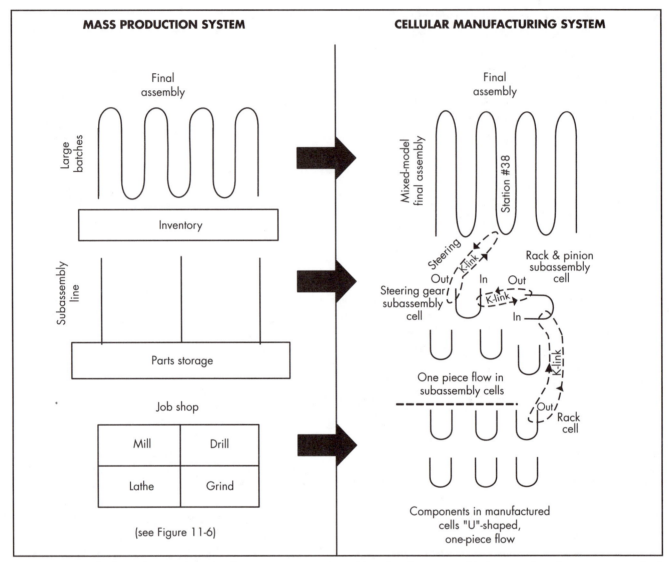

MASS PRODUCTION SYSTEM

CELLULAR MANUFACTURING SYSTEM

Final assembly

Large batches

Inventory

Subassembly line

Parts storage

Job shop

| Mill | Drill |
| Lathe | Grind |

(see Figure 11-6)

Final assembly

Mixed-model final assembly

Station #38

Steering

K-link

Out

In

Out

Steering gear subassembly cell

K-link

Rack & pinion subassembly cell

In

K-link

One piece flow in subassembly cells

Out

Rack cell

Components in manufactured cells "U"-shaped, one-piece flow

Figure 11-3. In the lean plant on the right, the components made in the rack cell are assembled into rack and pinion gears, which are assembled into a stationary gear, which is installed into car at station #38.

Between machines and filling the aisles are tote boxes filled with racks of bars in various stages of completion. Because it is difficult to count parts in inventory, it can be estimated that there are 97,000 racks in this area at any point in time, enough for eight days of production. The company calls this area a manufacturing cell, but in reality, it is a large job shop with a family of parts (rack bars).

Contrast the American plant with the Japanese transplanted factory that is manufacturing steering gears (see Figure 11-7). Again, observe how a lean plant makes the rack. This cell makes racks for the Toyota Camry. Machine tools that are not made by a traditional machine-tool builder are performing processing in the cell. Machines are custom-built for the cell. Each machine basically performs

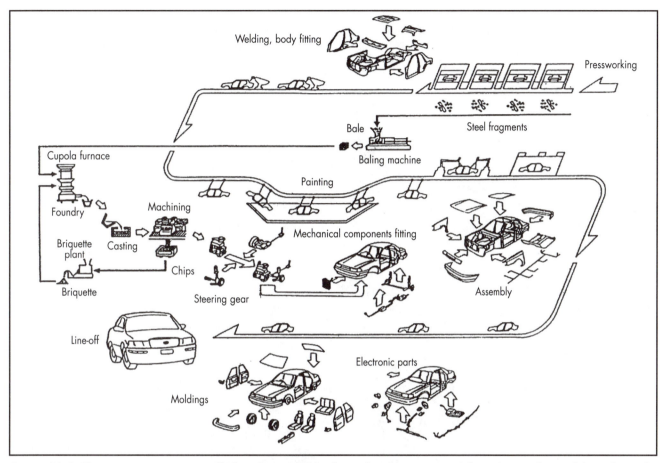

Figure 11-4. The steering gear is installed at Station #38 after it has been received from the vendor and brought to the assembly line.

one step on the bar. Then, the bar is moved to the next machine, which may have devices on it, such as poka-yokes or decouplers, to check what has been done in the previous step. Or, the worker may be checking the rack bar as part of the lean production methodology.

The machines that tool builders are making today are great examples of the super machine. Super machines are costly because they are complex with many capabilities. The user pays for these capabilities, but often never uses them. Machine tools in the cell are simple but precise, repeatable, reliable, and replaceable with narrow footprints to reduce worker-walking time between machines.

The lean manufacturing system has unique characteristics embodied in its manufacturing and assembly cells. Multifunctional workers man the cells. They can perform tasks other than handling material and operating manufacturing processes. Tasks include quality control and inspection to prevent defects from occurring, machine-tool maintenance, setup reduction, and problem solving for continuous improvement. Cells are usually in U-shaped or rectangular arrangements. The cells are designed so a worker can easily step across an aisle to work on machines located on the opposite side. This separates the machine's work and the operator's work. Changing the number of workers can vary the cell output.

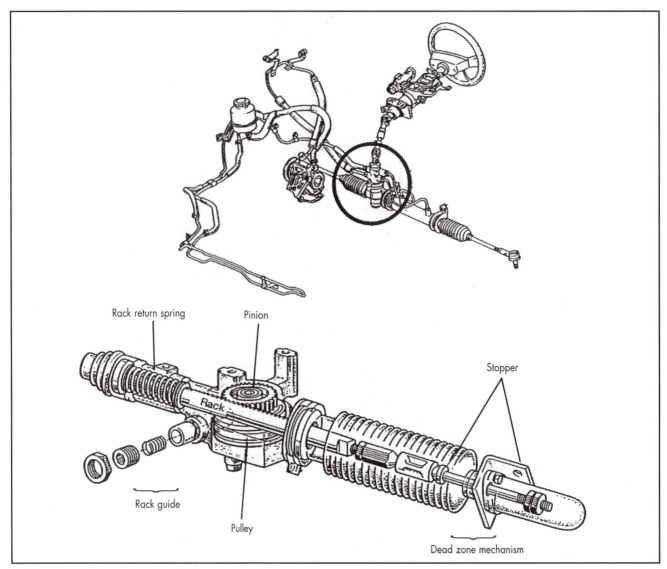

Figure 11-5. The steering gear shown has two major components, the rack bar and pinion. The pinion is contained in the valve housing.

To recap, implementation of a lean system requires work that is systematic and, many times, difficult. Lean manufacturing cells and a system's design must continue to evolve and improve over time. Continuous improvement is forced through the gradual removal of inventory from kanban links between cells. Most equipment in a cell operates untended; that is, it independently completes a cycle initiated by an operator. A lean manufacturing cell has built-in poka-yoke devices to prevent defects from occurring. Cells operate on the lean-production methodology of make-one, check-one, and move-one on. Within a cell, there are an exact number of parts that are either in machines or in decouplers between the machines. This is a lean operation, which points to there being no extra inventory within a cell. When a part is finished and exits a cell, another part starts into the cell. Lean production's secret is that manufacturing

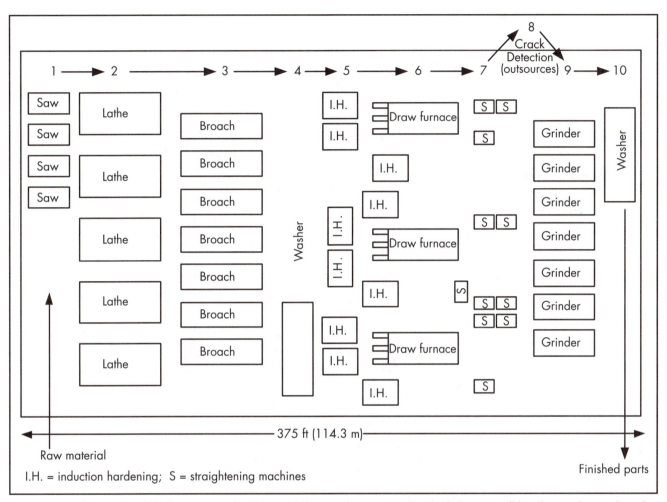

Figure 11-6. The overhead shafts are gone from this rack bar machining area but the lathes are still lined up in this modern day job shop, a functionally designed area that produces racks for rack-and-pinion steering gears. This area is about two acres (80,000 ft²) and the work-in-process is estimated at about 97,000 parts. The area is manned by 20 workers.

cells operate by a one-piece-flow philosophy (Sekine 1990). Lean manufacturing cells are at the heart of the Toyota production system.

How Lean Cells Operate

To understand the Toyota production system is to understand how manufacturing cells work. Manufacturing cells are the proprietary element in lean production. The typical lean manufacturing cell is shown in Figure 11-7. This is a fairly large cell capable of high throughput rates. The rack for a steering gear requires heat treating, inspection, and mechan-

ical straightening, in addition to numerous machining operations like drilling and tapping, hob milling gear teeth, deep-hole drilling, grinding, and broaching. All the processing required to produce a finished rack, ready for subassembly, is in the cell. This lean production cell can make nine different types of racks for the same automobile model. The changeover at any individual machine occurs with one touch when the worker unloads the previous part from the machine (Shingo 1985). Many machines are equipped with poka-yoke devices

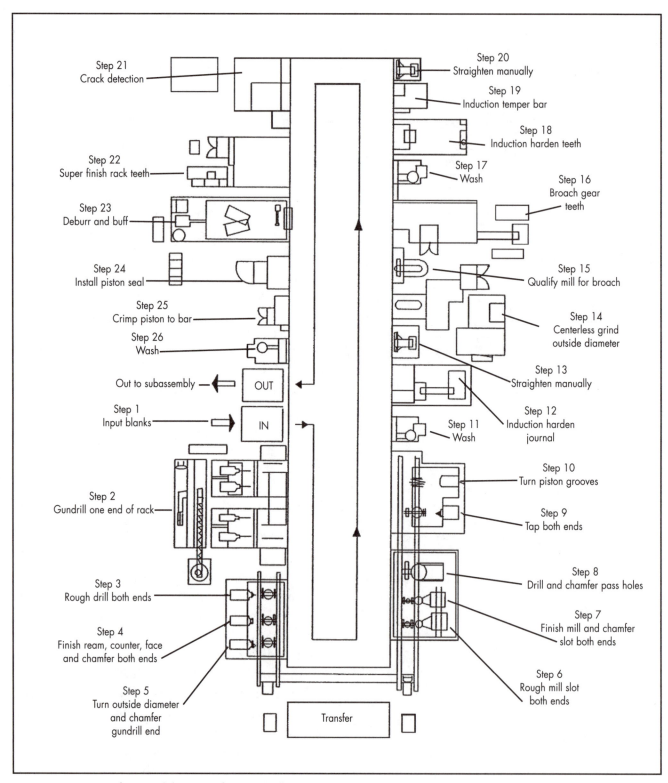

Step 21
Crack detection

Step 20
Straighten manually

Step 19
Induction temper bar

Step 18
Induction harden teeth

Step 17
Wash

Step 16
Broach gear
teeth

Step 22
Super finish rack teeth

Step 23
Deburr and buff

Step 15
Qualify mill for broach

Step 24
Install piston seal

Step 14
Centerless grind
outside diameter

Step 25
Crimp piston to bar

Step 13
Straighten manually

Step 26
Wash

Step 12
Induction harden
journal

Out to subassembly

OUT

Step 1
Input blanks

IN

Step 11
Wash

Step 10
Turn piston grooves

Step 9
Tap both ends

Step 2
Gundrill one end of rack

Step 8
Drill and chamfer pass holes

Step 3
Rough drill both ends

Step 7
Finish mill and chamfer
slot both ends

Step 4
Finish ream, counter, face
and chamfer both ends

Step 5
Turn outside diameter
and chamfer
gundrill end

Step 6
Rough mill slot
both ends

Transfer

Figure 11-7. Layout for a rack bar manufacturing cell.

to prevent processes or operators from making mistakes.

This cell is designed a bit differently from most others in that the work arrives and departs from the middle of the U-shaped cell. Operations at the start (the right end of the cell) are the same for all the bars in the family of parts. Therefore, a transfer line is used with automatic transfer devices, small robots, and mechanical arms and levers to move the part from machine to machine.

The machining time required for the deep-hole drilling is longer than the cycle time for the cell. That is, machine time is greater than cycle time. The cell produces one finished rack bar per minute. In other words, cycle time equals one minute per rack. Thus, one rack is started through the cell every minute and the processes of deep-hole drilling and tapping are divided into stages. On the average, machine times for each stage are less than one minute. In this area, the machines have automatic repeat-cycle capabilities, with automatic transfer devices moving parts to the next step. This is possible because parts in the family are identical in these areas. This is a common feature of lean manufacturing cells; a portion of the component is made on a small transfer line attached to a lean cell, with cell workers loading and unloading parts.

In total, the rack moves through 26 steps or operations. Most of these operations are machining with single-cycle-automatic machines performing the work. However, there are manual operations in the cell other than loading and unloading. These include Steps 13 and 20, to manually straighten the bar, which can warp after heat-treating. Step 21 inspects the bar using inline magnetic-particle inspection and Steps 24 and 25 assemble parts onto the bar. The times for these steps are variable.

The rack-bar lean manufacturing cell typically uses two operators. These workers are standing, walking workers who move from machine to machine in counterclockwise loops, as shown in Figure 11-8. Each operator makes the loop in about one minute. Operator 1 typi-

cally addresses 10 stations and Operator 2 addresses 11 stations. Most steps involve unloading a machine, loading another part into that machine, checking the unloaded part, and dropping it into the decoupler between the machines. After completing tasks at a process, a worker walks to the next machine, hitting a start switch for the machine that is being left. This switch is called a *walk-away switch*.

The stock-on-hand in decouplers and machines helps maintain the smooth flow of parts through the machines. Stock-on-hand is kept as small as possible. Sometimes decoupler elements inspect or check a part, but mostly they serve to transport parts from one process to the next. Sometimes a decoupler performs a secondary operation like deburring or remove residual magnetic fields. A steel bar can become magnetized, causing small chips to adhere to it and perhaps cause it to be incorrectly located in a subsequent process.

By design, one operator controls both the input and output of the cell and, thus, the volume of material going through the cell. This keeps the stock-on-hand quantity constant and the cell working in balance with the final or subassembly lines it is feeding. Operator 1 loads the centerless grinder, then moves across the aisle to unload the operation called "deburr and buff." Operator 2 unloads the centerless grinder and then loads the part in the next process, moving in a clockwise loop in the cell, from right to left.

At the interface between the two operators, either operator can perform the necessary operations depending on when they arrive and when the process in the machine is finished. That is, the region where the two operators meet is really not fixed, but changes or shifts depending upon the manner in which parts are moving about the cell. This is called the relay zone (Suzaki 1987), an added flexibility feature that requires workers who are cross-trained on processes in the cell. This cell can operate with one, two, or three workers.

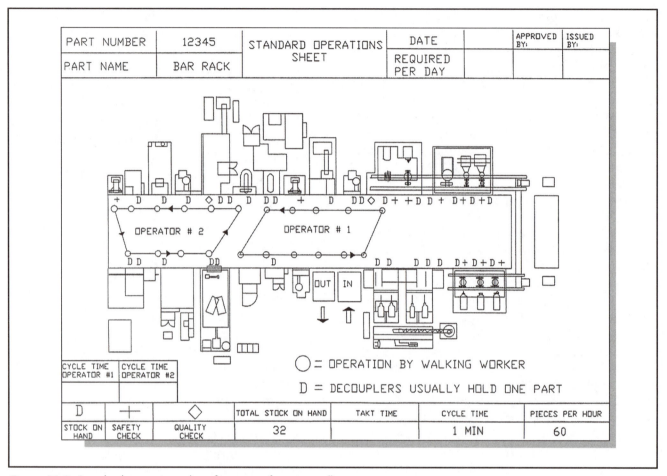

Figure 11-8. Standard operations sheet for a manufacturing cell.

Lean Versus Mass Production

In the mass-production system, reducing direct labor is the best approach to reducing production cost. The mass-production plant puts a high value on reducing direct labor and increasing machine utilization. Instead of focusing solely on labor reduction and machine utilization, the lean plant concentrates on a system design that simultaneously achieves all of the goals of the lean manufacturing system. The data in Table 11-1 compares an assembly cell at a lean plant to an assembly cell at a mass-production plant. The results indicate that the line at the mass production plant has a lower direct-labor rate, but that it requires more inventory, has a longer throughput time,

is more expensive to build, and generates more defects.

The data in Table 11-2 presents a comparison of rack machining in a lean manufacturing cell to machining areas at a mass-production plant. Again, the mass-production plant has a lower direct-labor rate, but requires more floor space, significantly higher inventory, longer throughput time, and more expensive parts. In addition, it results in more defects. So the mass production plant succeeds in achieving a lower ratio in direct labor in both machining and manual operations; but, if scrap rates and overtime are considered, both plants produce about the same amount of parts per labor hour.

Table 11-1
Assembly measurables for design comparison

	Lean Production	Mass Production
Floor area	1	1.10
In-cell inventory	1	2.80
Throughput time	1	1.60
Capital investment	1	1.30
Direct workers	1	0.70
Parts/labor-hour (with overtime)	1	0.99
Line returns	1	1.20
Warranty claims	1	9.20
(Cochran and Dobbs 1999)		

Table 11-2
Assembly measurables for design comparison

	Lean Production	Mass Production
Floor area	1	1.70
In-cell inventory	1	970
Throughput time	1	117
Capital investment	1	1.20
Direct workers	1	0.86
Parts/labor-hour (w/overtime)	1	1.00
Internal scrap	1	5.40
(Cochran and Dobbs 1999)		

While visiting both example plants, some intangible differences become evident. The worker attitudes are noticeably different. The push to reduce direct labor at the mass-production plant causes workers to be wary of goals set by management. Engineers at the mass-production plant seem reluctant to seek suggestions from the workers on the plant floor. They also tend to minimize the importance of internal customers' contributions. At the lean production plant, a close relationship between engineering and production departments is developed. Workers appreciate having their cell's engineer nearby and frequently provide suggestions for improvements. Likewise, the engineers respect workers, appreciate their suggestions, and often implement proposed solutions or improvements.

The lean-production plant's machine tools are custom-built and are a proprietary element of lean manufacturing. Figure 11-9 shows the differences between lean and mass production systems for the broaching process. In a lean cell, broaching is Step 16. Notice how much larger the broach is in the mass-production plant. It is immovable and takes 45 minutes to changeover. The broach in the lean cell is a rotary broach and requires a flip of a switch to change it from left- to right-hand rack teeth angles.

At the lean supplier plant for steering gears, there are about 14 cells for rack bars, with one cell for each Japanese transplant company. Each cell is dedicated to the company's specific design, but each has similar process technology. So, many of the machines for the Mitsubishi® rack cell are interchangeable with some modifications to the Camry cell. This interchangeability keeps production moving if a machine tool in the Camry rack cell breaks down. However, if there is a problem with the Camry rack bar, engineers from Toyota need only visit the Camry rack bar cell.

The cell design isolates processes, which must be redesigned so batch flow becomes one-piece flow. Notice that crack detection, the Step-8 process in a job shop that requires outsourcing, is incorporated directly into the cell as Step 21. Between Steps 21 and 22 is a decoupler, which transports and degausses parts before they go into superfinishing.

Other new processes are induction tempering, Step 12, and conduction hardening, Step 18, which replace quench and temper processes in a job shop. Drawing is done in batches with long processing times, 1.5 hours, while induction tempering is completed in the cell with a cycle time of about 54 seconds. See Figure 11-10.

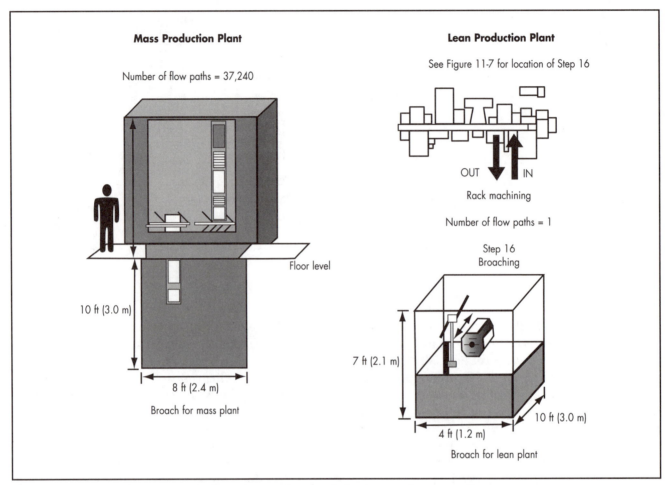

Figure 11-9. *The machine tools in the lean plant are homemade for the manufacturing cells.*

RULES FOR LEAN CELL DESIGN

The rules for the design of a lean manfuacturing cell include:

- Each machine, process, or operation in a cell should be ergonomically designed for a standing, walking worker to approach the machine from the right and leave it from the left.
- Material should pass from right to left because most people are right-handed and it is easier for them to load with the right hand and unload with the left.
- Machines should be designed to have walk-away switches that the worker hits when leaving the machine. The doors should then close so the machine can begin the processing cycle unattended. The machine should be at least a single-cycle automatic.
- Machines should be arranged in the sequence of operations needed to process parts.
- All the processes needed to make the part should be in the cell and have machine times less than the cycle time or the average time. This requires some unique process technology.
- The aisle in the cell should be about 4–ft (1.2 m) wide, so workers can pass each other in the cell, but also easily step across the aisle. Between each process there

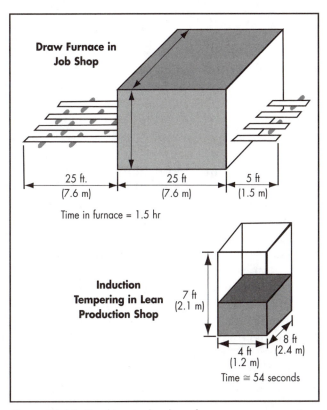

Draw Furnace in Job Shop

25 ft.
(7.6 m)

25 ft
(7.6 m)

5 ft
(1.5 m)

Time in furnace = 1.5 hr

Induction Tempering in Lean Production Shop

7 ft
(2.1 m)

4 ft
(1.2 m)

8 ft
(2.4 m)

Time ≅ 54 seconds

Figure 11-10. Batching in the draw furnace versus one piece flow in the induction tempering process (Step 19).

should be a decoupler that holds one part. The decouplers should be designed to connect the flow of parts, reorient the part, deburr the part, or degauss the part. The decoupler can also hold a part for heating, cooling, curing, drying, etc. Like machine tools and tooling, decouplers are custom designed to hold every part in a family with equal facility.

• The cell should be equipped with many poka-yokes performing self-inspections or successive inspections. Devices can be in the decouplers or in the workholding device of the next machine; they should be simple.

Ergonomics of Lean Cells

Ergonomics deals with the mental, physical, and social requirements of a job and how that job is designed or modified to accommodate human limitations. Considerations include:

• Are processes in a cell designed to be at an adjustable height to minimize lifting of parts?
• Are transfer devices designed for slide on/slide off?
• Are automatic steps equipped with interrupt signaling to help a worker monitor the process?
• When a job is defined primarily as loading/unloading, ergonomic concerns about lifting parts, placing parts in machines, and operating workholding devices must be addressed.

An operator's ability to detect and correct cell malfunctions establishes utilization and thus production efficiency. Machine design for maintainability and diagnostics is critical. The original designer of a cell should incorporate ergonomic issues initially, rather than trying to return later to implement fixes. Manufacturing cells designed correctly rarely result in cumulative-trauma problems for workers. This is because a worker's tasks and movements are varied from machine to machine. In assembly cells where workers control the operation of the machines, it is important that the machines are ergonomically identical. Sewing machines in a cell are a good example (Black and Schroer 1993). To an operator, the control of all sewing machines should feel the same.

Computer-integrated Manufacturing

There has been much discussion about flexible manufacturing systems and computer-integrated manufacturing. Many believe the only way that manufacturers can compete is to automate their systems. This is the computer-integrated approach that was renamed "agile manufacturing." Briefly, the concept is to integrate a system through computerization and automation. This often results in trying to computerize, robotize, or automate complex manufacturing and assembly processes. Most manufacturers know how to integrate a system when there is little or no variety in the products. Variety, however, is a fact of manufacturing life.

Lean-manufacturing cells take a different approach. First, the manufacturing system must be integrated, then it must be computerized and automated. The development of manufacturing and assembly cells is the first step of integrating a manufacturing system (Black 1991). Experts on computer-integrated manufacturing agree that lean manufacturing must occur before making an effort to computerize a system (Ayers and Butcher 1993). While system costs are difficult to obtain, early evidence suggests that a lean cell approach is significantly less expensive than the computer-integrated approach.

Continuous improvement requires continuous redesign through large and small problem-solving efforts in a manufacturing system. This is a way of life for lean-manufacturing companies.

FOURTH INDUSTRIAL REVOLUTION

The manufacture of weapons drove the first industrial revolution. The second industrial revolution was driven by the production of equipment and weapons for World War II. It should not be surprising, therefore, that the fourth industrial revolution has been assisted by technology developed to design airplanes, specifically the Boeing 747 that carries super-lasers that can shoot down enemy ballistic missiles from hundreds of miles away. The computer system that Boeing used to design the 777 was also used to design an airborne laser by combining the work of 22 design teams working in 11 states. Both the design and manufacturing system were simulated in the computer. This same technology is capable of designing manufacturing systems and products simultaneously. Products may be large subassemblies that are assembled on a final-

assembly line anywhere in the world. This means that the final assembly line for automobiles should be shorter (or leaner), and that it will have fewer stations and longer station times for the installation of larger but fewer subassemblies. The vendors would not only be responsible for the Just-in-time manufacture and delivery of subassemblies, but also be able to supply labor to perform an installation on a customer's assembly line. Some vehicle assembly plants in Brazil are operating in this manner and have become test beds for future designs of lean manufacturing systems.

Supercomputers will permit simulation of the assembly of an entire product, in this case the automobile, including simulation of each workstation with ergonomic subroutines for good workplace design on the line. Similarly, work cells with walking workers or robots that produce components for subassembly cells can be simulated in detail.

The enabling technology for the fourth industrial revolution is the supercomputer, which is capable of operating high-level, 3D-design software, including virtual reality capability. This powerful computer system is capable of designing products and processes, including entire manufacturing systems. Such systems, though not widespread in use yet, were in use in 2002 at Chrysler, Boeing, Lockheed, Electric Boat, and a few other large companies.

What will the manufacturing system design be for these factories of the future? They will be "e-lean," large subassemblies manufactured in sync with final assembly and delivered in sequence for installation. The final assembly plants will be smaller (leaner) and communicate with the suppliers via electronic methods for controlling material movement, accounting, ordering, planning, purchasing, billing, and so forth.

Chapter 12
Ergonomics in Cell Design

Lean production's success is critically dependent on the worker, the factory's most valuable resource. It is imperative that workers have safe and ergonomically correct workstations. There has been much written on the subject of workstation design and ergonomics, but little has been written about workstation design for manufacturing and subassembly cells.

LEAN PRODUCTION AND ERGONOMICS

Lean production is a productivity methodology; it shortens the lead time between customer orders and factory shipments. Lean production uses less of everything compared to the methods employed in a job shop (Womack 1991). Lean methods require less labor and manufacturing space, smaller investments in tools, fewer engineering hours to develop new products. Proper lean production implementation requires that less than half of the inventory-on-hand be kept. It also means that when a factory adopts lean production practices, it will manufacture products with fewer defects and, therefore, an increase in quality will result.

There have been numerous studies on the advantages of linked-cell systems. However, research into human-resources issues and manufacturing cells indicates that the integration of cellular-manufacturing systems with good human-engineering practices is still uncertain. Early computer simulations of linked-cell manufacturing operations do not reflect proper cellular functions. These functions include standing and walking while performing a make-one, inspect-one, and move-one-on operation. The simulations did not use a one-piece, inter-cell, parts-movement methodology with single-cycle-automatic processes, physical-inventory and production-control systems, decouplers, or kanban squares (Black 1991). There is little ergonomic research in linked-cell manufacturing and the implications of having standing, walking workers; and, almost no research, as well, on the ergonomic ramifications of this system. A systematic empirical investigation of the effects of cell manufacturing on worker jobs, attitudes, and work-related musculoskeletal disorders has not been undertaken (Jackson and Martin 1996). However, in 2000, there was an investigation that described a favorable analysis of three ergonomic simulations comparing linked-cell manufacturing to functional job shops.

Individual workstations in a linked cell environment must include typical ergonomic and safety considerations and functions to accommodate and enhance total-cell optimization (Figure 12-1). Manufacturing cells require that the worker be mobile; that is, able to move easily and freely from workstation to workstation. Individual tools and pieces of equipment must be designed or modified to meet these requirements, while also maintaining worker safety. The workstation must be designed for effortless and fast movement between cells and stock-on-hand areas.

Since employees are the top resource of a manufacturing organization, manufacturing-system designers are acutely aware of potential ergonomic and physiological dangers to factory

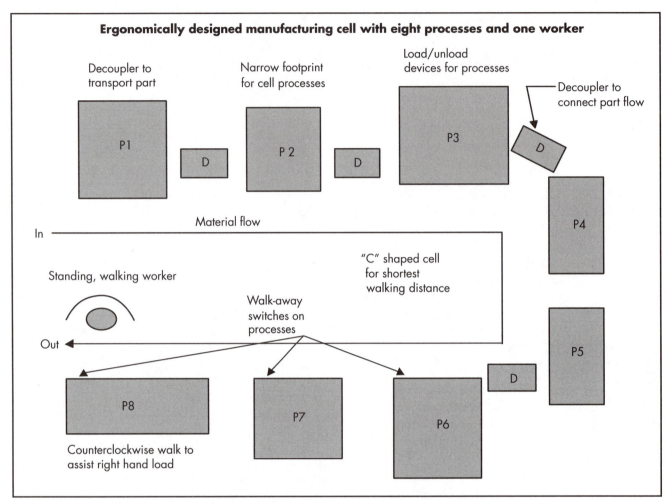

Figure 12-1. Ergonomic and safety aspects of a manufacturing cell.

workers. Government and private studies show that work-related musculoskeletal disorders are increasing. The resulting injury costs are staggering to industry. Therefore, it is important to design work that is safe and ergonomically sound. There are several ergonomic standards being proposed to eliminate human suffering and simultaneously reduce worker injuries and the economic burdens such injuries impose on industry.

The National Academy of Sciences has found a clear relationship between work-related musculoskeletal disorders and manufacturing jobs. It states that research clearly demonstrates that specific intervention can reduce reported musculoskeletal-disorder rates for workers who perform high-risk tasks. Therefore, ignoring moral and humanistic issues for a moment, it makes good business sense to design manufacturing and assembly cells within accepted ergonomic and physiological guidelines. Of course, the optimum cell or workstation design eliminates human suffering while, concurrently, saving a manufacturing organization significant workers' compensation and related expenses, along with maintaining productivity gains for which cellular systems are noted.

There is no more fundamental aspect of occupational ergonomics than the design of local workstations where workers spend considerable amounts of time and effort doing their jobs. Ergonomics and the laws of work, by science and custom, have focused primarily on the physical aspects of work such as force and energy requirements. It is well known that these factors are coupled with the specific design of workstations. The physical arrangement of tasks being performed in workstations defines the parameters necessary for ergonomic analysis and for design of the work area. This part of workstation and cell design and evaluation can be thought of as applied ergonomics, anthropometry, and safety.

In workstation design, one must look beyond ergonomics to broader factors of engineering for humans. While workstation designers look at the physical aspects of work, engineering for humans examines the total interface between workers and their work. In other words, designers are concerned with the interface of stimulus and the resulting response involving information processing and action initiation, that is, the senses and physical-muscular control. Workers use their senses. Actions are taken based on the dynamics of the processes around workers, from sensory-perception decisions. Good workstation design is critical for the actions of workers to result in positive outcomes.

HEALTH ISSUES

Job-related, chronic health issues are on the rise. According to the Occupational Safety and Health Administration (OSHA), work-related musculoskeletal disorders are presently the leading cause of lost-workday injuries and worker-compensation costs. In 1996, for example, work-related musculoskeletal disorders reportedly accounted for 647,000 lost workdays (OSHA 2000). Each year, work-related musculoskeletal disorders account for $15-20 billion in worker-compensation costs. The total costs, direct and indirect, may be close to $60 billion.

However it is accomplished, the designer's focus should be on the prevention or reduction of work-related musculoskeletal disorders resulting from working in manufacturing sys-

tems. An ergonomic response should include consideration of the hand, wrist, shoulder, neck, elbow, and back. The kilocalorie consumption of these muscle areas should be monitored and analyzed for repetitive motion, joint deviations, and reach-and-grasp motions. This is especially important since these particular body parts are primarily at risk in manufacturing environments.

Musculoskeletal Disorders

The two leading work-related musculoskeletal disorders are carpal-tunnel syndrome and back injury. Compared to other injuries, carpal-tunnel syndrome results, on average, in more days away from work. Typically, carpal-tunnel cases involve more than 25 days away from work (Khalil 1991). Work-related problems of the back occur primarily because of manual material handling; although problems can also occur from body movements without a load, such as pinched nerves, ruptured discs, pulled muscles, and many other conditions. Also, back problems can occur from lack of motion, such as sitting for long periods. Manufacturing-system designers must take into account these facts and other related physiological factors.

Work-related musculoskeletal disorders can occur from manufacturing tasks related to the hand and wrist, where the concerns are with tendons, muscles, or nerves (Figure 12-2). There are several cumulative-trauma disorders that may occur in these areas, including carpal-tunnel syndrome and tenosynovitis. Tenosynovitis results when tendons running through the wrist abrade on the bones. If the median nerve flowing through the wrist becomes pinched in the wrist's narrow carpal-tunnel area, thumb and index finger numbness and tingling result. Cumulative traumas of the upper extremities are physical ailments of the wrist, arm, and shoulder. The cumulative effects of repeated mechanical stresses cause disorders that develop gradually over time and are believed to be work-related.

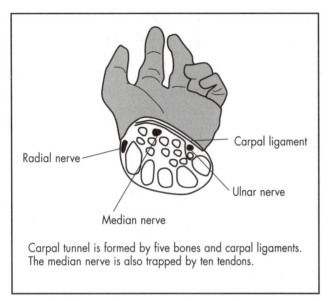

Carpal tunnel is formed by five bones and carpal ligaments.
The median nerve is also trapped by ten tendons.

Figure 12-2. Carpal tunnel syndrome is leading cause of upper body injury in the workplace (adapted from Putz-Anderson 1988).

Causes

Repetition seems to be the major contributing factor in cumulative-trauma disorders. Generally, a task is considered repetitive if the basic cycle time is less than 30 seconds. Repetition influences cumulative trauma more than force does. Therefore, a reduction in the lifetime use of the joint may be necessary to prevent carpal-tunnel syndrome. Various engineering solutions should be considered. In addition, joint deviation also influences carpal-tunnel syndrome. The goal is to keep the wrist in a neutral (handshake) position. Changing the job or changing the tool design accomplishes this goal. A job change may entail a simple change in operator posture. Changing the hand-to-tool angle is another option. Applied load influences carpal-tunnel syndrome as well. The cell designer should strive to reduce the force duration and the amount of force required to perform the work.

It is known that force at extreme deviations is worse for the body than force in the neutral position. It has been reported that highly repetitive jobs more than double the chances for worker injury, compared to low-repetition jobs. However, cumulative trauma may also occur when there is little repetitive work. Other possible causes include holding one position, a non-neutral posture, localized pressure, or the use of force, cold, or vibration. Muscles that hold a body part in position for long periods are more prone to fatigue than muscles that are moving a body part. A worker assembling awkward parts by extending and holding parts for alignment is an example. A non-neutral posture is the relative position of an individual joint, not an overall body posture. Any joint posture significantly different from a neutral position is considered to be at risk for musculoskeletal distress. Neutral is considered to be the position about halfway through the accepted range of motion for the joint. Cumulative trauma can occur when a joint is extended or flexed at the far end of a joint's range. Also, direct pressure on nerves or tendons can cause long-term damage. The wrist's carpal tunnel and the elbow are both of major concern. Hand tools must be designed with ergonomically correct handles. They also should be padded to prevent sharp surfaces from applying direct pressure to nerves and tendons (see Figure 12-3).

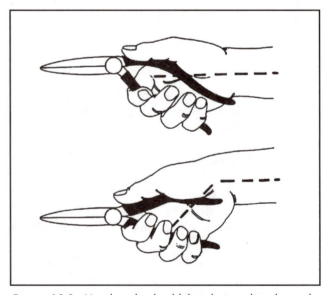

Figure 12-3. Hand tools should be designed to keep the worker's wrist straight, thus relieving many work-related musculoskeletal disorders.

Monitoring the Work Force

Carpal-tunnel syndrome and tenosynovitis indications and symptoms could be monitored in the work force before employees begin working in the cellular-manufacturing system. The test for carpal-tunnel syndrome involves the use of an electro-neurometer to measure nerve speed and conduction rates. This type of analysis should also be completed for shoulder and neck areas. The practice of monitoring for pre-existing work-related disorders should occur for every manufacturing employee before hire or at least as new hires.

Workers should be monitored on a periodic basis thereafter. Health-care providers can provide the metrics. Metrics should be charted for the work force based on the collected data. The metrics should be compared on a before-and-after basis and between the cell work force and remainder of the work force. The best plan, but still not ideal, would be to conduct a comparison of the cell work-force data before entering the cellular environment, then with ongoing data collection after workers enter the cell.

Work-related musculoskeletal disorders are a result of many factors that may apply on or away from the job. These factors are different for different parts of the worker's body. There are several formulas for the application of risk factors to the worker. However, as of 2002, these factors were not well defined and the formulas could not be applied to the probability that the risk factors would affect an individual worker.

Joint Deviation

Another important work-related muscu-loskeletal disorder is joint deviation. Cell designers and ergonomists can take steps to prevent joint deviation. Ideally, joints should operate in a neutral position, that is, *zero-joint deviation*. Specific joints naturally have different motion ranges. *Deviation* is usually defined as a percentage of maximum deviation for a particular joint. Posture affects joint deviation. Naturally, joint position affects stress or strain on a joint.

Venous Pooling

Venous pooling is a potentially serious aliment for workers who stay seated or standing in one place for long periods of time without walking. Deep-vein thrombosis, a condition with serious consequences, has the potential to result from venous pooling. Therefore, before a job shop is converted into a manufacturing cell, the job-shop worker should be monitored several times per day through the use of measured water displacement, with the worker standing in a bucket of water. The standing and walking cell worker is generally unaffected by this problem, since the walking muscle action pumps blood from a worker's lower extremities. Therefore, for walking workers in cellular environments, there is little risk, since these cell workers have little exposure to potential venous-pooling problems.

Healing

The human body is a self-healing bio-mechanism. *Repair* is defined as the body's ability to heal. The more time a body has to heal between repetitions, the better. The body heals muscles faster than tendons, ligaments, or nerves. This is because there is greater blood flow to muscles compared to other damaged areas.

Repetition is less harmful if the body has been trained or preconditioned for that particular work. For exercise or work, warm-up exercises are beneficial. The repair interval can be calculated as the ratio of exposure time over a certain period. Recovery rates decline exponentially over time. Insufficient movement can be as equally harmful as repetitive motion. Static loading, such as sitting at a workbench for long hours, minimizes nutrient and waste exchange from muscles. This minimal body or muscle activity leads to work-related musculoskeletal disorders.

ERGONOMIC SOLUTIONS

Ergonomic solutions for cell design are divided into engineering and administrative categories. Administrative procedures should be considered temporary, until permanent engineering solutions can be implemented. The primary concern should be with engineering solutions. These solutions follow scientific-analysis methods to address problem areas. Solutions often include (Konz 1995):

- automation,
- mechanization,
- cycle reduction,
- difficulty reduction,
- minimization of joint deviation,
- minimization of force, particularly duration, and
- job enlargement.

Job enlargement may play a particularly important function in the relationship between work-related musculoskeletal disorders and cellular-manufacturing systems.

Vibration is a risk factor because of its interference with blood flow, as well as its physical damage to an affected area. Also, vibration contributes to artery constriction, which may result in reduced blood supply. Insufficient blood supply results in less-than-optimum healing. Many cellular-manufacturing systems, especially assembly cells, must provide solutions to prevent injury from assembly-tool vibration.

Work-related musculoskeletal disorders may occur from manufacturing tasks where the hand and wrist are used. Carpal-tunnel syndrome is more a result of repetition, rather than loading factors. A reduction in the use of certain joints may be required to prevent carpal-tunnel syndrome. This is accomplished by adding mechanisms to machines to assist with loading and unloading tasks. This offers a permanent solution.

Solutions to possible awkward postures are decreasing repetition, joint deviation, and applied load. The best solution is to reduce the use and deviated angles of joints. A work task should be designed so both hands do the work, rather than just one hand. The upper arm should be kept in a vertical position aimed downward, not horizontal or elevated positions.

Load, magnitude, and duration factors also should be reduced. The use of suspended power tools will reduce static loading of the worker's shoulder and protect it from possible injury.

Tasks are many times more flexible in manual cells where workers can add or change processes. This, coupled with the slow repetitiveness characteristic of most manual-cell operations, provides reduced probabilities for repetitive-motion injuries. In one cycle, the worker may perform loading and unloading operations on five to 10 processes, with no repetition within the cycle. The fact that a worker may repeat a cycle 60 times an hour and 480 times per shift may be augmented by shifting the worker to a different set of tasks every two hours. Here again, joint deviation also influences carpal-tunnel syndrome. The worker's wrist must be kept in the handshake orientation to prevent harm. To implement this solution, workstations or tooling may need to be redesigned. Sometimes, all that is required is a hand-to-tool angle or a task change to modify an operator's wrist posture, along with implementing loading reductions for that operator.

Ergonomic-assessment Measures

The ergonomic benefits of an optimum manufacturing system are qualifiable. Possible metrics considerations include kilocalorie expenditure, joint deviation, reach and grasp factors, heart rate, bending and reaching factors, and repetitive motion. Specific tools used to gather and then analyze this ergonomic and physiological data include high-level computer-software programs and simulation tools, rapid-upper-limb assessment (RULA), time methods, and the National Institute of Health and Safety (NIOSH) lifting guides. These metrics are a means to an end; that is, they are tools to prevent or eliminate work-related injuries in the workplace. Therefore, manufacturers and their work force will reap two large benefits from using these tools:

- elimination or reduction of worker injuries on the job; and

- reduction of the expensive losses for manufacturers resulting from direct and indirect work-related injury costs.

Rapid-upper-limb Assessment

Rapid-upper-limb assessment can determine if there are posture problems that can lead to work-related musculoskeletal disorders. A RULA begins with an analyst making observations of a worker's limb and body postures for those parts of the work cycle that create the most frequent joint use or the most extreme joint angles. Rapid-upper-limb assessment uses two body regions for estimating the degree of posture correctness. These areas are:

- upper limbs (upper arm, lower arm, and wrist); and
- neck, trunk, and legs.

A RULA scoring form is provided in Figure 12-4.

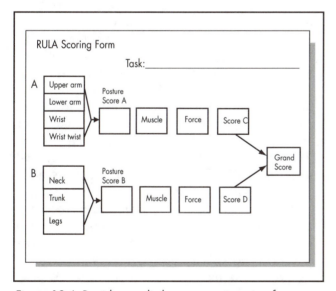

Figure 12-4. Rapid upper-limb assessment scoring form.

Rapid-upper-limb assessment also can be used to minimize the risk of back pain development as a result of poor work design. Work-related problems with the back occur primarily due to manual material handling, although problems can also occur from body movements without applied force, and lack of movement, such as sitting. Lifting guidelines from the NIOSH can be used to design jobs to minimize the risk of back injuries.

Energy Expenditure

Metabolic-energy expenditure or kilocalorie usage is a physiological measurement for determining the amount of task intensity that a worker can continuously carry out. By examining energy requirements for a task, the manufacturing-system designer can assess the worker's capacity to perform the task, establish duration and frequency of rest periods, and evaluate other work designs in case the proposed work is determined to be too strenuous.

The kilocalorie consumption prediction model can be used to provide an estimate of kilocalorie consumption for various job tasks. Kilocalorie-expenditure estimation directly confronts the issue of how much energy is required to carry out a worker's task. This is a tool to make sure that a proposed task is within a worker's capabilities. Thus, it evaluates the physiological difficulty a task presents to a worker. Since individual workers react differently to the same energy expenditures, the issue of kilocalorie usage, as with many ergonomic responses, is not the same for all workers. Nonetheless, data and results provide the manufacturing engineer and ergonomics expert a good indication of how much energy is expended, and hence, how an average worker may react to cellular and job-shop designs within a lean production system.

Analysis Methods

After a workstation is in place, the ergonomist or industrial engineer may use methods time measurement or 3D/virtual reality techniques to capture the exact motions of factory workers, and then simulate the results. The software reports potential problems with current work methods.

An organization should have a policy of pre-employment evaluation for work-related musculoskeletal disorders. The collected data could be used for comparison purposes. The company has two options:

1. digital comparison/analysis; and
2. physical comparison through physiological and medical work methods.

Heart rate is a medical parameter that could monitor workers in competing manufacturing systems. The worker's heart rate could be monitored periodically on the job and results charted individually for each worker in a workstation. This could be done in advance of cell implementation for a job-shop worker. Then, the results could be compared with the results taken after lean-cell implementation for a head-to-head comparison of how strenuous tasks are in these two manufacturing systems.

PHYSIOLOGY

Physiology is defined as the study of functions of human body parts; specifically, it is how these parts work or carry out their functions. Work physiology is defined as the study, description, evaluation, and explanation of the physiological changes in the human body that are a result of either a single or repeated series of exposures to work stress.

Industrial uses of work physiology include:

- confirmation that workers can safely accomplish a job;
- identification of the best methods to get a job done safely and productively;
- confirmation that a specific individual is able to carry out assigned work tasks safely;
- the ranking of jobs for wage and salary purposes and for work and rest cycles;
- an evaluation of whether the job tires the worker to the point that quality of life is affected; that is, if the job causes the worker to be adversely affected due to fatigue, sleep disorders, exhaustion, etc.

It is important for the cellular-system designer to be aware of physiology, and, in particular, how it applies to the standing, walking cell worker in the lean-production environment. The cell designer must be able to design a work cell that not only meets the factory's productivity demands, but that is also safe. Assigned work tasks must be within the physical means of the worker.

The human body's work capabilities are dependent on its internal ability to generate energy over various time periods, and at varying energy levels. The engineer determines the work required and how it is to be done and, thus, largely has control over the worker's external environment. To arrange for a suitable match between capabilities and demands, the engineer must adjust the work and the environment to the worker's physical capabilities.

Metabolism

As one can readily ascertain, the worker's ability to do assigned tasks is one of the first areas of concern for the cellular-system designer. Therefore, knowledge of human metabolism, which is the conversion of nutrients and oxygen into energy, is important to design success.

Metabolism includes the chemical processes in the living body. In the narrow sense, it describes energy-yielding processes. This is the ability to convert chemical energy into physical energy, or work. Skeletal muscles, moving body segments against external resistance, perform the work. By resting, muscles can increase their energy generation up to 50-fold. Such enormous variation in metabolic rate requires workers to be able to quickly carry supplies of nutrients and oxygen to the muscle. Muscle must also generate large amounts of waste products, mostly in the form of heat, carbon dioxide, and water, which must then be removed. Thus, the ability to maintain the body's internal equilibrium, while it is performing physical work, depends largely on circulatory and respiratory functions that service muscles.

Metabolism is divided into three types: basal, digestion, and activity. Basal metabolism maintains the basic body functions such as temperature and blood circulation. Digestive metabolism maintains the energy required to digest and transform food into energy and fat. The third type of metabolism is activity metabolism; it is the area that ergonomics is most interested in. There is an increase in metabolism that occurs when workers go from resting to working states. This increase above a resting level represents the amount of energy needed to perform work.

Walking metabolism, with and without a load, is of interest to the manufacturing-cell designer because the basic principle of cell manufacturing is to take a part to the next process and exchange parts. A new part is checked and the cell worker continues this process of exchanging parts from the previous process with the next process, while working around the cell. The cell designer and ergonomist are concerned with walking metabolism as it relates to carrying a load from workstation to workstation in the manufacturing cell. This area is also related to the possible cumulative-trauma effects of bending and twisting while carrying a workpiece from process to process.

At the start of physical work, oxygen intake slowly follows muscle demand. As shown in Figure 12-5, oxygen intake rises rapidly after a slow start and it gradually approaches the level necessary to meet the body's oxygen requirements. During the first minutes of physical work, there is a discrepancy between oxygen demand and available oxygen. During this period, energy yield is almost entirely anaerobic. This oxygen deficit must be repaid at some time, usually during rest after the workday. The amount of this deficit depends on several factors including the type of work being carried out and the worker performing the job.

If a workload exceeds roughly 50% of the worker's maximum oxygen intake, then the worker will not be able to maintain this high work level. Only if the worker's oxygen intake,

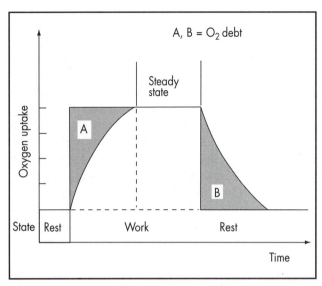

Figure 12-5. Graph showing oxygen uptake during a work cycle. Oxygen debt must be repaid during light duty or rest periods (Kroemer 1997).

heart rate, and heart output can achieve their required supply levels of oxygen can the worker maintain this high work state. This work plateau is called *steady state*. Thus, a well-trained person can attain this equilibrium between demand and supply, even faced with a relatively high workload.

Human-energy requirements, also called *kilocalorie usage*, allow the ergonomics expert to determine whether a job is light or heavy from a work-output point of view. This is due largely to the linear relationship between heart rate and kilocalorie usage. Light work is associated with a small energy expenditure and by a heart rate of approximately 90 beats per minute. At this work level, the oxygen available in the blood and the glycogen in the muscle cover the energy requirements of the working muscles. At medium work, with a heart rate of 100 beats per minute, the oxygen required is still sufficient. Lactic acid developed initially is re-synthesized to glycogen during the work process. During heavy work periods, requiring a heart rate of about 120 beats per minute, the oxygen required is supplied if the person is physically able to do the work.

Fatigue

Fatigue is another important factor in the workplace. It is an individual's temporary state of reduced ability to continue making physical efforts. This phenomenon occurs if work demands approach half of a person's maximum oxygen-uptake capacity. This results in accumulations of potassium and lactic acid, which are believed to be the primary reasons for the stoppage of muscular work. The length of time during which a person continues to carry out work depends on the individual's will to overcome feelings of exhaustion that coincide with consumption of glycogen deposits in the active muscles, drop in blood glucose, and increased blood lactate. This process is not completely understood because different workers react differently to the effects of fatigue. Fatigue varies by individual; some people push themselves because of ego or self-motivation.

The measurement of heart rate as an indicator of work requirements should be carried out during a steady-state phase. Often, the energy requirements of a job can be calculated by breaking the job into elemental subtasks for which the average energy requirements are known.

Acclimatization

Another physiological factor affecting work is acclimatization. This factor is typically only concerned with how heat affects the standing, walking manufacturing-cell worker. There are few manufacturing cells where a cold temperature is an issue. However, there are numerous manufacturing cells where heat stress can be a negative influence on worker health, safety, and productivity.

HUMAN AND MACHINE INTERFACING

To properly understand the importance of workstation design, a system must be defined not only by its hardware, but also by the operator and the interface between the two.

Humans carry out varying roles in manufacturing systems. In the dimension of control, or the degree that humans determine which way a process operates, their roles can vary from one extreme, that of monitoring or supervising, to the other extreme, that of controlling, meaning that no action takes place without human involvement. In many manufacturing systems, the control role is somewhat less extreme, most commonly an initiator role. This involves humans choosing the course and timing of a system's next action, based on its current state and knowledge applied in the analysis of control dimensions.

A second aspect of the human role in systems is that of performed manual work or the degree that a worker expends energy for the manual process. At one end of the spectrum, a human may not be required to provide any manual work. The other limit is where a worker provides all of the manual work necessary for a task's completion. The more likely scenario is a combination of tasks involving both ends of the manual work spectrum.

The machine aspects are extensive. It includes not just the process, but also tooling and fixtures, materials, and finished goods. The information and control necessary for the process is also a part of the machine. The interface between the human and machine can be viewed as the physical characteristics of the interface between the two. The physical characteristics include controls, ergonomic coupling, process location, size, shape, manual loads, and access.

Environment

Although often difficult to control due to both technical and nontechnical issues, the environment can play an important role in the success of a process. Environmental issues include: engineering concerns such as noise, vibration, temperature, humidity, and lighting. In addition, there are sometimes social and political factors at work such as malfunctioning teams, workplace esthetics, communication issues, local community considerations, management goals, strategies, workplace policies and rules, performance measures, and workers' goals, motivations, and morale levels.

Workstation Design

For workstation design, existing anthropometric data may determine specific design dimensions. This information is found in many sources, such as the National Aeronautics and Space Administration (NASA) human-factors standards (NASA-STD-3000T) and SSP 50005 Revision B, so a designer can readily employ these dimensions. Workstation-design dimensions are determined for industrial tasks such as sitting, standing, and sit/stand positions. In the case of manufacturing-cell design, relevant issues are standing and walking workers. Sitting situations are not particularly relevant.

In the past, manufacturing-workstation design was often an arbitrary process, with little consideration of the anthropometric sizes of workers in the design methodology. The physical dimensions in the design of a manufacturing workstation are of major importance from the viewpoint of productivity, as well as an operator's physical and mental well being. Small changes in workstation dimension can have a huge effect on worker productivity, health, and safety. Poor design can result in a decrease in productivity and an increase in related health problems.

A challenge of designing manufacturing workstations is the complication caused by human variability in size and capability. It is difficult for designers to discover solutions that are optimal fits for the diverse body sizes of internal customers, while still satisfying workstation and manufacturing-cell task demands. An ergonomic analysis of workstation design is concerned with working space, accommodation, posture, reach, clearance, body-segment interference, field of vision, worker strength, and environment (Karwowski and Salvendy 1998).

Gather Information

It is necessary to gather relevant information or data on task performance, equipment, work-

ing posture, and the environment to design a lean-production workstation. For a new workstation design, it is best to obtain this information from similar existing tasks or pieces of equipment. Several methods, such as direct observation, interviews with workers, videotaping, and other industrial-engineering methods can be used. Before redesigning an existing workstation, a survey is often beneficial to determine the effect of the equipment or the cell design on employee health, comfort, ease of use, and productivity. Survey results can be useful in reinforcing the recommended modifications to an existing workstation design based on ergonomics principles and scientific data.

Form a Design Team

As in cell design, workstation design requires concurrent design with continuous input from cell workers. Thus, a design team consisting of engineers and workers should be formed at the beginning of the design process. This design methodology lays the groundwork for continuous improvement brought about by the design team's cooperative endeavors.

Determine Work Methods

From the start, decisions should be formulated regarding task sequence, available space, equipment, and tools. Work methods should be established before embarking on a new design. The workstation design procedure usually begins with the collection of data by direct observation and with input from experienced operators and supervisors. It is then necessary to identify and gather data for the appropriate user population based on such factors as ethnic origin, gender, and age. Necessary anthropometric dimensions of the population are then obtained.

Determine Optimum Work Height

In developing a manufacturing workstation, a designer should take into account the worktable height. Worktable height must be compatible with worker height, whether standing or sitting.

The height of the working surface should maintain a definite relationship with the operator's elbow height, depending on the type of work. The nature of the work to be performed also must be taken into consideration in determining the proper work height of the worktable. In addition, frequently used hand tools, controls, and bins must be located within the maximum-reach space. Standing and walking workers must have an adjustable work surface.

Workstation Simulation

Operator workstation fit should be evaluated with a workstation mock-up or virtual-manufacturing simulation done with an appropriate user population. This ensures that the task demand and layout will not impose an undesirable working posture on the worker. It is desirable as well to check for interference of body groups with workstation components. The four essential dimensions for the physical design of manufacturing workstations are:

- work height,
- normal and maximum reaches,
- lateral clearance, and
- angle of vision and eye height.

The thumb tip defines a normal reach, while the forearm moves in a circular motion on a table surface. During this motion, the upper arm is kept in a relaxed, downward position. The maximum reach can be considered as an imaginary outer circle on the work surface that a worker can obtain without bending the body. If carrying out repetitive tasks, hand movement should be limited within a normal working circle. Controls as well as any other items of occasional use may be placed beyond the normal working area, but should still be located within the maximum working circle. The normal and maximum working circles both define the working area in a horizontal plane at elbow level. The frequently used area on the workstation should be within the normal reach circle of the worker.

For angle of vision and eye height, trigonometry can be used to calculate the measurement. The angle of sight can be calculated from the horizontal distance of the work surface from the worker's eye position.

Equipment Adjustment

Previous design criteria assumed that workplace components, such as workbenches, bins, equipment height, etc., were fixed and could not be adjusted. However, there is an alternative design criteria, and that is to provide for adjustments in the cell or workstation design. The advantage of this alternative is that a large proportion of the work force can be accommodated. Offsetting disadvantages include higher design and manufacturing costs, adjustment times, and the likelihood of an adjustment-component failing.

While adjustment is a practical approach, the proportion of the population to be accommodated must be determined. Typically the range of adjustment includes the middle 90%, or more, of the population.

CONCLUSION

A good ergonomic approach to the design of manufacturing-cell workstations strives for an adequate balance between worker capabilities and workstation requirements. The goal is to optimize worker productivity and the total lean-production system, while still enhancing worker well being, job satisfaction, and safety.

Chapter 13
Automation and Autonomation

Autonomation is the development of devices and methods in manufacturing that automatically prevent a process from producing defects or overproducing. This should not be confused with the word "automation."

The word *automation* was first used in the early 1950s as a definition for automatic material handling. As automation technology progressed, the term gained wider usage. Today, automation refers to both services performed and products produced automatically. In other words, human intervention is unnecessary for handling tasks. The dictionary defines automation as "the technique of making a process or system automatic."

AUTOMATICITY

A yardstick for automation appears in Table 13-1 (Amber and Amber 1962). The automation order is based on human attributes that are mechanized or automated into the manufacturing process.

Work requires energy and information. A human being, or the human's substitute, provides these elements. As a machine assumes higher levels of human attributes, it advances to the next automation stage. The more the machine performs the human attributes, the higher the machine is in order of "automaticity." *Automaticity* is thus defined as the self-acting capability of the device. In this classification, it is observed that ten levels are sufficient to describe the present machines and those that will be invented (see Table 13-1).

"A(0)" represents hand tools and manual machines where no human attribute is mechanized. Such a process is without self-action properties. It does not replace human energy or any basic control, but may include built-in guides and measurements. A(0) tools include hand tools. Hand tools and manual machines increase worker productivity, but they do not replace human functions. The group includes muscle-energized machines; that is, machines that give mechanical advantages but do not replace a person's energy or control. Some examples of A(0) machines are a lever, an inclined plane, a wheel and axle, a screw, a pulley, and a wedge.

An A(1) machine is a powered machine or tool. The human attribute that is mechanized is energy. The basic machine function replaces muscle. Machine action and control are completely dependent upon the operator. These tools or machines use mechanical power (windmill, waterwheel, steam engine, electric motor, etc.), but the operator positions the work and machine for the desired action.

The "A(2)" machine is a single-cycle automatic or a self-feeding machine. The human attribute mechanized is dexterity. These machines complete an action when an operator initiates the action. The operator must set up, load, initiate actions, adjust, and unload the machine. A(2) machines are common in the kitchen as well as the factory. The toaster and dishwasher are A(2) level machines. A drill press that, once activated by a worker, completes the drilling cycle and then automatically cuts itself off is a good factory example of an A(2) level machine.

Table 13-1
Yardstick for automation

Orders of Automation	Human Attribute Replaced	Examples	Common Terms and Concepts
Level A(0)	*None*; level, screw, pulley, wedge	Hand tools, manual machines	
Level A(1)	*Energy*; muscles replaced	Powered machines and tools Whitney's milling machine	Electric motors
Level A(2)	*Dexterity*; self-feeding	Single-cycle automatics	Unload, load, start by operator
Level A(3)	*Diligence*; no feedback	Repeats cycle; open-loop machine control; automatic screw machine	Older transfer lines; no feedback; automatic unload and load
Level A(4)	*Judgment*; positional feedback	Closed loop; numerical control; self-measuring and self-adjusting	NC machine invented in 1959. Machining centers available in 1962 with tool changers
Level A(5)	*Evaluation*; adaptive analysis; feedback from the process	Computer control; model of process required for analysis and optimization	CNC machines with sensors feeding data to computers to "optimize" the process using algorithms
Level A(6)	*Learning*; by experience	Limited self-programming	Expert systems and neural networks (computer software) provide learning by experience
Level A(7)	*Reasoning*; exhibits intuition; relates causes from effects	Inductive reasoning	Artificial intelligence; few examples in factories
Level A(8)	*Creativeness*; performs design unaided	Originality	No machines or computers at this level on factory floor
Level A(9)	*Dominance*; super-machine; commands others	Machine is master (Hal from "2001: A Space Odyssey")	Only sci-fi material at this point

(Amber and Amber, 1962, updated by Black)

An A(3) machine is an automatic machine that repeats the cycle. The human attribute mechanized is diligence. These machines carry out routine instructions without human aid. They start cycles and repeat the actions automatically. The machine loads, goes through a sequence of operations, then unloads to the next station or machine. They are open loop, not self-correcting, and obey internal (fixed) or external (variable) programs, such as cams, tapes, or cards. These machines include all automatic machines and many transfer machines such as classical "Detroit" automation. In the home, a CD player with an automatic changer is an A(3) machine. A factory example would include a manufacturing transfer line that automatically and sequentially processes a raw casting into a completed engine block, without ever having a human hand touch the block.

The A(4) is a self-measuring and self-adjusting machine with feedback. The human attribute mechanized is judgment. These machines measure and compare results to the desired size or position and make adjustments to minimize any error. Although feedback control of the workpiece surface is preferable, positional control of the machine table or tool is also valuable. A process may use more than one A(4) subsystem operating independently. Figure 13-1 presents examples of A(1) through A(4) machines found on the factory floor. Numerical control (NC) and computer numerical control (CNC) machine tools are widely used in almost every factory.

A(5) machines have computer process control or automatic cognition. The human attribute mechanized is evaluation. These machines are cognizant of multiple factors on which the machine or process performance is predicated, and a computer model (analysis) determining the proper control action evaluates and reconciles the proper control action. Any process or problem that can be expressed as an equation can be computer-controlled. Such a control system can adapt to variations in materials, process conditions, and the job. Limited-purpose, on-board computers are used to accomplish A(5) computer control. The computer must have a process "model" describing its behavior in words or equations. The A(3), A(4), or A(5) control systems are superimposed on A(2) machines to reduce the dependence on operator skills.

An A(6) machine has limited self-programming capability. The control algorithm contains an expert system or neural networks. The human attribute mechanized is learning. These machines may be set up to try subroutines based on the general program. By remembering which actions were most effective in obtaining the desired results, the machine learns by experience or trial and error.

A(7) machines relate cause and effect or have artificial intelligence (AI). The human attribute mechanized is reasoning. These machines forecast trends, patterns, and relationships from incomplete facts. They exhibit "intuition" by going beyond available data. The control software has subroutines programmed with artificial intelligence models. Other strategies may be the basis of operation. The inductive reasoning of A(7) machines is not the same as the deductive reasoning of A(8) machines. Analysis requires deduction; synthesis requires induction.

An A(8) machine has originality. The human attribute mechanized is creativeness. These machines originate work to suit human tasks and preferences. They do not copy, imitate, and follow plans or instructions. A program for an A(8) machine only designates the general form of the desired action and eliminates clashes, discords, and disharmonies. The result is original.

A(9) machines command. The human attribute mechanized is dominance. These machines govern the actions of people, machines, and other systems. They act as a "commanding general" or as a "dictator" to achieve results. The machine is no longer a servant, but the master. An A(9) super-machine is capable of superior energy, dexterity, diligence, judgment, evaluation, learning, reasoning, and creativeness (that is, the other automation levels replace the human attributes) and would be able to dominate humanity.

Currently, A(4) machines are typically computer numerically controlled and are commonplace on the factory floor. This machine class adaptively controls processes. A(5) machines use mathematical equations and problem-solving capabilities as part of their control system. This requires the process be mathematically modeled and some process aspect is then optimized. For example, varying feed or depth of cut may maximize the metal-removal rate per unit force. More typically, cutting forces are either minimized or held constant during the cuts, which usually reduces the variation in part size; that is, it improves the precision. In newer machines, dynamic models have been implemented to control chatter and vibration that can ruin the newly machined surface. At the A(6) level, an expert system or neural network is incorporated allowing experience to teach the computer control system, which then becomes the "expert." The A(7) machine requires computer software to have artificial intelligence or the ability to reason. The computer logic for levels A(5), A(6), and A(7) are still in the developmental stages. Extremely

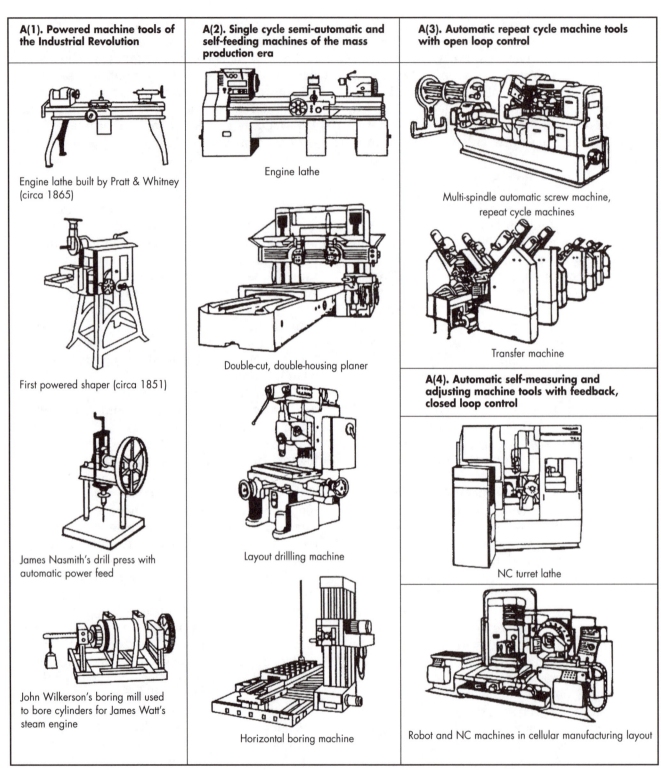

A(1). Powered machine tools of the Industrial Revolution

Engine lathe built by Pratt & Whitney (circa 1865)

First powered shaper (circa 1851)

James Nasmith's drill press with automatic power feed

John Wilkerson's boring mill used to bore cylinders for James Watt's steam engine

A(2). Single cycle semi-automatic and self-feeding machines of the mass production era

Engine lathe

Double-cut, double-housing planer

Layout drillling machine

Horizontal boring machine

A(3). Automatic repeat cycle machine tools with open loop control

Multi-spindle automatic screw machine, repeat cycle machines

Transfer machine

A(4). Automatic self-measuring and adjusting machine tools with feedback, closed loop control

NC turret lathe

Robot and NC machines in cellular manufacturing layout

Figure 13-1. Machine tools of the first industrial revolution (A1), the mass production era (A2), and examples of levels of automation (DeGarmo, 7th ed).

few machines with adaptive control are found on the factory floor, although they exist in other human endeavors. Machines using expert systems and artificial intelligence in their control logic are found mostly in research laboratories.

AUTOMATION IN LEAN MANUFACTURING

To obtain maximum benefits from automation, the manufacturing areas must be redesigned into an integrated manufacturing production system. The restructured system is further refined through continual improvement efforts. Once the system is running at peak efficiency, it can be automated to give maximum return on investment for complex, sophisticated equipment. Productivity improvements in the individual processes have a stronger impact on the bottom line when the system is at peak efficiency. Within the lean manufacturing philosophy, automation is not buying super-machines, complex machines capable of producing thousands of parts per day, but is, instead optimizing the performance of the existing equipment and improving its efficiency through preventive maintenance.

As the process of converting the factory to lean manufacturing is best done in stages, the process of automating the plant is basically an evolutionary and incremental process. The need to solve a problem in quality or capacity, such as eliminating a bottleneck, initiates the process. It can begin with mechanization of simple operations like loading, unloading, inspecting, and clamping, and later move toward emulating the human attributes of sensing and correcting problems.

Before proceeding from simple mechanization to complex, programmed automation, consider exactly what automation is designed to achieve. Automating just to avoid human processing of products is not the objective. As the ninth step in the lean manufacturing strategy, autonomation is developed when it becomes clear that manual means do not increase productivity. Establishing a factory with tightly linked processes is not easily accomplished. Trivial matters never considered in a job shop create serious problems in automated cells. When automating the lean production system consider the following:

- The manufacturing system should move materials as quickly, precisely, and efficiently as possible from raw material to finished product. The time from start to finish is as short as possible. If this goal is accomplished, whether tasks are performed by humans or automatically is secondary. In fact, humans can easily perform tasks designed for the robot.
- Preview potential problems to prepare for the advancement to the next higher stage of machine automation. Incremental, continuous improvements rather than radical changes must be made—large and small—everyday.
- Maintain proper roles for people and machines. Automation should not degrade people. In other words, machines should be used in such a manner that the operators remain fully involved. Progressively building the level of automation requires revising the interaction of the workers, machines, and materials making up the manufacturing system. Once modifications to old equipment no longer create viable returns, the system automatically tells the users what modifications are needed.
- Buying a machine having more capability than needed is wasteful. Purchase or build flexible equipment (low-cost, small) or equipment capable of being modified and maintained in-house. Flexibility is in the ability to handle the parts family with little or no setup for part changeovers. The equipment should be easy to move (not bolted to the floor) and linked for automatic feeding and unloading.
- Remember that the quality, flexibility, and reliability of equipment, processes, and people are important.

Automation in lean manufacturing means converting manned cells into automated cells using an evolutionary process where automation solves problems in setup, part loading, quality (inspection), or capacity (eliminate a bottleneck). Automating the entire manufacturing system is not easy. It may not even be possible. Automating the manufacturing system without first redesigning it into a highly productive, integrated manned system is unadvisable.

Automating does not necessarily mean buying highly sophisticated equipment with greater capacity than actually required. The emphasis should be on integrating the best abilities of the processes and the people in the system.

The task of automating any manufacturing system involves automation of all elements: product design, process design, product manufacture, the material handling system, and final assembly. Conversion of manned cells into automated cells requires devices to perform functions that a worker performed in the manned cell. A decoupler is such a device. Decouplers separate the processes when they are functionally dependent on each other. Hence, they are important elements for maintaining flexibility of the unmanned cell.

The ultimate goal of automation in any system is to achieve the highest possible level of automatic mechanical processing, that is, to infuse attributes such as evaluation and reasoning, human characteristics, into the machine. The main obstacle for implementing adaptive control into a process may not be the unavailability of technology, but a lack of knowledge about the process that needs to be adaptively controlled.

Final Assembly

Most products involve some assembly before the product is ready to be shipped to the marketplace. However, final assembly lines have resisted automation for many years. One of the reasons assembly processes were not automated is concern over the design and quality of the manufactured components. If individual components reach final assembly and are defective, then it is necessary to inspect and rework the defective parts. Making the parts correctly the first time and every time (that is, integrating quality control) corrects the situation.

Designing the product for final assembly eliminates a high percentage of direct labor. Innovative product and process designs for assembly can bring a new flexibility level to the manufacturing system. A design accommodating automation performs a greater variety of manufacturing steps without delay or unnecessary product handling in the process. The functional requirements of an automated final assembly are:

- uniqueness and creativity necessary to develop technical competitiveness;
- flexibility in the ability to handle changes in volume and product mix;
- responsiveness and adaptability to product changes;
- integration of components and simplification/standardization of product design to minimize the number of assembly steps;
- one step, one machine (small, special, simple machines);
- multiple functions at each step; and
- minimize equipment size.

The best method to achieve automated assembly is to perform a detailed study of each specific product component. A product designed for automated assembly must have component parts of consistent quality. Parts of nonuniform character and widely varying dimensions must be assembled by hand. Thus, manufacturing methods are critical. Parts produced and assembled by machines must have less variability and more precision than parts assembled manually.

Robotic Manufacturing Cells

In an unmanned cell, robots, conveyors, and gravity chutes accomplish the material handling. Simple operations like picking, loading, and unloading a process are the preliminary operations that can be automated. For these simple operations, robots can be readily employed. After a certain efficiency level is reached in performing these simple tasks, the robots can perform more intelligent tasks, such as picking up the correct-size barstock or checking the surface finish. At the current state of robot development, these are difficult tasks for robots to carry out.

In an unmanned cell, the machines are programmable, CNC, or other automated equipment, and there are no workers. Unmanned cells are typically U-shaped or circular allowing the robot to access the processes. Figure 13-2 shows a typical example of an unmanned cell. The robot's full range of motion is required so it can reach every machine. At each machine, the robot performs critical unloading and loading tasks, properly orienting the parts. This requires the robot to have a certain level of accuracy and repeatability. This is called *robotic process capability* and this must be known prior to designing the cell.

An examination of Figure 13-2 reveals that the robot cell operates on a pull basis; that is, when a part is removed from the output chute, the process creates a demand for another part. The empty place on the output chute is the autonomous signal for the cell to make another part. Decoupler Two holds parts already processed through machines M1 and M2. If the part family was comprised of four parts, then D2 holds four parts. Pulling a part out of D2 trips a chain of commands back through M2, D1, and M1, and finally another part is removed from the input conveyor for processing on M1.

Decouplers

In unmanned cells, the robot replaces the worker. It is not an easy task to replace human flexibility. To deal with this problem, a new element, called a *decoupler*, can be introduced into automated cell designs to increase the system's capability and flexibility.

Looking at the various functions a decoupler can carry out, it is observed that decouplers are needed to replace many functions that workers perform in a manned cell. Typically, these are functions that neither the processes nor the robots can adequately perform. Clearly, the check-one and move-one-on functions are prime decoupler functions.

When machines are placed next to each other in a cell, the processes become functionally dependent on each other. Many times the workers service multiple machines. The decoupler breaks the dependency of the processes on each other in a cellular environment. Decouplers typically hold one part and have specific input and output points. Decouplers can perform the following functions:

- production control;
- functionally decouple processes;
- poka-yoke inspection;
- freedom of movement for the robot;
- intracell transportation;
- part manipulation;
- handling of a family of parts;
- automatic production control; and
- branching.

Production control. The simplest type of decoupler exists in a manned assembly cell—the kanban square. Figure 13-3 shows an electronic assembly cell with kanban squares between each workstation. Kanban squares provide for production control within the cell, control the operational timing, and create flexibility in the cell staffing, thus providing flexibility in the cell production rates. The decouplers hold only one part so an empty decoupler is the signal to perform the upstream operation to fill the space. As shown, two workers are operating the cell with the workers sharing station six to achieve balance in time. Do not confuse decouplers with buffers. Buffers only store parts. In robotic cells, the decoupler performs various functions that a worker in a manned cell performs routinely, imparting flexibility back into the system.

Functionally decouple processes. Decouplers separate or decouple processes so they are not dependent on each other. This relaxes the

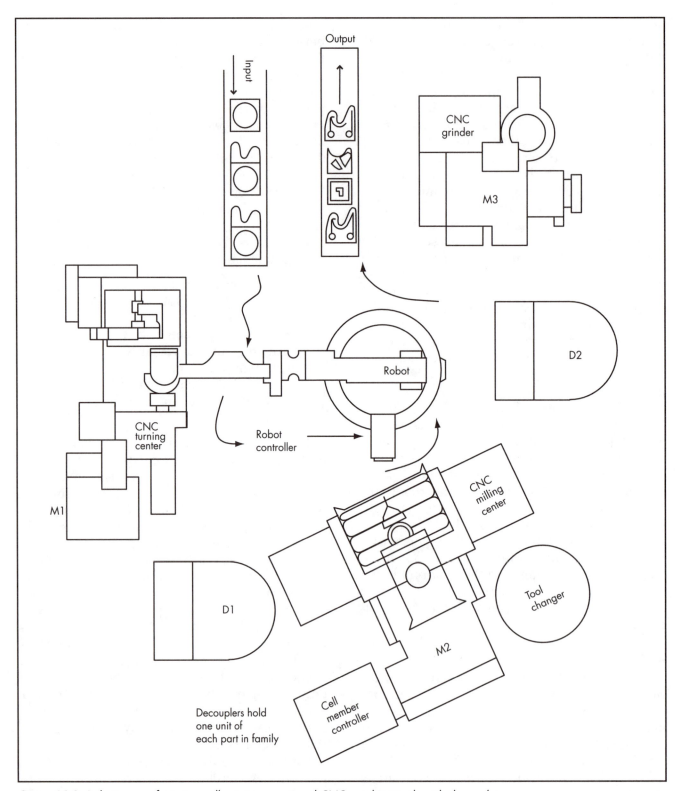

Figure 13-2. Robotic manufacturing cell using conventional CNC machine tools with decouplers.

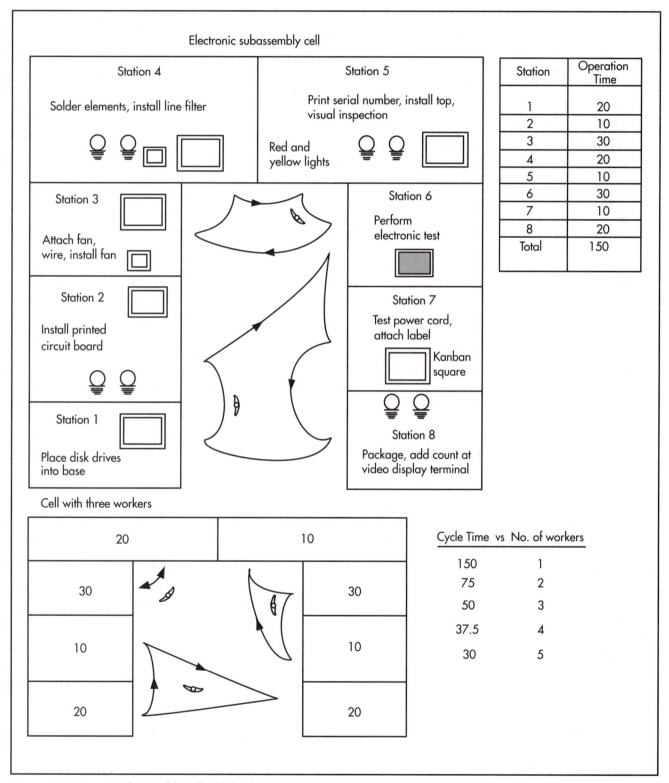

Figure 13-3. A manned assembly cell with kanban squares (decouplers) with two or three workers.

need for precise line balancing when the work in the cell is redistributed. Also, decouplers can overcome the problem of variations in manual process time or machine time.

When workers have increased variation in their processing times about the mean, processing time output from the cell decreases. That is, variability in processing time decreases the output but increasing the decoupler capacity improves output.

Poka-yoke inspection. A decoupler checks critical part dimensions. The feedback signal from sensors is sent to the process controller so the process can be modified or corrected before any defects are made. Thus only good parts are pulled to the next station. This is an example of 100% inspection. Figure 13-4 shows a decoupler for inspection. This decoupler is designed for handling a parts family that the cell is producing.

Suppose the family has three basic sizes of parts—small (S), medium (M), and large (L). Just as the machine tools must have flexible fixtures to handle the different part sizes and the robot's gripper must adapt to different part sizes, the cell must have flexible decouplers to handle a family of parts. This flexible decoupler chute is designed for a family of three parts (S, M, and L).

Freedom of movement for the robot. The robot's freedom of movement is the most important function of the decoupler as far as cell automation is concerned. In staffed cells, the addition of the decoupler allows the human worker to move upstream, which is opposite to the part-flow direction. That is, the decoupler allows the worker to move in any direction within the cell. The same is true for the robot. Remember, most robots have only one arm and cannot walk, so compared to a human, robots are severely handicapped.

Intracell transportation. Decouplers in the form of gravity slides or chutes can transport parts from process to process within the cell. This eliminates the need for precisely locating the part on the decoupler's input side. Precise location on the output side ensures cor-

rect, repeatable registration of the part for the robot's gripper. The transportation process can be automated. Figure 13-5 shows a decoupler chute transporting and reorienting parts.

Part manipulation. In an unmanned robotic cell, decouplers handle a parts family and can locate a part for the robot gripper. Often parts must be manipulated or reoriented for insertion into the next process. Figure 13-6 shows a simple decoupler designed for part reorientation. The robot places a part in slot "A." Before rotation, surface One is at the top. After rotation, surface Two comes to the top so a new orientation is obtained. The wheel holds four slots, one slot for each part in the family of four parts.

Handling a parts family. In a cell, handling a parts family requires flexible decouplers along with flexible workholders. A decoupler designed with a family of chutes (as shown in Figure 13-4) allows parts to pass each other in the cell or to skip a process. The simple rotary device shown in Figure 13-6 can handle a family of parts while providing part reorientation.

Automatic production control. Decouplers act as automatic production control devices between two processes when automatically shutting off an upstream process that cycles faster than the downstream machine. An example of a decoupler performing this function is shown in Figure 13-7. The decoupler consists of an inspection station, a gravity chute, and a limit switch. The limit switch automatically stops the operation of process "A" when three parts are in the chute. One part has been inspected, the second part is being inspected, and the third part is ready for inspection. Process "A" makes no additional parts until they are needed, that is, until the controller for process "A" receives a signal from the decoupler that the previous part has passed inspection. In Figure 13-7, machine "A" is not being adjusted based on the output inspection. Instead a light is turned on that attracts the worker's awareness of the problem.

Branching. When two or more processes are being fed by one machine or one machine is

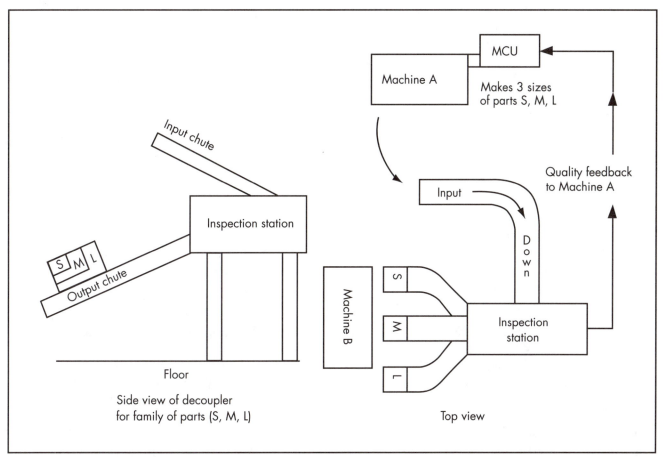

Figure 13-4. Decoupler for a family of parts with inspection station.

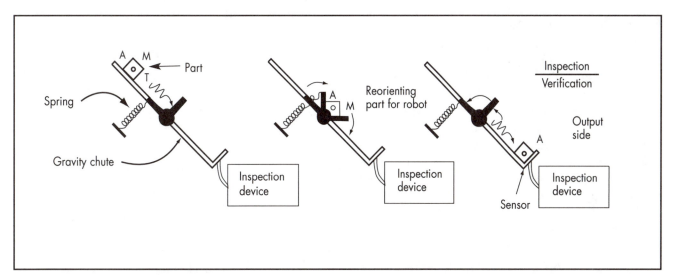

Figure 13-5. This decoupler transports the part and also reorients and inspects the part with feedback to the previous process, detecting the part's presence or absence as part of the control system for the cell.

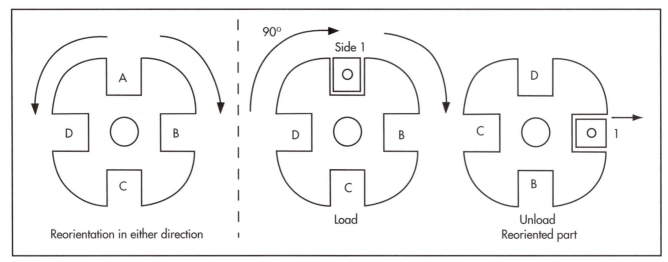

Figure 13-6. Decoupler reorients by the rotation of the part and provides exact registration (location) of the part for a robot doing the unloading.

being fed by two or more processes, this is called *branching*. When branching occurs in automated cells, a decoupler is needed to control the branching function. In general, this situation should be avoided since it clearly presents a violation of the lean production philosophy. The lean production reasoning is clear. The branching methodology induces variability into the system. Sometimes this is unavoidable but other times preventable.

Robot Process Capability

Machine-tool process capability is defined as the natural capability of the process. That is, the machine's ability to consistently perform a job with a certain degree of accuracy, precision (repeatability), reproducibility, and stability. In studies, which traditionally were performed on metal-cutting machine tools, the parts made on the machine could be examined to determine the machine tool's process capability. However, in many robot tasks (for example, material handling or assembly) there is no product or output that can be directly examined or measured to determine the robot's process capability. Therefore, the problem of how to measure robotic process capability is important.

The lack of adequate robot process capability can lead to robot installation failure. It is embarrassing to remove a robot from an assembly line or manufacturing cell because the robot was not able to accomplish desired tasks. Manufacturers and users need more effective techniques for measuring robot process capability so they can evaluate a robot's ability to perform required tasks and select a robot meeting the company's needs. Robot tasks or processes requiring process capability measurements include:

- assembly,
- insertion,
- spot welding,
- inspection, and
- loading and unloading parts.

In unmanned cells, equipment is placed anywhere within the robot's reach, but the robot's ability to perform the task within its reach is highly variable.

Robot process capability is a function of:

- move speed,
- move position,
- arm orientation, and
- the weight being transported.

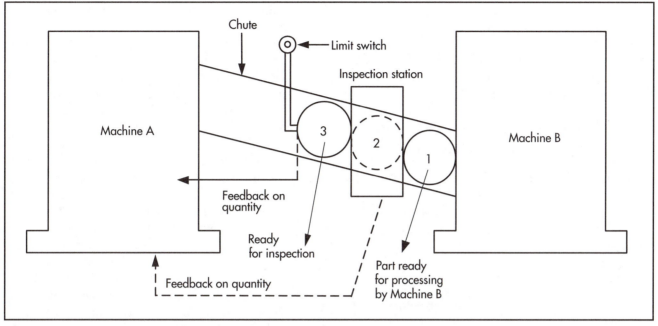

Figure 13-7. Automatic process-control function of a decoupler, combined with quality control.

Therefore, a method providing an independent measurement of the spatial location of the robot's end effectors under a variety of operating conditions determines robot process capability.

Although the terms *accuracy, repeatability* (precision or process variability), *reproducibility*, and *stability* seem clear, disagreement exists about their proper meanings. This discussion uses the following definitions.

- Accuracy: A robot's ability to move to an exact point that was programmed offline the first time, and to hit where it is aimed. It is the degree of agreement between independent measurements and the target value being measured.
- Precision: A robot's ability to return to an exact or repeatable point from the same starting point. It is the degree of mutual agreement between independent measurements under specific conditions.
- Stability: The robot's ability to return to a point and hit its target over time without drifting off target. It is measured as percent error in a given period of time.

- Reproducibility: The robot's ability to return accurately to a point from different starting points. In general, the farther away the end effector is from the end point, the poorer the reproducibility.

Generally, one or two of the process's operational characteristics dominates or has the strongest influence on process capability. Process capability measurements must therefore reveal both dominant and interactive characteristics. For example, a manufacturer should specify not only a robot's weight-handling and velocity capabilities, but also the relationship between weight handling and arm velocity. If the relationship is mutually interactive, a change in either factor affects the robot's subsequent positional accuracy, precision, and reproducibility accordingly.

Measurement and improvement techniques. Most manufacturers provide specifications for static or extreme conditions but not for the robot's process capability of performing specific tasks. Both users and manufacturers need acceptable techniques for measuring and improving robot process capability to achieve quality-control objectives. Techniques that are currently available are contact sensing and noncontact sensing devices. Some robot process capability measurement and improvement techniques are compared in Table 13-2.

Test procedure. To determine a robot's accuracy and precision before installing the robot in the workplace, a test procedure must be developed. Statistical methods such as experimental designs and Taguchi methods allow a designer to examine different factors and determine their effect on the robot's process capability. Factors to be considered include:

- weight transported,
- speed of translation,
- location point in the robot's envelope, and
- reach distance.

Frequently, significant interactions are found in these factors. In general, the weight and speed are significant and most robots perform best with short reaches.

Calibration. Studies prove that robot-positioning errors can be significantly reduced with the introduction of calibration techniques. However, a calibration study is intended to develop no-load data, whereas a process capability study is intended to determine operational or performance characteristics. Furthermore, in a robot process capability study, the measurement system must be independent of the robot. Calibration systems, however, can be part of the robot, which can cause intrinsic errors.

Measurement equipment requirements. To conduct periodic process capability checks, ideally before robot installation, companies require access to low-cost, high-speed robot process capability measurement equipment, and a simple, effective checking procedure. In selecting measuring equipment, the following factors should be considered:

- Processing speed—the computer's processing speed usually limits the measuring system's processing speed. For example, a

commercially available high-speed camera can take thousands of pictures per second, but the fastest computer can only process up to 50 frames per second.
- Precision and accuracy—the measurement device should be 10 times more precise than the variability to be measured and 10 times more accurate.
- Linearity—this refers to the calibration accuracy of the measurement device over its full working range. Is it linear? What is its degree of nonlinearity? Where does it become nonlinear and what is, therefore, its real linear working region?
- Stability—how well does this device retain its capability over time? Does it drift off target and need realignment?
- Resolution—this refers to the smallest dimensional input that the device can detect or distinguish.
- Magnification—this refers to amplification of the device's output portion over the input dimension. The better the resolution of the device, the greater the magnification required of the measurement so it can be read and compared with the desired standard.

Measurement system costs. A trade-off exists between measurement system performance and cost. For example, a low-resolution, low-speed video-based system may cost a few thousand dollars, while a sophisticated laser-based system may cost hundreds of thousands of dollars. Measurement equipment selection should be based on the robot performance and task requirements. Unfortunately, most measurement systems are expensive or do not have sufficient accuracy for use in measuring robotic process capability. Future research should be directed toward developing a low-cost, high-speed, portable system to measure robot process capability.

THE FACTORY WITH A FUTURE

After the vendor has been integrated into the lean manufacturing system, the manufacturing

Table 13-2
Summary of measuring techniques

Method	Resolution	Accuracy	Repeatability	Advantages	Disadvantages
Contact Sensing					
Dial indicator	0.0025 mm	n/a	n/a	a. low cost b. easy to setup for one dimensional measurement	a. for point to point only b. measuring range limited by dial construction c. difficult to set up for accuracy test
Extensible ball bar	5×10^{-6} m	32×10^{-6} m	20×10^{-6} m	a. simple in operation b. both positioning and patch accuracy can be measured	a. limited to one dimensional measurement b. measuring speed is limited
Latin square	n/a	n/a	±0.15 mm	a. experimental setup is defined by statistical procedure	a. slow speed b. for point to point test only c. velocity must be very slow when the probe contacts the tooling balls
LVDT sensor	0.0025 mm	n/a	n/a	a. both position and orientation can be measured	a. slow speed b. for point to point only c. measuring range is limited (2 mm)
Noncontact Sensing					
Acoustic-based system; acoustic-range sensor	0.2 mm	n/a	n/a	a. uses lightweight sensor b. can improve accuracy by using ultrasonic sensor	a. environmental effects are likely
Optical-based system; active-video system: SELSPOT and WATSMART	12 bits (1:4,096)	1 mm	Point: 0.005% Path: 0.01%	a. high speed (4,700 Hz) multiple markers b. can be used for both PTP and continuous path c. pre-surveyed calibration frames are available	a. lighting environment should be controlled to avoid reflection b. LED position may cause inaccuracy c. high temperature due to extensive use may cause innaccuracy
Theodolite	13×10^{-6} m	n/a	n/a	a. simple algorithm and operational procedure b. system capability is good enough for industrial robots	a. method very slow (about one point/min) b. manual operation may cause eye fatigue for a long operation c. for point to point only
Proximeter	25×10^{-6} m	n/a	n/a	a. can measure both position and orientation	a. linear measure range is limited (2 mm) b. for point-to-point only c. difficult to set up for accuracy test

and computer link the assembly. The cells also are linked to the production system. Questions to consider include:

- Will the unmanned manufacturing cells be able to produce 100% perfect quality?
- Will the processes have computerized adaptive control?
- Will the system have a short lead time and low unit cost?
- Will machines run perfectly and never break down?
- Will setups be eliminated?
- Will all the material be transferred one at a time, from process to process, automatically?

Likely, no factory can operate in a perfect manner, but perfection can be a goal. Continuous improvement of the products and processes are within reach, and the better the manufacturing system prior to automating and computerizing, the better it will be afterward.

The kanban method used in cellular manufacturing is still valid in a computerized manufacturing environment, except that the computer monitors the progress of materials and bar codes are substituted for kanban cards. Automated guided vehicles (AGV) may replace kanban carts because they can be computer controlled and are flexible. New methods for transferring parts between devices will be devised along with flexible modular fixtures and decouplers to handle the diverse product mixture made in the factory. However, trouble lights will still flash in the factory with a future when the monitoring computers beep to notify maintenance personnel that something has gone awry.

Information systems in the factory with a future will be capable of data interpretation in more than a conventional data-processing sense. Instead of merely performing repetitive calculations on data, the system can understand the inherent relationships in the data. For example, an engineering-design change related to a product would automatically be propagated throughout the databases affected by the change. New process plans and tooling would then be automatically brought into the manufacturing system. Ultimately, automatic changes in flexible fixtures needed to accommodate process change would be made as well.

The factory with a future substitutes machines for human workers. The implications for future employment in factory operations are clear. As automation is implemented, there will be a shift from direct to indirect labor jobs. Human workers will not participate directly in manufacturing and assembly processes, but will be required to manage and maintain the processes. This will require more highly educated people. Included in that education must be an understanding of technology and manufacturing systems. Education is the keystone to survival for a manufacturing nation.

The new era in manufacturing-systems design is here. New manufacturing giants have emerged. Honda and Toyota are examples of such giants. The development of lean and integrated-manufacturing systems chiefly fuels these giants. In Alabama, Mercedes Benz, Honda, and Hyundai have constructed a plant that embraces the tenets of lean production. Volkswagen has such plants in Brazil. Honda has exceptionally lean manufacturing plants in Ohio and Canada. In total there are now 16 auto assembly plants on U.S. soil representing 10 foreign car companies. These are factories with futures.

Chapter 14
Simulation

Factories are turning to high-powered 3D graphic-simulation software and low-cost powerful desktop computers for manufacturing-system design and ergonomic analysis. There are several commercial software packages available. These software programs generate as well as analyze human engineering, anthropometry, and physiological functions of a simulated human model. With these software packages, engineers and ergonomists collect data and analyze potential problem areas during design or after system or cell implementation.

The power of using 3D simulation and the virtual environment for solving manufacturing and ergonomic problems can be extraordinary. It gives engineers the ability to see the interactions of moving people, machines, and parts across the intended factory floor (see Figure 14-1). The factory floor can be brought to life from the original CAD data, and the user can model the accurate physical characteristics of entities and human motion.

Simulation in a virtual manufacturing environment allows multiple disciplines within an organization to contribute to better solutions. It is a safe, low-cost method to verify product design and manufacturing related factors for human engineering, process, tool, material flow, and safety. Computer simulation is a powerful tool for communication. The power of visually communicating design or process plans to management, providing visual instruction to workers, process evaluation for the manufacturing engineer, or ergonom-

ics feedback for the industrial engineer cannot be overstated.

Simulation efforts have increased significantly as the personal computer has evolved. The personal computer's emergence as a viable graphics workstation has had a significant impact on the application scope of technology. There are increasing numbers of companies participating in high-level simulation. Simulation of the system, work cell, and human tasks can be economically generated and run alongside other computer applications.

An engineer with graphic simulation capabilities has an opportunity to contribute to manufacturability or assembly analysis, and process, layout, factory throughput, and ergonomics analysis while in the cell design stage (see Figure 14-2). Computer technology allows all engineering groups to participate in the product life cycle.

Traditionally, industrial engineers handled workstation design, layout, productivity, quality, and human-factor analysis. Workstation design often focuses on a single cycle of operation to address layout, process, ergonomics, and safety issues. Discrete event simulation models, which are 3D-graphics-based, are used for many manufacturing activities including final assembly, subassembly, manufacturing cells, various flow lines, material handling, or entire factory-production operations. Metrics such as throughput, production rates, process utilization, ergonomics analysis, and standards can be accurately determined.

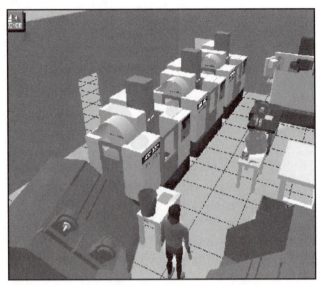

Figure 14-1. High-level 3D simulation of a manufacturing cell.

Figure 14-2. Simulated worker fitting large fabricated panel into position prior to welding.

HISTORY

Computer simulation began around 1960 when NASA pioneered computer use for satellite design. By 1970, larger manufacturing operations, especially in aerospace, used computers and proprietary software that they developed or contracted from engineering software companies. Other companies followed the lead of aircraft manufacturers and soon most medium- and larger-sized companies had computers for processing business data and numeric control (NC) machine-tool programming.

In 1973, Richard Muther was one of the first to apply a systematic methodology to the manufacturing systems planning process. Muther considered the planning process a loop that had to be executed twice; once for the general overall layout and a second time to detail the layout plans.

Early manufacturing cell designers were primarily concerned with cell layout. Two major studies of manufacturing cell implementation in 46 U.S. factories were conducted in 1989 (Wemmerlov 1997). The researcher reported that the formation of manufacturing cells was not especially problematic, but the equipment placement within the cell had a high impact on cell performance. Accordingly, the process layout function was found to be critical to manufacturing cell performance; and is, therefore, best completed with computer simulation's aid.

In the early 1990s, several studies indicated that the purposes of simulation of manufacturing systems are to better understand the dynamics of the proposed system. This ensures that the designed system satisfies the constraints outlined in the problem definition, and that it protects workers' health. In 1988 it was reported in a study that simulation models could increase comprehension and improve insight into the performance of a manufacturing system (Kamrani et al. 1998). The process of constructing the simulation model forces the system's designer to question to foster this insight. Analysis of the numerical results of the simulation runs could identify true performance indicators for the system. Table 14-1 illustrates manufacturing engineering areas particularly suited for evaluation by simulation models. A systematic simulation methodology was developed in the study, which outlined how to design and execute a simulation. The methodology began with the design engineer defining the problem and ended with solution documentation. An outline of the methodology is listed in Table 14-2.

ADVANTAGES AND LIMITATIONS

Computerized methods permit an easy and relatively low-cost method of constructing and evaluating alternative cell and workstation designs. Also, they make it easy to evaluate several iterations with the assistance of variable human simulations. These methods allow the 3D evaluation of human/machine interfaces from the earliest stage of design. Conventionally, this type of operator compatibility check is only possible at the later stages of the workstation design process. It is completed through a mock-up or prototype construction of the workstation. Computerized models, with their ability to produce a multitude of variable anthropometry human models in standard user-defined postures, can provide a relevant and standardized fitting trial, eliminating the difficulty of selecting representative personnel.

The conventional design aids, such as line drawings, mannequins, 3D dummy human models, and mock-up workstations, can virtually be replaced by the 3D/VR simulated and anthropometrically correct workers. As the human attributes—body size, volume, joint movement ranges, strength, mass, and inertial properties—are embedded within the computer program, the necessary calculations required to evaluate posture, clearance, spatial compatibility, visual requirements, biomechanical loads, and body balance can be handled by programmed routines. However, the computerized workstation or cell design does not work like an expert system. It cannot by itself generate an optimum workstation design from a set of given conditions. The designer must determine posture, working height, preferred line of sight, body clearances, and other pertinent physiological factors. Thus, for effective use of such computer programs in workstation design, the designer must be knowledgeable of the relevant ergonomical principles and guidelines.

Digital or virtual humans are computer generated, graphically represented entities that represent either imaginary characters or real humans. Virtual human models are of particular interest to the workstation and manufacturing cell designer. These virtual humans exist in a 3D graphical simulation environment for the purpose of engineering evaluation.

Table 14-1
Simulation evaluation areas

1	Cellular, flow line, and system layouts
2	Process technologies
3	Line balancing assistance for flow lines
4	Cellular, flow line, and system designs
5	Early identification of potential design process problems
6	Ergonomic and human engineering analysis
7	Expected benefits

(Kamrani, et al. 1998)

Table 14-2
Kamrani Simulation Methodology

1. Formulate the problem and plan the study
2. Collect data for the existing physical system (if any) and define the model
3. Validate the collected data and any assumptions made in the model definition
4. Construct the computer program for the model and verify its operation or use commercially available software
5. Make pilot runs of the program and validate the results
6. Design experiments and perform simulations
7. Analyze the output data from simulation runs
8. Document, present, and implement the results of the study

(Kamrani, et al. 1998)

Though they may vary in anthropometry, size, shape, and capability, they are intended to mirror human characteristics. Virtual humans can be programmed to carry out the tasks required by their human counterparts. They act within simulated environments, manufacturing components, assembling, and maintaining processing equipment. The computer models also can be used to train real workers on how to perform future assignments.

The growth in the interest and development of digital humans can be traced to at least two major factors. First, the advances in computer graphics technology have delivered the speed and performance necessary to efficiently duplicate and visualize human motion. In fact, ability to run human simulations on middle- to high-end personal computers has put this technology into the mainstream of engineering design tools. Second, engineers are becoming increasingly aware that ergonomically correct designs are critical and must be accounted for in every phase of the product life cycle. From concept to production, the application of ergonomics principles helps ensure that the product can be safely made.

High-level simulation has achieved formal recognition by many major manufacturers. Within these companies, the design engineer, manufacturing engineer, and industrial engineer need a set of human-factor tools to supplement the business process, just as they need design tools, dynamic analysis tools, and costing tools. Whereas most early human-modeling packages were aimed primarily at ergonomics professionals, today they are used to solve the complex human/product-related issues of many different engineering functions.

Several major industries have embraced human modeling and simulation. Among the first to apply the technology were the aerospace, automotive, and shipbuilding industries. These industries were driven by long product development cycles, high-cost startups, and intense manual labor demands. These are also industries where the use of computer-aided-design (CAD) technology to develop digital mockup of products was well-established engineering practice. A simulated manufacturing environment, complete with human models interacting with existing layout data, was extremely important to avoid the time and expense of costly physical mockups of processes and tasks.

Cellular manufacturing systems are quite complex and their successful implementation requires development of a sound, replicable design methodology for cells and systems (Massay et al. 1995). Therefore, animation-enhanced simulation plays an important role in the logical design of manufacturing cells and other manufacturing and production systems. Real-time, 3D animation technology is used to simulate, analyze, and provide optimization capabilities for the manufacturing system designer. Today, simulation is an even more valuable tool due to globalization of world markets, where industrial firms, in an ever-increasing competitive environment, are required to reduce their production costs, produce superior quality, and shorter delivery times. This must be accomplished in a flexible manner. Computer design and analysis employing high-level graphic software adds to that flexibility.

Manufacturing design simulation helps engineers identify design errors, make better decisions, and more quickly evaluate the effects of those decisions (McLean 1998). By improving process specifications and simulation capabilities, a much greater percentage of products are produced correctly the first time with better use of production resources. The best resources for the job are selected more often and nonproductive work consumes less time. Also, the overall time to perform the engineering function is reduced if fewer changes to plans and programs are required once a product goes into production. These improvements result in less scrap and rework. The integration of software packages and common databases ensures that less time is wasted re-entering the same data into multiple engineering tools.

The utilization of mathematics models appears to be more optimistic in predicting manufacturing cell performance (Mital 1995). While it seems that simulation models that incorporate a high degree of realism are more pessimistic. However, the simulation models are fairly flexible and can be modified to reflect changes in the workstation or cell; such as changes in the processing rate of machine tools, increases/decreases in machine reliability, and changes in part-type mix. These changes result in cell parameters that the simulation model can evaluate, providing engineering and management with valuable information on which to make decisions.

An integrated-production-system engineering environment provides the functions to specify, design, engineer, simulate, analyze, and evaluate a production system or workstation design (McLean 1998). Industrial models, interfaces, and techniques for integrating production system engineering tools have been developed. Table 14-3 lists the areas in which simulation software assists the manufacturing engineer. However, software packages have a poor ability to move data from one package to another. This is an important point as there is a trend toward teaming between various organizations using different simulation software packages.

Simulation is a good tool for communication between the varied groups in an organization. For example, 3D simulation allows companies to bring employees from many functions of the manufacturing organization into the design process much earlier, from those involved in the initial conceptualizing to post-production maintenance. High-level 3D simulation is also used for training purposes.

3D COMPUTER SIMULATION TOOLS
Simulation of Assembly

It has been said that a drawing is worth a thousand words. However, a computer-aided design (CAD) drawing of a complex assembly is more than worthwhile. Further, a simulation showing how the components fit together is worth a thousand times more than an ordinary 2D drawing. In recent years, many powerful simulation tools have become available. The advances previously mentioned have made it

Table 14-3
Simulation Uses

1	Identify product specifications and production-system requirements
2	Producibility analysis for individual products
3	Models and specification of manufacturing processes
4	Measurement and analysis of process capabilities
5	Plant layout and facilities planning
6	Simulation and analysis of process capabilities
7	Modification of product designs to address manufacturability issues
8	Consideration of various economic/cost tradeoffs
9	Manufacturing processes, systems, tools, and materials
10	Analysis supporting selection of systems/vendors
11	Procurement of manufacturing equipment and support systems
12	Task and workplace design
13	Management, scheduling, and tracking of projects

(McLean 1998)

possible to run many of these software tools on the new, powerful desktop computers instead of expensive workstations and mainframes. Combined with the improvements in the tools themselves, these are the main reasons that simulation use is beginning to increase in manufacturing plants. The most popular software applications deal with the movement of raw material and finished goods, and manufacturing operations.

Ergonomic Analysis

One type of simulation tool is 3D graphics with ergonomic function analysis. This type of simulation can be used to design and investigate a new product or manufacturing system design, and then perform ergonomic analysis. Also, 3D simulation can carry out various analytical and verification functions such as finite-element analysis and time studies. Such analysis can be useful for system safety issues.

Graphical 3D-simulation modeling facilitates engineering's ability to design both tooling and equipment, and validates human capabilities such as reach, clearance, and vision. Simulation allows human motions or labor elements to be prototyped for a range of operator sizes so many of the ergonomic aspects of a task or job can be evaluated prior to purchasing tooling or equipment. Some software packages have the ability to rapidly prototype human motion using entire libraries of whole-body and hand postures, and point-and-click routines to generate walking, lifting, and carrying. The use of such software, with ergonomic functions, allows engineers to quickly and effectively evaluate manual assembly tasks to improve cycle times and eliminate or reduce injuries.

While using simulation software, engineers and ergonomists may proactively address human/manufacturing system interface issues. A wide anthropometrical range of simulated humans is used to carry out tasks while maintaining a proposed product or work cell design. Four immediate benefits are found:

1. While in the design stage, designers may virtually eliminate the time and costs of expensive tooling rework or changes in design.
2. Simulation eliminates costly and time consuming physical mockups.
3. Manufacturing engineers reduce time-to-market by visualizing and validating processes digitally before the product design is frozen, previous to committing resources, and before purchasing or modifying equipment and tooling. After the simulation is validated, engineers may use the product and process models for training, maintenance, and documentation.
4. Ergonomics, anthropometry, physiology, and safety issues can be analyzed and addressed, while the system is still in the design stage.

Most leading software programs predetermine time standards using the cycle times derived from the motions created within the worker simulation. These software packages include techniques for determining safe postures, lifting, energy-expenditure evaluation, and physiological analysis.

Ergonomic and physiological functions included in many of the 3D and virtual reality simulation packages are listed in Table 14-4. These are most frequently used for ergonomic studies that relate to manufacturing-system design. There are several types of simulation software programs available and they range from the relatively simple to complex. Some use mathematics models while more sophisticated models use 3D and virtual reality simulation coupled with sophisticated analytical subroutines.

Metrics

The ergonomic benefits of an optimum manufacturing system, whether it is a job shop workstation or a manufacturing cell, can be observed by several metrics to monitor and track the health and well-being of the work force. Some of the ergonomic and physiology metrics are: joint deviation, nerve conductivity rate, venous pooling, energy expenditure, reach and grasp, heart rate, bend and reach, and repetitive motion. The tools used to gather

**Table 14-4
Ergonomic and physiological functions needed
in simulation programs**

1	Visualize the feasibility of certain tasks
2	Reach and grasp
3	Bend and reach
4	Eye windows to view what the model sees
5	Kcal prediction model for energy expenditure
6	Motion time measurement
7	Rapid upper-limb assessment posture analysis
8	National Institute of Safety and Health lifting guidelines
9	Anthropometry switching for human models

(Deneb 1998)

and/or analyze this data include rapid upper-limb assessment (RULA), motion time measurement, and National Institute of Safety and Health lifting guides, high-level ergonomic simulation software, and other means. These metrics are tools to identify and prevent or eliminate work-related musculoskeletal disorders from the workplace. Doing so, manufacturers and their work force reap two significant benefits: (1) elimination or reduction of worker injuries on the job and (2) reduction of the incredibly expensive financial losses that burden manufacturers resulting from direct and indirect costs of work-related musculoskeletal disorders.

Software

Since the worker is the most important aspect of workstation and manufacturing cell design, more leading-edge technology, such as computer modeling, has been developed to assist in human engineering and manufacturing. Computerized ergonomic and physiological simulation programs for workstation and manufacturing-cell design provide a convenient interface for the user to generate and manipulate 3D images of human and workstation characteristics graphically. Through the use of high-level ergonomics software, the designer can construct many anthropometric combinations to represent human workers. The programs give the user complete control over the development of the digital model. They provide comprehensive analysis to evaluate human/machine interaction through programmed commands. The user is not required to be a computer expert to use these programs. However, most require either a reasonable learning curve or professional instruction to be used productively.

The cell and workstation designer must analyze and choose carefully to determine if a given program fulfills the designer's requirements. Four broad criteria should provide the basis for comparison.

1. usability in terms of hardware and software;
2. anthropometry and the structure of the human model;
3. model manipulation, reach, and visual analysis functions; and
4. other ergonomics evaluative functions.

From a manufacturing-engineering point of view, the programs must include machines, equipment, and the tools necessary for a real manufacturing cell to work. The various programs currently available have varying system requirements, operating characteristics, applicability, and ergonomics evaluation functions for ergonomic simulation and analysis.

Delmia Software

The primary tool used in the following case study was the 3D ergonomic analysis simulation software produced by Delmia Corporation based in Auburn Hills, Michigan. The software, Delmia Envision ERGO, has these capabilities: drawing in two and three dimensions; design working models of processes and tooling; and design, simulate, and analyze manufacturing systems. It is an interactive, 3D simulation-based tool for ergonomic analysis that uses anthropometrically correct digital human models (Deneb 1998). The software also supports virtual reality devices where designers can immerse themselves and virtually manipulate a product or walk through a manufacturing workstation or system.

The human simulation tool can be used for workplace design and analysis, allowing the manufacturing-systems designer to prototype human motion within a work area using proprietary graphical motion programs. This allows the manufacturing engineer to design and/or set up the motion sequences for the simulated workers of the manufacturing cell. With the graphical motion programs, a motion sequence consists of an ordered collection of worker postures generated by the designer. Computer software manipulation of the worker's limbs generates simulated worker postures. The software program uses a combination of forward and inverse kinematics. If the worker posture exceeds the reach of the worker's arm, the inverse kinematics provide a solution by automatically bending the worker's torso. Capabilities are provided for developing time standards and studying the ergonomics of a job, including parameters related to lifting, energy expenditure, and posture analysis using percentile-based, fully articulated 3D human simulated models.

The simulated human worker is central to the case study, just as real workers are the essential resource in a manufacturing facility. Anthropometrically, the simulated worker utilized was a 50th-percentile female, and is used for both the manufacturing cell and each of the five functional system workstations.

The design of the manufacturing cell or workstation, jigs and fixtures, and workstation support equipment could only be done after examining the inherent human factor interface in the design process. Design and industrial engineers traditionally relied upon expensive and time-consuming mock-ups to evaluate their designs and workplaces. To avoid these expenses, it was important to evaluate available design alternatives early in the initial design stage. Three-dimensional simulation of human workers where the software carries out human motion, reach ability, anthropometry, biomechanics, cycle times, and ergonomic analysis was extremely important. This methodology was used to eliminate or reduce human suffering and the many upfront costs associated with product and new system development. The utilization of such simulation software can result in significant reduction of the design effort and related costs in both time and financial resources.

Before the designer can analyze the product, manufacturing system, and ergonomic functions, they must draw or import into the software programs a product, workstation, or system. Next, for ergonomic functions, the designer must teach the digital worker how to carry out the designed tasks. The teaching process, for Delmia software, is done through a dedicated human-motion-programming interface. This interface provides utilities to manip-

ulate the simulated worker's body joints. Drop-and-pick screens code program tasks such as walking, stooping, squatting, bending, and grabbing.

The human-motion-programming interface is based on the graphic programming method. A main objective of software designers was not to burden the cell designer, engineer, or ergonomist by having to write extensive computer code; but to allow simplified methods to govern the actions and motions of the product, system, or worker. Commanding worker action and work elements was done by selecting drop-and-pick commands then manually manipulating the worker via mouse movements. Thus, the designer was able to exactly program the worker-motion sequences and form them into a series of postures. A motion sequence is an ordered collection of postures where the user manipulates the model worker's limbs using task-based and graphic programming. A posture contains information regarding the joint values, attachments, and analysis. There are no limits to the number of postures in a motion sequence or the number of sequences attached to the worker. The interface allows quick selection for moving back or forward through postures for quick visual verification and editing of motion sequences (Deneb 1998).

Kilocalorie prediction. The Delmia ERGO software provides a kilocalorie prediction tool that is used to obtain kilocalorie consumption estimates for various manual industrial and assembly tasks that simulated workers carry out. This tool is primarily designed to ensure that work designed by the manufacturing engineer is within the worker's energy capabilities. Metabolic-energy expenditure is a physiological measurement used to accurately estimate the task intensity that a worker can continuously execute. Thus, by examining the energy requirements for a task, the manufacturing engineer or ergonomist can assess the capability of the worker to perform a given task. Then they can use this data to assist in the establishment of duration and frequency of rest periods and evaluate alternative work methods in case the task is too intense. The kilocalorie prediction model provides strong support for manual handling activities that involve walking, carrying, lifting, pushing, or pulling. For this study, it was arbitrarily determined to use a work classification endurance limit of four kilocalories per minute as the maximum limit for female workers, who are engaged in light industrial tasks.

The way the simulation software works is relatively simple. It uses designer inputs and then breaks the motion sequences into subtasks that the energy expenditure prediction model understands. Once the user supplies this input, the system computes the geometric distances and energy requirements from the simulation data. An energy-expenditure log from the prediction model is written to a file. The file contains the data in report form; there, it sums the total energy expenditure and time, and averages the rate for the motion sequences in the analysis.

Rapid upper-limb assessment (RULA). The Delmia simulation software has a posture analysis system to investigate the workers exposure to risk associated with work-related upper limb disorders brought about by stressing postures. The RULA tool can be used to reduce or eliminate workplace hazards due to workstation design and layout. RULA-based analysis examines the following risk factors: number of movements, static muscle work, force or load, working posture (body-part angles away from neutral), and time worked without a break. These factors are combined to provide a final score for a worker's particular posture. For working postures, RULA focuses on the use of arms and wrists, head position, and upper-body posture. RULA also takes into account the worker's legs.

The designer provides input to the system regarding muscle use for arms and body loading. The system combines this information with the posture category, based on a comfortable joint range of motion, to give an action level for the posture. A color change of the simulated worker's body part stressed by the posture sig-

nals the action level. However, in use, the color-code scoring appeared to be conservative. Delmia engineers confirmed that this was the case, so a combination of 3D simulations that generated postures carried out the RULA analysis for this study. Then the postures were viewed at various points of view and manual RULA assessments were made based on simulated joint angles. Analysis was then carried out manually on the worst-case selected posture for a given task. This was done by decomposing the individual process jobs into work elements. Then, by posture flipping the simulation, the worst-case posture for each job element was found. This relatively simple procedure froze the simulated worker in the worst-case posture and the postures were then manually scored.

With the manual/simulation analysis technique, the simulation records the position of the upper limbs and head, then the trunk and legs using two separate number codes derived from the worker's postures. The procedure requires that segments of the human body be rated on a simple scale that produces a series of numbers, which, in turn, were matched against a grid. The value of the numbers and their position on the grid determines the severity of the posture. The engineer or ergonomist can then take action based on this data to reduce or eliminate the problem.

NIOSH lifting tool. This analysis function of the software is based upon the NIOSH lifting equation. It analyzes the two-handed-lifting activities of workers. The lifting equation is aimed at reducing lower back injury and related musculoskeletal disorders. The output can alert manufacturing cell and workstation designers to the need for assist devices for workers to perform their jobs without back injury risk.

The NIOSH lifting equation gives a measure of human lifting capacity. The output of the equation is a weight limit suitable for men and at least 67% of women. The NIOSH limit is 51 lb (23 kg) under ideal conditions and if all lifting risk factors are 1.0. The Delmia software calculates the risk factors associated with the lifting task by computing the input variables from the postures. Based on the computed risk factors, the system outputs recommended weight limits for the specific task. The weight limit takes into consideration the risk factors at the lift's beginning and ending. The Delmia system also allows the design engineer to carry out "what if" scenarios.

Cycle time. The Delmia simulation software comes with an accurate performance analysis subroutine for rapid evaluation of work measurement. This module determines time standards for tasks to support productive task planning. The standard for this simulation tool is methods time measurement.

Case Study: Ergonomics Simulation

In the following investigation, which utilized the simulation-driven cycle-time calculation feature of the Delmia software, the manufacturing cell and the five job-shop workstations were analyzed for potential repetitive-motion injuries based on the 30-Second Rule. The software was used heavily for cycle-time calculations and the kilocalorie energy-expenditure function. In addition, rapid upper-limb assessment and repetitive motion analysis via the 30 Second Rule were performed.

The research for this case study used Fourth Industrial Revolution technology along with traditional industrial and manufacturing engineering methods for data collection and analysis to answer the question as to whether manufacturing system design has an impact upon worker ergonomics.

The research plan included simulating two competing manufacturing systems, lean production and the job shop, in which the modeled human carries out various computer-generated tasks. These identical manufacturing tasks allow the modeled worker to be exposed to various physiological stressors while carrying out simulated cell or job-shop manual tasks. The manufacturing processes are simulated using two manufacturing system designs: (1) an interim lean manufacturing cell; and (2) a tra-

ditional functional job shop. In both cases, the simulation software generated and collected data on the various ergonomic stressors and reported those back for further analysis.

The 30-Second Rule

Cumulative trauma disorders of the upper extremities are physical ailments of the wrist, arm, and shoulder caused by the cumulative effect of repeated mechanical stresses. They develop gradually over time and are believed to be work related. Typically, a task is considered repetitive if the basic cycle time is less than 30 seconds—hence, the 30-Second Rule (Konz 1995). The 30-Second Rule is primarily concerned with repetitive motion of the hand, wrist, shoulder, and back. Repetition occurs when exertions, motions, recovery, vibration, or cold temperature exposure are repeated by the worker in the course of carrying out a task. Of particular concern are repetitive motions that involve force and result in extreme deviations for the body part carrying out the task. It has been reported that highly repetitive work has a 2.8 times higher risk of injury than the same work with longer cycle duration (Silverstein 1986). Also, work that involved extreme deviations coupled with high force had a 30 times higher risk of worker injury.

Fourth Industrial Revolution

Some believe that the state-of-the-art tools and analysis now being used in the manufacturing design process are catapulting manufacturing into the Fourth Industrial Revolution. Teams of design, industrial, manufacturing, quality assurance engineers, and ergonomists will design and test a product and the processes to produce it. These teams will use powerful desktop computers that run high-level simulation, design and analysis software packages; and, everyone will be working off the same database. In the Fourth Industrial Revolution, a virtual product will be designed and tested; the manufacturing system will be built and workstations designed; subsystems built and tested, such as product quality assurance; and ergonomic and safety factors ensured; all in a 3D/virtual environment. This completed and tested system will be finished before the first chip is cut, the first piece of metal bent, the first die made, or the first prototype is actually produced. Design and analysis facets will be completed via computer simulation. When the first part is made, it will be to specification with no scrap, rework, or starting over.

The Cylinder Manufacturing Cell

The manufacturing cell used for the 3D simulation model in this study is a viable and mature interim machining cell. The cell is a vital part of the John Deere Corporation facility located in Greer, South Carolina. Figure 14-3 shows a schematic of the cell. The cell produces cylinders for small gasoline engines. The engines power string trimmers, leaf blowers, and chain saws. The factory is located in a 240,000 ft^2 (22,297 m^2) building and operates with roughly 160 people, including two manufacturing engineers. The cylinder cell and its processes form the core of the study. Both the cell and job shop simulations were designed from the Deere cylinder cell; thus the comparisons and analysis have this cell as a common origin.

The Greer plant produces about one million cylinders a year from two manufacturing cells. These cells replaced two former transfer lines; there is still one other cylinder transfer line in operation. The two manufacturing cells have cycle times that are greater than the transfer line. However, tolerance problems, machine breakdowns, and an array of other technical problems continually plagued the transfer line. Therefore, the quantity of acceptable cylinders produced by the transfer line is below either of the two manufacturing cells.

The completed cylinders are assembled into small gasoline engines for consumer products designed and built for the commercial market. The cylinders are also produced for aftermarket spare parts. The cylinder is die cast from aluminum alloy and weighs approximately 14 oz. (0.4 kg). The cast cylinder blanks are shipped from the die caster to Greer for final machining.

The John Deere cell and functional job shop were modeled using Delmia software. The John Deere manufacturing cell was simulated and verified first. Then, the job-shop processes were redesigned using the exact manufacturing cell's processes as simulated for the modeled cell. The processes are exactly the same for both the cell and job shop. Only the methods employed for process usage were different.

Decomposition of the Job Shop

Typically, lean manufacturing cells are designed using the former job shop's processes. The process was reversed for this research where each cell process was decomposed or redesigned into a typical job-shop workstation. As is the normal practice, job-shop workers stay with the process the entire shift, tending the process by loading and unloading parts, and waiting for the machining cycle to end to initiate another round of servicing. The simulated job-shop workstations were designed with typical functionality for that manufacturing system.

At each job-shop workstation, the worker has two boxes of parts, input and output; one is for raw material or semi-finished parts and the other for completed parts. The normal job-shop processing cycle for any one of the five processes redesigned into the functional system would include unloading a just-finished part, then loading a new part into the process. Some workstations may include other manual tasks such as cleaning the machine tool's chuck or workholding device with an air gun and dipping the finished part into a bucket of coolant solution to wash off chips. After starting the machine tool, the worker may give the just-finished part a visual inspection and then wait for the machining cycle to end. Once the process has completed the machining cycle, the job-shop worker/machine cycle starts over.

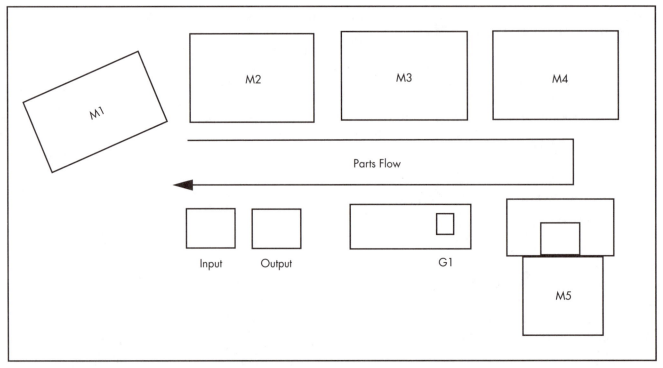

Figure 14-3. Schematic of John Deere manufacturing cell.

Comparisons

For an ergonomic comparison of the manufacturing cell and the job shop workers, walk time between processes was included in the cellular computations. While walking is an important aspect of cellular manufacturing, the functional job shop has little required walking. Another important aspect was that the five job-shop processes were modeled with the same simulation worker, so, there were five identical workers utilized for the functional job-shop-designed system. The manufacturing cell was modeled with only one simulated worker. Here the worker tends each of the five cell processes in sequence while walking around the cell; this is the normal lean manufacturing methodology.

Next, the job-shop processes with five workstations were modeled and simulations completed. The total cycle time for the manufacture of one part utilizing the job-shop manufacturing system model was 221.1 seconds. This system utilized five identical workers with one at each of the five functional workstation simulations designated WS1-WS5.

The cycle-time differences between the lean manufacturing cell and the traditional job shop are dramatically clear. Referring to Table 14-5, in every case, the cellular manufacturing system possesses faster process times ranging from 20.8-48.1 seconds faster than the corresponding job-shop-designed workstation. The process cycle-time differences of the cell over the job shop are significant, ranging from 53.6-91.6% better than the job shop.

One of the reasons that the job-shop cycle time is greater is because of the one-worker, one-process parallel methodology. In the job-shop design, the worker must wait while the process completes its cycle; whereas, in the cell, the worker starts one process and walks to the next cell process. The single-cycle process continues automatically after the worker leaves and shuts itself off at the end of one processing cycle. The cell operates in parallel while the job-shop workstations work in series. Therefore, there is zero idle time for the cell worker. Table 14-5 does not indicate the total idle time difference for the workers operating the five machine tools in the job shop. However, the idle time component of the total job-shop cycle time was calculated at 91.66 seconds. So, the five workers' total idle time accounted for 41.4% of the total job-shop cycle time.

Ergonomic Analysis

The primary purpose of this study was to concentrate on the ergonomic ramifications of lean manufacturing cells versus the functional design. The use of high-level 3D simulation focus and ensuing analysis provided the data.

Kilocalorie expenditure. The amount of energy used by the workers working in each manufacturing system type was measured and the results compared. According to Delmia Corporation, the kilocalorie analysis model assumes that the work can be broken into simpler tasks. Once the work has been divided, the average kilocalorie rate for the whole job can be estimated by summing the energy requirements for those individual tasks. Also, the energy required to maintain the posture is added in and then averaged over time for the completed work.

A kilocalorie prediction model was programmed in this Delmia simulation software package used for this study. The software was extremely useful for calculating the amount of energy expended by these two manufacturing systems during simulation. Also, on an ongoing basis, the energy expended could be collected by time periods and charted to track progress of continuous-improvement projects

and its effects on the workers in a work cell or other system.

Kilocalorie expenditure estimation directly confronts the issue of how much energy is required to carry out a worker's task. Thus, it is a gage of how difficult, physiologically; a task is to a worker. Since individual workers are going to react differently to the same energy expenditure, the issue of kilocalorie usage, as with many ergonomic responses, will not be the same for all workers. Nonetheless, the data and results presented will give the manufacturing engineer and ergonomist a good indication as to how much energy and hence how the average worker may react to the cellular and job-shop designs.

Table 14-6 illustrates the kilocalorie energy-expenditure data generated from the worker operating the five processes in a cellular manufacturing methodology, and the five workers operating each of the five workstations in a functional job-shop design.

Both sets of simulated workers serviced the identically same simulated processes with the only difference being the manufacturing-system design. To manufacture one part, the cell worker consumed 1.1674 kilocalories, as compared to the job shop, where five workers expended a total of 7.2705 kilocalories or 1.4541 average kilocalories per worker. These calculations yielded a 19.7% decrease in kilocalorie expenditure for one worker going from the job shop to the cellular system. If the total kilocalorie expenditure of the cellular system versus the job shop is compared, then the five job-shop workers use 622.8% more kilocalories than the one cell worker.

Table 14-5
Cellular manufacturing system versus job shop cycle times

	M1 (sec)	M2 (sec)	M3 (sec)	M4 (sec)	M5 (sec)	Totals (sec)
Cell	18.05	2.64	2.68	4.38	11.99	39.75
Job Shop	38.89	47.92	30.50	52.50	51.30	221.11
Difference	20.84	45.28	27.82	48.12	39.31	181.36
% Difference	53.6%	94.5%	91.2%	91.6%	76.6%	82.0%

Table 14-6
Cellular manufacturing system versus job shop worker's kilocalorie expenditure comparison

	M1	M2	M3	M4	M5	Total	Kilocalorie/ worker
Cell	0.8151	0.0908	0.1045	0.1569	0.7091	1.1674	1.1674
Job Shop	1.2680	1.4278	0.9894	1.5529	2.0322	7.2705	1.4541
Difference	0.4529	1.3371	0.8849	1.3960	1.3231	6.1031	0.2867
% Difference	35.7%	93.6%	89.4%	89.9%	65.1%	83.9%	19.7%

The simulated expenditure rate for the cell worker was 2.292 average kilocalories per minute, while the job-shop workers expended 2.479. This data indicates that the job-shop worker was utilizing energy at an 8.2% faster rate than the manufacturing-cell worker.

Another interesting comparison was the number of kilocalories required to produce one part under the two different manufacturing systems. For instance, the simulation model indicated that the job-shop workers (a total of five) must expend 12.4033 kilocalories per finished part. The manufacturing cell worker (a total of one) used 1.1674 kilocalories per finished part. This difference reflects 10.6 times per part more kilocalorie usage. In other words, the five job-shop workers must use 1062.5% more energy to produce one component when compared to the one cell worker.

The simulation proved that the lean cell system consumed fewer kilocalories in every workstation comparison. Therefore, in this study, the criterion for determining the better manufacturing system was the selection of the system that was less stressful to the workers, that is, the system that used fewer kilocalories. The cellular manufacturing system was shown to expend significantly fewer kilocalories per worker to achieve the same output. Therefore, it is readily apparent that a lean production cellular system design can lower the risk of human suffering while possibly saving the manufacturing organization a significant amount of workers' compensation, medical, and related expenses.

Rapid upper-limb assessment (RULA). This study was concerned with harmful worker postures associated with the following: chronic musculoskeletal injuries to the hand, wrist, shoulder, neck, elbow, and back; and repetitive-motion injures related to overuse and excessive force. The ergonomic features of the Delmia software and other analytical means assisted with the evaluation of those body parts that were subject to work-related musculoskeletal injuries. The RULA tool was also employed to evaluate postures relating to the ergonomic differences between the lean shop and the job shop manufacturing system designs.

The focus of the RULA analysis was to determine whether there was any advantage from an ergonomics and physiological standpoint to choose a cellular manufacturing system over the functional job-shop-manufacturing system or vice versa. Although both systems could produce the exact same product, the methods employed were completely different. The data was generated by manually completing the RULA assessment worksheets for each task in both systems. Both manufacturing designs were subdivided into five major processing tasks and further division resulted in a subset of elements for each major task and for each system. Naturally, each process task and the resulting elements were different; this is inherent for different manufacturing system methodologies. Once the two system tasks were decomposed into elements, then the process of applying RULA took place on each systems' elements. Then it was only a matter of compiling the information into tabular form for analysis.

Summarizing the data in Table 14-7, it is apparent that the cellular manufacturing system is much less stressful on the worker than the same work performed under the job shop system. The scoring is based on the RULA action levels, which range from one, indicated by a final score of one or two, to an increase in severity level of four, indicated by a final score of seven or more. In almost every case, the cellular manufacturing system scored fewer points and the points were less severe than the job shop. Thus, Table 14-7 indicates that the cell should be much less harmful from an ergonomic postural standpoint.

A comparison of the total number of RULA task elements of the total job shop versus the cellular system is significant. In this case, there were a total of 56 RULA points. The job shop scored 33 points as compared to 23 for the cell. This indicated that for the same tasks performed in the cell and the job shop, the job shop required 43% more assessment than was required by the cell to capture the potential harmful postures. Further, the average scores for the job shop were more severe than the corresponding scores from the manufacturing cell.

Table 14-8 gives the average RULA scores for the individual body parts by manufacturing-system design. The final RULA score averages both the job shop and the cell workstations. The difference scores of the job shop over the cell design average from a low of -6.0%, indicating that the job shop faired more favorably than the cell for the neck column, to 25.6% in favor of the cell over the job shop. All but the -6.0% score showed that the cell was superior as far as RULA assessments were concerned.

The final score for the job shop is 3.348; clearly the average RULA final score for the functional design is in the unacceptable action level. The cellular design final score is 2.664, and still below the unacceptable 3.0 action level. The difference between the two scores represents a 25.7% increase of the job shop over the cell. Since lower is better, the higher job-shop average score represents a substantial increase and is viewed as having a greater potential for ergonomic problems associated with poor work-related postures.

Conclusion. Although the Delmia software incorporates a RULA function, the RULA function had limited utilization for this study. Mainly because it only highlighted the simulated work-

Table 14-7
Summary of RULA assessment element data

Area	Number of Elements	Total RULA	Average	Standard Deviation	Range	Score
Job Shop 1a	10	35	3.50	0.972	2–5	8
Cell 1	7	18	2.57	0.535	2–3	4
Job Shop 2a	5	16	3.20	1.304	2–5	3
Cell 2	3	7	2.33	0.577	2–3	1
Job Shop 3a	4	13	3.25	1.500	2–5	2
Cell 3	2	6	3.00	0.000	3–3	2
Job Shop 4a	5	16	3.20	1.304	2–5	3
Cell 4	3	8	2.67	0.578	2–3	2
Job Shop 5a	9	35	3.89	0.928	3–5	9
Cell 5	8	22	2.75	0.707	2–4	5

Table 14-8
RULA element comparison

	Upper arm	Lower arm	Wrist	Twisted Wrist	Neck	Trunk	Leg	Final Score
JS 1a–5a	2.983	2.191	1.982	1.150	2.073	2.747	1.230	3.348
Cell 1–5	2.375	2.070	1.804	1.000	2.198	2.236	1.000	2.664
Difference	0.608	0.121	0.178	0.150	–1.250	0.511	0.230	0.684
% Difference	25.6%	12.1%	17.8%	15.0%	–6.0%	22.9%	23.0%	25.7%

er's stressed body part with different colors during the simulation run to indicate the Action Level of the postural stress. This reason dictated the manual RULA assessment along with the use of the Delmia 3D simulation to determine exact body-part angles, etc. Nonetheless, the graphics generated by the simulations of the system designs were essential, and played an extremely important role in the analysis process. Therefore, there is assurance that the utilization of an ergonomic computer simulation with powerful ergonomic and physiological functions during the design state for a manufacturing system, workcell, or workstation would ensure lower postural stress in the worker.

Virtual Reality

Virtual reality (VR) is a special kind of simulation that depends upon a human/computer interface technology. It allows three-dimensional, multi-sensory interaction between the user and the computer. With VR, instead of looking at the flat computer screen, the user interacts with a 3D computer-generated environment, based on the way manufacturing or design areas look in the real world.

VR is a real-world-grounded, business-oriented technology of particular interest to many areas of product design, manufacturing, safety, and ergonomics. For example, VR allows companies to bring employees from the manufacturing side into the design process much earlier. This includes those involved from conceptualization to post-production maintenance. VR is used for training purposes, allowing a company's best technol-

ogy and personnel to be widely used in several locations simultaneously.

The Virtual Factory

The idea of a virtual factory is not new. But in the past, the development and application of large usable simulations of factory operations have been almost universally unsuccessful. This is in the face of the fact that local simulations, for example, those simulations at the process or workstation level focusing upon manufacturing and ergonomical situations, have been successful. The past models have not had the detail to properly capture factory operations. These early models were too poor to provide solutions that benefited factory demands. Even small events may produce large fluctuations in factory operations, and adequate models must be capable of reflecting these subtle influences. Also the early simulations were too slow to provide usable solutions. Often graphic representations of the process were inaccurate, which lead to wrong solutions. The user interfaces were complicated and/or incomprehensible and were unusable to manufacturing and human factors engineers. A requirement for manufacturing models is that detail levels be consistent since small factor variables at local levels may have a significant impact at the highest factory level.

Powerful simulation programs to capture the entire manufacturing environment while being detailed enough to simulate and analyze the individual details of human and machine interface are required. Simulation software running on low-cost, yet powerful, computers, using manufacturing and ergonomically correct software with a short learning curve, is the key. The simulation, whether two-dimensional or three-dimensional, must provide fine-detail modeling of work cell or factory conditions. Software must be powerful to emulate complicated factory operations. Computers driving this state-of-the-art software must be powerful and fast to produce solutions to real-world problems in real time. There are such VR simulation systems being developed and used in various manufacturing operations, primarily in the aerospace and automotive industries.

INDUSTRY SUCCESSES

In the aerospace area, many organizations including Boeing, Lockheed, as well as NASA, are using human simulation to dramatically decrease the time and expense associated with the design, redesign, prototyping, production, and maintenance phases. In the competitive aerospace industry, one design or production mistake can be costly. Every competitive edge must be used and virtual prototyping capabilities provide a huge advantage by eliminating the need to build multimillion-dollar mockups. To eliminate building a prototype, the company must have considerable confidence in the accuracy of the digital prototype. Human simulation provides that assurance by graphically demonstrating worker interactions with products and processes, and delivering analysis on the worker's productivity and physical capabilities.

Lockheed has had great success with the application of virtual manufacturing in the aerospace and defense industries. Human simulation activities are ongoing in many of its companies. For example, an analysis of manual labor tasks on an F-16 fighter's vertical fin involves a simulation of maneuvers required of astronauts aboard a space shuttle. The objectives are wide ranging, from pure visualization of human activity to more advanced productivity and ergonomics analysis.

In the automotive industry there is a highly defined, repetitive cycle of activity that occurs with each new car program. At the General Motors' North American Operations, engineering activities are associated with the product life cycle, from concept to production. For the most part, many individuals who are currently performing this type of work are either design or manufacturing engineers who must validate a product and process design plan several years before production begins.

Many of General Motor's divisions now incorporate worker simulations as part of a strategy to evaluate manufacturing and robotic processes. In addition, engineering groups contracted to develop processes and tooling for specific manufacturing cells are required to deliver robotic and worker simulations prior to process implementation. The design of a manufacturing cell; the interaction of workers with parts, equipment, and tooling; and the cycle time of operations are all important issues addressed through the use of 3D human simulation.

Shipbuilding is another area where virtual manufacturing has been utilized successfully. Within the shipbuilding industry, human simulation is a key component to what the Navy refers to as simulation-based design. Historically, shipbuilding, as an industry, has one of the longest product life cycles, with submarines in particular taking as long as 14 years to go from design to launch. Traditional prototyping methods may include several iterations of producing wooden mockups of submarine sections. These physical prototypes are expensive, time-consuming efforts. Eliminating or reducing the number of prototypes will save development time and millions of dollars.

General Dynamics' Electric Boat Corporation uses a 3D virtual environment to build digital prototypes of nuclear attack submarines. Working with CAD packages, Electric Boat is able to simulate the kinematics, dynamic, mechanical, and ergonomics aspects of the submarine and its components. The simulation creates an environment in which to evaluate a wide range of parameters, including ergonomics, and then optimizes the preliminary design based on the results. Virtually tested activities, such as torpedo loading and engine maintenance, are prominent examples of where human simulation contributes to better design.

Electric Boat Corporation was one of the first to demonstrate the use of motion capture and immersion techniques to enable engineers and their naval customers to "walk through" a digital submarine; this includes visual feedback. Motion-capture techniques, coupled with virtual reality and human simulation, are expected to provide solutions to real-world training and design problems at Electric Boat.

SUMMARY

Successful organizations continue to build upon their digital enterprise, drawing upon product, manufacturing, plant, and operations data to simulate the entire product life cycle. The benefits received from the CAD revolution have enabled companies to shorten the time required to bring new products to market.

However, in spite of the benefits of computerized human modeling, it has been used to prove few industrial workstation designs.

The use of 3D high-level simulation continues to gain additional following. Human interface to a product or process is critical to the success or failure of that process. The ability to predict human performance enables correct engineering decisions to be made earlier and at less cost.

For industrial and manufacturing engineers with an outlook toward proactive participation in the product life cycle, virtual manufacturing may be the perfect partner. Computer simulation can assist the engineer in seeing the environments in which real humans will later be placed. It can help engineers and designers experience, in a virtual workstation or manufacturing cell, the physical characteristics of parts to be handled and the effort required to execute production processes. Simulation will ensure that the manufacturing cell or workstation will be successful from the productivity, quality, ergonomic, and safety points of view.

Chapter 15
The Toyota Production System Today

INTRODUCTION

Companies today need to be more productive than the competition at providing external customers with high-quality goods and services. If these goods are provided at a low cost and in a timely fashion, a company will thrive and become a factory with a future. Companies that are less productive than their competitors are likely to decline rapidly into oblivion.

The globalization of markets means customers have more choices. Customers expect world-class quality and prompt delivery at a reasonable price. They will not accept anything less.

Lean production is a manufacturing methodology based on a new system design. It has enabled companies to achieve continual gains in productivity (low unit costs), which satisfy customer expectations for superior quality and prompt delivery. These benefits are the result of a well-planned, agile, and flexible lean manufacturing system. The watchwords for the Toyota production system (TPS) are "better," "faster," and "less expensive."

ELIMINATING WASTE

The lean production system arranges all assembly processes, subassemblies, and components (from raw materials to finished products) into a single, smooth flow. Employees and managers at companies that employ the system learn to identify and eliminate any waste that occurs in the flow. Eliminating waste, thereby raising quality, reduces cost. Basically, the lean production system provides for eliminating waste or excess in human resources, equipment, and materials. Managers and employees learn to question the need for every element of motion; square foot of space; item of in-process stock; and amount of time that people, material, or machines spend moving or not moving through the production system. By eliminating waste in these and many other categories, companies concentrate resources on making and delivering only what customers want, when they want it, and in the amounts they want.

There are two groups of customers: those who purchase the product (external customers) and those who make the product (internal customers).

Superior quality comes with productivity when internal customers learn to identify and eliminate all forms of waste. That is because a big part of eliminating waste consists of preventing defects. Defective products entail a grievous waste of human resources, equipment, and material. Measures for eliminating waste by preventing defects are a definitive and paramount feature of the lean production system.

By identifying waste and eradicating it, companies can reduce costs. Many managers have regarded costs as a "given" that are largely beyond their control, and prices as a variable that they can adjust to accommodate fluctuations in costs. But in the intensely competitive global markets of today, external customers rather than the sellers are the arbiters of price based on their perceived value of the product. The only way for companies to survive and secure profits is to get costs under control, thus lowering the price that external customers are asked to pay.

The lean production system results in productivity gains by highlighting waste. It results in quality gains by making problems visible when and where they occur and then by having the internal customer take measures to solve the problems to prevent recurrence. Lean manufacturers learn how to get continuous improvements in productivity and quality by continuously redesigning and making the manufacturing system simpler. The critical element in that redesign is the internal customers who are truly empowered and trained to analyze, resolve, and prevent problems. Everyone who works in the lean production system understands how the system works.

ROOTS IN FORD'S SYSTEM

TPS evolved from the flow-line production system concept developed by Henry Ford's manufacturing engineers. Henry Ford's system had its roots in the American Armory System, also called the functional job shop. The distinguishing elements of Ford's system, all of which still can be seen today in any modern automobile plant, are:

- A moving conveyor moves vehicles through the assembly process. In other words, the work comes to the workers, rather than the workers coming to the work.
- There is a division of labor in which workers each handle only a single step in the assembly sequence. Early automobile plants were project shops for assembly of the cars coupled with job shops for components. Individual workers put together entire assemblies, such as the engine, by themselves. Ford greatly improved productivity by breaking down the assembly sequence into simple, repetitive tasks and arraying those tasks along a flow or conveyor line. See Figure 15-1.
- There is an integrated organization of vendors for parts and materials. Ford kept each process in the production sequence supplied with all the parts and materials needed.

Figure 15-1. Ford Motor Company's assembly line in 1913, showing the marriage of the body to the chassis.

Ford's mass-production system provided the historical and technological foundations for the TPS. Ford brought a Swedish engineer, Carl Johanson, to the United States to introduce gage blocks and the concept of standard measurements so everyone's inch was the same length. True component interchangeability evolved as Ford's production engineers pioneered advances that reduced variation in part dimensions through standardization and thereby ensured that parts would fit together properly.

Even the vendors for nuts and bolts were required to deliver their hardware in wooden boxes made from specified grades of wood in specified sizes with the location of holes exactly predetermined. Upon receipt at the Ford plant, the bolts were dumped out and the box disassembled. The sides of the boxes became an automobile floorboard. The holes were already drilled and ready to be bolted in place with the bolts used to hold the box together. Because Ford's system had no variety in the product line, that is all automobiles were the same, black with no options, there was no variation in the components either.

After World War II, in Japan, production volumes were minuscule compared with automotive output in the U.S. Those small production volumes did not allow Japanese automakers the luxury of using specialized equipment for each model. Nor did they allow for stocking huge inventories of parts. Automakers in Japan thus needed to develop flexible methods for adapting the same machines to different vehicle models. And they needed to find ways to ensure reliable supplies of needed parts and materials without maintaining large inventories.

Another factor involved the deterioration of labor-management relations. Severe recession buffeted Japan's rebuilding effort in the early postwar years. Adverse economic conditions had catalyzed an ugly cycle of strikes and lockouts. Toyota experienced the same labor strife that was endemic in Japanese industry in the early 1950s. Ultimately, labor and management at Toyota came to an understanding. Labor would cooperate with drastic restructuring, including job cuts, which were necessary for the company's survival. Management would guarantee lifetime employment for about 30% of the employees. Together, they would refrain from increasing employment casually, even in good times. Instead, they would hire temporary workers and try to find ways to accommodate upturns in the demand using the minimum number of employees.

Mutual trust between labor and management at Toyota developed over the years. Management rewarded employees for productivity gains with improved compensation and working conditions. Employees took the initiative in activities for raising productivity and otherwise enhancing the company's competitiveness.

Trust has enabled management to delegate authority to the workplace. The people who run the TPS are the ones on the line, those who can see problems when and where they occur and who can act immediately to resolve them. Workers are empowered and provided with pull cords to stop the assembly line. Line-stop problems are then permanently resolved.

Trust in the company encourages employees to acquire whatever skills are necessary to perform the work that needs to get done. By mastering a wide range of skills, they equip themselves to help and fill in for each other as necessary. Employees also reinforce their job security by acquiring diverse skills. The versatility of multi-skilled employees gives management the flexibility to redeploy people in response to changes in demand. However, to be able to deploy people, the design of the manufacturing system must be changed. The three basic parts of the manufacturing system are the final assembly line, the subassembly lines, and the component-part manufacturers. Each of these areas must be redesigned to change the functional job shops and flow-line systems into the Toyota lean manufacturing system.

So, TPS has inherited Ford's practice of breaking down work into simple steps and distributing those steps among employees along the line. This is called the "division of labor". But employees in the Toyota system are in charge of their own jobs. Through their teams, they manage their own work sites. They identify opportunities for making improvements and take the initiative in implementing those improvements under the umbrella of cooperation with management. And they share fully in the fruits of their own labor via a profit-sharing system.

Yet another element of Ford's system that remains critical in the Toyota production system is the concept of one-piece flow. On Ford's final-assembly-line conveyor, vehicles were manufactured one at a time. TPS extends that methodology to the rest of the manufacturing system, so it is like a vast machine that starts with customer orders and culminates in deliveries of finished products (Figure 15-2).

TPS HISTORY

Four men figured prominently in creating TPS and bringing the revolution to the U.S. The first was Sakichi Toyoda, the inventor of automatic looms, who later founded the Toyota group. In 1902, he invented a loom that would stop automatically if any of the threads snapped. His invention opened the way for automated loom works where a single operator could handle dozens of looms.

ROOTS OF AUTONOMATION

Sakichi Toyoda's invention reduced defects and raised yields, since a loom would not go on producing imperfect fabric and using up materials and production time after a problem occurred. The principle of designing equipment to stop automatically and calling attention to problems immediately is crucial to TPS. It is evident on every production line at Toyota and at other companies that use the system.

When Toyota set up an automobile manufacturing operation in the 1930s, Toyoda's son, Kiichiro, lead the new venture. Kiichiro traveled to the United States to study Ford's system of operation. He returned with a strong grasp of Ford's flow-line system and an even stronger determination to adapt that system to the small production volumes of the Japanese market.

Kiichiro's solution was to provide the different processes in the assembly sequence with only the kinds and quantities of items needed and only when they were needed. Production and transport activities took place simultaneously and synchronously throughout the production sequence, inside and between all the processes. Kiichiro thus laid the groundwork for Just-in-time (JIT) production and gets credit for coining the term JIT.

The man who did the most to structure TPS as an integrated framework was Taiichi Ohno. In the late 1940s, Ohno was in charge of a machining shop. He worked his way up to become an executive vice president at Toyota. He experimented with various methods of setting up the equipment to produce needed items in a timely manner. But he got a whole new perspective on JIT production when he visited the U.S. in 1956.

Ohno went to the U.S. to visit automobile plants, but like many Japanese who came to visit, he made two side trips. One was to an

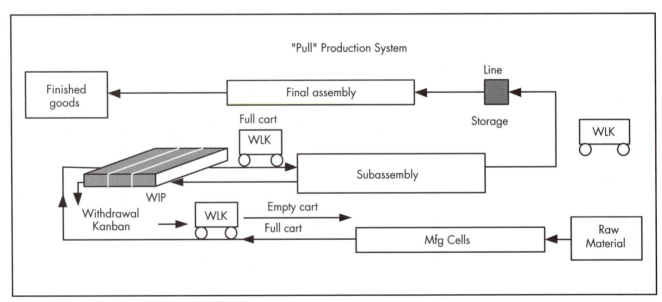

Figure 15-2. The lean production system provides for arranging all the processes from the raw materials to finished products in a single, smooth flow. Employees and managers at companies that employ the system learn to identify and eliminate any waste that occurs in the flow.

American supermarket. Japan did not have many self-service stores at that point and Ohno was impressed. He marveled at the way customers chose exactly what they wanted and in the quantities that they wanted. Ohno admired the way supermarkets supplied merchandise in a simple, productive, and timely manner.

In later years, Ohno often described his production system in terms of the American supermarket. Each Toyota production line arrayed its diverse output for the next line to choose from, similar to merchandise on supermarket shelves. Each line became the internal customer for the preceding line; each line became a supermarket for the following line. The downstream line would come and choose the items it needed and only those items were chosen. The feeder line would produce only the replacement items for the ones that the following line had selected. This format, then, was a pull system, driven by the needs of the following lines. It was in direct contrast with conventional push systems, which were driven by the output of the feeder lines.

Ohno developed a number of tools for controlling his production system in an integrated way. The best known of those tools is the kanban system, which provides for conveying information in and between processes by the utilization of instruction cards.

Ohno's other American side trip was to ride the cable cars in San Francisco. Here, he observed riders pulling an overhead cord when they wanted to get off the trolley car. Pulling the cord sounded a bell and the cable car operator stopped the car and the customer would disembark. Ohno later implemented a system of pull cords on the final assembly line for the operators to stop the line whenever they found a problem.

Another contributor to the development of the TPS was a consultant, Shigeo Shingo. He developed a methodology for setup-time reduction and wrote one of the earliest books detailing the TPS. In the 1980s, Dr. Shingo visited many companies in the U.S. demonstrating his single-minute-exchange-of-dies (SMED) system. The key to SMED was simplification of the setup process so workers could perform setups quickly and routinely as part of their daily routines. This was critical in the press forming area of the plant where sheet-metal body parts were produced. Also, it was critical in manufacturing cells where families of components were being made on the same set of processes. The machines were arranged in U-shapes according to the sequence of operations needed to make the family of components. The processes were extensively modified so that a changeover from one component in the family to the next was simple and quick.

GETTING READY FOR LEAN

Companies around the world have demonstrated the value of lean production in making automobiles and many other products. Some have even used the concepts of the lean production system successfully in service sectors.

As applied to lean production, the basic concepts of the original TPS are unchanging. But all companies implement those lean concepts differently. This has been true for all manufacturing-system implementations, but the TPS is particularly adaptable for many different products in many different countries. Some common threads are apparent in the experiences of many companies that have implemented the lean system successfully. To benefit from the TPS, companies must satisfy three basic conditions:

- Top management must make a strong and visible commitment to the system, participate directly in implementing the system, and instruct middle-level managers to do likewise.
- All employees must participate in the system (100% participation). The workers must be committed, not just involved. This requires enlightened management leadership. In the manufacturing of a ham and egg breakfast, the hen is involved but the pig is committed.

- Companies must put in place a solid framework for cultivating capable leaders and providing internal customers with necessary practical skills to do the job.

The commitment by top management is especially crucial. It is a beacon for everyone in the company, a clear and compelling mandate for change.

Companies often introduce new schemes for raising productivity and quality. But they rarely stick with demanding regimens unless required to do so. Even inefficient companies can get by when business conditions are good. And all but the most nonproductive companies can muddle through the modest economic downturns.

It usually takes a company-threatening crisis, a severe market slump, for example, or a technological breakthrough by a competitor, to put mortal fear into management and their employees. It usually takes a crisis to put the fear of going out of business into everyone. Only in crisis do people fully awaken to the need for fundamental change.

Once top executives see the gallows and recognize that corporate survival depends on fundamental change, they will lead that change. They must venture onto the factory floor. They must let employees know what kind of change they envision, how they will be involved in change, and why the change is important to the long-term survival and success of the company. And they must put middle management on notice that their tenure will hinge on active cooperation in promoting these changes. Middle management has the most to gain and the most to lose.

Companies need to develop programs for the training of everyone, from managers to employees, to operate and maintain a new lean production system. The natural teachers are the people who have participated in lean manufacturing with other companies. They should impart their skills to the other managers and employees through classroom instruction and hands-on sessions.

The second prerequisite for adopting the lean production system is participation by all employees. This requires a strong commitment from those in top management, in addition to those in the rest of the organizational framework. Full participation is essential because the lean production system works by establishing a smooth, continuous flow of material through the entire production sequence. For example, streamlining work and eliminating inventories at one work site means little if work just piles up at the next stage of the production sequence. Lean production generates the greatest benefits for companies when it is implemented throughout the entire manufacturing system, including all of the companies' suppliers. Companies strengthen each other by developing a smooth flow of material that extends all the way from suppliers of raw materials to assemblers of finished products in the final assembly line.

Vendors

Suppliers who participate in the lean production system enjoy the same benefits that the main company does from the system. Lean production can reduce inventories at part suppliers just as readily and effectively as it does at main assembly plants. Product quality improves as well. This is because the lean production system includes measures for exposing defects whenever and wherever they occur.

Suppliers who become lean producers also report improvements in their employee-management relations. This is mainly because the system provides for expanding their employee roles in designing their own workplace and managing their work areas. It brings employees and management together in the joint pursuit of improving the quality of the product and working conditions, thus reducing the unit cost of the product and throughput time, and increasing the overall flexibility of the factory.

The Internal Customer

Responsibility and authority are motivational. Nothing is more demoralizing over the long term than spending time in an unproductive manner. Experience has proven that the more authority employees have to manage their own work, the more inclined they are to pursue improvements in that work. Employees who can translate their own ideas into visible improvements in production flow and product quality take pride in their work, jobs, and companies.

In lean manufacturing, teams of employees undertake tremendous responsibility for designing standardized work procedures for their own jobs and strive continuously to find ways to improve those procedures. Team members use kanban to manage workflow and obtain parts and materials. They each work to master every job in their cell or on their line so that any member of the team can help or fill in for any other member of the team. This means that the factory must be redesigned so that the processes and operations can be operated by just enough people to meet demand. For example, take a look at Wendy's, a fast-food restaurant that can be considered a manufacturing cell for hamburgers. At lunchtime, Wendy's has numerous workers in the cell to meet the daily demand. By mid-afternoon, one person can handle the demand. Wendy's burger cell is designed for flexibility in handling changes in customer demand and product design, or making the burger to the customer's specifications.

For people who have worked in regimented job/flow shop manufacturing systems, the lean production system and the broad-ranging responsibilities it assigns to employees can come as a shock. Many conventional systems are rife with rigid job designations. The lean production system cultivates employee flexibility by having employees acquire multiple skills. Conventional manufacturing systems buffer schedules for many tasks with so-called "reserve" time. Lean leaves no time in the work cycle for any task that is not absolutely necessary to generate value.

The lean production system enforces a creative attitude in the workplace. Employees do not coast. Lean production demands continuous vigilance. Continuous improvements demand unflagging efforts to find better ways of doing things. The lean manufacturing system structures a workplace environment that nurtures employee initiative. The overall result is a stimulating workplace where employees can take charge of their own destinies.

JIT PRODUCTION

Customers want the best possible products at the lowest possible prices and they want them as soon as possible. The Toyota production system provides for fulfilling customers' demands productively and promptly by linking all production activity to marketplace sales.

In the lean manufacturing system, all the processes in the manufacturing sequence are arranged to produce in a single, smooth line of flow. Basically, each process produces items for the next downstream process to withdraw and use as needed. Each process withdraws items from some preceding process and produces items to replace ones that the following process has withdrawn. Each process only makes additional items to replace items that the following process has withdrawn. All the processes are connected by kanban links. A kanban link is a set of containers, cartons, baskets, boxes, etc., which hold a specific number of parts. The system's work-in-process (WIP) inventory is held in the kanban links.

JIT manufacturing, another term for lean production's cellular manufacturing, means making only what is needed, when it is needed, and in the amount that is needed. It eliminates many types of waste and the need to maintain large inventories, which reduces storage costs. JIT eliminates waste that occurs when changes in specifications or shifts render stocks of old items worthless. It also eliminates waste that occurs when defects go undetected in the manufacture of large batches.

Cellular manufacturing, though simple in principle, requires dedication and hard work to implement properly. Once managers and employees have mastered the basic concepts, they can learn how to devise various tools and techniques for putting those concepts into practice. Notably, they learn to:

- distribute production of different kinds of items evenly throughout the day and week, allocating work evenly and thereby using resources optimally;
- link each process using kanban to the preceding and following process (pull system);
- make items one at a time whenever possible, emulating one-piece flow;
- establish a time frame for linking the pace of work in every cell to the pace of final assembly (system takt time); and
- where batch processing is necessary, such as stamping sheet-metal components, reduce batch size to as small as possible by reducing setup time between batches.

In summary, lean production requires a level demand for subassembly and component parts. This level demand is accomplished by making the same mix of products in small quantities every day. The output from feeder processes is balanced then to match the daily demand. This process seems easy, but is often difficult to accomplish.

LEVEL PRODUCTION

Lean production can help companies achieve spectacular gains in productivity and quality. It is impossible to attain, however, unless companies distribute work evenly by leveling production.

At Toyota, leveling can be looked at (based on customer sales) by examining how the planning department gets information each month about the number and kinds of vehicles it expects to sell in the following month. This information is then passed on to vehicle plants and suppliers to provide a rough basis for production planning. Dealers give Toyota information every 10 days about actual orders they have received. Based on that information, plants and suppliers draft detailed 10-day production plans. Dealers also provide Toyota with daily information about customer orders and requests. Production plans can be adjusted up to three days before production begins to accommodate requests for changes in some specification, such as body color. Based on the daily production plan, an exact sequence of items to be produced at the plant is determined. Different specifications are distributed evenly over the day.

At a Toyota vehicle plant, a variety of body types can be seen moving along the same assembly line at the same time. The production of different body types is staggered evenly over the course of the day to make efficient use of the basic elements of production processes, including machine tools, tooling, equipment, and material-handling devices.

Suppose Toyota spends all morning producing one item, all afternoon producing another, and all evening on a third item. This might seem productive, since it would enable Toyota to run larger batches without changing paints, tools, and dies. However, it would distance the pattern of production from the pattern of sales in the marketplace. Even worse, it would impose a disproportionate burden on one team at times in the upstream processes. Some teams might be idle, while others would be busy, and this would be an unproductive utilization of resources.

Production should be scheduled evenly in the final assembly processes. Leveling and scheduling final assembly to evenly distribute various models of the cars and their options throughout the day is also called *smoothing of production* in Toyota literature. Leveling enables suppliers to distribute components evenly in their manufacturing processes. It enables workers to function with a minimum of manpower and equipment.

PULL SYSTEM

The most important feature of the Toyota production system is the way it links all production activity to real demand. Everything that happens in the system happens only in the name of fulfilling actual orders from dealers. The system works that way because it is a pull system.

In push systems, manufacturers produce goods and then try to find buyers for those products. Processes inside the manufacturers' plants turn out batch after batch of items according to the schedule developed by the production-control department using material-requirements-planning (MRP) scheduling. The items are passed on to the next process, regardless of the pace of work in the following process.

Inevitably, a lot of time and effort ends up being wasted in push systems. The material-requirements-planning system is a computer-based system designed for planning. If this computer system were designed for control, it would be called material-requirements control. Using material-requirements planning causes the manufacturing system to turn out streams of products without regard for the needs and wants of the intended customers. As a result, semi-finished goods pile up between processes inside plants and between parts makers and assembly manufacturers. The piles of WIP are a sure indicator that the WIP inventory is not under control.

Kanban

Toyota uses a production-control tool, kanban, to operate a pull system. Every item or box of items that flows through a production process carries its own kanban card. Kanban cards are removed from items that have been used or transported, and these cards go back to preceding processes to serve as orders for additional items. Kanban cards bear lettering and bar codes that identify items, locations of work sites where the items are used, and the production lines or suppliers from which they come.

There are two basic types of kanban cards used at Toyota: parts withdrawal kanban (WLK) as shown in Figure 15-3, and production ordering kanban (POK) as shown in Figure 15-4. WLK is used for communication between processes; POK is for communication within processing.

Operators remove withdrawal kanbans from parts and materials they have used. These kanban cards are carried back to preceding processes to withdraw additional items. Production ordering kanbans come off of items that subsequent processes have withdrawn. They go back into their processes as instructions to make additional items and replace those that have been withdrawn.

The homely kanban is an unlikely candidate for fame. Though its name means signboard or signal in Japanese, the kanban is no marquee. Kanban at Toyota is usually no more than a printed piece of cardboard sandwiched between clear plastic covers. Yet this nondescript item has become the best-known element of TPS. Some people think that the kanban system is the essence of TPS.

Actually, the kanban is a production-control tool that enables employees to operate the TPS by taking responsibility for managing their own work. Envision an operator who removes a kanban card from a basket of components before mounting the components on vehicles. The operator sends the kanban card back to the upstream process to order additional components that replace the ones that have been used. That operator is then shouldering an important part of the management function of ordering parts and managing inventory.

Kanban helps enforce an organic linkage between work in preceding and following processes. Employees maintain that linkage by handling the kanban properly and abiding by established work procedures. Every large assembly shop at Toyota has two or more kanban stations, each of which processes about 10,000 kanban cards per shift. Suppliers then affix identifying kanban cards to the items they deliver. Suppliers receive orders via kanbans that are removed from boxes at the stations on the way out. The paperwork is minimal and the

An operator removes the kanban from a new box of items when he or she uses the first item from the box.

The operator deposits the kanban that he or she should be removed from boxes of parts in a kanban mailbox nearby.

Team leaders gather the contents of the kanban mailboxes at pre-scribed times—several times a day—and place them in collection boxes. The kanban postman picks the kanbans up from the collection boxes...

...and takes them to a sorting room. There, an automatic sorter places the kanbans in separate boxes for the different suppliers.

The drivers that bring parts from the suppliers stop in at the sorting room after unloading their trucks and pick up kanban to take back to their plants.

Back at the suppliers' plants, the drivers deposit the kanban in collection boxes for subsequent sorting.

A withdrawal kanban goes onto a new box of parts in place of the production instruction kanban. The latter goes back into the plant as a production order for a like quantity of the same part.

Then, the supplier delivers the new box of parts to the plant indicated on its kanban.

Here is a withdrawal kanban that Toyota used with an outside supplier. It indicates the name of the supplier, the receiving area at the plant, the location in the plant that will use the item, the part number, the part name, and the quantity. This kanban also has a bar-code label to permit automatic invoicing.

Figure 15-3. Kanban Flow: Withdrawal kanban (courtesy Toyota Motor Company).

productivity is maximal. And the employees are completely in charge.

LEAN MANUFACTURING

In the lean production system, work is arranged in a single, smooth flow. That means arranging work inside each cell to flow smoothly from one step or operation to the next. It means redesigning the factory floor so that work proceeds directly from one cell to the next without any detours to storage. It means devising logistics so that work moves smoothly and on schedule from raw materials plants through machining cells, to subassembly cells, to assembly lines, and on to distributors, dealers, and customers, like water flow through a pipe.

Production at the supplier proceeds in accordance with the production instruction kanban (circled) that flows back to the manufacturing line.

Boxes of finished parts at this Toyota supplier go into a rack to await pickup and delivery. Note the arrows. They indicate which boxes to pick up first when more than one box of the same kind of part are awaiting delivery. This first-in, first-out system avoids the collection of dust and other problems that can occur when items sit idle. Shipment orders, of course, are in the form of withdrawal kanban. Those kanbans go onto the boxes in place of the production instruction kanbans. The production instruction kanbans go back into the manufacturing line as production orders.

Kanban flows echo each other throughout the production sequence. The materials that the operators use at this supplier each carry their own withdrawal kanban for ordering additional materials from the suppliers' suppliers.

Kanban do not need to be printed cards. They can be triangular metal plates and color-coded washers, like the ones above. They even can be colored balls, like those used in some processes at Toyota.

Figure 15-4. Kanban Flow: Production instruction kanban (courtesy Toyota Motor Company).

Ideally, items should proceed one at a time through the entire production sequence. This is the fastest way to translate raw material into a finished product because it minimizes the amount of material in process at all stages of production. One-piece flow is impractical, however, for work where dies, molds, or other tools are changed to produce different products, as in forging, castings, stampings, as well as moldings. Other batch-type processes, such as plating and chemical milling, must be continued until technology catches up and single-piece production is feasible. A good first step is to use the smallest possible batches. Since changing dies or molds is time-consuming, manufacturers traditionally will favor large batches in batch-processing machines and also in upstream stages of production sequences.

Inventories can be reduced and flexibility increased by using smaller batches or lots. Suppose 1,000 units per day each of Parts A and B are needed. Can these be produced in four batches of 500 units, rather than two batches of 1,000 units? To do this without compromising productivity, ways must be found to shorten the changeover or setup time for the dies or molds. That is, the increased number of production runs must not greatly increase the total time the machines are idle for setup.

Historically, advances in decreasing changeover times have been an important dynamic of TPS. Those advances are easy to achieve once internal customers in the workplace recognize the importance of decreasing changeover time to reduce batch sizes. The trick is to analyze changeover work systematically using the single-minute-exchange-of-dies system.

Example

Here is a look at the difference in throughput time between one-piece-flow processing and conventional batch processing for 100 pieces. This example is of three consecutive processes, each of which requires one second to complete one item. Batch processing entails a production lead time of 300 minutes because parts sit idle at upstream processes while work is under way on whole batches in the following processes. One-piece flow allows for completing 100 parts in 102 minutes, just enough time to produce all 100 parts, one at a time, in turn, through the three processes.

In Figure 15-5, Operators A, B, and C are performing successive steps in an assembly sequence. Work begins for each operator when receiving a box of 100 semi-finished units from a preceding process. Workers perform additional work on each of the assemblies and then take the 100 assemblies to the next operator. This approach entails inefficiencies of the following types:

- Each operator has 100 items at a time, which is resulting in extremely long lead times.
- It is difficult to balance the distribution of work.
- The large amount of items per operator means extra handling on the workbench.
- If Operator B discovers an improperly assembled workpiece, the operator cannot determine exactly when or how this problem occurred. Operator B knows only that it has happened at some point during the processing of 100 items.
- When production shifts to a different kind of assembly, operators must remove all parts for the previous assembly from the shelves to avoid mixing them with parts for a new assembly.

Assuming the time for Jobs A, B, and C are equal, a company can avoid problems in the preceding example by placing workers next to each other in an assembly cell and having each operator handle parts one at a time. Workers perform their work on an assembly and hand it over to the next operator before reaching for the next workpiece. This is one-piece flow in assembly operations. This change, which requires no increase in the number of operators for the same span of work, yields the following improvements:

Functional job shop design

One-piece flow cell design

Figure 15-5. How one-piece flow cell design cuts lead time by reducing inventory.

- The number of items on the line, from raw material to finished product, becomes the same as the number of operators on the line.
- When Operator B discovers a defective item, that operator along with Operator A can determine the cause of the problem immediately, since it is the item that Operator A has just handled.
- Operators need not arrange or convey large numbers of parts on the workbench.

- Differences in workloads between operators are readily apparent, and a company can often find ways to reduce its manpower needs.
- A company can switch production to different items without interrupting flow.

Takt Time

TPS links all production activity to actual customer demand through the design of the linked-cell manufacturing system. The key aspect of this linkage is takt time. *Takt* is the German word for meter, as in musical meter, or heartbeat. In TPS, takt time is based on the pace of sales in the marketplace. Takt time in plants is calculated as the quotient of daily working hours divided by the number of vehicle orders to be filled each day.

Here is how takt works. Assume a plant operates with two shifts a day of 460 minutes each, for a total of 920 minutes. If the need were to fill orders for 400 vehicles per day, the takt time would be about 2.3 minutes per vehicle. If an increase in sales volume were to raise the daily requirement to 500 vehicles, the takt time would shrink to 1.84 minutes. Takt time at final assembly yields cycle times for subassemblies and component manufacturing.

If the takt time for a vehicle model is two minutes, the cycle time for the engine also will be two minutes. The cycle time for the cell making crankshafts for an engine is also two minutes, while the cycle time for a cell making the piston rod is 30 seconds, since each engine needs four rods. The cycle time for 20 locknuts used to mount the four wheels would be six seconds per nut (120 seconds/20 nuts).

Workflow

Once a takt time has been determined, the most efficient workflow and procedures, with due consideration to quality, safety, quantity, and cost, can be determined. Work is allocated to maintain a steady optimal workload for each operator and machine. Using substantial changes in daily workloads for individual operators does not accommodate changes in takt times. Instead, when the takt time for a production line becomes shorter and more demanding, the flow of work is streamlined and additional workers are added as necessary. When takt time becomes longer, fewer workers are assigned to a line. Assigning more people to a line means that each operator handles a narrower range of work. Assigning fewer people means that each operator handles a broader range of work. Flexibility in allocating work is possible because the cell is designed for standing, walking workers. People master a much broader range of skills, and multiprocess handling (instead of multi-machine) is employed.

Traditionally, manufacturers assigned their operators to several machines of the same type. That is, a lathe operator might process five items on lathes and then pass them on to a milling machine operator, who processes them on milling machines. The items then might move on to drilling and tapping in the same manner. Even if the lathe operator runs multiple lathes, multi-machine handling entails long lead times and excessive handling. The item that the lathe operator processes on the first lathe, for example, sits idle until the operator has finished processing the other items on the other lathes. Overproduction occurs frequently, and feedback on quality problems is difficult to obtain.

In manufacturing cells, an operator handles different kinds of machines to keep work moving in a continuous flow. The operator might use a lathe, a milling machine, a drill press, and then a tapping machine on each item in a sequence.

Multi-skilled operators and multiprocess handling thus enable the accommodation of changes in takt time while maintaining short lead times with one-at-a-time production. In the example, an increase in demand could be accommodated by assigning two operators, instead of one, to the four processes. The first operator might narrow his or her scope of work to the lathe and milling machine, and the second operator would handle the drill and tapping machine. Turning all four processes back over to one operator would accommodate a subsequent decline in demand.

INTEGRATED QUALITY

The principle of stopping work immediately when problems occur and preventing the production of defective items is basic to the Toyota production system. In Japanese, this principle is called *jidoka*. We call it *autonomation*.

When under the Toyota production system, equipment is designed to detect abnormal conditions and to stop automatically whenever they occur. Operators in the assembly cell can stop the production flow whenever they note anything suspicious. Mechanical and human autonomation prevent defective items from progressing into subsequent stages of production, prevent the waste that would result from producing a series of defective items, and prevent overproduction (see Figure 15-6).

Another advantage of autonomation is that it exposes the causes of problems by stopping the equipment exactly as it is when a problem first occurred. Autonomation also calls attention to the problem immediately with a signal light or some other kind of indicator. The most fundamental effect of autonomation is the way it changes the nature of cell management: it eliminates the need for an operator to watch over each of the machines continuously, since machines stop automatically when abnormalities occur. It therefore opens the door to major gains in productivity.

Autonomation is thus partly a humanistic approach to configuring the human-machine interface. It liberates the operators from the tyranny of the machine and leaves them free to concentrate on tasks that enable them to exercise skill and judgment.

Line Stop

On the final assembly line, the fixed position is clearly marked for work in each station. Operators in the process assume responsibility for

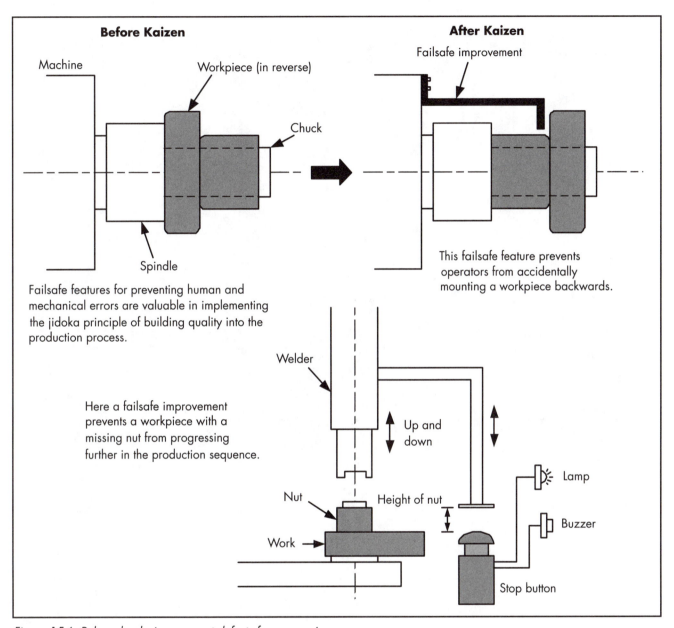

Before Kaizen

Machine

Workpiece (in reverse)

Chuck

Spindle

Failsafe features for preventing human and mechanical errors are valuable in implementing the jidoka principle of building quality into the production process.

After Kaizen

Failsafe improvement

This failsafe feature prevents operators from accidentally mounting a workpiece backwards.

Here a failsafe improvement prevents a workpiece with a missing nut from progressing further in the production sequence.

Welder

Up and down

Nut

Height of nut

Work

Lamp

Buzzer

Stop button

Figure 15-6. Poka-yoke devices prevent defects from occurring.

guaranteeing the quality of all work up to that line. They make sure no defective items progress beyond that line and into the next process. When an operator signals a problem by pulling on the line-stop cord, the line keeps moving until it reaches the fixed position. That gives the team leader and operator a chance to resolve the problem before the line stops (see Figure 15-7).

Operators would be hesitant to pull the line-stop cord if pulling it stopped the line immediately; they might be subconsciously inclined to let minor imperfections pass rather than take responsibility for stopping the line. Employees are more inclined to call attention to possible problems when they know that summoning help will not stop the line at that

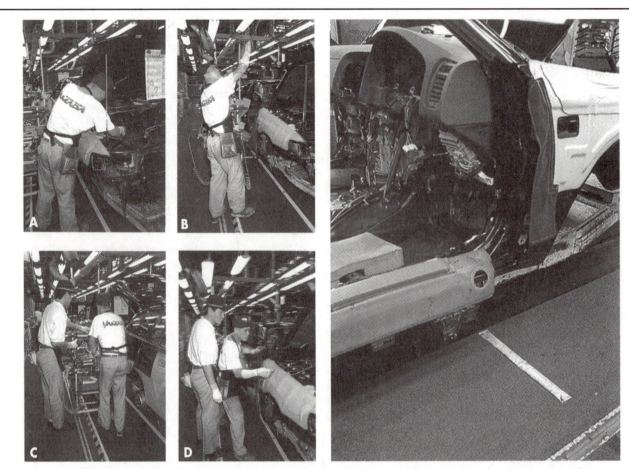

Operators in the Toyota production system can stop the production line whenever they spot anything suspicious. Along the conveyor on this assembly line, an operator (A) has noted a part that does not fit correctly. He pulls on the line-stop cord (B). That lights the andon lamp and summons the operator's team leader to have a look (C). The line will continue moving until it reaches the next "fixed position"— the position where each process on the line has completed one work cycle.

When the team leader arrives, the operator explains the problem. The team leader discovers a fitting that has slipped out of place and is able to resolve the problem (D) before the line reaches the fixed position. If the leader required more time to resolve the problem, the line would stop at the fixed position.

Figure 15-7. The fixed position is clearly marked for work in each station with a yellow line. Stopping work movement at the line assures all tasks on the line will be completed when stoppage occurs (courtesy Toyota Motor Company).

instant. This methodology results in more rigorous quality control.

Another reason for keeping the line moving until it reaches the fixed position is that stopping the line in the middle of a work cycle would be disruptive to all the other stations. Stopping the line at the fixed position ensures that all processes along the line will have completed their work cycles when the stoppage

occurs. Thus the errors and quality problems that happen all too easily when interruptions occur in the midst of work are avoided.

INTERNAL CUSTOMER SATISFACTION

External customer satisfaction is a reflection of employee (the internal customer) satisfaction. In that sense, the Toyota production system has been successful in earning customer satisfaction because it provides employees with fulfilling work.

Measures for enhancing employees' sense of job fulfillment are an important emphasis in the new ways Toyota is implementing its production system. For example, Toyota knows that work is more fulfilling when employees can take part in completing an entire product or assembly. Employees take pride in their work when they can see their efforts take shape in a functional unit.

Assigning a single small team to assemble a whole vehicle would be grossly inefficient. But work can be arranged so teams can handle all the steps of assembling complete systems. For instance, Toyota traditionally has installed electrical wiring a small portion at a time at different stages in the vehicle assembly sequence. This also has been the case in the installation of exhaust systems and other important systems. Recently, Toyota began concentrating the installation steps for such systems at single work sites. This heightens the sense of teamwork among the 20-or-so workers at each work site. It reinforces their sense of accomplishment by enabling them to complete a crucial and integrated part of each vehicle.

The ultimate responsibility for raising quality and productivity lies with the operators in the workplace. Success in implementing the TPS hinges on earning their trust, securing their active participation, and providing them with sufficient skills and understanding to fulfill their role fully.

STANDARDIZED WORK AND CELL DESIGN

Standardizing work is a way to maintain productivity, quality, and safety at high levels. It provides a consistent framework for performing work at the designated takt times and for illuminating opportunities for making improvements in work procedures. Three elements are used for structuring standardized work:

1. takt time, which is set by the pace of marketplace sales;
2. working sequence for the manufacturing cell, which is the series of steps that are determined to be the best way to perform a task; and
3. standard stock-on-hand, which is the minimum number of workpieces needed to be on hand for a process to maintain a smooth flow of work.

Standardized work results in detailed, step-by-step guidelines for every job in the lean production system. Team leaders determine the most efficient work sequence. They make continuing improvements in the work sequence with their team members. Continuous improvement thus begets new patterns, or new cell designs of standardized work.

The operator in the series of photos in Figure 15-8 is abiding by a carefully designed working sequence. The sequence appears in a standardized work chart posted at the workplace. The chart shows the sequence of 12 operations for the right half of the manufacturing cell. It shows the location of the quality checkpoints, stock-on-hand, and cycle time compared to the takt time.

Because standardized work involves following procedures consistently, any inherent problems in the working sequence surface repeatedly and, therefore, conspicuously. This allows cell team leaders and members of the team to identify and fix problems easily. Similarly, monthly changes in production volumes require changes in the standardized work. Standardized work allows team leaders and members to devise new standardized work procedures to accommodate monthly changes in production volumes.

Kaizen

Kaizen furnishes the dynamism for continuous improvement and encourages individuals to take part in designing and managing their own jobs. Kaizen improvements in standardized work help maximize productivity at every work site.

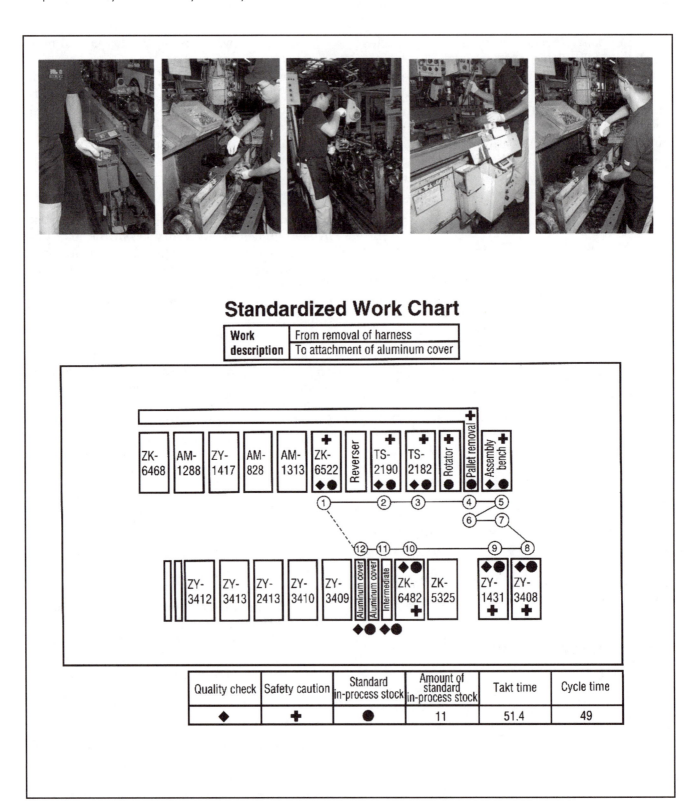

Figure 15-8. Standardized work chart for a lean manufacturing cell (courtesy Toyota Motor Company).

Kaizen activities include methods for improving equipment, as well as techniques for improving work procedures. But implementing kaizen improvements for work tends to be easier, faster, and less expensive than for equipment. Toyota usually starts with work kaizen when trying to resolve a problem. If modifying a working sequence is not sufficient to resolve a problem, possible solutions through equipment kaizen are then considered.

TOYOTA SUPPLIER SUPPORT CENTER

The Toyota Supplier Support Center was opened in Kentucky in 1992 to work with companies adopting TPS. Local Toyota plants work with suppliers, while the support center lends a hand to companies regardless of whether they are doing business with Toyota. This center even assists manufacturers in industries beyond the automotive industry.

Several companies that have worked with the Toyota Supplier Support Center have demonstrated the effectiveness of TPS in an American setting. Figure 15-9 shows an example of a handout from TRW/Koyo, a first-tier supplier to Toyota in Kentucky. Another example is the automotive parts manufacturer, Grand Haven Stamped Products Company, located in Michigan.

Case Study

In 1993, Grand Haven began working with the Toyota Supplier Support Center. Its core competencies are centered on stamping, welding, and assembly. This company makes floor-mounted transmission-control systems, hood- and deck-lid hinges, and clutch, brake, and accelerator pedals.

Like most companies that adopt TPS, Grand Haven began in one segment of its operations. It set up a continuous flow line in a cell for assembling luggage arms. The improvements in productivity and quality were immediate and dramatic, and have continued (Table 15-1).

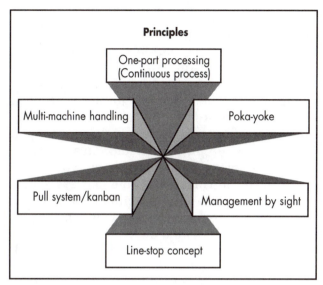

Figure 15-9. TPS principles practiced by suppliers.

Grand Haven extended its continuous flow processing to stamping, an upstream process. Grand Haven's press department traditionally operated under the classic principles of mass production. This resulted in long changeover times for the stamping machines. Hence, the department processed large batches between die changeovers. Large batches resulted in huge inventories. Stoppages occurred frequently in the downstream processes because of improper part mixes from the stamping department.

Table 15-1
Luggage arm assembly
Results of implementing the Toyota
production system (first two years)

Productivity	
Output/person	0.84%
Overtime hours/week	−100%
Personnel needs on line	− 45%
Inventory (on production line)	
Work-in-process	− 93%
Raw material	− 92%
Finished goods	− 68%
Floor space	− 60%
Quality	
Customer complaints/month	−100%

With the assistance of engineers from the Toyota Supplier Support Center, Grand Haven, discovered ways to shorten changeover times. Notably, it began doing of lot of preparation and follow-up work offline, instead of online, for changeovers. The company formerly stopped the presses while bringing up and positioning new dies for mounting. It also stopped machines while returning old dies to their storage spaces. By revising its work procedures, Grand Haven was able to prepare new dies while stamping machines were still running and restart the stamping machines before putting away old dies.

Grand Haven standardized changeover work systematically and trained workers to follow the standardized format faithfully. This allowed for using small batches on a continuing basis. The company succeeded in producing only the amount of items actually needed, which meant lasting gains in productivity.

The company also streamlined its presswork by implementing a signal kanban system. Formerly, planning and prioritizing jobs for each sheet-metal press was a difficult process subject to chronic confusion. The use of kanban eliminated this confusion by linking the job sequence to the needs of the downstream processes.

Productivity gains were just as dramatic in stamping work as they were in the assembly areas (Table 15-2). Grand Haven has since introduced lean production principles in several other cells that include processes for serving customers besides Toyota. Implementing the principles of TPS has strengthened the company's

**Table 15-2
Stamping work
Results of implementing the Toyota
production system (first two years)**

Die changeover	
Average time required	– 94%
Average monthly changeovers	+300%
Inventory	– 82%
Output	1.38

overall competitiveness. It is continuing this momentum by helping its suppliers implement elements of JIT production. The company is concentrating on setting up pull systems between its plant and suppliers.

Summary

The message is clear to all who will listen and learn. Toyota has evolved a new manufacturing system design that has carried this company to the top of the automobile manufacturing world and changed the way the world makes cars and many other consumer goods. This book was written to explain how manufacturing cells work to produce superior-quality parts at the lowest cost, with the shortest lead time. The Toyota system is easy to understand. Now, many are trying to figure out how to apply this system to large complex assemblies like boats, planes, and the like. Like TPS, this will happen and the outcome will benefit internal and external customers alike.

References

Alexander, D.C. and B.M. Pulat. 1990. *Industrial Ergonomics: A Practitioner's Guide*. Norcross, GA: Industrial Engineering and Management Press.

Amber, J.S. and P.S. Amber. 1962. *The Anatomy of Automation*. Englewood Cliffs, NJ: Prentice Hall.

American National Standards Institute (ANSI). 1998. "Proposed Standard for Control of Cumulative Trauma Disorders." No. Z-365. Washington, D.C.: *Accredited Standards Committee*.

Armstrong, T.J., R.G. Radwin, D.J. Hansen, and K.W. Kennedy. 1986. "Repetitive Trauma Disorders: Job Evaluation and Design." *The Journal of the Human Factors and Ergonomics Society*.

Askin, Ronald G. and Charles R. Standridge. 1993. *Modeling and Analysis of Manufacturing Systems*. New York: John Wiley & Sons. p. 461.

Astrand, Per-Olof and Kaare Rodahl. 1986. *Textbook of Work Physiology*. New York: McGraw-Hill.

AT&T Technical Journal. 1990. "Striving For Manufacturing Excellence." Vol. 69, No. 4, July/August.

Ayres, Robert U. 1991. *Computer Integrated Manufacturing, Vol. IV*. London: Chapman Hall.

Badler, Norman I., C.B. Phillips, and B.L. Webber. 1993. *Simulating Humans: Computer Graphics Animation and Control*. New York: Oxford University Press.

Baily, R.W. 1982. *Human Performance Engineering: A Guide for Systems Designers*. Englewood Cliffs, NJ: Prentice-Hall.

Banerjee, A., P. Banerjee, and S. Mehrotra. 1996. "An Enabling Environment for Inputting Qualitative Information in MS Layout Design." *Proceedings of Virtual Reality in Manufacturing Research and Education Symposium*. Chicago, IL: University of Illinois at Chicago.

Banister, E.W. and R.S. Brown. 1968. "The Relative Energy Requirements for Physical Activity." *Journal of Applied Physiology*. Vol. 33, p. 674-676.

Baron, J.J. 1991. "Tips on Tackling GT-based Cells." *Manufacturing Engineering*. Vol. 106, p. 46-49.

Black, J T. 1988. "The Design of Manufacturing Cells." *Proceedings of Manufacturing International*. p. 143-157.

—— 1991. *The Design of the Factory with a Future*. New York: McGraw-Hill.

—— 1999. "Black's Blueprint for Lean Manufacturing." Unpublished manuscript. Auburn, AL: Industrial and Systems Engineering Dept., Auburn University.

Black, J T., B.C. Jiang, and G.J. Wiens. 1991. "Design, Analysis and Control of Manufacturing Cells." New York: American Society of Mechanical Engineers (ASME). PED-Vol. 53.

Black, J T. and B.J. Schroer. 1988. "Decouplers in Integrated Cellular Manufacturing Systems." *Journal of Engineering for Industry*, Transactions. ASME. Vol. 110, p. 77-85.

—— 1993. "Simulation of an Apparel Assembly Cell with Walking Workers and Decouplers." *Journal of Manufacturing Systems*. Vol. 12, No. 2, p. 170-180.

Burbridge, John L. 1975. *The Introduction of Group Technology*. New York: John Wiley & Sons. p. 149-188.

—— 1997. *Production Flow Analysis for Planning Group Technology*. Oxford, England: Clarendon Press.

Burgess, J.H. 1982. *Designing for Humans: The Human Factor in Engineering*. Princeton, NJ: Petrocelli Books.

Buzacott, John A. 1995. "A Perspective on New Paradigms in Manufacturing." *Journal of Manufacturing Systems*. Vol. 14, No. 2, p. 118.

Carter, C.F. Jr. 1971. "Trends in Machine Tool Development and Application." *Proceedings of the Second International Conference on Product Development and Manufacturing Technology*. University of Strathclyde.

Castillo, Adelina, H. Seifoddini, and Jeffrey Abell. 1997. "The Development of a Cellular Manufacturing System for Automotive Parts." *Computers & Industrial Engineering*. Vol. 33, No. 1-2, p. 243-247.

Chaffin, Don B. 1997. "Human Simulation Modeling—Will It Improve Ergonomics During Design?" *Proceedings of Human Factors and Ergonomics Society*, 41st Annual Meeting. Santa Monica, CA: Human Factors and Ergonomics Society. Vol. 1, p. 685-687.

Chan, Felix and K. Abhary. 1996. "Design and Evaluation of Automated Cellular Manufacturing Systems with Simulation Modeling and AHP Approach: A Case Study." *Integrated Manufacturing Systems*. Vol. 7, No. 6, p. 39-52.

Cochran, David. 1994. "Manufacturing System Design and Control." *Ph.D. Dissertation,* Auburn University.

Cochran, David S., J.F. Arinez, J.W. Duda, and J. Linck. "A Decomposition Approach for Manufacturing System Design." *Journal of Manufacturing Systems*. Vol. 20, No. 6, 2001/2002.

Cochran, David S. and D.C. Dobbs. "Evaluating Manufacturing System Design and Performance Using the Manufacturing System Depomposition Approach." *Journal of Manufacturing Systems*. Vol. 20, No. 6, 2001–2002.

Cochran, David S., Walter Eversheim, Gerd Kubin, and Marc L. Sesterhenn. "The Application Axiomatic Design and Lean Management Principles in the Scope of Production System Segmentation." *International Journal of Production Research*. Vol. 38, No. 6, 2000, p. 1377-1396.

Crosby, Philip. 1979. *Quality is Free: The Art of Making Quality Certain*. New York: McGraw-Hill.

Das, Biman and Arijit K. Sengupta. 1996. "Industrial Workstation Design: A Systematic Ergonomics Approach." *Applied Ergonomics*. Vol. 27, No. 3, p. 157-163.

Das, Biman and R.M. Grady. 1983. "Industrial Workplace Layout Design: An Application of Engineering Anthropometry." *Ergonomics*.

Deming, W.E. 1982. *Quality, Productivity, and Competitive Position*. Boston, MA: Massachusetts Institute of Technology.

Deneb Robotics, Inc. 1998. "IGRIP/ENVISION/ERGO Software Manual." Auburn Hills, MI: Deneb Robotics.

DeVor, Richard, R. Graves, and J.J. Mills. 1997. "Agile Manufacturing Research: Accomplishments and Opportunities." *IIE Transactions*. Norcross, GA: Institute of Industrial Engineering. Vol. 29, p. 813-823.

Eastman Kodak Company. 1986. *Ergonomics Design for People at Work*. Vols. I and II. New York: Van Nostrand Reinhold.

Eckstein, A.L.H. and T.R. Rohleder. 1998. "Incorporating Human Resources in GT/CM." *International Journal of Production Research*. Vol. 36, No. 5, p. 1199-1222.

Ehrhardt, Ina, H. Herper, and H. Gebhardt. 1994. "Modeling Strain of Manual Work in Manufacturing Systems." *Simulation Conference Proceedings*. Institute of Electrical and Electronics Engineers. p. 1044-1049.

Feyen, Robert, Yili Liu, Don Chaffin, Glenn Jimmerson, and Brad Joseph. 1999. "New Software Tools." *Ergonomics in Design*. No. 5, p. 24-30.

Ford, Henry. 1919. *My Life and Work*. North Stratford, NH: Ayer Company Publishers, Inc.

—— 1988. *Today and Tomorrow*. Cambridge, MA: Productivity Press.

Fry, T.D. 1995. "Japanese Manufacturing Performance Criteria." *International Journal of Production Research*. Vol. 33, No. 4.

Geller, T.L., S.E. Lammers, and G.T. Mackulak. 1995. "Methodology for Simulation Application to VM Environments." *Proceedings of the 1995 Winter IEEE Simulation Conference*. Institute of Electrical and Electronics Engineers. p. 909-916.

Gilad, Issachar and Reuven Karni. "Architecture of an Expert System for Ergonomic Analysis and Design." *International Journal of Industrial Ergonomics*. Vol. 23, No. 3, p. 205-221.

Goldtouch Technologies. 2001. "Injury Costs Support the Need for a Federal Ergonomic Standard." *August Goldtouch Newsletter*.

Grandjean, E. 1988. *Fitting the Task to the Man*. London: Taylor and Francis Publishing.

Hall, Robert W. 1982. "Kawasaki U.S.A.: A Case Study." Alexandria, VA: American Production and Inventory Society.

—— 1983. *Zero Inventories*. Homewood, IL: Dow Jones-Irwin.

Helander, Martin. 1995. *A Guide to the Ergonomics of Manufacturing*. Bristol, PA: Taylor and Francis Publishing.

Hitomi, K. 1979. *Manufacturing Systems Engineering*. Bristol, PA: Taylor and Francis Publishing.

Hopp, W.J. and M.K. Spearman. 1996. *Factory Physics*. Boston, MA: Irvin/McGraw-Hill.

Hunter, Steve L. "Ergonomic Evaluation of Manufacturing System Designs." *Journal of Manufacturing Systems*. Vol. 20, No. 6, 2001/2002.

Hunter, Steve L., J T. Black, and Robert E. Thomas. "An Ergonomic Study of Worker Kcal Expenditure: Lean Manufacturing Versus Functional Designed Manufacturing Systems." *Proceedings: GT/CM World Symposium 2000*.

—— 2000. "Ergonomic Evaluation: 3D Simulation of Cellular Versus Function Manufacturing Systems." Ph.D. Dissertation. Auburn, AL: Auburn University.

Iyer, Anand and Ronald G. Askin. 1998. "Modeling and Simulation Operating Policies for Manufacturing Cells." *IIE Transactions*. Norcross, GA: Institute of Industrial Engineers. Vol. 30, p. 785-794.

Jackson, Paul R. and Robin Martin. 1996. "Impact of JIT on Job Content, Employee Attitudes and Well-being: A Longitudinal Study." *Ergonomics*. Vol. 39, No. 1, p. 1-16.

Kamrani, A. K., K. Hubbart, and H.R. Leep. 1998. "Simulation-based Methodology For Machine Cell Design." *Computers and Industrial Engineering*. Vol. 34, No. 1, p. 173-188.

Kaplan, R. and D. Norton. 1992. "The Balanced Scoreboard—Measures that Drive Performance." *Harvard Business Review*, January/February.

Karmakar, U. 1989. "Getting Control of Just-in-Time." *Harvard Business Review*, September/October. p.122-131.

Karwowski, Waldemar and Paul Gaddie. 1995. "Simulation of the 1991 Revised NIOSH Manual Lifting Equation." *Proceedings of the Human Factors and Ergonomics Society, 39th Annual Meeting*. Santa Monica, CA: Human Factors and Ergonomics Society. Vol. 1, p. 699-703.

Karwowski, Waldemar and W.S. Marras, Eds. 1999. "Rapid Upper Limb Assessment (RULA)." *The Occupational Ergonomics Handbook*. New York: CRC Press, p. 437-440.

Karwowski, Waldemar and Gavriel Salvendy, Eds. 1998. *Ergonomics in Manufacturing*. Dearborn, MI: Society of Manufacturing Engineers.

Khalil, T. 1991. "Ergonomic Issues in Low Back Pain: Origin and Magnitude of the Problem." *Proceedings of the Human Factors Society*. Santa Monica, CA: Human Factors and Ergonomics Society. p. 820-824.

Konz, Stephen. 1967. "Design of Workstations." *Journal of Industrial Engineering*.

—— 1990. "Workstation Organization and Design." *International Journal of Industrial Ergonomics*, p. 175-193.

—— 1995. *Work Design: Industrial Ergonomics*, Fourth Edition. Scottsdale, AZ: Publishing Horizons, Inc.

Kroemer, K.H.E., H.J. Kroemer, and K.E. Kroemer-Elbert. 1994. *Ergonomics: How to Design for Ease and Efficiency*. Englewood Cliffs, NJ: Prentice Hall.

—— 1997. *Engineering Physiology: Basis of Human Factors/Ergonomics*, Third Edition. New York: Van Nostrand Reinhold.

—— 1997. *Engineering Physiology*. New York: Van Nostrand Reinhold.

Laughery, R. 1990. "Simulation Changes the Way Industry Thinks About Planning." *Industrial Engineering*. Vol. 22, No. 6, p. 50-85.

Marcotte, Andrew J., Sheri Marvin, and Troy Lagemann. 1995. "Ergonomics Applied to Product and Process Design Achieves Immediate, Measurable Cost Savings." *Proceedings of the Human Factors and Ergonomics Society*. Santa Monica, CA: Human Factors and Ergonomics Society. Vol. 1, p. 660-663.

Maskell, B.H. 1991. *Performance Measurement for World Class Manufacturing*. Cambridge, MA: Productivity Press.

Massay, Lorace L., S.J. Udoka, and C.O. Benjamin. 1995. "A Simulator-based Approach to Cellular Manufacturing System Design." *Computers & Industrial Engineering*. Vol. 29, No. 1, p. 327-331.

McAtamney, Lynn and E.N. Corlett. 1993. "RULA: A Survey Method for the Investigation of Work-related Upper Limb Disorders." *Applied Ergonomics*. Vol. 24, No. 2, p. 91-99.

McLean, Charles. 1998. "Production System Engineering Using Virtual Manufacturing." Washington, DC: National Institute of Standards and Technology. p. 1-7.

Mital, Anil. 1995. "The Role of ERGO in Designing for Manufacturability and Humans in General in Advanced Manufacturing Technology: Preparing the American Workforce for Global Competition Beyond the Year 2000." *International Journal of Industrial Ergonomics*. Vol. 15, No. 2, p. 129-135.

Monden, Yasuhiro. 1998. *Toyota Production System*. Norcross, GA: Industrial Engineering and Management Press.

Muther, Richard. 1973. *Systematic Layout Planning*, Second Edition. Boston, MA: Cahners Books.

Nakajima, Seiichi. 1990. *Introduction to TPM*. Cambridge, MA: Productivity Press.

Nalgirkar, Makarand and Anil Mital. 1999. "A User-friendly 3-Dimensional Kinetic Model for Analyzing Manual Lifting Tasks." *International Journal of Industrial Ergonomics*. Vol. 23, No. 4, p. 255-268.

Nandkeolyar, Udayan, M.U. Ahmed, and A.R. Pai. 1998. "Simulation Study of a Manufacturing Cell Application." *Production and Inventory Management Journal*. Vol. 39, No. 2, Second Quarter, p. 29-36.

National Safety Council. 1988. Itasca, IL: "Making the Job Easier: An Ergonomics Idea Book."

National Academy of Sciences. 2001. "Musculoskeletal Disorders and the Workplace." *Institute of Medicine Report*. February. Washington, DC: National Academy of Sciences.

Nayar, Narinder. 1995. "DENEB/ERGO, A Simulation Based Human Factors Tool." *Proceedings of the 1995 Winter Simulation Conference*, Association for Computer Simulation. p 427-431.

Occupational Safety and Health Administration (OSHA). 2000. *Ergonomics Standard Proposal*. www.osha-slc.gov.

Ohno, Taiichi. 1988. *Toyota Production System: Beyond Large-Scale Production*. Cambridge, MA: Productivity Press.

Orady, Elsayed, T.A. Osman, and Clark P. Bailo. 1997. "Virtual Reality Software for Robotics and Manufacturing Cell Simulation." *Computers & Industrial Engineering*. Vol. 33, No. 1, p. 87-90.

Porter, J.M., M. Freer, K. Case, and M.C. Bonney. 1995. "Computer Aided Ergonomics and Workplace Design." London: Taylor & Francis. p. 574-620.

Rubenstein, M.F. and I.R. Firstenberg, 1995. *Patterns of Problem Solving*. Englewood Cliffs, NJ: Prentice Hall.

Salvendy, Gaviel, Ed. 1997. *Handbook of Human Factors,* Second Edition. New York: John Wiley and Sons, Inc.

Schonberger, R. 1982. *Japanese Manufacturing Techniques: Nine Hidden Lessons in Simplicity*. New York: The Free Press.

—— 1986. *World Class Manufacturing: The Lessons of Simplicity Applied*. New York: The Free Press.

Sekine, Kenichi. 1990. *One-Piece Flow: Cell Design for Transforming the Production Process*. Cambridge, MA: Productivity Press.

Shafer, S.M. and J.M. Chanes. 1993. "Cellular Versus Functional Layouts Under a Variety of Shop Operating Conditions." *Decision Science*. Vol. 23, No. 3, p. 665-681.

Shewhart, W.A. 1931. *Economic Control of Quality of Manufactured Product*. New York: Van Nostrand.

Shingo, Shigeo. 1985. *A Revolution in Manufacturing: The SMED System*. Cambridge, MA: Productivity Press.

—— 1986. *Zero Quality Control: Source Inspection and the Poka-Yoke System*. Cambridge, MA: Productivity Press.

—— 1989. *A Study of the Toyota Production System*. Cambridge, MA: Productivity Press.

Shinn, A. and T. Williams. 1998. "Stitch in Time: A Simulation of Cellular Manufacturing." *Production & Inventory Management Journal*. Vol. 39, No. 1, p. 72-77.

Smith, Leighton L. 1994. "High Technology and Manufacturing: Work Physiology Improvements via the Ergo Simulation Analysis System." *Proceedings of the Human Factors and Ergonomics Society*. Santa Monica, CA: Human Factors and Ergonomics Society. No. 1, p. 664-667.

Suh, Nam P. 1990. *The Principles of Design*. New York: Oxford University Press.

—— 1992. "Design Axioms and Quality Control." *Robotics and CIM*. Vol. 9, No. 4/A, August/October, p. 367.

Suh, Nam P., David S. Cochran, and Paulo C. Lima. 1998. "Manufacturing System Design." *CIRP Annals Manufacturing Technology*. Paris, France: Institution for Production Research. Vol. 47, No. 2, p. 627-639.

Suzaki, Kiyoshi. 1987. *The New Manufacturing Challenge*. New York: The Free Press.

Taguchi, Genechi. 1987. *Systems of Experimental Design*. New York: Kraus International Publications.

Thomas, Robert E. 1998. Personal communication. Auburn, AL: Industrial and Systems Engineering Department, Auburn University.

Quinn, Roger, G.C. Casey, and F.L. Merat. 1997. "Agile Manufacturing Workcell Design." *IIE Transactions*. Norcross, GA: Institute of Industrial Engineers. Vol. 29, No. 10, p. 901-909.

Wemmerlov, U. and N.L. Hyer. "Cellular Manufacturing in the U.S. Industry: A Survey of Users." *International Journal of Production Research*. Vol. 27, No. 9, p. 1511-1230.

Whitney, Dan. 1992. *Scientific Information Bulletin*. Vol. 17, No. 3.

Wilson, John. 1997. "Virtual Environments and Ergonomics: Needs and Opportunities." *Ergonomics*. Vol. 40, No. 10, p. 1057-1077.

Womack, James and Daniel Jones. 1996. *Lean Thinking*. New York: Simon & Schuster.

Womack, James, Daniel Jones, and Daniel Roos. 1991. *The Machine That Changed The World*. New York: Harper Perennial.

Index

A

accidents, 248
acclimatization, 270
accuracy, 285
Amber and Amber, 1
American Armory System, 3
andon, 212
assembly cells, 83, 94, 257
automatic production control, 282
automaticity, 273-277
automation, 4, 184, 273
autonomation, 31, 41, 273, 310-311

B

balancing, 35, 199, 206
    cells, 206-207
    plant, 208-210
benchmarking, 186-187
branching, 282-284
build to sequence, 199
business process reengineering, 42

C

calibration, 286
case studies, 249-253, 298, 325-326
cells, 25-28, 83-84, 98, 112, 207, 210-211, 258-260
    262, 281, 299
cellular manufacturing system, 250
cleanliness, 197
CNC machine tools with decouplers, 280
coding/classification methods, 111
computer-integrated manufacturing (CIM), 259-260
computer maintenance management system, 187
constraints, 78
continuous improvement, 187-191
    charts, 188-189
    combination tables, 188
    employee involvement, 189-190

control charts, 241
controllability, 74
conversion, 113
corollaries, 79
creativity, 74
cultural change, 12
cycle time, 100, 188, 203, 298
cylinder manufacturing cell, 299

D

decouplers, 93, 279-286
Delmia, 295-298
design
    axioms, 79
    for customers, 108
    for flexibility, 62
    process hierarchy, 76
dual-card kanban system, 219-225, 234-235

E

economic order quantity equation, 5
eliminating waste, 307-308
empowered workers, 8
environment, 270-271
EOQ, see: economic-order quantity
equipment, 193, 272
ergonomics, 248, 259, 261-272, 301-302
    analysis methods, 267-268
    assessment measures, 266-267
    energy expenditure, 267
    rapid-upper-limb assessment (RULA), 267
    scoring form, 267
exchange of dies, 30

F

factory with a future, 286-288
fatigue, 270
    kilocalorie usage, 269

metabolism, 268-269
oxygen intake, 269
steady state, 269
final assembly, 278
first industrial revolution, 1-3, 276
five pillars, 185-186, 195
Five-S, 190-191
flexibility, 74, 102
Ford system, 1, 308-309
Fourth Industrial Revolution, 7-8, 260, 298-299
freight consolidation programs, 245
frequent deliveries, 245
functional
decoupler processes, 279-282
requirements, 78
structure, 46

G

group technology, 59, 110

H

hardware systems, 192-194
Harley-Davidson, 217
healing, 265
health issues, 263-265
heijunka, 201
Honda's uniqueness requirement, 75
housekeeping, 197
human and machine interfacing, 270-272
determine optimum work height, 271-272
determine work methods, 271
environment, 270-271
equipment adjustment, 272
form a design team, 271
gather information, 271
workstation, 271-272
hydraulic inspection, 187

I

improvement techniques, 285-286
independent control variable, 230-236
industrial revolutions, 1, 2-8, 276
industry successes, 305-306
in-house-built equipment, 246
inspection form for hydraulic and pneumatic systems, 187
integrated quality, 320-322
interim cell design, 84
interim manned cell, 27

internal customers, 182-183, 207-208, 313, 322-323
intracell transportation, 282
inventory control, 215, 230, 237

J

job shop, 9, 18, 299
joint deviation, 265
Just-in-time (JIT), 6, 215, 313-314

K

kaizen, 191-192, 321, 323-325
kanban, 209, 215-226, 227, 228, 229, 230, 232, 233, 235-236, 315-316, 317
dual-card system, 219-225
Harley-Davidson, 217
integrated manufacturing production system, 217
limitations, 225-226, 230
material, 227, 229
production ordering, 221
push production control system, 216
rules, 221
signal, 227
single-card system, 218-220
special types, 226, 228
stock on hand, 217
systems, 218
withdrawal, 221, 316
work-in-process inventory, 217, 233
kilocalorie, 269, 296, 301-302

L

lead time and expediting, 243-244
lean, 1, 2, 62, 186, 199, 243-260, 253, 258, 259, 261-262, 277-286, 310, 311-313, 316-320
automation in, 277-286
evolution of, 11-12
introduction to, 12-14
success, 25-43
supply chain, 244-246
versus mass production, 256-257
leveling production, 199-203, 213, 314
advantages, 201-203
disadvantages, 201-203
production leveling, 201
smoothing final assembly, 199-201
life cycles, 22, 23
line balancing, 203-204
line stops, 320-322
linked-cell systems, 2, 8, 59, 84, 106, 213

long-range forecasting, 205
long-term contracts, 244-245

M

machine-tool process capability, 284
maintenance, 33, 181-183, 185-187, 197, 206
manned cell, 83, 207, 281
manufacturing cell, 98, 262, 299
manufacturing systems
    background, 14-15
    classifications, 49
    cost, 15
    defined, 47
    design trends, 45
    engineering, 184-185
    optimization, 46
    processes, 16
    production, 16-19
mass production, 1, 5, 250
material requirements planning, 235
measurement
    equipment requirements, 286
    system costs, 286
    techniques, 285-287
metabolism, 268-269
methods analysis, 140
mixed model final assembly, 200, 203-205
    determining cycle time, 203
    determining sequence schedule, 203, 205
    line, 200
    line balancing, 203-204
    precedence diagram, 203
movable equipment, 248-249
musculoskeletal disorders, 263

N

NIOSH lifting tool, 297-298

O

Ohno, 2, 213, 311
one-piece flow, 31, 319
oxygen intake, 269

P

paperless factory of the future, 238-241
    management by sight, 238-239
    visual control at standard operations, 239-240
    workplace organization, 239
physiology, 268

pilot cells, 112
plant trip, 246-257
pneumatic inspection, 187
poka-yoke inspection, 282
power clamps, 138
precedence diagram, 203
predictive maintenance, 187
preventive maintenance, 33, 181-183
process
    cells, 210
    drift, 182
product
    cells, 210-211
    life cycles, 22
    production system, 217
    reliability, 181
    systems, 237
production
    control, 33-36, 215, 279
    flow analysis, 110
    leveling, 201, 314
    ordering kanban (POK), 221, 315
    systems, 16, 18, 48, 58
profitability, 249
pull system, 310, 315-316
push production control system, 216

Q

quality, 30-33, 101

R

rack-and-pinion assembly, 220, 252, 254
rapid-upper-limb assessment (RULA), 267, 297, 302-304
reliability, 192-195
repeatability, 285
reproducibility, 285
robot process capability, 284-285
robotic manufacturing cells, 278-286
rules for lean cell design, 258-260

S

safety, 262
scoring form, 267
second industrial revolution, 4-6
second shift, 195-197
self-inspection devices, 248
sensing, 287
sequence schedule, 199, 203, 205

setup reduction, 28-30, 117-118, 128
simulation, 289-306
    3-D, 289
    evaluation areas, 291
    history, 290-291
single
    card kanban system, 218-219
    minute exchange of dies (SMED), 29, 117, 125, 143, 311
    sourcing, 244
    units, 248
smoothing
    final assembly, 199-201
    production, 314
software, 194, 198, 295
special kanban, 226
stability, 285
standard operations, 107, 212-213, 256
standard packaging, 245-246
standard work, 88, 159, 323-326
station design, 197, 271-272
steady state, 269
steps to lean production, 25-43
    1, 25-28
    2, 28-30
    3, 30-33
    4, 33-34
    5, 34-35
    6, 35-36
    7, 36-40
    8, 40-41
    9, 41
    10, 42-43
stock-on-hand, 94, 188, 217
studies, 192
subassembly flow lines, 10
suggestion system, 192
suppliers, 40-41
supply-chain management, 236-238
support routines, 198
synchronizing, 199, 211-213
system design tools, 109

T

takt time, 8, 100, 203, 319
teams, 43, 191
test procedure, 286
throughput time, 20
total preventive maintenance, 206
total productive maintenance, 185-186, 197

Toyota production system (TPS), 205, 307-326

UVW

U-shaped cells, 25-28
vendors, 243, 312
venous pooling, 265
virtual factory, 304-305
walkaway switch, 26, 255
waste, 201
withdrawal kanban (WLK), 221, 315
work
    flow, 319-320
    force, 198, 265
    height, 271-272
    in-process, 36-40, 94, 226-230, 253
    methods, 271
    sequence, 188
    simulation, 272
    station design, 197, 271-272

XYZ

yo-i-don, 31, 211-212
zero downtime, 186